DECOLONIZING CONSTITUTIONALISM

The modern state, law, and constitution result from a legal canon that (re) produces the abyssal lines dividing the world that is validated from the world whose humanity and epistemological validity are denied. This book aims to contribute to a post-abyssal reflection on law and constitutionalism by considering the structural axes of power that are constitutive of modern law "capitalism, colonialism, and heteropatriarchy" alongside the legal plurality of the world. Is it possible to decolonize, decommodify, and depatriarchalize the constitution? The authors speak from multiple geographies, raise different questions, resort to differentiated theoretical approaches, and reveal varying levels of optimism about the possibilities of transforming constitutions. The readers are confronted with critical perspectives on the Eurocentric legal canon, as well as with the recognition of anti-capitalist, anti-colonial, and anti-patriarchal legal experiences. The horizon of this publication is the expansion of the possibilities of legal and political imagination.

Boaventura de Sousa Santos is Emeritus Professor of Sociology at the University of Coimbra (Portugal) and Distinguished Legal Scholar at the University of Wisconsin-Madison. He is also Director Emeritus of the Center for Social Studies at the University of Coimbra. He has written and published widely on the issues of sociology of law and the state, epistemology, intercultural democracy, social movements, postcolonialisms and global citizenship. Among his most recent publications in English are: *Epistemologies of the South: Justice against Epistemicide* (Paradigm Publishers, 2014); *If God Were a Human Rights Activist, Stanford University Press* (Stanford University Press, 2015); *The End of the Cognitive Empire: The Coming of Age of Epistemologies of the South* (Duke University Press, 2018); *Toward a New Legal Common Sense. Law, Globalization, and Emancipation*

(Third edition, Cambridge University Press, 2020); *Decolonising the University: The Challenge of Deep Cognitive Justice* (Cambridge Scholars Publishing, 2021).

Sara Araújo is a researcher at the Centre for Social Studies (CES) and invited assistant professor in sociology at the Faculty of Economics, University of Coimbra. She holds a PhD in Law, Justice and Citizenship in the 21st century and co-founded the PhD Programme in Sociology of the State, Law and Justice (CES and FEUC) that she now co-coordinates. After four years at the Permanent Observatory for the Portuguese Justice (2000–2004), she was part of the research team of the Legal and Judicial Training Centre of Mozambique (2005–2006) and associated researcher at the Centre for African Studies of the Eduardo Mondlane University (2008–2010) (Mozambique). In 2015, she was a visiting scholar at the Law School of the University of Wisconsin-Madison (USA). Between 2011 and 2016, she was a member of the Coordination Board of the ERC Alice project, which was transformed into the Research Programme in Epistemologies of the South (CES). Within this, Sara co-coordinated four editions of the Epistemologies of the South Summer School and co-organized several workshops of the Popular University of Social Movements (UPMS).

Orlando Aragón Andrade is a professor and researcher at the National Autonomous University of Mexico (in Morelia) where he is the coordinator of the Laboratory of Legal Anthropology and of the State. His research focuses on the study of indigenous peoples' collective rights, legal pluralism, counter-hegemonic uses of law, law's decolonization, epistemologies of the South and, relevantly, the construction of a militant legal anthropology. Along his academic work, he is also a legal advisor and accompanies several autonomy and self-government processes in Mexico, as part of the Emancipations Collective, of which he is a founding member.

Epistemologies of the South

The Global North has faced growing difficulty in making sense of the broad changes sweeping the world, from the financialization and neoliberalization of the world economy to the growth of inequality on an unknown scale in its persistence, extension and diversification of segregation, discrimination and violence. Uneasiness has been growing within the social sciences at the feeling of inadequacy and even irrelevance of current work and established theory in its attempt to get to grips with such a world.

The main idea underlying this series is that the experience of the world is much broader than the Eurocentric understanding, and what is known as the Global South has been for centuries – and remains in contemporary times–an inexhaustible source of experiences, knowledges, political and social innovations, and celebrations of difference. Challenging the canonical and Eurocentric epistemological tradition, including the social sciences and humanities themselves, this series innovates through the encounter and dialogue with other epistemologies that have historically emerged in the South.

Series Editor: ***Boaventura de Sousa Santos***, University of Coimbra (Portugal)

The Pluriverse of Human Rights
The Diversity of Struggles for Dignity
Edited by Boaventura de Sousa Santos and Bruno Sena Martins

From the Pandemic to Utopia
The Future Begins Now
Boaventura de Sousa Santos

DECOLONIZING CONSTITUTIONALISM

Beyond False or Impossible Promises

Edited by Boaventura de Sousa Santos, Sara Araújo and Orlando Aragón Andrade

Routledge
Taylor & Francis Group
NEW YORK AND LONDON

Cover Image: "Golden Future", Mário Vitória 2013

First published 2024
by Routledge
605 Third Avenue, New York, NY 10158

and by Routledge
4 Park Square, Milton Park, Abingdon, Oxon, OX14 4RN

Routledge is an imprint of the Taylor & Francis Group, an informa business

ISBN: 9781032490311 (hbk)
ISBN: 9781032490274 (pbk)
ISBN: 9781003391920 (ebk)

DOI: 10.4324/9781003391920

Typeset in Bembo
by Newgen Publishing UK

CONTENTS

PREFACE

Boaventura de Sousa Santos, Sara Araújo and Orlando Aragón Andrade

The epistemologies of the South are based on two basic premises which are very relevant to the theme of this collection. The first premise is that our understanding of the world is much broader than the European understanding. The second premise rests on the fact that the available epistemological diversity is infinite and no general theory can aim to understand and explain it. This means that it is not possible to offer a universal response to the questions that will be raised or to exhaust those questions that are relevant.

As a cosmopolitan epistemological and pedagogical project, the epistemologies of the South have staked their claims on the possibility of social groups or movements, academics, political actors and others working in different regions of the world being able to share political agendas, experiences and knowledge by recognizing and celebrating diversity and promoting exercises in reciprocal learning. For this to be possible, it is necessary to recognize that all knowledge is incomplete, thereby challenging the hierarchies that have naturalized Western options and legitimized the exclusion of everything that lies beyond the limits of the Eurocentric canon. In other words, it is necessary to recognize and learn from the diversity that has been classified by default and crystallized through the negative impact of modern dichotomies (the ignorant, the primitive, the traditional, the local, the unproductive, the barbarian, the savage, the underdeveloped).

The epistemologies of the South propose to denaturalize Eurocentric theories with their outdated questions and binomials, subjecting them to a sociology of absences which seeks to identify their limits. On this basis, a sociology of emergences becomes viable, one that validates other knowledges (and with it the possibility of links with scientific knowledge), promotes the expansion of the canon of knowledge and, by identifying and recognizing anti-capitalist, anti-colonial and anti-patriarchal experiences, contributes to extending the possibilities of liberation and self-determination. The horizon which this publication sets out to enhance is the extension of the possibilities of legal and political imagination.

The concept of the abyssal line, which represents a denial of humanity and the epistemological validity of the experience of much of the world, is of central importance to this book. Constituted through a shifting combination of capitalism, colonialism and patriarchy, the impact of the abyssal line is evident not only in the physical violence meted out to those isolated by the divide but also in the knowledge and experiences they have. The 14 chapters within this publication contribute to a post-abyssal reflection on law and constitutionalism. The authors come from various backgrounds, raise different questions, resort to differentiated theoretical approaches and reveal varying levels of optimism regarding the possibilities of decolonizing, decommodifying and depatriarchalizing constitutions. Some chapters present reflections on the development of democratic legal cultures, open to intercultural dialogue and operating within the framework of the rule of law. Others assert the need to radicalize discussion and practices, holding modern constitutional principles up to the cruel mirrors of the colonialist and patriarchal capitalist world in which we live. The issues range from the degree of success or failure of the constitutional struggles waged by excluded groups and their allies, aimed at enlarging and deepening social inclusion, to the possibilities of reframing a constitution by dismantling the modern hierarchies that structure the legal plurality of the world.

The title reflects the complexity and ambition of the general objective which permeates the book: to explore the experiences of the world, beyond incomplete or unambitious projects or impossible promises sustained by the belief that it is possible to decolonize without eliminating the hierarchies imposed by modernity. The contribution to the debate is thus based on two exercises: (1) Reflection on what we can learn from imperfect experiences, identifying absences and developing the progressive dimensions; (2) Identifying ambitious questions that challenge modern hierarchies, enabling us to formulate possibilities for promoting decolonization, decommodification and the depatriarchalization of law and justice.

The book is not only aimed at those who are dedicated to sociolegal studies but also students and academics from other fields, including sociology and political economy, world activists, jurists, magistrates, politicians, NGO members, officials from international organizations and all those interested in understanding the power which legal institutions exert and which enables them to reproduce the modern oppressive triad – capitalism, colonialism and patriarchy – and in reflecting on the possibilities of decolonizing, decommodifying and depatriarchalizing societies and their institutions.

This is one of the eight volumes[1] in the collection 'Epistemologies of the South', in which the results of the Alice project – *Strange Mirrors, Unsuspected Lessons*[2] – are presented and questions are raised that continue to fuel discussions and debates within the Epistemologies of the South research program hosted by the Center for Social Studies (CES) at the University of Coimbra, coordinated by

Boaventura de Sousa Santos, with Bruno Sena Martins, Cristiano Gianolla, João Arriscado Nunes, José Manuel Mendes, Maria Paula Meneses, Sara Araújo and Teresa Cunha.

Our profound thanks are extended to activists and academics around the world who have collaborated in the various volumes that make up the 'Epistemologies of the South' collection and have thus responded to the challenge of establishing an emancipatory science that is capable of defending dignity and restoring hope. The authors of the chapters in this book have our immense admiration and gratitude. However, the people who contributed to the realization of this publication are not limited to those named above. Various activities have played a key role in the realization of the Alice project, the reflections that have led to this collection, including academic meetings, the workshops of the Popular University of Social Movements (UPMS), the 'Conversations of the World', discussion forums and countless individual and collective interviews. We wish to thank all the people, movements and organizations who agreed to participate in, share and launch the challenges.

Special mention should be made of the Center for Social Studies, given that it is the institutional space in which the Alice Project has been based, but above all for the generous support of the scientific and administrative structures that have contributed to the success of the project and its subsequent materialization as a research program. We also wish to highlight the dedicated collaboration of Lassalete Paiva and the tireless work of Rita Kácia Oliveira, who has given her heart and soul to the philosophy of the project and made an invaluable contribution to its realization. With specific reference to this volume, we would like to extend our special gratitude to our colleagues Agustin Grijalva, Bryan Vargas, Bruno Sena Martins, José Luis Exeni, José Manuel Mendes, Maria Paula Meneses and Patrícia Branco and, last but not least, a word of thanks to Victor Ferreira for his diligent and competent revision of the texts, as well as to Neil Walker for translating works written in other languages into English.

Notes

1 The books are published in Portuguese, Spanish and English. The following volumes are published in Portuguese: *Demodiversidade – Imaginar Novas Possibilidades Democraticas*, coordinated by Boaventura de Sousa Santos and José Manuel Mendes (Lisbon; Issue 70, 2017; Belo Horizonte: Authentic Editor, 2018); *O Pluriverso dos Direitos Humanos: A Diversidade das Lutas pelas Dignidade*, coordinated by Boaventura de Sousa Santos and Bruno Sena Martins (Lisbon: Issue 70, 2019; Belo Horizonte: Authentic Publishing House, 2019). The following are published in Spanish: *Demodiversidad. Imaginar Neuvas Possibilidades Democráticas*, coordinated by Boaventura de Sousa Santos and José Manuel Mendes (Ciudad de México: Akal, 2017) and *El Pluriverso de los Drechos Humanos*, coordinated by Boaventura de Sousa Santos and Bruno Sena Martins (Madrid: Akal, 2019). The following are published in English: *Knowledges Born in the Struggle. Constructing the Epistemologies of the Global South*, coordinated by Boaventura de Sousa Santos and Maria Paula Meneses (New York and London: Routledge, 2019); *Demodiversity: Toward Post-Abyssal Democracies*, coordinated by Boaventura de Sousa

Santos and José Manuel Mendes (New York and London: Routledge, 2020) and *The Pluriverse of Human Rights: The Diversity of Struggles for Dignity*, coordinated by Boaventura de Sousa Santos and Bruno Sena Martins (Routledge, 2021). Volumes on other economies, methodology and health are to be published subsequently.

2 *Alice – Strange Mirrors, Unsuspected Lessons; Leading Europe to a New Way of Sharing World Experiences*, coordinated by Boaventura de Sousa Santos, with funding from the European Research Council – 7th European Union Framework Programme (FP/2007–2013)/ERC Grant Agreement no. [269807] and realized between 2011 and 2016 at the Center for Social Studies (CES) at the University of Coimbra <www.alice.ces.uc.pt>.

ACKNOWLEDGEMENTS

This book was developed in the context of the research project ALICE – Strange Mirrors, Unsuspected Lessons – coordinated by Boaventura de Sousa Santos at the Centre for Social Studies of the University of Coimbra, Portugal, between 2011 and 2016. The project was funded by the European Research Council, 7th Framework Program of the European Union (Fp/2007-13)/ERC Grant Agreement n. [269807].

INTRODUCTION

The Constitution, the State, the Law and the Epistemologies of the South

Boaventura de Sousa Santos, Sara Araújo and Orlando Aragón Andrade

The concept 'epistemologies of the South' was coined in a special issue of the *Revista Crítica de Ciências Sociais* in 2008, but the background to the proposal dates back to Boaventura de Sousa Santos' ethnographic experience of legal pluralism in a Rio de Janeiro favela in the 1970s (Santos, 1977). In the division between Pasargada law and asphalt law presented in this first work, we can see what would, decades later, come to be formulated as a constitutive concept of the epistemologies of the South, namely the abyssal line which divides the world that counts from the one which, in light of the five monocultures constituting modern thought,[1] is irrelevant, local, residual, inferior and non-productive (Santos, 2014, 2018).

As such, legal pluralism was not only a theoretical and analytical issue but also an epistemological and political problem concerning the definition of what counts as truth:

> What is the truth or validity of an official scientific-legal knowledge which considers that which is 'of worth' to vast sectors of the popular classes, as another law or alternative legal knowledge, to be non-law or ignorance of the law?
>
> *Santos, 2003: 43*

The aim of this book is to extend the debate, bringing together a set of post-abyssal reflections in the field of socio-legal studies with an emphasis on discussions concerning the limits and possibilities of critical constitutionalism.

The South, as the founding metaphor of an emerging subjectivity, appears in a 1995 publication in a chapter entitled 'Don't Shoot the Utopist' (Santos, 1995). It established a challenge in three phases: learning that there is a South, learning to go South and learning from the South (Santos, 1995: 508). Learning from the South

DOI: 10.4324/9781003391920-1

is currently the greater challenge. It requires a process of unlearning the social sciences which have divided the world between those who produce knowledge and those who are the object of study. Making this statement is different from proclaiming the irrelevance of the knowledge produced in the geographic North or romanticizing the South. The South is a metaphor for knowledge born of capitalist, colonial and patriarchal violence, and the social struggles that have opposed them (Santos, 2014, 2018). Unlearning the North involves questioning the hierarchies imposed by the Eurocentric canon and provincializing theories which, due to their distorted self-image, start from a premise of immunity to context (Chakrabarti, 2000; Santos, 2014, 2018).

The epistemologies of the South, which are incompatible with general theories, do not offer a formula but propose a combination of epistemological instruments that serve not only to denounce epistemicide (Santos, 1995) and juricide (Santos, 2011) but also to identify silenced knowledge and expand the political imagination. The social sciences are, from the outset, invited to develop a sociology of the absences in theories, concepts and long-established questions, and to raise questions and identify concepts that allow for the production of a sociology of emergences.

When Boaventura de Sousa Santos defines the concept of the abyssal line, he identifies absences produced through the regulation/emancipation dichotomy hitherto central to his work:

> Indeed, the regulation/emancipation dichotomy only applied to metropolitan societies. It would be unthinkable to apply it to colonial territories. There, another dichotomy would apply, the appropriation/violence dichotomy which, in turn, would be inconceivable if applied on this side of the line.
>
> *Santos, 2014: 119*

The tension between regulation and emancipation is relevant where the social contract is valid. The other side of the abyssal line is the state of nature, the zone of non-being (Fanon, 2008 [1952]), which can be subjected to violence and appropriated, either through the elimination of subjects or through a civilizing process (Santos, 2014). This dividing line was identified by Mamhood Mamdani, in the context of the African continent, as a 'bifurcated state', a colonial heritage separating humans and lesser humans, linguistic discourse and vernacular conversation, art and crafts, modern law and customary law: in short, the civilized and the savage (Mamdani, 1996: 61). The abyssal division, however, crosses other locations, namely the geographical North. In Europe too, the development project was based on the elimination of the Souths, with all the knowledges and alternatives they contained. This waste of experience is constitutive of modernity, which only recognizes the knowledge of a science favourable to capitalist development and the capitalist order, as an exportable legal model compatible with this project.

Having identified the abyssal line, the incompleteness of the theory of regulation and emancipation becomes visible. Hence, a core question is revealed as incomplete: can the law be emancipatory? (Santos, 2002). This question is formulated from this side of the line, a sphere in which cultural differences fit within modern codes of interpretation and inequalities can be translated into modern legal language. It is not a case of declaring the question irrelevant, but of arguing for the need to broaden its terms. Legal thinking must consider both sides of the line and the three structural axes of power within modernity that are constitutive of modern law – capitalism, colonialism and patriarchy. Thus, the question has become: is it possible to build a post-abyssal law? In other words, is it possible to decolonize, decommodify and depatriarchalize the law? This is a very broad question which can be translated into multiple questions, whose answer can only be found in the convergence of very different knowledges.

I.1 Epistemologies of the South and Constitutionalisms

The modern-Western hegemonic project identifies the constitution as a set of basic elements that establish and regulate political and legal agreements in the social life of a given community and sees it as the legal scale *par excellence* for political unity within Western modernity: the nation state. In turn, the modern state, which began to be constructed in Europe in the seventeenth century, was mainly conceived as a machine for political and social engineering from the mid-nineteenth century onwards. Its formal, mechanical and artificial constitution has given it a strength and plasticity unprecedented in any other political entity. Its plasticity resulted from its virtually infinite institutional and legal manoeuvrability, which provided the state with the ability to define the normal and abnormal means, as well as the normal and abnormal ends, of social transformation (Santos, 2000: 170). The modern state, as an exclusive unit of social intelligibility and political imagination, reduced law, which had previously been plural, diverse and dispersed, to a single monolithic type of law, namely state law. This reduction was safeguarded by scientifically legitimized codification processes (Santos, 1995, 2014).

The constitution has been predominantly conceived of as an expression of a united dualism, composed of 'the legal' and 'the political', a privileged place for perceiving the relationship between politics and law (Bobbio, 1984).[2] Constitutions are imagined as a more or less crystallized synthesis of the legal and political bases that uphold the life of a given community as a collective. Most approaches in the dominant field of Western legal studies are characterized by the technical-scientific reductionism of the constitution. This reductionism fails to take into account the political projects and divergent social forces interested in the success or failure of the constitution and ignores or devalues the asymmetric power relations that globally traverse past and contemporary constitutions and constitutionalisms.

The state, the law and the constitution, as well as the strong interconnections they establish, are the central pillars in the construction of the economic, social and political structure generated by the dominant modern-Western project. From the perspective of the epistemologies of the South that we have been proposing (Santos, 2014, 2018), this project is based on three main forms of domination: capitalism, colonialism and patriarchy. Thus, much of what is present in and around contemporary constitutions reproduces the capitalist (classist), colonialist (racist) and patriarchal (sexist) dynamics that characterize this project. Thinking about the state in this context involves, on the one hand, finding ourselves situated in the field of a legal sociology of absences – the sociology of absences is one of the main conceptual devices of the epistemologies of the South – and assuming a hermeneutic of suspicion in relation to the alleged neutrality and technical superiority attributed to the modern state and law, thereby positioning them within a colonial, capitalist and patriarchal civilizational project. On the other hand, it involves engaging with the sociology of emergences and identifying legal alternatives based on the wide range of legal maps of the world that pave the way for the construction of new utopias. These are supported by real experiences and knowledges which have been thought through and constructed by those who have personally suffered the effects of structural violence while engaging in political struggles against the various forms of oppression (Santos, 2014, 2018).[3]

When commencing with a study of the constitution, we are confronted, on the one hand, with the paradoxical conjunction between the polysemic and contentious nature of the term itself and, on the other hand, the constitutional homogeneity which produces abyssal exclusions. The polysemy results from the possibility of understanding, and even contesting, the constitution in different ways. For example, from some standpoints it is seen as a reflection of a minimum consensus on the basic norms governing community life, while others consider it from the viewpoint of dissent; there are those who see it as a mechanism for preserving a particular social agreement or *status quo* and others who see it as the basis for transformation or innovation; there are also those who consider it the foundation of 'unity' and those who, in contrast, interpret it as recognition of plurality and diversity beyond homogenizing unitarisms. In short, the same word can assume different and even contradictory meanings.[4]

Hence, the constitution is a disputed term.[5] The origins, understanding, contours, potentialities and usefulness of the constitution, as well as the problems associated with it, are controversial. In this sense, its meanings depend to a large extent on the social actors who dispute them and the power relations synthesized in a given context that ultimately configure what is considered to be a constitution. It is a dispute which implies that the political, theoretical and epistemic positions and projects, and even the world views of the dominant social and political subjects, carry significant weight. The understanding of what is, or what may be, a constitution is structurally traversed by dynamics that reveal ethnocentrism and the hegemony of the global North. Thus, what is considered part of the 'minimum elements of validity' of a constitution, as well as its purposes and objectives, is also traversed by abyssal dynamics (Santos, 2010a, 2014, 2018). This condition translates, on the one hand, into the invisible status of conceptions, experiences and practices that do not fit within the dominant Western 'constitutional canon', or the impossibility of these 'other forms' and 'other experiences' becoming known and valued. At best, they are reduced to mere 'particularisms', relevant only to thinking about the reality of countries and regions of origin, but not for thinking about constitutions or constitutionalism on a global level.[6]

I.2 The Hegemonic Constitutional Project

Constitutionalism, which establishes the limits and form of the state, is based on the ideas of unity, uniformity and homogeneity: one state, one nation, one law. The nation is the set of individuals who belong to the same geopolitical space and share a culture. However, the homogeneity of the nation state was artificially constructed, resulting from a violent rupture with the past. Although immersed in a fictional account of inclusion and homogeneity, the history of the relationship between vast social groups and the modern nation state is constituted by violence which targets different social groups or dissidents and a monocultural understanding that covers up the destruction or marginalization of nations, laws, cultures and identities that coexisted in the same geopolitical territory (Chatterjee, 1991, 1998; Yuval-Davis, 1993; Tully, 1995; Marx, 2002; Comaroff and Comaroff, 2003; Anderson, 2006; Roy, 2008; Santos, 2014, 2017).

Modern law is administered by the state, operating exclusively on a national scale and presiding over a bureaucratic and professional administration. Compatible with the fiction of the homogeneous nation, law is a globalized localism (Santos, 2008), that is to say, a Western initiative that acquired the status of universality through colonial power. In the words of Peter Fitzpatrick (1992), the law is a Eurocentric myth, allegedly immune to context and politics, which sustains the claim of Western superiority and linear historical narrative, progressing from disorder to order and combining the latter with the rule of law.

According to the author,

> [M]odern law emerges, in a negative exaltation, as universal in opposition to the particular, as unified in opposition to the diverse, and as omnicompetent in contrast to the incompetent, and as controlling of what has to be controlled [...]. Law is imbued with this negative transcendence in its own myth of origin where it is imperiously set against certain 'others' who concentrate the qualities it opposes. Such others are themselves creatures of an Occidental mythology, a mythology which denies its own foundation by consigning myth in general to the world of these others. This combined denial of myth does not mean that

> the mythology which operates in the West is qualitatively different from that attributed to these other ignorants.
>
> *Fitzpatrick, 1992: 10*

For James Tully,

> The great tragedy of the modern constitutionalism is that most European philosophers followed Hobbes and turned their backs on dialogue just when non-European peoples were encountered and dialogue and mediation were needed to avert the misunderstanding and inhumanity that followed.
>
> *Tully, 1995: 116*

The jurist Kenneth B. Nunn, co-founder of the Center for the Study of Race and Race Relations, a law school centred on the issue of race, argues that Western European culture, when compared to others, is highly materialistic, competitive, individualistic, narcissistic and focused on the consumption of natural resources and material goods, and that law is part of a broader cultural effort that promotes European values and interests at the expense of everyone else (1997). Law is understood by Nunn to be a 'European enterprise' which affirms and celebrates the Eurocentric cultural experience, contributing to its hegemony:

> Law contributes to Eurocentric hegemony in three concrete ways. First, law 'controls the beast' by organizing and directing white institutions and cultural practices. Second, law 'polices' white culture. That is, law operates to help determine which ideas and practices are valued in Eurocentric culture and which can be identified as 'threats' subject to the use of coercion or force. Third, law works to legitimate white institutions and practices by helping to place the imprimatur of universality on European practices and champion the desirability and inevitability of white dominance.
>
> *Nunn, 1997: 351*

Although there are examples of social achievements through law in the history of the twentieth century, the truth is that it was conceived as an instrument for protecting private property and for collective submission to the terms of capitalist productivity as conceived by the bourgeoisie in the West (Abel, 1990; Santos, 2002, 2017; Castro-Gómez, 2005; Roy, 2008). It is characterized by a set of assumptions essential to the ambitions of this economic model, such as uniformity (applied invariably), universality (reproducible and predictable), territoriality (law is territorial and non-personal) and logical–formal rationality (borrowed from modern science) (Galanter, 1966; Wolkmer, 1994; Santos, 2000). Its allegedly rational, neutral, objective and fair language promotes a fictionalized natural order legitimizing the values and goals of capitalism.

In the book *Colonial Lives of Property*, Brenna Bhandar (2018) shows how the appropriation of indigenous lands was based on ideologies that claim European racial superiority and on legal narratives that equate civilized life with private property. The evolution of modern property laws and the justifications for the possession of private property 'were articulated through the attribution of value to the lives of those defined as having the capacity, will and technology to appropriate, which in turn was contingent on prevailing concepts of race and racial difference' (Bhandar, 2018: 4). For the author,

> The colonial encounter produced a racial regime of ownership that persists into the present, creating a conceptual apparatus in which justifications for private property ownership remain bound to a concept of the human that is thoroughly racial in its makeup.
>
> *Bhandar, 2018: 4*

Moreover, the link between capitalism and patriarchy has long been the subject of research work and feminist theories. In Silvia Federici's well-known study *The Witch and Caliban*, the author presents what the epistemologies of the South would call a sociology of the absence of the role of women. It advocates the importance of reading events not only from the point of view of production but also in terms of reproduction, and shows the intersection between women's history – the naturalization and devaluation of their role, the violence targeted at their bodies and the social struggles they have fought – that is, the history of the other (in another modern artificial dichotomy) and the history of capitalism (Federici, 2009; Federici, 2014).

The transformation of women's bodies into machines that produce workers required universal, formal, binding legislation and complicit institutions that would ensure abortion was penalized and would only recognize binary bodies and a bourgeois, heteronormative family design at the service of a single productivity (Peterson, 2013; Federici, 2014). It was this form of productivity that established itself as one of the five monocultures of modernity: the capitalist monoculture (Santos, 2014). Naturalizing the heteropatriarchal family model means denying the history of the power relations at the origins of capitalism and the construction of states. The type of relationships constituted in extended family networks was based on different kinds of relationship and logics of authority, respect and resources. As V. Spike Peterson argues,

> [E]ffective centralization required a reconfiguration of social arrangements, which typically involved states establishing relatively independent heteropatriarchal 'family'/households as the basic socio-economic unit; the latter facilitated resource extraction, military conscription, regulation of property (including women), and centralized control more generally.
>
> *Peterson, 2013: 57–59*

The modern legal paradigm survived the national independence processes, which failed to change the way the West viewed the colonies. The world order negotiated by the United Nations at the end of World War II was based on a Charter of Rights and a set of principles which reflected European history, even though they were granted universal validity. The model state law was presented as a neutral device, the universal archetype of a linear development project (Mattei and Nader, 2008; Roy, 2008; Madlingozi, 2010; Araújo, 2016). The 'other' could only aspire to independence and recognition by the Westphalian international order when it conformed to the only state model recognized, the nation state (Roy, 2008). Within the same project, civil society was created, in many contexts an entity even more artificial than the state itself. The many social processes (ethnic divisions, local cultures, legal pluralism, etc.) that were excluded from civil society were translated by the hegemonic powers into explanatory factors for the 'weakness' of civil society (Santos, 2000), the same type of approach that often resulted in the classification of states as fragile, failed or collapsed (Barros-Varela, 2017).

As Dianne Otto states, 'to become a member of the UN community and to obtain full international citizenship and sovereign legal personality, an entity must generally qualify as a state' (1996: 341). She continues: 'Decolonization repeated imperialism, but with a new legal and moral appearance' (1996: 343). Despite all their differences, the countries of Eastern Europe and those of the West converged in recognizing the Eurocentric canon and saw history as a global evolutionary movement, whether in the direction of global capitalism or international socialism. In both cases, Europe symbolized the most advanced stage of development (Otto, 1996: 340). The international principle *utis possidetis juris* (the inalterability of colonial frontiers), a construct as colonial as that of the nation state, ensured the continuity of highly artificial borders, ignoring the affinities and forms of organization that existed prior to colonial invasion (Roy, 2008; Otto, 1996).

In a text on the rule of law in African contexts, Makau Mutua summarizes the continuity of the colonial scenario in one paragraph:

> Soon after Africa's independence, cadres of Western academics and policy-makers believed that Africa's new states would be 'civilised' by the rule of law. Western thought viewed pre-colonial Africa as pre-law, and thus argued that emergent states needed formal Western legal regimes to enter modernity. No credit was given to pre-existing African legal systems, which were often referred to as 'customary law', 'traditional', 'savage' or 'uncivilized'.
>
> *Mutua, 2016: 163*

Contemporary legal transplants are fuelled by the disparity within modernity between experiences and expectations, an unbalanced form of management that results from the great unfulfilled promises based on the idea of progress and abstract prognoses (Galindo, 2014). In this introduction, we will not detail the complexity resulting from these top-down processes which fail to recognize what exists and produce unexpected results. The excessive weight attributed to international agents and their impositions, marked in legal historiography, was called the 'diffusionist model of reception' because it is based on blindness to the complexity of legal encounters (Duve, 2014: 8, 9).

Colonialism is translated into academically validated, apparently neutral concepts, as is the case with 'transitional justice'. Mechanisms designed to depoliticize the past, the present and the future are hidden beneath the celebration of the rule of law. Transitional justice rests on a legality that promotes a less controversial version of the past. 'Transitional justice entrepreneurs' occupy the space dedicated to local voices and seek to reconstruct the world in the image of Western liberal democracies (Madlingozi, 2010). Sociopolitical claims tend to remain in the background in a debate that is now about criminal facts, in which clashes based on race and class are tempered by a legal language that brings victims and perpetrators face to face (Bowsher, 2018).

Our arguments are not concerned with the intentions of the people involved in these cases, which certainly vary. The purpose of this reading, and many others we have addressed, is to foreground a part of the narrative that the hegemonic version of modernity has rendered invisible. The monoculture of modern science, which has infected the sphere of law, has narrowed our perception of the world, alienating people and knowledges and reducing the political imagination to a very controlled sphere. Law has been increasingly contaminated by economics, in turn increasingly recognized as an exact science, promoting what Capra and Mattei (2015) call an 'obsolete mainstream view, rooted in the duopoly of property and state', which 'feeds ecologically destructive practices'. According to the authors, 'So-called economic laws produce major distortions because they are based on the assumption that it is natural and desirable for an institution to set growth targets that induce extractive individual behavior while discouraging virtuous practices' (Mattei and Fritjof, 2015: 8).

Neoliberal globalization has not been questioning the capitalist, colonial and heteropatriarchal model, despite the advances (and setbacks) in social struggles. The alleged neutrality of modern law has always been sustained through science oriented towards the domestication of nature and people, and this linear path has not been eroded. Ugo Mattei and Marco de Morpurgo refer to an 'imperial rule of law' which lies above the state, 'a dominant layer for the worldwide legal systems' (Mattei and Morpurgo, 2009). This law, presented as neutral, scientifically legitimated and produced in the interests of international capital by a huge variety of institutions, both public and private, has been fuelling important discussions on legal pluralism on a global scale, as well as global economic constitutionalism (Santos, 2002; Schneiderman, 2008; Michaels, 2009; Berman, 2012; Peters, 2015). The impact of global legal systems is not homogeneous, that is to say, it is not a question of scale, but of power camouflaged beneath the idea of good economic governance (Baxi, 2013):

> With all the profusion of General Comments of the UN human rights treaty bodies and the MDG, and the right to development talk, there exists no human right against fiscal and monetary policy regimes. Thus, there is no human right directed against price-rise (inflation) which mocks the smooth languages of the right to affirm, protect and promote socio-economic rights. There is no human right whatsoever against policies and programmes of 'structural adjustment' or 'devaluation' of national currency which ruins the everyday lives of millions of peoples in the global South.
>
> *Baxi, 2013: 41*

In this context, what is the role of the constitution? What is the role of the state? The erosion of the state has been highly selective, considering only the components of the social state that regulate markets and promote distribution. The old values of private property, the individual, and contractual security are celebrated, and distribution practices are presented as an attack on the rule of law. More than ever, law assumes the form of a neutral technology, while political intervention is identified as a legal correction (Mattei and Morpurgo, 2009). The state is the instrument for applying neoliberal economics presented through technocratic language, cloaked in a neutral and universal appearance. In the case of classical liberalism, the state should have limited intervention; in the case of neoliberalism, the state must be regulated internally and externally by the logic of the market (Ferreira, 2016). A recent comparative study on austerity discourses in Europe concludes that

> Since 2010, Europe has converged to a neoliberal vision in overcoming the crisis and promoting competitiveness, becoming increasingly aligned with international institutions such as the IMF in terms of structural adjustment and austerity measures. Therefore, for most countries of the EU, namely those under the Troika interventions, or others under IMF Stand-By Arrangements, the recipe has become similar.
>
> *Meneses et al., 2018*

As Robert Knox points out, 'the anti-statist and "free market rhetoric" of the original theorists of neoliberalism is vastly at odds with the expansion and reconfiguration of state power that was needed to birth and secure it' (2017:93). In the same vein, Brabazon argues that

> if the state is increasingly acknowledged – at least in academic circles – to have been restructured in the neoliberal period rather than restrained, this is

typically seen as a re-orientation of the state away from social concerns and toward facilitating market transactions: 'profit over people'.

Brabazon, 2017: 5

In this context, public law is modelled according to the principles of private and market law, as the public and the private merge within the concept of governance (Tzouvala, 2017: 132).

I.3 The Dilemmas of Critical Constitutionalism

Within the hegemonic project, constitutionalism can be understood as a field of legal and political knowledge anchored in the historical processes of Eurocentric modernity, in which the legitimate differences between the continental European and the Anglo-Saxon are accommodated (McIlwain, 1947: 1–22; Bobbio, 1986: 124; Fioravanti, 2001: 85–100; Comanducci, 2002: 90–93; Bovero, 2006: 22–23; Wittington, 2009: 1–2; Ferrajoli, 2011: 16–21; Medici, 2016: 29–30). When viewed from this perspective, constitutionalism can be considered a set of doctrines, namely an intellectual and political movement which aimed to build a series of ideas that would explain, and even legitimize, the centrality of the constitution as a way of restricting public power by imposing on governments respect for the rule of law over force, as well as limiting the exercise of power. This positioning is also constructed from the primacy of the individual over the community and the state, hence the importance of establishing some form of respect for the rights of the individual vis-à-vis state power. Based on the epistemologies of the South and the concept of the abyssal line, it can be affirmed that all these developments occurred in the metropolitan area and that modern constitutionalism comprised the juridification of relations of domination, violence and appropriation on the 'other side of the line', in the colonial zone. This is why the dominant modern-Western project, with strong roots in individualism and liberalism, necessarily coexists with the dynamics of capitalist, sexist and colonial oppression.

In limiting ourselves to more recent times, it is important to mention the constitutional designs after World War II: the neoconstitutionalisms. It should be emphasized that, in tracing the path of modern constitutional history, changes have affected the metropolitan area. This is why the debates taking place have paid very little attention to the colonial issue, even though much of the African continent remained under the colonial rule while they were in progress. The prefix 'neo' refers to the need to go beyond previous constitutional designs, which were not sufficient to prevent the atrocities committed during World War II. For this reason, neoconstitutionalisms coincide with the need to defend the constitutional principles of justice and, as a rule, do not deny the connection between law and morals, while defining fundamental rights as insurmountable limits for public authorities (Dworkin, 1996; Comanducci, 2002: 96–112; Zagrebelsky, 2013; Alterio, 2014: 232–253). This relates to the aforementioned constitutional rigidity, which plays a key role in the expression of the 'unbreakability' of the protection of fundamental rights. It also explains the attention paid to guaranteeing fundamental rights by various means which are difficult to modify, precisely in order to ensure that this protection is maintained. Thus, guarantee-based constitutionalism is conceived of as a reinforced positivism (Ferrajoli, 2011: 24–34). The role of judges in ensuring constitutional supremacy and exercising constitutional control is central in this design for the constitutional system.

Another of the relevant contemporary proposals is founded on the so-called 'popular constitutionalism' which, instead of advocating the 'closure' of constitutional issues (as in 'legal constitutionalism'), advocates opening up these issues to popular participation. It should be clarified that such participation is, as a rule, restricted by an understanding that limits it to the representation of the legislative power. The emphasis is placed on questioning the democratic legitimacy of the constitutional designs for legal constitutionalism (Kramer, 2004; Waldron, 2006, 2012), and it can be said that it provides for (1) a loosening of the constitution and its exercise; (2) the challenging of judicial supremacy and, in certain cases, even the challenging of some form of judicial control over constitutionality; (3) the extrajudicial interpreting of the constitution; (4) democratization and participation in political and economic institutions; and (5) recovering the relationship between law and politics (Alterio, 2014: 253–255).

In short, it can be said that popular constitutionalism focuses its attention on questioning several of the central postulates associated with positions that can be considered 'elitist' because they close constitutional issues to public debate and democratic challenges. However, it is necessary to question the extent to which popular constitutionalism 'opens up', since, as previously mentioned, several interpretations of this constitutionalism do not seem to question the fact that popular participation only occurs through the state legislative power, thereby excluding many other possibilities for participation in constitutional issues.

In addition to neoconstitutionalisms and popular constitutionalism, there are other variants which come under the category of the 'constitutionalism of diversity' (Uprimny, 2011), a reference to the social and cultural diversity in different regions of the world. Specifically in the case of Latin America, with its emphasis on the relationship between indigenous peoples and the state, a kind of constitutional progression[7] was contemplated, which developed from a 'multicultural constitutionalism', far more embodied in the Western liberal paradigm, to a 'pluricultural constitutionalism' and finally a 'plurinational constitutionalism' (Yrigoyen, 2011). Obviously, these constitutional designs and reflexive proposals can have systemic impacts, at least in the case of plurinational constitutionalism, since while directly questioning colonial law, it also questions the foundations of the state, both in its nineteenth-century liberal form and the social form of the twentieth century (Yrigoyen, 2011: 139–141). However, it is important to question how far these constitutional recognitions have effectively reconfigured the pillars of constitutionalism. From the perspective of epistemologies of the South, it is also important to determine the extent to which plurinational constitutionalism calls into question or denounces the abyssal line separating the metropolitan area from the colonial zone. It is necessary to devote increasing attention to establishing and regulating the exercise of public power and to verifying whether or not this design helps to address social problems that extend beyond the dominant modern-Western paradigm.

Another discussion that may be relevant to this theme involves questioning the purpose and social function of constitutions. In this regard, a 'conservative constitutionalism' would become evident, rather than an 'aspirational constitutionalism'. The former intends that the constitution and constitutional dynamics should serve to 'preserve' a certain state of affairs and a certain agreement on the functioning of social relations. In this sense, constitutions resemble a 'reflection of what really exists'. In contrast, aspirational constitutionalism does not view constitutions as a reflection of reality, but as a set of minimal bases that point towards what reality needs to be. This is a constitutionalism which resonates strongly in contexts where there is 'a great dissatisfaction with the present and a strong belief in the possibilities of a better future' (García Villegas, 2013: 77).

Finally, 'transformative constitutionalism', which is found in the global South and has a strong presence in Latin America, seeks to establish constitutional dynamics, evolving through instruments that aim to bring about social transformation and human emancipation, set against capitalist, colonialist and patriarchal oppression. In Latin America, this is known as new Latin American constitutionalism (NCLA). Since the 1990s, in different latitudes of Latin America, social mobilizations have emerged and developed, managing, through democratic means, to assume state power with the aim of transforming it, resulting in new constitutional texts with such distinctive characteristics that they may be considered pioneers of something different. For this reason, the expression NCLA is used by several authors (Gargarella and Courtis, 2009; Uprimny, 2011; Viciano Pastor and Martínez Dalmau, 2011). Other authors, focusing on the expression of a counter-hegemony, prefer the term 'transformative constitutionalism' (CT) (Santos, 2010b). NCLA began to be theorized mainly through constitutional law, while transformative constitutionalism takes the theoretical work of Boaventura de Sousa Santos as its gravitational centre. Both perspectives provide important elements, either for a structural analysis of the political implications of the content of the new constitutional texts or for thinking about counter-hegemonic social transformations, that is, the need for a new political and legal culture that seeks to overcome forms of sexist, colonial and capitalist systemic oppression.

These social processes find their maximum expression in the constitutions of Ecuador (2008) and Bolivia (2009).[8] Understanding them as expressions of transformative constitutionalism requires placing special emphasis on plurinationality, decolonization, depatriarchalization and legal, cultural, political and linguistic pluralism as principles that emerge when subalterns, namely those that are historically invisible, come to power with the aim of overhauling the state. They require new ways of understanding law and politics, both inside and outside the constitutions, which are often opposed to the liberal and Eurocentric legal culture that prevails in several countries in the global South.

Regarding the constitutions of Ecuador and Bolivia, textual recognition of the reality of legal pluralism entails the challenge of making visible what abyssal thinking has actively produced as invisible (Santos, 2010a) or, in other words, visualizing indigenous justices and understanding them as one of the cornerstones of the new plurinational states (Santos, 2007, 2010b, 2012). It also implies a change in ordinary justices, to enable an ecology of legal knowledges to emerge, built from an intercultural dialogue with indigenous justices (Grijalva Jiménez and Exeni Rodríguez, 2012). It is therefore necessary for intercultural translation to be produced not only in relation to the knowledge of indigenous justices and ordinary justice but also in relation to their practices (Bazurco Osorio and Exeni Rodríguez, 2012), in order to build a 'legal culture of conviviality', the ideal expression of legal pluralism as classified by Boaventura de Sousa Santos (Santos, 2012).

As with the 'constitution', 'constitutionalism' is expressed in multiple ways through contemporary reflections and realities. These expressions are not always compatible, given that they emphasize different aspects, focus on the various problems with different degrees of concern and attribute different levels of centrality to the various subjects. However, it can be argued that, as a whole, they represent a mosaic or collage of the constitutional reflections present today in various parts of the world.[9] As previously mentioned, just as there have been voices and proposals which try to explain or justify constitutional projects in line with the dominant modern constitutional paradigm, there have also been several critical voices. Some criticisms, even within the dominant constitutional canon, recognize the great limitations of constitutional designs in addressing contemporary problems and the need to control powers affecting people's lives which exceed those which have been constituted (Grimm, 2016: 249–251). Others denounce the functional relationship between the dominant constitutional design and relations based on capitalist domination, arguing that it has coexisted alongside inequality and the exclusion of multiple realities and social subjects which the system considered disposable (De Cabo Martín, 2014). Finally, voices critical of constitutional North-centrism, emanating specifically from Africa and Latin America, have singled out the importance of extending beyond the dominant constitutional canons, encouraging the construction of refocused proposals, as a constitutionalism of the global South (Medici, 2016). The chapters included in this book are critical voices associated with the latter, with varying nuances.

I.4 The Chapters

The chapters are organized into three parts. The five chapters that make up the first part theoretically situate the discussion around the decolonization, decommodification and depatriarchalization of constitutions. The second part combines the perspectives of three South African authors with different experiences and approaches, comprising a reflection on the constitutional processes that came after apartheid. The third part contains six chapters, two by indigenous Ecuadorian authors, on the recent constitutional processes in Latin America.

The first chapter, by Issa Shivji, introduces the theme by asking the question: Do constitutions matter? The author believes there is a lack of clarity in the idea that constitutions are a terrain for struggle, yet stops short of rejecting this conviction, instead choosing to focus on lawyers outside elitist circles who are driven by a passion for social justice and the struggle for the rights, dignity and livelihoods of those who work. Shivji recognizes the limits of bourgeois law and constitutions, while also recognizing the possibilities and identifying the conditions by which radical lawyers can be involved in the struggle for the recognition of rights, thus keeping a passion for social justice and social transformation alive.

In Chapter 2, Asifa Quraishi-Landes outlines the plurality which formed the basis of the constitutional structure of Islamic societies before the European model of the nation state superimposed itself. The Islamic conception of law is structurally different from the Western one. Classical *sharia* does not constitute a singular monolithic code and, as such, is far removed from the process of configuring law in the strict Western sense, which only recognizes the centralist logic. The state has never held the exclusive role of producing and imposing law associated with *sharia*. Before colonial intervention, *sharia* was based on a non-centralist structure, accommodating legal plurality through two types of law, two branches of *sharia*, two components of a holistic rule of law structure and two sources of legitimacy charged with different purposes: *fiqh* (law not codified by the state but created by legal experts through a heterogeneous, plural interpretation of scripture) and *siyasa* (law based on the authority of the state, unrelated to personal life). In addressing a dimension of a history that has effectively been rendered invisible, Asifa Quraishi-Landes positions herself beyond the nation state, within the renowned '*many rooms*' of the law. In this sense, her position poses a question that Western pluralists rarely manage to ask: What would a constitution look like if it started with the idea of legal pluralism as its founding principle, rather than as an add-on critique of existing legal monism? The author argues that the strong presence of legal pluralism throughout the history of Islamic law shows the extent to which it is possible to build a constitutional system without the premises of uniformity embedded in the nation state and where the balance between equality and difference can be achieved without subsuming every right to the authority of the state. In this sense, she proposes that modern Islamic constitutionalism should be inspired by the deep legal pluralism of pre-colonial *sharia*, comprising two pillars: (1) state lawmaking (*siyasa*) based on the public good; (2) the plurality of *fiqh* (and other religious rights), available as a voluntary opt-out from state law.

In Chapter 3, Upendra Baxi reflects on old and new constitutionalisms, formulates a set of issues that deepen the debate on decolonizing constitutionalism and proposes theoretical instruments that consolidate the analysis. Recognizing the importance (and the enormous challenge) of studying constitutionalisms from a subaltern or worm's-eye view, Baxi engages with the proposal of the epistemologies of the South, analysing how the concept of abyssal line might be useful in addressing theories of constitutionalism. In this sense, a broad question is maintained as a common thread in the text: Do constitutions matter at all for what Franz Fanon called the 'wretched of the earth' or Boaventura de Sousa Santos called the abyssally excluded? The author recognizes the multiplicity of forms of subaltern constitutionalism and the fragility of the 'new constitutionalism' category, as well as acknowledging that comparative constitutional studies (COCO) compare the incomparable. Interpreting the Indian context, Baxi argues that constitutionalism itself and all 'new' constitutions are faced with contradictions which can be studied on the following levels: aspirational/institutional; normative/institutional; civilizational/cultural; material/symbolic or performative. Constitutional innovation has traditionally been attributed to the West, whose civilizational mission led to the spread of the four Cs – conquest, Christianity, commerce and civilization. Among the set of questions raised in the context of COCO, this study focuses on the following: How are we to grasp the varieties of postcolonial experience? Are the constitutionalisms of non-Euro American others always mimetic and never otherwise? Where can we place certain astonishing examples of judicial creativity in the global South? May we conceive of the world as a Western shopping mall or arcade from which countries in the non-West assemble their constitutions? Do history and context matter and if so, how? Can anomie and contradiction be transplanted, transferred and compared? What kinds of constitutionalism does a movement-led struggle produce? How do we reconcile the imperatives of the global market with those of elite or mass-conceived religion? Is constitutional secularism the best possible answer? How far may the constitutional courts impose their demos prudence over their jurisprudence? What may be the future constitutional promise and peril of this different modernity? For the author, what matters is perhaps not the way constitutions are written, but the contradictions of constitutionalism and, crucially, the forms of 'insurgencies' that characterize life under the constitutions.

In Chapter 4, Rosalva Aída Hernández Castillo combines a feminist and pluralistic approach to transformative constitutionalism, extending the boundaries of the Latin American debate beyond the experiences of Bolivia and Ecuador to include the voices of indigenous women who have been protagonists in internal and external political debates. Drawing on experiences in the Mexican states of Chiapas and Oaxaca – the former an autonomous entity not recognized by the state, where Zapatista support bases pursue their own justice with no state intervention; the latter a space that has recognized legal autonomy in the context of the constitutional reforms that have taken place in Oaxaca within the last decade – Hernández identifies sites for legal and political dispute where resistance strategies are discussed and indigenous and gender identities are negotiated. By refuting an essentialist conception of local legal structures, she develops a sociology of emergences, highlighting the dynamic nature of indigenous constitutions and the possibilities that result from interlinked struggles.

In Chapter 5, Sara Araújo discusses the possibilities and limits of the concept of legal pluralism expanding the recognized legal reality and the possibilities of political imagination. Building on the challenges and conceptual instruments of the epistemologies of the South, she explores the extent to which theories and empirical studies of legal pluralism, as well as different recognition policies, have contributed to decolonizing the Eurocentric legal canon. By adding categories to Sally Engle Merry's widely accepted typology, five approaches to legal pluralism are defined: classical legal pluralism, new legal pluralism, global legal pluralism, instrumental legal pluralism and intercultural legal pluralism. The chapter concludes by discussing the possibilities of constructing a post-abyssal legal thinking through a sociology of emergences which addresses the diversity of legal maps of the world.

The second part brings together three distinct reflections on recent constitutionalism in South Africa. In Chapter 6, Heinz Klug introduces the discussion, arguing that it is not possible to understand the complexity of the present without considering the legal continuities of colonialism and apartheid, the legacy of anti-apartheid social struggles and the form which the process of democratic transition has assumed. The author begins by situating the discussion within some of the main concepts and theoretical developments associated with the state and constitutionalism in Africa, recognizing the common colonial legacy, as well as the historical, cultural and constitutional heterogeneity of the continent. Klug focuses on a set of conditions that result from continuities with the past, which marked the first 20 years of post-apartheid governance: social inequality; the preservation of apartheid in the public sector; the extension of non-democratic transition to local government; recognition of the traditional authorities; the limited role of the Truth and Reconciliation Commission. For the author, the constitution, 'the crowning achievement of that historic moment', represents an opportunity for social transformation, with the potential to act as an instrument for anti-corruption and anti-nepotism.

In Chapter 7, Albie Sachs presents an exercise in self-reflection regarding his work as a judge in the South African Constitutional Court. Sachs actively participated in the drafting of the democratic Constitution of the Republic of South Africa and was appointed a Constitutional Court judge by Nelson Mandela. In this text, which draws on his own experience, Sachs discusses the limits and possibilities of law as an instrument for social transformation. In sharing cases in which he intervened as a judge and defender of the new post-apartheid constitutional order, the author reflects on transformative constitutional jurisprudence and the possibilities for establishing social and economic rights, as well as the construction of a true interculturality, respecting the right to equality and the right to difference. For the author, the constitution should function as an active source of regulation – combining common law and customary law, and allowing for emancipatory readings in situations in which constitutional principles are at odds with each other (such as dignity and private property, or the right to equality and the recognition of customary law).

In Chapter 8, Tshepo Madlingozi presents a highly critical reading of what he describes as neo-apartheid constitutionalism. The author links the concept of the abyssal line to the South African philosopher Mogobe Ramose's proposal for a post-conquest constitution. Seeking not to lose sight of the perspective of the historical victims of settler colonialism, Madlingozi is not optimistic with regard to the horizon of possibilities unlocked by the 1994 Constitution. Neo-apartheid constitutionalism, he argues, shifts the abyssal line without overcoming it, promoting a transition from settler domination to settler hegemony. The author examines the extent to which a constitution can embody the decolonizing project and its sensibilities. In deliberating on what remains to be deconstitutionalized in the world created by the colonizer, Madlingozi reflects on the possibilities of building a constitution that promotes epistemic justice, sustains its authority through Ubuntu philosophy and replaces the monoculture of constitutional law with intercultural dialogue.

The final part, which focusses on constitutional processes in Latin America, is introduced by Salvador Schavelzon. In Chapter 9, the author offers a detailed narrative of the constituent process in Bolivia, based on the ethnographic record of the debates within the Constituent Assembly and the identification of the translational challenges involving different civilizational, epistemological and ontological universes. A number of topics are addressed in this text, including the following: the issue of recognition for multiple historically excluded identities (namely class and ethnicity); problems with the process for approving the constitution; colonial continuities; challenges regarding the implementation or interpretation of the constitutional text, such as issues related to recognition of indigenous justice and demodiversity; and modern criticisms of plurinationality. Through the idea of a 'constituent silence', the author illustrates the difficulties inherent in constructing dialogues based on different world views when colonial hierarchies are not definitively questioned and the modern legal language retains the power to impose limits on the dialogue.

In Chapter 10, Raúl Llasag, a Quechuan jurist from Cotopaxi, views plurinational constitutionalism from a highly critical perspective, distinguishing between plurinationality from above, which is a Eurocentric continuity, and plurinationality from below, arguing that it cannot be built on the basis of modern-Western theories of constitutionalism or understood through colonial conceptions of modern social sciences. For Raúl Llasag, plurinationality from above is not an end in itself but a transitional tool which must be monitored without losing sight of the initial proposal, namely plurinationality from below. This proposal does not focus on taking state power, but on exercising autonomy in the daily life of grassroots communities, and on expanding these bases beyond indigenous spaces with a view to simplifying life and recovering political, economic and epistemological autonomy.

In Chapter 11, Nina Pacari, a Quechuan jurist from Cotacachi and a former judge in the Constitutional Court of Ecuador, provides another critical reading of constitutional advances in Ecuador from the perspective of indigenous peoples. It is a testimonial and a critical reflection constructed from her experience as a jurist, an activist working for the recognition of indigenous peoples, and a member of the National Constituent Assembly, the National Assembly of Ecuador and the Constitutional Court. Pacari draws attention to the continuity of power structures based on Western hegemony imposed on the originary peoples and seeks to show the epistemic complexity underlying indigenous claims. She discusses the processes of deconstitutionalization, the construction of plurinationality, the recognition of legal pluralism and the challenges to the independence of the Constitutional Court, arguing that interculturality has to involve an epistemic dialogue in plurinational societies which will oblige the state to implement consultation procedures through an exercise in 'command obeying'.

In Chapter 12, Agustín Grijalva discusses the relationship between participation, (hyper)presidentialism and extractivism in the context of the NCLA, specifically analysing the case of Ecuador a decade or so after the great constitutional change. The 2008 Constitution nominally strengthened citizen participation in public management, monitoring and combatting corruption. However, the reality failed to correspond to the expectations provided by law. Grijalva introduces an important distinction between participation as legitimation and participation as democratization. In order to illustrate the difference, the author examines the popular consultation of 2011 convened by Rafael Correa, as President of Ecuador, and the blocking of other consultations, such as the one concerning the Yasuní-ITT project. In the end, Grijalva argues that extractivism is not just a model for economic policy, but also influences policy fields as diverse as participation, education, labour and the justice system. From a position compatible with that of other authors, Grijalva argues that the constitution is not the end, but rather the beginning of a process for social change. It must therefore be seen as a political program to be defended at any given moment.

Chapter 13, by Orlando Aragón Andrade, broadens the discussion on Latin American transformative constitutionalism, questioning the limits of the debate and the horizons of possibilities imposed by colonial legal terms. Extrapolating the terms of Eurocentric scientific research in assuming his dual role as a lawyer and militant academic, Andrade discusses the possibilities of building transformative constitutionalism from below on a national scale, based on a local Mexican experience: the insurrection of the Pureecha people of San Francisco Cherán and the establishment of a new municipal government founded on local organizational principles. The author challenges the limits of abyssal legal thinking, proposing a broadening of the constitutional discussion through local legal diversity and the construction of an ecology of trans-scale legal knowledges. What makes constitutionalism transformative? Does Cherán's Constitution have the potential to become part of a transformative constitutionalism project? Is it possible to say that indigenous justices have their own constitutions? Can a local constitution challenge the hegemonic model of the nation state?

In the final Chapter 14, Boaventura de Sousa Santos shows the relevance of research on law and justice as a window to understanding the dynamics of social transformation. The indigenous struggles aimed at constructing plurinational societies are addressed in light of the author's extensive theoretical work in the sociology of law, together with his proposal for the epistemologies of the South, presenting an overview of the main concepts. Among the tensions he analyses, the following are the most salient: judicial monism and judicial pluralism; multicultural liberalism and interculturality; the nation and the plurination; Eurocentric political pluralism and intercultural political pluralism; dependent developmental capitalism and *Sumak Kawsay* or *Suma Qamaña*. The construction of a plurinational state will have to challenge the cognitive, economic, social and political injustice at the core of the nation state. This is a slow path which involves suffering and struggle and also requires transforming dualisms into ecologies of judicial knowledges. Santos concludes the chapter with a set of lessons derived from the processes that were studied, which can serve as beacons along this path.

Notes

1 On the monoculture of valid knowledge, the monoculture of linear time, the monoculture of social classification, the monoculture of the superiority of the universal and the global and the monoculture of productivity, see Santos (2018).
2 Although the author does not make explicit reference at this point to the constitution, he does refer to 'politics' and 'law' as being two sides of the same coin (Bobbio, 1984).
3 We will return to these concepts later when outlining the socio-juridical proposal of the epistemologies of the South.
4 Another reference to constitution and complexity can be found in Medici (2016).
5 One reflection on the constitution as a space that includes several 'fundamentally controversial concepts' can be found in Waldron (1994). In the same vein, see Ortega Soriano (2017).
6 An eloquent example is provided by the work *Constitutionalism: Past, Present and Future* published by the Oxford University Press in 2016. In this 400-page volume, Grimm makes less than ten references to constitutions and constitutionalisms of the state beyond the global North, although several years have elapsed since constitutions such as those of Ecuador and Bolivia, considered relevant from other perspectives on a constitutional present and future, were promulgated (Grimm, 2016: 249–251).
7 This progression should not necessarily be read in terms of 'evolutionism' or 'improvement' since, on many occasions, all these 'constitutionalisms of diversity' coexist in the same country, in the same region and, of course, in the world.

8 For further discussion on the similarities and differences regarding the premises of neoconstitutionalism and other constitutional developments, see Uprimny (2011) and Alterio (2014: 275–293).

9 For a more focused approach to debates on the reality of the United States of America, see Wittington (2009), where normative constitutionalism, descriptive constitutionalism and empirical constitutionalism are distinguished. For constitutional reflections aimed at a dialog between Europe and the Latin American region, see von Bogdandy (2015). Although the latter focuses on Latin America, reflecting on exclusion and inequality, he uses a comparative perspective in analysing the dynamics of institutions and law.

References

Abel, Richard L. (1990), 'Capitalism and the Rule of Law: Precondition or Contradiction?' *Law & Social Inquiry*, 15(4): 685–697. DOI: https://doi.org/10.1111/j.1747-4469.1990.tb00600.x.

Alterio, Ana Micaela (2014), 'Corrientes del Constitucionalismo Contemporáneo a Debate', *PROBLEMA. Anuario de Filosofía y Teoría del Derecho,* 8: 227–306. DOI: https://doi.org/10.22201/iij.24487937e.2014.8.8166.

Anderson, Benedict (2006), *Imagined Communities*. London: Verso.

Araújo, Sara (2016), 'O Primado do Direito e as Exclusões Abissais: Reconstruir Velhos Conceitos, Desafiar o Cânone', *Sociologias,* 43(18): 88–115. DOI: https://doi.org/10.1590/15174522-018004304.

Barros-Varela, Odair (2017), *Crítica da Razão Estatal. Estado Moderno em África nas Relações Internacionais e Ciência Política. O caso de Cabo Verde.* Praia: Pedro Cardoso Livraria.

Baxi, Upendra (2013), 'Preliminary Notes on Transformative Constitutionalism', *in* Oscar Vilhena, Upendra Baxi, Frans Viljoen (eds.), *Transformative Constitutionalism. Comparing the Apex Courts of Brazil, India and South Africa*. Pretoria: Pretoria University Press.

Bazurco Osorio, M.; Exeni Rodríguez, J. L. (2012), 'Bolivia: Justicia Indígena en Tiempos de Plurinacionalidade', *in* B. de S. Santos and J. L. Exeni Rodríguez (eds.), *Justicia Indígena, Plurinacionalidad y Interculturalidad en Bolivia*. Quito: Fundación Rosa Luxemburg/Abya-Yala, 49–144. HDL: http://hdl.handle.net/10316/44166.

Berman, P. S. (2012), *Global Legal Pluralism: A Jurisprudence of Law Beyond Borders.* New York: Cambridge University Press.

Bhandar, Brenna (2018), *Colonial Lives of Property: Law, Land, and Racial Regimes of Ownership.* Durham, NC: Duke University Press.

Bobbio, Norberto (1984), 'El Poder y el Derecho', *in* Norberto Bobbio and Michelangelo Bovero (eds.), *Origen y Fundamentos del Poder Político.* Mexico: Grijalbo, 19–36.

Bobbio, Norberto (1986), *El Futuro de la Democracia*, Mexico: FCE—Fondo de Cultura Económica.

Bovero, Michelangelo (2006), 'Prefacio', *in* Pedro Salazar Ugarte (ed.), *La Democracia Constitucional. Una Radiografía Teórica.* Mexico: FCE, IIJ- UNAM.

Bowsher, Josh (2018), 'Law & Critique: Transitional Justice as "Omnus et Singulatim"', *Critical Legal Thinking.* Available at http://criticallegalthinking.com/2018/06/07/law-critique-transitional-justice-as-omnus-et-singulatim.

Brabazon, Honor (2017), 'Introduction. Understanding Neoliberal Legality', *in* Honor Brabazon (ed.), *Neoliberal Legality. Understanding the Role of Law in the Neoliberal Project.* Abingdon: Routledge, 1–21.

Capra, Fritjof; Mattei, Ugo (2015), *The Ecology of Law. Toward a Legal System in Tune with Nature and Community.* Oakland, CA: Berrett-Koehler.

Castro-Gómez, Santiago (2005), 'Ciências Sociais, Violência Epistêmica e o Problema de "Invenção do Outro"', *in* Edgardo Lander (ed.), *A Colonialidade do Saber: Eurocentrismo e Ciências Sociais. Perspectivas Latino-Americanas*. Buenos Aires: CLACSO, 169–186. Available at http://biblioteca.clacso.edu.ar/ar/libros/lander/pt/lander.

Chakrabarty, Dipesh (2000), *Provincializing Europe. Postcolonial Thought and Historical Difference*. Princeton, NJ: Princeton University Press.

Chatterjee, Partha (1991), 'Whose Imagined Community?' *Millenium*, 20(3): 521–525. DOI: https://doi.org/10.1177/03058298910200030601.

Chatterjee, Partha (1998), 'Beyond the Nation? Or Within?', *Social Text*, 56: 57–69. JSTOR: www.jstor.org/stable/466770.

Comanducci, Paolo (2002), 'Formas de (Neo)Constitucionalismo: Un Análisis Metateórico', *Isonomía*, 16.

Comaroff, Jean; Comaroff, John (2003), 'Reflections on Liberalism, Policulturalism and ID-ology: Citizens and Difference in South Africa', *Social Identities*, 9(4): 445–473. DOI: https://doi.org/10.1080/1350463032000174632.

De Cabo, Martín (2014), *Pensamiento Crítico. Constitucionalismo Crítico*. Madrid: Trotta.

Duve, T. (2014), 'Introduction', *in* T. Duve (ed.), *Entanglements in Legal History: Conceptual Approaches*. Frankfurt am Main: Max Planck Institute for European Legal History, 3–25. DOI: https://doi.org/10.12946/gplh1.

Dworkin, Ronald (1996), *Freedom's Law*. Oxford: Oxford University Press.

Fanon, Frantz (2008 [1952]), *Black Skin. White Masks*. New York: Grove Press.

Federici, Silvia (2009), *Caliban and the Witch*. New York: Autonomedia.

Federici, Silvia (2014), 'The Making of Capitalist Patriarchy: Interview with Silvia Federici', *in* Tessa Echeverria and Andrew Sernatinger (eds.), *The North Star*, 24 February. Available at: https://marxismocritico.com/2014/02/24/the-making-of-capitalist-patriarchy.

Ferrajoli, Luigi (2011), 'Constitucionalismo Principialista y Constitucionalismo Garantista', *DOXA, Cuadernos de Filosofía del Derecho*, 34: 15–53. DOI: https://doi.org/10.14198/DOXA2011.34.02.

Ferreira, António Casimiro (2016), *Política e Sociedade. Teoria Social em Tempo de Austeridade*. Porto: Vida Económica.

Fioravanti, Maurizio (2001), *Constitución. De la Antigüedad a Nuestros Días*. Madrid: Trotta.

Fitzpatrick, Peter (1992), *The Mythology of Modern Law*. London: Routledge.

Galanter, Marc (1966), 'The Modernization of Law', *in* Miron Winer (ed.), *Modernization*. New York: Basic Books.

Galindo, G.R.B. (2014), 'Legal Transplants between Time and Space', *in* T. Duve (ed.), *Entanglements in Legal History: Conceptual Approaches*. Frankfurt am Main: Max Planck Institute for European Legal History, 3–25. DOI: https://doi.org/10.12946/gplh1.

García Villegas, Mauricio (2013), 'Constitutionalismo Aspiracional', *Araucaria. Revista Iberoamericana de Filosofía, Política y Humanidades*, 15(29): 77–97. Available at: www.redalyc.org/pdf/282/28225781004.pdf.

Gargarella, R.; Courtis, C. (2009), 'El Nuevo Constitucionalismo Latinoamericano: Promesas e Interrogantes', *Políticas Sociales*, 153. HDL: http://hdl.handle.net/11362/6162.

Grijalva Jiménez, Agustín ; Exeni Rodríguez, J. L. (2012), 'Coordinación entre Justicias, ese Desafío', *in* B. de S. Santos and J. L. Exeni Rodríguez (eds.), *Justicia Indígena, Plurinacionalidad e Interculturalidad en Bolivia*. Quito: Fundación Rosa Luxemburg/Abya-Yala, 699–732. HDL: http://hdl.handle.net/10316/44166.

Grimm, Dieter (2016), *Constitutionalism. Past, Present, and Future*. Oxford: Oxford University Press.

Knox, Robert (2017), 'Law, Neoliberalism and the Constitution of Political Subjectivity. The Case of Organised Labour', *in* Honor Brabazon (ed.), *Neoliberal Legality. Understanding the Role of Law in the Neoliberal Project*. Abingdon: Routledge, 92–118.

Kramer, Larry (2004), 'Popular Constitutionalism, circa 2004', *California Law Review*, 92(4): 959–1011. DOI: www.jstor.org/stable/3481314.

Madlingozi, Tshepo (2010), 'On Transitional Justice Entrepreneurs and the Production of Victims', *Journal of Human Rights Practice*, 2(2): 208–228. DOI: https://doi.org/10.1093/jhuman/huq005.

Mamdani, Mamhood (1996), *Citizen and Subject. Contemporary Africa and the Legacy of Late Colonialism*. Princeton, NJ: Princeton University Press.

Marx, Anthony W. (2002), 'The Nation-State and Its Exclusions', *Political Science Quarterly*, 117(1): 103–126. DOI: https://doi.org/10.2307/798096.

Mattei, Ugo; Morpurgo, Marco (2009), 'Global Law and Plunder: The Dark Side of the Rule of Law', *Bocconi School of Law Student-Edited Papers, No. 2009-03/EN*. DOI: https://doi.org/10.2139/ssrn.1437530.

Mattei, Ugo; Nader, Laura (eds.) (2008), *Plunder: When the Rule of Law Is Illegal*. Malden, MA: Blackwell.

McIlwain, Charles H. (1947), *Constitutionalism. Ancient and Modern*. New York. Cornell University Press.

Medici, Alejandro (2016), *Teoría del Nuevo Constitucionalismo Latinoamericano*. Aguascalientes/San Luis Potosí: Centro de Estudios Jurídicos y Sociales Mispat Maestría en Derechos Humanos de la UASLP.

Meneses, Maria Paula; Araújo, Sara; Ferreira, Sílvia; Safradin, Barbara (2018), 'Comparative Report on the Types of Distributive Claims, Interests and Capabilities of Various Groups of the Population Evoked in the Political and Economic Debates at the EU and at the Nation State Level', *ETHOS, Work Package 6, D6.2*. HDL: http://hdl.handle.net/10316/87019.

Michaels, Ralf (2009), 'Global Legal Pluralism', *Annual Review of Law & Social Science*, 5: 243–262. DOI: https://doi.org/10.1146/annurev.lawsocsci.4.110707.172311.

Mutua, Makau (2016), 'Africa and the Rule of Law', *Sur 23*, 13(23): 159–173. Available at: https://sur.conectas.org/wp-content/uploads/2016/09/13-sur-23-ingles-makau-mutua.pdf.

Nunn, Kenneth, B. (1997), 'Law as a Eurocentric Enterprise', *Law & Inequality: A Journal of Theory and Practice*, 15(2): 323–371. Available at: https://scholarship.law.umn.edu/lawineq/vol15/iss2/2.

Ortega Soriano, Ricardo A. (2017), *La Seguridad Jurídica en el Estado Constitucional: Hacia la Renovación de un Ideal*. PhD thesis. Universidad Nacional Autónoma de México, Mexico (UNAM), Mexico City. Available at: https://repositorio.unam.mx/contenidos/64954.

Otto, Dianne (1996), 'Subalternity and International Law: The Problems of Global Community and the Incommensurability of Difference', *Social & Legal Studies*, 5(3): 337–364. DOI: https://doi.org/10.1177/096466399600500304.

Peters, A. (2015), 'Global Legal Constitutionalism', *in* M. T. Gibbons (ed.), *The Encyclopedia of Political Thought*. Wiley. Available at: www.mpil.de/files/pdf5/Peters_Global_Constitutionalism__Encyclopedia_of_Political_Thought_20151.pdf.

Peterson, Spike V. (2013), 'The Intended and Unintended Queering of States/Nations', *Studies in Ethnicity and Nationalism*, 13(1): 57–68. DOI: https://doi.org/10.1111/sena.12021.

Roy, Alpana (2008), 'Postcolonial Theory and Law: A Critical Introduction', *Adelaide Law Review*, 29: 315–357. Available at: http://classic.austlii.edu.au/au/journals/AdelLawRw/2008/10.html.

Santos, Boaventura de Sousa (1977), 'The Law of the Oppressed: The Construction and Reproduction of Legality in Pasargada', *Law & Society Review*, 12(1): 5–126. JSTOR: www.jstor.org/stable/3053321.

Santos, Boaventura de Sousa (1995), *Toward a New Common Sense. Law, Science and Politics in the Paradigmatic Transition*. New York: Routledge.

Santos, Boaventura de Sousa (2000), *A Crítica da Razão Indolente. Contra o Desperdício da Experiência*. Porto: Ediçoês Afrontamento.

Santos, Boaventura de Sousa (2002), *Toward a New Legal Common Sense*. London: Butterwords.

Santos, Boaventura de Sousa (2003), 'Introduction', *in* Santos, Boaventura de Sousa (ed.), *Conhecimento Prudente para uma Vida Decente. 'Um Discurso sobre as Ciências'Revisitado*. Port: Afrontamento, 15–54.

Santos, Boaventura de Sousa (2007), 'La Reinvención del Estado y el Estado Plurinacional', *OSAL*, 22: 25–46.

Santos, Boaventura de Sousa (2008), 'The World Social Forum and the Global Left', *Politics & Society*, 36(2): 247–270. DOI: https://doi.org/10.1177/0032329208316571.

Santos, Boaventura de Sousa (2010a), *Para Descolonizar Occidente: Más Allá del Pensamiento Abismal*. Buenos Aires: CLACSO/Prometeo Libros. HDL: http://hdl.handle.net/10316/44177.

Santos, Boaventura de Sousa (2010b), *Refundacíon del Estado en América Latina: Perspectivas desde una Epistemología del Sur*. Lima: Instituto Internacional de Derecho y Sociedad. HDL: http://hdl.handle.net/10316/44161.

Santos, Boaventura de Sousa (2011), *Para uma Revolução Democrática da Justiça*. São Paulo: Cortez.

Santos, Boaventura de Sousa (2012), 'Cuando los Excluidos Tienen Derecho: Justicia Indígena, Plurinacionalidad e Interculturalidade', *in* B. de S. Santos and J. L. Exeni Rodríguez (eds.), *Justicia Indígena, Plurinacionalidad e Interculturalidad en Bolivia*. Quito: Fundación Rosa Luxemburg/Abya-Yala, 11–48. HDL: http://hdl.handle.net/10316/44166.

Santos, Boaventura de Sousa (2014), *Epistemologies of the South*. Boulder, CO: Paradigm.

Santos, Boaventura de Sousa (2017), 'The Resilience of Abyssal Exclusions in Our Societies: Toward a Post-Abyssal Law', *Tilburg Law Review*, 22(1–2): 237–258. DOI: https://doi.org/10.1163/22112596-02201011.

Santos, Boaventura de Sousa (2018), *O Fim do Império Cognitivo*. Coimbra: Almedina.

Schneiderman, David (2008), *Constitutionalizing Economic Globalization: Investment Rules and Democracy's Promises*. Cambridge: Cambridge University Press.

Tully, James (1995), *Strange Multiplicity. Constitutionalism in an Age of Diversity*. Cambridge: Cambridge University Press.

Tzouvala, Ntina (2017), 'Continuity and Rupture in Restraining the Right to the Strike', *in* Honor Brabazon (ed.), *Neoliberal Legality. Understanding the Role of Law in the Neoliberal Project*. Abingdon: Routledge, 119–139.

Uprimny, R. (2011), 'Las Transformaciones Constitucionales Recientes en América Latina: Tendencias y Retos', *Revista Pensamiento Penal*, 122: 1–22. Available at: www.pensamientopenal.com.ar/system/files/2011/04/doctrina28469.pdf.

Viciano Pastor, R.; Martínez Dalmau, R. (2011), 'El Nuevo Constitucionalismo Latinoamericano: Fundamentos para una Construcción Doctrinal', *Revista General de Derecho Público Comparado*, 9: 1–24. Available at: www.researchgate.net/publication/349029222_El_nuevo_constitucionalismo_latinoamericano_fundamentos_para_una_construccion_doctrinal.

von Bogdandy, Armin (2015), 'Ius Constitutionale Commune na América Latina: Um Olhar para um Constitucionalismo Transformador', *Revista Derecho del Estado*, 34: 3–50. DOI: https://doi.org/10.18601/01229893.n34.01.

Waldron, Jeremy (2006), 'The Core of the Case Against Judicial Review', *The Yale Law Journal*, 115(6): 1346–1406. JSTOR: www.jstor.org/stable/20455656.

Waldron, Jeremy (2012), 'Constitutionalism: A Skeptical View', *Public Law and Legal Theory Research Papers Series*, 10–87. Available at SSRN: https://ssrn.com/abstract=1722771

Wittington, Keith (2009), 'Constitutionalism', *in* Gregory A. Caldeira, R. Daniel Kelemen, and Keith E. Whittington (eds.), *The Oxford Handbook of Law and Politics*. Oxford: Oxford University Press, 281–299.

Wolkmer, Antônio Carlos (1994), *Pluralismo Jurídico. Fundamentos de uma Nova Cultura do Dereito*. São Paulo: Editora Alfa Omega.

Yrigoyen Fajardo, Raquel (2011), 'El Horizonte del Constitucionalismo Pluralista: Del Multiculturalismo a la Descolonización', *in* César Rodríguez Garavito (ed.), *El Derecho en América Latina. Un Mapa para el Pensamiento Jurídico del Siglo XXI*. Buenos Aires: Siglo Veintiuno Editores, 139–159.

Yuval-Davis, Nira (1993), 'Gender and Nation', *Ethnic and Racial Studies*, 16(4): 621–632. DOI: https://doi.org/10.1080/01419870.1993.9993800.

Zagrebelsky, Gustavo (2013), 'Constitucionalismo', *Derechos y Libertades*, 29 (Época II): 19–38.

PART I

The Vast Landscape of Constitutionalisms

1

DO CONSTITUTIONS MATTER?

The Dilemma of a Radical Lawyer[1]

Issa G. Shivji

Constitutions don't make revolutions. Revolutions make constitutions. No constitution envisages its own death for that is what a revolution entails. But constitutions matter. Some of the finest constitutions have been erected on ugly socio-economic formations wrought with extreme inequalities and inequities. South Africa and Kenya are examples. But constitutions do matter. Constitutions rarely herald fundamental transformations. They are the product of major transformations to consolidate the new status quo. Yet constitutions do matter. Why do constitutions matter? Why do we need constitutions? Why do every revolution and major change in modern societies birth new constitutions? This is the question I want to reflect on: why do constitutions matter?

A constitution is as much a political as a legal document. It is a power map. Deeper structures of a constitution reveal, albeit partially, the constitution of the state, the primary repository of political power. The constitution defines the citizen and expresses the authority of the state over her. It defines and demarcates the rights of the citizen and limits his or her freedom. In turn, the state demands unquestionable loyalty to itself. State's authority and citizen's loyalty are sanctioned by criminal law which stands for the use of force. Citizen's rights and freedoms are sanctioned by civil law which censures individuals and organs, never the state. Citizen's loyalty to the state is taught in our schools as Civics. State's authority over citizens is political, not civic, and politics are embargoed from schools. In the mystified language of politics, the absolute loyalty to the state is called patriotism. It is in the name of patriotism that wars are fought, and conflicts between and among ruling classes are played out, all at the expense of the lives and freedoms of the people.

I said the constitution is a political document. Now I extend it—it is also an ideological document. It mystifies citizen's loyalty to the state as a civic duty

DOI: 10.4324/9781003391920-3

while it mesmerises state's authority over the citizen as necessary in the interest of society. Rights and freedoms are given by the grace of the state—they are gratuitous. Restrictions and abbreviations of rights and freedoms are a necessity, which, the otherwise benevolent, state has to enforce in the interest of social stability (read state's stability). All liberal and liberal-left discourses, whatever their nuances and however anti-establishment they may sound, ultimately reflect and reinforce the ideological apparatus of the state to justify, mystify and mesmerise the state's monopoly of authority and violence to maintain the status quo.

1.1 Why Do Then Constitutions Matter?

Constitutions are a terrain of struggle, as progressive lawyers like some of you and me would say. It is a cliché but a cliché with some truth and much mystification. Permit me briefly to deconstruct the cliché by asking the following rhetorical questions. Who fights that struggle? At what site? In whose interest? For what purpose? Under what perspective and set of values (which is really a euphemism for ideology!)? Lawyers fight that struggle in courts through litigation in the interest of their clients with the purpose of winning, driven or motivated by a set of liberal values—human rights, accountability, checks and balances, limitation of power and so on—values that are anchored in liberal democracy which is the staple on which we have been trained and fed and brought up. What is there in it for lawyers? Fees in the pocket, status in society, reputation at the bar, appeasement of the conscience and inflation of the ego. That is a bit harsh. For there are some who do *pro bono* work probably funded by liberal donor organisations including such dubious funders as George Soros' "Open Societies". (Some of you may know that Soros made his money through speculation on the financial markets or what is better termed as "casino capitalism".)

But, to be fair, on the margins of such a coterie of elitist lawyers, there exist sincere, well-intentioned and self-sacrificing lawyers who are motivated by their passion for social justice and fight for the rights, dignity and livelihoods of the working people. It is to this group of radical lawyers that I wish to address my following remarks. (And I include myself in this group.)

It is important for us, radical lawyers, to recognise the limits of bourgeois law and constitutions.

Firstly, law, by its very nature, *individualises* collective demands as individual grievances and disputes. It thus *fragments* social struggles and undermines solidarity of the working people.

Secondly, in a litigation, it is the lawyer who is the hero while the people are victims or spectators. The hero fights while the spectators cheer. It deprives the people of their self-esteem and militancy. It subverts people's agency.

Thirdly, the struggle moves from the barricades to the barristers thus robbing the people of their schools of struggle which are streets, neighbourhoods and places of production.

Fourthly, while victory goes to legitimise the status quo and the system, defeat results in despondency and hopelessness and, not infrequently, surrender.

Finally, the progressive lawyer is infected even more deeply by the liberal virus, to use Samir Amin's phrase, holding high the placard of change and reform while simultaneously holding down the banner of fundamental transformation.

So, then, the question for the radical lawyer is: why fight for rights and freedoms and constitutionalism? Why, at all, do constitutions matter? I am sure many a radical lawyer has agonised over this, as I have, over the years in my legal aid and trade union practice. Let me think aloud with you on how a radical lawyer may engage in the rights struggle while keeping his passion for social justice and transformation alive and undented.

First, a radical lawyer must disinfect herself or himself of the liberal virus. And the most effective vaccine is revolutionary theory and conscientious practice.

Second, a radical lawyer must disabuse himself or herself of the notion that law is neutral and apolitical. It is not. If politics is the concentrated form of economics, as Lenin said, I add, law is the concentrated form of politics. The question is: what kind of politics? Radical politics are not on offer and cannot be picked up from workshops and seminars. Rather, they should be learnt from the masses for real politics are where the masses are.

Third, a radical lawyer must humbly acknowledge that legal struggles are only one front of the social struggles of the working people. Therefore, it cannot be waged in isolation from other fronts of struggles.

Fourth, a radical lawyer should not stop at chanting that constitution is a terrain of struggle. He or she must go beyond to identify sites of struggle. The sites of struggles which matter to the people are where they live (urban neighbourhoods and village communities) and where they get their livelihoods (land and factories).

Fifth, and finally, radical lawyer must recognise that the sites of struggle are also sites of organising working people. Unorganised masses are like steam that evaporates into air and disappears. But the same steam when captured in an engine pushes the piston and moves the engine.

Stating these guidelines in the abstract rightly sounds esoteric and perhaps unrealistic. It behoves on me to concretise them. I will do so by broadly painting one possible scenario.

Let me use what they call triangulation. My three points will be right to life, freedom of expression and freedom of association. Right to life can be further resolved into right to live with dignity and right to decent livelihood—in short, right to be human, as Upendra Baxi would have it. It is around these rights that local struggles are strategised and people are mobilised and organised. It is around these rights and freedoms that litigation strategies are worked out. This way of highlighting and focusing on a selected number of strategic rights and freedoms allows one to move away from the fragmented rights' discourse.

This way of crystallising the rights' struggle on the ground also gives radical activists a handle on the demands that should be made of the state at the national level. And here I draw in the concept of commons, both traditional commons—land, water, underground and over-ground natural resources and new commons which are often called public goods. In this I include education, health and sanitation, energy, communications and finance. Here the strategic demand would be to de-commodify and de-privatise the commons. In other words, for the working people to reclaim the commons and liberate them from the clutches of monopoly finance capital assisted by our comprador states. This way of conceptualising, operationalising and strategising on different fronts the rights struggle and the struggle for the commons would strike an immediate chord in the consciousness of the masses for it is a struggle for their decent livelihoods and human dignity. It is a struggle to facilitate production where energy and finance are important factors. And it is a struggle for the education and health of their children. It also becomes a struggle to bring strategic sectors of the economy in the public domain. It is thus a struggle against local compradorial classes and imperialist capital.

Friends and comrades, I have overstepped my boundaries and said more than what you bargained for! Let me end with two remarks. You are commemorating ten years of your constitution and launching my friend Willy Mutunga's new edition of the book *Constitution-making from the Middle.* No doubt, in the new constitution you have a fine product. Many commentators have analysed and will continue to comment on the product. My interest, though, is not so much in the product but the process of making the product, so well captured in Willy's book. I had the taste of that process when I was invited to address the National Convention Assembly (NCA), I think, sometime in 2001. I was amazed at the composition of the delegates attending that convention. They were all elected at the grassroots level, mostly working people in their ragtag clothes and women in *baibui.* The deliberations were in Kiswahili. Willy reminds me that at that meeting I warned *walalahoi* (working people) not to leave the process in the hands of the *walalahai* (petty bourgeoisie or the middle class) for they will be betrayed. Apparently, that is what Mutunga's book documents in his book for the process was driven by the middle class. But—and this is an important "but"—NCA mothered so many social justice centres which have continued the struggle for social justice in slums and communities. Their demands go beyond constitutional reforms to social reforms. That is the path towards fundamental transformation. Willy tells me that he is planning a sequel which will capture this process in what he wants to call *Constitution-(un)making from the bottom.* "Un" is my addition. I say this so that blame is laid at the right quarters. It would be blasphemous to attribute the *unmaking* of the constitution to a former Chief Justice!

With these many words, I thank you for inviting me from across the border to join you in this commemoration. Truly, you are breaking new ground to ground a new African intellectual community; a community of "Intellectuals without Borders".

Asanteni sana na kila la heri

Note

1 Keynote address on the 10th Anniversary of Kenya Constitution Celebrations.

2

HEALING A WOUNDED ISLAMIC CONSTITUTIONALISM

Sharia, Legal Pluralism, and Unlearning the Nation-State Paradigm

Asifa Quraishi-Landes

2.1 Introduction

Constitutionally speaking, colonialism did more than just transform the political and legal systems of Muslim-majority societies: it ruptured the connection to their own constitutional theory. The European nation-state model of government changed Muslim ways of thinking about legal and political authority so successfully that most are unaware that before the western intrusion they were governed by a very different rule of law, one that might today be called legal pluralism. Contrary to the legal monism and centralism of the nation-state, the Islamic constitutional ordering for centuries of Muslim societies involved two types of law: ruler-made (*siyasa*) and jurist-made (*fiqh*), or—to use the terminology of legal pluralism—state law and non-state law, operating in a parallel but interdependent relationship with each other.

Today, legal scholars seem unaware that Muslim history provides one of the earliest real-life examples of legal pluralism. There is, of course, a strong critique of legal monism in the established and growing scholarship of legal pluralism, but pre-colonial Muslim history has apparently not been noticed by the scholars undertaking that critique. Sharia does appear (quite frequently, in fact) in the literature of legal pluralism, but only in its doctrinal form (*fiqh*)—that is, as local/customary rules that were accommodated by colonial rulers. There is no attention to sharia in its macro form, as an Islamic rule of law organizing an overall legal and political system. In other words, whenever the field has addressed sharia, it has seen it as a subject of legal pluralism, not as an inspiration for it. More broadly, comparative legal theory, especially constitutionalism, does not treat Islamic legal theory as an equal partner in public discourses thinking about law and government. This is especially unfortunate for legal pluralism, a field

DOI: 10.4324/9781003391920-4

particularly open to comparative insights and new approaches, because pre-colonial era Muslim history offers abundant material for exploring new models of legal pluralism.

The omission is not completely the fault of legal pluralists. There is little in contemporary work on Islamic government to draw their attention in this direction. This is largely due to the fact that modern political Islamism has adopted the legal monism of the nation-state wholesale, with virtually no critique. Islamically oriented political movements, many born in colonial resistance, generally focus on "Islamizing" their inherited nation-state systems; they do not offer an Islamic alternative to the nation-state itself. For example, they often look to a centralized legislature to enact *fiqh* rules (disregarding *fiqh* diversity) as the law of the land (Quraishi-Landes, 2015a). But this presumes (as did colonial rulers) that sharia equals the rules of *fiqh*, ignoring the historical role of sharia as a holistic Islamic rule of law encompassing the two very different *fiqh* and *siyasa* realms of legal authority. In other words, while there is much talk about the "Islamic state,"[1] there is little attention to Islamic constitutional theory.

It is thus no wonder that scholars of legal pluralism have been unable to see the potential presented by sharia as an Islamic rule of law built on both state and non-state law. This chapter will reveal that potential. It will show how Islamic constitutionalism based on the legal pluralism of the *fiqh-siyasa* bifurcation of law offers a better model for Islamic government than those that exist today. It will also demonstrate that Islamic constitutionalism itself offers a new contribution to constitutional theory by illustrating a qualitative alternative to the nation-state: constitutionalized legal pluralism.

Section 2.2 reviews the history of western encounters with sharia, pointing out how the colonial version of legal pluralism stunted its growth through codification and centralization. It then follows the evolution of legal pluralism through independence and ultimately to the post-colonial West, where new awareness of plural legal structures has created an appreciation for legal pluralism as a feature of all societies, even ostensibly monist ones. Now that legal pluralism is understood as not just a phenomenon of colonialism and indigenous peoples, westerners have become used to seeing it in places where we did not see it before. Section 2.3 takes this new appreciation as an indicator that western legal theorists may be ready to see sharia for what it was before the colonial mutations. We now have a language to understand sharia without forcing it into monist terms, seeing it as a form of legal pluralism operating at a macro level, with a bifurcation of two types of law, *fiqh* and *siyasa*. Using this language, this section explains how pre-colonial Muslim legal and political systems worked, explaining the realms of *fiqh* and *siyasa* and their interdependency in more detail. Section 2.4 then reviews the rupture that occurred with colonialism and how the combination of nation-state legal monism with Muslim fidelity to sharia ultimately created the theocratic Muslim governments we see today. It argues that these Muslim governments' use of state power to force selected and uniform *fiqh* rules on their populations is contrary to the sharia-based constitutionalized legal pluralism that existed before the colonial era. Muslim ignorance of this understanding of sharia represents a deep gash in the collective Muslim body that has been hemorrhaging oppression and authoritarianism in the name of sharia since the middle of the twentieth century. Section 2.5 then offers a way to heal this wound: by describing a theory of Islamic constitutionalism built on its history of legal pluralism. This new Islamic constitutionalism includes two key components: (1) state lawmaking (*siyasa*) must be based on the public good (i.e., not an app peal to religious scripture), and (2) a diverse marketplace of *fiqh* (and other religious law) should exist in a parallel legal realm, available as a voluntary opt-out of state law. Section 2.6 explains how a constitution built on these two principles would provide a powerful challenge to dominant beliefs about Islamic government, because this constitution is sharia-mindful but it is not theocratic. It also suggests new ways of thinking about legal pluralism, decolonizing the state, and constitutionalism without a nation-state.

2.2 Colonialism, Legal Pluralism, and Sharia

Colonialism and legal pluralism have an interconnected history. Indeed, legal pluralism was, in the words of John Griffiths, "a fixture of the colonial experience"[2] (Griffiths, 1986: 6). When European countries established colonies abroad, they usually imposed their legal systems there, creating complex questions of overlap with existing law and culture. As a pragmatic measure, colonial rulers often created plural legal orders, applying different rules to different populations under their control, usually according to ethnic, racial, or religious identity (Griffiths, 1986: 5).[3] In addition, non-official indigenous custom and conflict resolution often continued to operate, separate from the centralized colonial legal system. When legal anthropologists and sociologists began to study the complex experiences of colonized peoples living with both indigenous law and European law and the unequal power relations in that arrangement,[4] this became known as the field of legal pluralism (Merry, 1988: 869). Importantly, plural legal orders in these societies have persisted even after independence, making this one of the "most enduring legacies of European expansion and characterizing at the present day the larger part of all of the world's national legal systems" (Griffiths, 1986: 6). Simply put, legal pluralism is a product of the colonial experiment.

Muslims are no strangers to this experiment. In fact, one might even say they were featured front and center as one of the first examples of how to do colonial legal pluralism. Griffiths traces the modern history of legal pluralism to the British East India Company's 1772 judicial system providing that "the laws of the Koran" would be applied to the "Mohamodans" (and those of the "Shaster" to the "Gentoos") (Griffiths, 1986: 6). British, French, and Dutch colonial powers took different approaches to accommodate Muslim law for their Muslim subjects, but they all generally involved a flurry of translations of classical texts into European languages, the creation of "sharia courts" under colonial direction, publication of manuals for lawyers and judges serving in them, and the compilation and enactment of selected (usually marriage and divorce) *fiqh* rules to be enforced on all Muslims in the territory.[5]

But this accommodation of Muslim law for Muslims wasn't so much an accommodation as it was an invention. It reconceptualized sharia to fit the European nation-state understanding of law—that is, legal centralism. According to legal centralism, law is the law of the state, exclusive to it, and does not exist without it.[6] With this ideology, colonials undertook extensive scholarship, legislation, and institution-building to craft a system of Islamic law[7] that was administered, maintained, and supervised by the new state hierarchy (Buskens, 2014: 218).

But sharia is not "law" as legal centralism defines it. The state has never been the exclusive location for the rules associated with sharia. Before the colonial era, sharia in Muslim societies was always made up of two types of law: *fiqh* and *siyasa*. *Fiqh* is non-state law, created by jurists interpreting scripture to articulate Islamic rules of right action.[8] While profoundly relevant to Muslim lives, much of *fiqh* was not enforced by Muslim rulers. Most *fiqh* was (and is) self-enforced by individual Muslims, often through fatwas from scholars, sometimes by community practice.[9] *Fiqh* was enforced by Muslim rulers only through the appointment of judges to adjudicate *fiqh*-based disputes, but even then, rulers did not control the content of the *fiqh* applied by those judges. The law that rulers did control, called *siyasa*, was quite different from *fiqh*: it was based on service of the public good, not interpretation of scripture.

So, the term "law"—if understood as state law—is both under- and over-inclusive as a way to understand sharia. To use Colin Imber's words,

> in the sense that it regulates both worldly and religious matters, the shari'a is an all-embracing law but, in the sense that many of its provisions have no application in practice, much of it is not, in the modern sense, law at all.
>
> *Imber, 1997: 30*

So, if law is state law, it straddles both *fiqh* and *siyasa*, because parts of *fiqh* and all of *siyasa* can be enforced by the state. But *fiqh* also includes many things that are not state-enforced. *Siyasa*, on the other hand, is all state law but it does not address Muslim personal lives, making it incomplete as a depiction of "Islamic law" and largely irrelevant to the colonial project of accommodation. Simply put, it is an oversimplification to equate the sharia with law (Weiss, 2010: 1). Even the commonly used phrase "Islamic law" is ill-fitting, for, as Ahmad Ahmad points out, "[t]he concept of law in the term 'Islamic law' has no equivalent in the concept of law as applied to any modem Western legal system" (Ahmad, 2006: 44). Classical Arabic does not even have a true equivalent to the English word "law" (Weiss, 2010: 1, 6).

All this means that when it accommodated sharia, colonial legal pluralism viewed it through a distorted lens. As a result, the colonial "'positivization' of Sharia into Islamic law was a misunderstanding of how Islamic normativity had functioned" (Buskens, 2014: 212). Driven by legal centralism, but also the economic and policy needs of colonial administration, sharia was contorted to fit into a nation-state model, in both normative-political and scholarly terms. The project is a perfect example of this insight from Norman Calder: "Western scholarship (even when written by Muslims) has rarely presented Islamic law in such a way as to demonstrate its values rather than the values of the observer" (Calder, 1996: 979). The irony, of course, is that legal pluralism under colonialism was justified as dispensing justice to Muslims according to their own law, all the while disconnecting them from it.

Of course, this treatment was not unique to Muslims. Scholars of the field have long noted colonial disregard for and misunderstanding of the complexities of indigenous legal orders around the globe (Merry, 1988: 869). As Marc Galanter said over thirty years ago, "'legal centralism' has impaired our consciousness of 'indigenous law'" (Galanter, 1981: 18). Today, decades of scholarship in legal pluralism have moved many western scholars past legal centralism. There is now an appreciation for legal pluralism as a feature of all societies, even industrialized western ones that claim to be legally monist. Legal pluralism is now understood as not just a phenomenon of colonialism and indigenous peoples, and westerners have become used to seeing it in places where we did not see it before.[10] This new appreciation sees legal monism and legal centralism not as descriptive facts of any society, but rather an ideology (Galanter, 1981: 21), one that has had such a hold on western lawyers and social scientists that it has been able to "successfully to masquerade as fact and has formed the foundation stone of social and legal theory" (Griffiths, 1986: 4) But, says Griffiths, "Legal pluralism is the fact. Legal centralism is a myth, an ideal, a claim, an illusion" (*Ibidem*). More and more western legal scholars are taking this seriously, looking outside the official legal order to see that law is not all about the state and that official law is often secondary in affecting behavior.[11]

With these new lenses of legal pluralism, perhaps western legal theorists are now ready to see sharia differently. Now that we have a language with which to talk about sharia without forcing it into monist terms, it may finally be time for us in the west to fully understand sharia as it was before the colonial mutations. Just as westerners had to reject legal centralism before we could see legal pluralism at home, legal pluralism may also be the key to seeing sharia as an Islamic rule of law. This will then open up our vision to see its constitutional implications. If we can make this paradigm shift—if we can benefit from legal pluralism as a "useful sensitizing and analytical tool," as Benda-Beckmann (2002: 40) puts it—we may find that we have missed the most constitutionally and politically interesting aspect of sharia: the separation of and relationship between *fiqh* and *siyasa* law. This bifurcation of legal authority between *fiqh* and *siyasa* is fundamentally and structurally different from nation-state legal monism. It represents one of the strongest forms of legal pluralism because it was an essential building block for the whole legal-political system. This cannot be seen through a legal monist filter, which sees sharia only as a collection of positivistic rules available for state legislation. Instead, with our vision adjusted to see sharia as a legally pluralist Islamic rule of law, we might be prompted to ask a question that pluralists in the west rarely get the opportunity to ask: what would a constitution look like if it *started* with the idea of legal pluralism as its founding principle, rather than as an add-on critique of existing legal monism? Islamic history provides some interesting food for thought.

2.3 Classical Sharia Rule of Law: Constitutionalized Legal Pluralism

Muslim legal-political systems from the ninth through the nineteenth centuries had one common structural feature: a separation of lawmaking power between (1) *siyasa* laws made by rulers and (2) *fiqh* laws articulated by religious legal scholars. This was not an accident or convenience. It grew from the core epistemology of Islamic jurisprudence, namely, the principle that sharia, God's Law, cannot be known with certainty. To understand how this led to a bifurcated legal system, a short summary of Islamic legal theory and history is necessary.

2.3.1 Fiqh Diversity

Literally meaning "street," or "way," sharia in the Quran denotes the perfect Way of God—that is, the way God advises people to live a virtuous life. This Way of God is described in the Quran and Prophet Muhammad's life example (sunnah), but because not everything is clearly answered in those two sources, Muslim religious scholars undertook ijtihad (rigorous legal reasoning) to extrapolate more detailed guidance from those sources, articulated as Islamic rules of right action called *fiqh*.

The epistemology of *fiqh* is important. *Fiqh* lawmaking happens with an awareness that, as a product of human endeavor, it is fallible (Weiss, 1978: 199). The scholars' use of the term "*fiqh*" (literally, "understanding") is telling. It linguistically signals that every *fiqh* rule is only a scholar's best understanding of God's Law, nothing more. In short, although their job is to articulate God's Law, the *fiqh* scholars are careful never to speak for God.

This attitude created a diversity of *fiqh* doctrines: because there is no way to know for sure which *fiqh* conclusions are correct (and there is no Muslim "church" to designate favorites); all *fiqh* rules are deemed to be equally valid understandings of sharia, even though they often contradict each other. In short, for a Muslim, there is one Law of God (sharia), but there are many different understandings (*fiqh*) of that Law here on earth. Thus, the tangible reality of sharia in the world is not a monolithic single code of law, but rather the different doctrines of many *fiqh* schools, none more important than another.

In Muslim-ruled societies for most of Muslim history, the application of *fiqh* was mediated through this diversity. *Fiqh* was accessible to the public in a way that gave individual Muslims choice over which school of *fiqh* they would follow. To summarize a vast temporal and geographic history, individual Muslims typically identified with one *fiqh* school and sought out scholars of that school for guidance in their specific legal questions, such as whether or not a contract was valid, or how to distribute inheritance. The *fiqh* scholars' answers to these individual questions came in the form of legal responsa (fatwa) which were voluntarily self-enforced by the questioners themselves. When a *fiqh*-based dispute arose between two or more Muslims (e.g., a property dispute between adjacent neighbors), they would typically go to a ruler-appointed qadi (judge) of a mutually agreed *fiqh* school to resolve the dispute. The qadi's ruling would then be enforced by the Muslim ruler. This was possible because Muslim rulers generally accommodated the *fiqh* diversity of their populations by appointing a variety of qadis from different *fiqh* schools, according to the demographics of each geographic area. Importantly, rulers did not alter the content of the *fiqh* applied in these courtrooms, nor did they consolidate the rules of divergent *fiqh* schools to create one *fiqh* code applied by all the qadis in the land. *Fiqh* always has been diverse, and that did not change even with ruler enforcement. Thus, the structure created a "to each his own" quality of religious law in these societies that included not just the many Muslim *fiqh* legal schools, but also the religious laws of Christians, Jews, and others. In this way, individuals in these Muslim legal systems could receive official recognition of their preferred religious law without having to impose it on everyone else.

2.3.2 Siyasa Public Service

Muslim rulers were making laws too, but unlike *fiqh*, their laws were not extrapolations from scripture. The laws of Muslim rulers, called *siyasa* (literally "administration" or "political order"), were made according to their own philosophies of government and ideas about how best to maintain public order. *Siyasa* laws were typically pragmatic, governance-related laws, covering topics like taxes, security, marketplace regulation, and public safety—that is, things necessary for public order, but about which the scripture says little.[12]

Siyasa lawmaking by temporal holders of power ultimately came to be seen as Islamically legitimate because of the widespread consensus among *fiqh* scholars that the ultimate purpose of sharia is to promote the welfare of the people.[13] Because rules extrapolated from scripture cannot cover all the day-to-day public needs of civil society, the *fiqh* scholars recognized that another type of law besides *fiqh* was necessary to fully serve the public good (maslaha 'amma). Scriptural study cannot identify, for example, what is a safe speed limit or what regulations will ensure food safety. The only institution capable of creating and enforcing these sorts of rules is the power that controls the use of force—that is, the *siyasa* power held by rulers. Thus, in the literature of Muslim political science that came to be known as *siyasa* shariyya, it was agreed that Muslim rulers should have the power to make and enforce law to serve the public good (maslaha 'amma).[14] Though the *siyasa* shariyya scholars differed widely about the proper scope of that power, the overall impact of this discourse was that the concept of sharia includes pragmatic considerations of good governance; it is not just limited to *fiqh* elaboration of scriptural rules. It includes *siyasa* too. This gave not just pragmatic but also Islamic legitimacy to Muslim rulers to issue laws and "perform the duties of everyday governance and law enforcement without specific reference to, or grounding in, the sacred texts" (Reza, 2007: 27).

Siyasa's lack of direct grounding in sacred texts is important for Islamic constitutionalism because it illustrates how sharia can work as an Islamic rule of law rather than just a collection of (*fiqh*) rules. That is, even though *siyasa* laws were not derived directly from scripture, pre-modern Muslims did not think of *siyasa* as "outside" of sharia. Instead, they considered *fiqh* and *siyasa* both to be components of a holistic rule of law system. Thus understood, *fiqh* and *siyasa* are two arms of a sharia rule of law: rulers and religious legal scholars together serve sharia, each serving different roles based on their different sources of legitimacy.

This means that legal pluralism formed the constitutional structure of these pre-colonial Muslim governments. In Sherman Jackson's words, "legal pluralism was to the premodern Muslim state what legal monism has become to the modern nation-state" (Jackson, 2013: 46). Moreover, it was inevitable. Muslim legal systems had to come up with a legal system that could accommodate the inherent diversity of *fiqh*, so legal monism was just not an option. That is, the different *fiqh* schools are all equally valid, so it would be impossible to simply declare one of them the law of the land—and those who tried, failed. So, quite different from the evolution of law and religion in Europe, Muslims crafted systems based on legal pluralism: two types of law, *siyasa* (made by rulers) and *fiqh* (made by religious legal scholars) both had authority over the people, but in very different ways. *Siyasa* existed to serve general public needs such as safety and justice and order, whereas *fiqh* provided rules of right action for Muslims seeking to live by sharia. Law and order in Muslim lands depended upon the separation of and relationship between these two types of law.

For those concerned about the theocratic implications of religious government, there is something significant here: *all fiqh* is non-state law. That is, all of the scripturally based rules of Muslim life (what we might call "religious law") exist in the non-state realm of *fiqh*. Moreover, this realm is inherently and unavoidably diverse. Because of this fact, Muslim history tells a very different story of religious government than the state churches of Europe. Simply put, Muslim rulers were not theocratic because they did not have the ability to dictate and enforced a uniform religious law (*fiqh*) on their populations. Instead, *fiqh* was exclusively the province of private scholars, in their diverse schools, and they insisted that it not be codified by the state. Moreover, this arrangement was respected by both rulers and scholars. For nearly all of Muslim history in nearly every Muslim land, *fiqh* scholars did not seek to control state power, and Muslim rulers did not control *fiqh*. That this separation of *fiqh* and *siyasa* was not a separation of "church" and "state"; Muslim rulers were still very much religious rulers. But they were not theocratic ones. This is often difficult for westerners to get their heads around because we are so used to thinking of law as state law, so, mutatis mutandi, religious law will naturally be imposed by a religious state. But if we release our presumptions of legal centralism, then it becomes clear that religious government is not necessarily theocratic. This realization is a crucial starting point for building a workable Islamic constitutional theory for the modern world.

Another important thing to recognize about the relationship between *fiqh* and *siyasa* is that, while neither controlled the other, they weren't hermetically sealed off from each other either. *Fiqh* was non-state law, but it had full respect and acknowledgment from the *siyasa* rulers, including being facilitated through qadi appointments. To use some modern pluralist references, *fiqh* did not operate in the "shadow" of *siyasa*, or in unofficial mediations and board rooms, as most other non-state law does today.[15] Rather, *fiqh*—a nuanced body of law covering many fields, such as property, marriage, inheritance, and contracts—operated autonomously in arenas recognized and respected by *siyasa* powers. But the state had little to no influence over which laws applied to which groups and had no control over *fiqh* content or mufti fatwas. Thus, this was a strong, deep legal pluralism, in which the entire legal system was built upon the reality of a fully formed *fiqh* realm of non-state law living alongside *siyasa*. These two legal realms, moreover, were interdependent. Either one alone could not serve all the legal needs of the society. *Siyasa* and *fiqh* thus operated with a mutual awareness of each other, sometimes in cooperation, sometimes in tension, but always interdependently.[16]

This interdependent relationship has often been misunderstood, usually because western observers often try to understand it in western terms. For example, the detailed doctrine elaborated in *fiqh* texts often does not address the relationship between that doctrine and the social practices of the time, suggesting that *fiqh* scholars were uninterested in social reality.[17] Thus emerged the well-known orientalist trope that "Islamic law" was aspirational, largely impractical, and idealistic (Emon, 2004: 3).[18] Seen this way, *fiqh* appears to be the quintessential "law in books" unconnected to (indeed unconcerned with) "law in action." Challenging this depiction are anthropological studies describing "Islamic law" exclusively in terms of human agency and *qadi* discretion, "to the detriment of any notion of legal authority, objectivity and legitimacy in the adjudicatory process" (Emon, 2004: 3). This is the famous "kadijustiz" of intuitive case-by-case judgment unbounded by "law." Both and neither of these descriptions are accurate. *Fiqh* is "law in books," but they are not state books. It is applied "in action" but not always through state institutions. Take, for example, fatwas as distinguished from qadi judgments: fatwas are "action" in the sense that they could (and often do) motivate human behavior, but they are only aspirational in the sense that they are not binding (either politically or theologically)—a Muslim may disregard a fatwa with no consequences. This is very difficult to understand if we insist on thinking in western categories. Without a nuanced understanding of sharia as a complex interconnection of *fiqh* and *siyasa*—of academic (*fiqh*), self-applied (*fatwa*), and enforced (*qadi*) rules of right action as well as social ordering—it is difficult to make sense of sharia's varying manifestations as "law in books" and "law in action."[19]

2.4 The Colonial Rupture

Nearly everything changed with colonialism. In countries colonized by European powers, the *fiqh-siyasa* bifurcation of authority was dismantled and replaced with national legal codes and judicial systems modeled on (sometimes borrowing wholesale from) that of the colonial homeland. Legal pluralist arrangements were created within this structure—applying different laws to different indigenous peoples—but these still operated within a centralist structure: the content of the laws applied, to whom they applied, and to what extent were all controlled by the central state. This included the transformation of sharia into a body of "Islamic law" that could be (selectively) codified and administered by colonial administrations. Moreover, colonial transformation of the preexisting sharia rule of law into a positivized Islamic law was so successful that it survived far past the end of colonial rule.[20] With independence in the mid-twentieth century, the new Muslim-majority states in Arabia, Africa, Asia, and Eastern Europe retained the systems set up by their former European rulers, now woven into the socioeconomic infrastructure of these countries.[21] Thus, virtually every Muslim-majority country today still operates with a legal centralist constitutional model.

Even those calling for an "Islamic state" do not seek an alternative to the nation-state. Political Islamic movements (also called "Islamism") regularly look to state lawmaking bodies to officially recognize sharia—usually in the form of legislating it.[22] Having completely internalized the colonial transformation of sharia into a positive and legislatable "Islamic law," they often support "sharia legislation" and constitutional provisions requiring sharia to be a source of legislation and a check on state action.[23] The "Islamic state" of modern political Islamism is thus one of legal centralism—it starts with the central state as the location of all legal authority and the guardian of society's orthodoxy, which is why they seek to "Islamize" it. Remarkably, they do not question the European nation-state structure itself. In Sherman Jackson's words, "the Islamic state is a nation-state ruled by Islamic law" (Jackson, 1996: xiv).

This approach represents a rather stunning amnesia. Rather than looking to Islamic history and taking inspiration from the *fiqh-siyasa* separation of legal authority, political Islamist movements have reinforced the colonial idea that state power is what gives law its authority, and worse is that the state has the responsibility of interpreting scripture and articulating sharia in these countries (Jackson, 2003).[24] Far from restoring sharia to now-independent Muslim lands, these sharia legislative projects have fundamentally transformed the nature of sharia's engagement with these societies. In pre-modern Muslim systems, the sharia mandate of *siyasa* power was *not* to enact and impose *fiqh* doctrine on everyone but, rather, to maintain public order and serve the public good. In other words, state lawmaking for the public good—*not* legislating *fiqh* doctrine—is the duty of an Islamic state.

Moreover, the inability to differentiate the respective roles of *siyasa* and *fiqh* has caused many Muslim-majority countries to create near-theocratic rule. These governments can now declare "the" Islamic law of the land, often discriminating against those who disagree. For a religion that has never had a "church," this is a dangerous and ill-fitting change. Muslim governments can now occupy the powerful position of being both author and enforcer of what is sharia. This creates a dangerous potential for state-enforced religious dogma, a situation exacerbated by the creation of "sharia courts" with final authority to interpret the authoritative meaning of state-enacted "sharia law." Seen in greater historical and theological context, this is an odd thing for Muslims to do. For centuries, Muslims rejected the establishment of a church with the power to declare Islamic orthodoxy. Today, however, "sharia courts" have the sole authority to interpret the meaning of sharia for the public (and if it follows stare decisis, the future public). This is arguably the closest thing to a Muslim "state church" that has ever existed (Quraishi-Landes, 2015a).

Moreover, the so-called "sharia legislation" does not really legislate "sharia" at all. It merely legislates one (or several) among many *fiqh* possibilities. That is, because every *fiqh* rule is fallible, no Muslim government can claim that the *fiqh* rule they have enacted is in fact God's Law. The most that can be claimed of so-called "sharia legislation" is that it has enacted its preferred *understanding* of sharia from among many equally valid options. To call such legislation "sharia" is to use religion in a politically manipulative manner—implying a divine mandate for rules that are actually fallible human interpretations of divine law.

But, sadly, it works. Widespread support for political Islamic movements and sharia legislation in many Muslim-majority countries indicates that most Muslims are not aware of *fiqh* diversity, nor the relationship it had with *siyasa* rule before the colonial mutations. The colonial project was so pervasive and successful that the majority of Muslims today think about law and legal authority in nation-state terms, and thus that the only way for sharia to exist in their countries is for it to be legislated by the government. This is reflected in polls documenting widespread support for sharia as the "law of the land" in Muslim-majority countries around the world.[25] In short, legal centralism has shrunk the Muslim constitutional horizon to just the narrow realm of positive law, creating dangerous power vortexes manipulated by contemporary Muslim governments.

In other words, it is nation-state legal centralism—not sharia—that is the source of authoritarian religious politics in Muslim-majority countries today. The nation-state is not the victim of religious overreach; it is its cause. It is not sharia that has caused this situation; it is rather, the result of failing to think of sharia as a rule of law, encompassing both *fiqh* and *siyasa* realms. The idea of "sharia legislation" itself is a wholly modern, post-colonial invention: it depends upon the centralized power and legal monism of the nation-state to operate. These governments would not be able to uniformly enforce their selected *fiqh* rules if the classical bifurcation of *fiqh* and *siyasa* had survived. The theocratic consequences of this status quo should offend not just secularists who feel that state law should be separated from religion but also religious Muslims because it disrespects *fiqh* diversity and lets the state claim control over what used to be left to the autonomy of an independent *fiqh* realm. There is no widespread Muslim rejection of these systems because Muslims are disconnected from their own constitutional history. This has left a large gap in Muslim consciousness of what sharia means as a constitutional organizing principle.

2.5 Healing the Wound: Islamic Reconstitutionalism

There is a way to close this gap: by developing a theory of Islamic constitutionalism that really is a uniquely Islamic constitutional theory, not just nation-state constitutionalism dressed up in Muslim garb. This requires identifying and reclaiming the essential aspects of the structure of authority found in sharia-based systems throughout history and building a modern Islamic constitutional theory around them. Looking at this history, it becomes clear that the most prominent structural feature of pre-colonial Muslim systems was the pluralist separation of *fiqh* and *siyasa* law. Looking a bit closer, we can see some essential characteristics about the nature of each of these legal realms. First, *siyasa* legitimacy is based on service of the public good. This is emphasized in the *siyasa* shariyya literature identifying *siyasa* power as an essential part of a sharia rule of law system and that the sharia responsibility of a Muslim ruler is to serve the public good. Second, the *fiqh* realm was not a monolithic code of *fiqh* doctrine. It existed in all of its diversity and Muslims had freedom of choice between the *fiqh* schools. If we reclaim those two facts as essential elements for a new theory of Islamic constitutionalism, we can create a viable Islamic alternative that is sharia-faithful, authentically resonates with Muslim history and practice, and also provides a real alternative to the colonial nation-state paradigm. Recall the question asked earlier: "what would a constitution look like if it *started* with the idea of legal pluralism as its founding principle, rather than as an add-on critique of existing legal monism?"[26] Here we begin to answer that question.

I propose that a modern Islamic constitutionalism inspired by the deep legal pluralism of pre-colonial sharia systems must have two key pillars: (1) state lawmaking (*siyasa*) must be based on the public good (and not *fiqh* doctrine) and

(2) a diverse marketplace of *fiqh* (and other religious law) should exist in a parallel legal realm, available as a voluntary opt-out of state law. A constitution built on these two pillars[27] would powerfully challenge misguided yet dominant beliefs about Islamic government because it provides a constitutional model that is sharia-based but it is not theocratic.

2.5.1 Pillar One: State (Siyasa) Action Must Be Based on the Public Good

The first pillar comes from the classical Islamic legal-political literature known as *siyasa* shariyya addressing the sharia power of Muslim rulers. This literature centered the legitimacy of *siyasa* power upon its service of the general good (maslaha 'amma). Today, *siyasa* power comes in the form of presidents, parliaments, and kings rather than sultans and caliphs, but the essential nature of the power is the same—*siyasa* authority is held by whoever holds temporal police power, that is, the state.[28] Putting these together, the first pillar of the present framework for Islamic constitutionalism provides that all state action must be based on the public good. That public good could be determined in a variety of ways, but the overwhelming desire for democracy among the world's Muslims[29] indicates that democratic means would likely be the most effective.[30]

Serving the public good may not seem like a very Islamic demand to make of a Muslim government, especially given the dominant belief that lawmaking by an Islamic state should be all about implementing laws already made by God, probably via religious experts reading divine scripture. In a word: theocracy. But, as presented earlier, this is an extremely narrow understanding of sharia. It limits it to only the doctrinal rules of *fiqh* and ignores the entire field of *siyasa* shariyya. It also perpetuates oppositional politics between secular and religious forces rather than seeing past them to imagine sharia in a broader context. When sharia is understood as a rule of law system that includes *siyasa* service of the public good, it becomes clear that "sharia legislation" is not the way to make a government Islamic. Instead, it is the service of the public good that gives sharia legitimacy to state action.

More specifically, if it is appreciated—as an *Islamic* matter—that the government should not be selectively enforcing its preferred *fiqh* doctrine but instead should be serving the public good, this could cause a revolutionary change in political discourse in Muslim-majority countries. Rather than debating "should we have religious law or not?" or "what is the sharia rule on this issue?" people would instead be asking "what serves our public good?" This opens the processes of public lawmaking open to everyone regardless of religion, reducing tensions of identity politics that have been part of "*sharia* politics" in these countries.[31] Public discourse could focus on practical evaluations of social need rather than oppositional arguments about the role of Islam and Islamic law. As Mohammad Fadel has said, "Muslims should not ask whether the human rights standard is the same as that under Islamic law, but only whether the human rights standard represents a legitimate act of government" (Fadel, 2008: 69). Moreover, sharia-minded Muslims should support this shift as the proper sharia role for their state, rather than as a concession to secularism or international pressure.

This shift is also the key to solving the purported conflict between Islam and democracy. Democratic decision-making is, after all, one method by which a society decides the public good. Accordingly, a sharia-based rule of law system could choose to use democracy in the lawmaking process in the *siyasa*/state realm. Keeping this in mind can help explain to western observers why Muslim affinity for both democracy and sharia is not an oxymoron.[32] Muslims' support for democracy and sharia is only confusing if we insist on limiting the meaning of sharia to *fiqh*. However, once we recognize that sharia is larger than *fiqh*—that it also encompasses *siyasa* state lawmaking based on the public good—then the paradox disappears. In short, if human lawmaking in the interest of the public good is part of a sharia rule of law, then there is no inherent conflict between human lawmaking and sharia.

This first pillar thus enables Muslims to have sharia as the "law of the land," but without creating a theocracy because it does not allow a state to impose its preferred religious doctrine upon the entire population. To skeptical secularists who believe that *any* recognition of religion always threatens theocracy and religious oppression, this pillar suggests that (while this is probably true of a legally monistic state) it does not necessarily follow for a pluralist one that maintains a separation of *fiqh* and *siyasa* law. In short, if Islamic constitutional theory insists that a Muslim state cannot use its police power to claim to be enacting God's Law, then theocracy is not the inevitable result of every religious government.

The first pillar sets up an Islamic constitutional theory in which religion is important, but not in a way that combines "church" and state. In doing so, it answers the concerns of both secularists and religious Muslims. For religious Muslims, it bases the legitimacy of state action directly on sharia principles. For secularists, it requires state lawmaking to be justified on something other than religious pedigree. Moreover, this Islamic constitutionalism includes—indeed, expects—an integral role in democratic lawmaking for the public good, situating it as *part* of a sharia-based system, not in opposition to it. Finally, to political Islamists who have been agitating for Islamic government, it says: this is not your father's Islamic state, but it could be yours.

2.5.2 Pillar Two: A Diverse Non-State Realm Fiqh (and Other Religious Law) Is Available as a Voluntary Opt-Out of State Law

The second pillar sees the preexisting *fiqh-siyasa* legal pluralism as the most important structural feature of pre-modern Muslim systems and builds it into the foundation of the constitutional theory. Thus, it requires that a modern Islamic constitution protects individual access to *fiqh* (and other religious laws, as needed) existing in a parallel non-state legal realm for those who choose to use it. Recognizing the importance of non-state *fiqh* is especially important for Islamic constitutionalism because of the importance of *fiqh* in Muslim lives. *Fiqh* exists as a vast and sophisticated body of legal doctrine with a recognized internal system of qualification, application, and evolution. It covers a wide range of legal topics, from marriage and divorce to property, and thus there will always be an enduring desire among Muslims to make it legally effective in their lives. In a legal monist system, the only way for an individual Muslim to have her legal disputes resolved according to the *fiqh* school of her choice is for her *fiqh* school to be the law of the land for everyone. If, however, a parallel *fiqh* realm is available, she does not need "sharia legislation" in order to make her *fiqh* choices formally enforceable.

By bringing constitutional attention to this non-state legal realm, the proposed Islamic constitutionalism rehabilitates the *fiqh* realm as a vibrant parallel sphere of legal practice and innovation. Sadly, the uniformity demanded by a centralized legal system in today's Muslim-majority countries, combined with their penchant for "sharia legislation," has muted the colorful diversity that was once the hallmark of Islamic jurisprudence. In most Muslim-majority countries, there is no official recognition of *fiqh* rules different from those enacted into state law, and consequently most Muslims are unaware of *fiqh* diversity altogether.[33] Further, codification of *fiqh* by Muslim states has resulted in freezing what was once a dynamic and evolving body of law—especially in issues related to women. In contrast, a *fiqh* realm constitutionally protected from state law could provide the space necessary for dynamic and sophisticated *fiqh* to again grow as more *fiqh* experts directly engage with a wider swath of the Muslim public. This could actively invite old and new *fiqh* scholars to undertake new levels of legal analysis, engage in new debates with *fiqh* colleagues, and thus dramatically expand the available corpus of *fiqh* laws. This could result in generating not only new *fiqh* rules but also a wider marketplace for the application of those rules, and this in turn could influence their further evolution. Importantly, established and conservative *fiqh* doctrine would still exist and be available to Muslims opting into the *fiqh* realm, but they would exist alongside new and reformed ones, and all of these *fiqh* choices—new and old—would be available in the marketplace of *fiqh*.[34]

Diversity is a necessary attribute of the *fiqh* realm.[35] This respects the epistemology of Islamic jurisprudence as well as ensuring meaningful choice for those selecting the *fiqh* realm. As described earlier, all *fiqh* understandings of sharia are equally valid, making the world of *fiqh* inherently and unavoidably diverse. Thus, individual Muslims should be free to choose whichever *fiqh* school best fits them. To borrow a modern constitutional concept, *fiqh* choice is part of *Islamic* religious freedom.[36]

By protecting a parallel *fiqh* realm, the second pillar creates a constitutional structure that is not only different from political Islamist discourse but also from all constitutional discourse that presumes a nation-state template. In stark contrast to the legal centralism of governments in the Muslim world, the proposed Islamic constitutional model creates a system of legal pluralism, with a realm of *fiqh* law that is facilitated (but not controlled) by the *siyasa* state power. This offers a way to return *fiqh* back to its proper place—not mined as raw material in support of political agendas, but existing independently offering a variety *fiqh* choices serving the needs of all sorts of Muslims.

Combined with the first pillar, this second pillar provides a workable and non-theocratic way for *fiqh* to exist—even thrive—in Muslim lives. Thus, if someone strongly believes in a *fiqh* rule, but cannot convince the rest of the public that it serves the general public for everyone, then it would fail the test of the first pillar and would not become the law of the land. But that would not mean that the person must relinquish her desire to live by *fiqh* in her own life; she would just turn to the *fiqh* realm to exercise her opt-out right to resolve her legal issue according to her selected *fiqh* school. And for those not choosing to opt out, state laws (enacted to serve the public good) exist as their default.[37]

2.6 Islamic Reconstitutionalism as Decolonized Constitutionalism

This chapter began with a review of colonial legal pluralism, with special attention to its treatment of sharia. Colonial legal pluralism was "weak" legal pluralism as it is understood in the field: its plural legal systems (customary, Islamic, and European) were all administered by the state (Griffiths, 1986). Weak legal pluralism is actually a form of legal centralism. As John Griffiths puts it, weak legal pluralism is merely "a particular arrangement in a system whose basic ideology is centralist" (1986: 8). Strong or deep legal pluralism, on the other hand, is said to exist when unofficial legal systems with no official authority nevertheless have real influence over behavior within certain groups in society.[38] Strong legal pluralism also does not typically involve unequal power relations, as is the case with state-law pluralism (Van Niekerk, 2001: 352).

Weak legal pluralism exists in many modern nation-states today. Several countries have parallel court systems for different minority groups, all controlled and supervised by the central state (Van Niekerk, 2001). In stark contrast to these systems, the Islamic constitutionalism proposed here is one of strong, deep legal pluralism. It starts not from the nation-state, but from a fact urged by legal pluralists for decades: law exists and operates in many "rooms" of society, not just official ones (like courtrooms and legislatures).[39] It takes that fact seriously and builds a constitutional structure around it. Therefore, it posits a separation of legal authority between state (*siyasa*) and non-state (*fiqh*) realms. These two realms are set up in an interdependent, not hierarchical, relationship with each other, with individuals passing between them at their own discretion.

This sort of strong legal pluralism directly challenges the ideology of legal centralism, where uniformity and predictability of law are heralded as necessary attributes of the rule of law. That is, it is commonly expected that the job of constitutionalism is to "provide for the hierarchy and unity of the law" (Viellechner, 2012: 607). As legal pluralism, multiculturalism and diversity enter social and legal discourses, one of the primary challenges is the question of relativism:[40] How to deal with the inherent tension between unity and diversity that inevitably arises? (Viellechner, 2012: 608). Not insignificantly, Islamic jurisprudence has spent considerable ink on this topic. Because no *fiqh* rule could ever claim with certainty to be the correct understanding of sharia, Muslim legal systems had to figure out how to accommodate *fiqh* diversity. Their answer was *fiqh-siyasa* bifurcation of legal authority: all *fiqh* schools of law were available in the *fiqh* realm, separated from the lawmaking realm of *siyasa* rulers. This strong legal pluralism of Muslim history illustrates that it is possible to build a constitutional system without nation-state presumptions about the predictability and uniformity and that the challenge of balancing unity and diversity can be accomplished without subsuming all law under state authority.

I am certainly not the first to challenge the nation-state constitutional model. Globalization and technology have caused many to consider the Westphalian state in decline and, as Neil Walker puts it, "the increasing marginality and distorting effect of a state-centred constitutionalism has become a familiar refrain of legal and constitutional thought" (2002: 320). Decolonial and post-colonial studies are a growing field, decades after the official end of European colonialism,[41] and with decolonialism comes further critiques of the nation-state. Thus, there is much academic and social interest today in exploring alternatives to the nation-state, and legal pluralism features prominently in this exploration.[42]

Muslims are strong voices in these fields,[43] not surprising given the large number of colonized Muslim countries. But what *is* surprising is that these voices do not seem to be speaking in the language of a unique Islamic constitutionalism. Despite all the anti-colonial resistance, independence, political Islamism, and obsession with an Islamic state, Muslims have yet to advocate a theory of Islamic constitutionalism that provides a structural alternative to the nation-state. This absence in the world's conversations about post-nation-state constitutionalism might create the impression that Islamic legal theory simply has nothing new or interesting to offer. But, as this chapter has outlined, that is not true. There *is* a uniquely Islamic approach to constitutionalism, and it is grounded in strong legal pluralism, but Muslims have been so cut off from their history that most are unable to appreciate it, let alone articulate what it might look like in the modern world. This chapter is part of an effort to repair this disconnect.

The rich history of centuries of Muslim rule demonstrates a unique way of allocating legal authority that can best be described as strong legal pluralism.[44] To fully appreciate this, we must decolonize our understanding of sharia itself. We must realize that sharia is more than just the positive rules of *fiqh* doctrine, but it is a holistic organizing principle for an Islamic rule of law, comprised of the *fiqh* and *siyasa* legal realms. When we broaden our spectrum of thinking about sharia in this way, we can see its constitutional potential, both then and now.

The Islamic constitutional theory proposed here is a normative theory. It thus provides one answer to the popular critique of legal pluralism that, while it may be useful as a descriptive tool, it is not normative.[45] The Islamic constitutionalism proposed here is a decidedly "normative" theory of legal pluralism, arguing that its constitutionalized legal pluralism is the key to dislodging the hold of nation-state centralist norms. To show that such a system is not just hypothetical, it draws on Muslim history to demonstrate that this could actually work, because it did work in Muslim lands for centuries.

The proposed Islamic constitutionalism is also normative in another important way: it is addressed directly to today's Muslim-majority countries, confidently asserting that this model would serve them better than their current nation-state European import. For those claiming to be "Islamic states," it argues further that this model is more sharia-faithful than the "Islamized" nation-state under which they are currently operating. More aggressively, it asserts that any honest sharia-based constitutionalism must *necessarily* be pluralistic—with separate legal realms for *fiqh* and *siyasa*—because of the inherent epistemology (and hence diversity) of *fiqh*.

2.7 Conclusion

How does this chapter fit into a book on "transformative constitutionalism"? After all, it does not address ways to use constitutional clauses to transform legal doctrine or practices in Muslim societies. Instead, it speaks of transformation in the sense of transforming the entire structure of power in societies that claim sharia legitimacy. It is transformative in insisting that we think about sharia beyond *fiqh*. It is transformative in thinking about legal pluralism at its most macro level, building a constitutional model on strong legal pluralism, rather than as an add-on to nation-state centralism. And it is transformative in expanding the global conversation about what is a constitution, what is legal pluralism, and what is sharia. It asks us to transform our idea of what Islamic constitutionalism is or can be.

All of this might or might not change the doctrine on the ground. A Muslim country following this model may very well end up with the same dress code or divorce laws. But this new vision of Islamic constitutionalism *will* transform the basis upon which they are enacted. No longer can Muslim state lawmaking be justified by claiming it is "sharia" and dictated by God; it must now be justified as serving the public good. This transformation would create huge obstacles to theocratic Muslim state authoritarianism, to which many are prone today. In sum, the Islamic constitutionalism proposed here would be transformative, but not in the form of micro-changes in particular rules; it would be at the macro level—in the structure and nature of Muslim political and legal authority.

This proposal focuses on constitutionalism as directing the structure of government—who has what power and what are the checks and balances on that power. In other words, it addresses "constitution" in the sense of a body's "healthy constitution." As described earlier, Muslim governments right now, especially those seeking to be sharia-mindful, do not have a healthy constitution. The Muslim political body has been devastatingly wounded—by colonialism, legal centralism, and a variety of political events since independence. More than that, Muslims have been disconnected from their own pre-colonial constitutional thinking, so it is not just actual structures within tangible constitutions that need repair, it is the very idea of Islamic constitutional*ism*—that is, what *is* Islamic constitutional theory—that has been wiped from the conscious memories of Muslim political and social actors.

To heal this wound, I articulate an Islamic constitutional theory based on lessons from Muslim legal and political history, understanding sharia as an Islamic rule of law rather than a collection of (*fiqh*) rules. This takes sharia all the way up the theoretical ladder to the rung of constitutional theory, opening up new ways of thinking about the allocation of legal and political power and how to create checks and balances on that power. More specifically, the Islamic constitutionalism proposed here involves two necessary features (1) state (*siyasa*) action based on the public good and (2) a parallel opt-in realm of *fiqh* (and other religious law). Taking sharia as an Islamic rule of law comprised of two legal realms (*siyasa* and *fiqh*), one state and the other non-state, this constitutional theory is an example of strong legal pluralism, making it a powerful alternative to the dominant (but currently challenged) nation-state model of legal centralism.

The Islamic constitutionalism articulated here is based on sharia but is not about "Islamizing" the nation-state. It is directed by sharia-based literature and the pre-colonial practices of Muslim governments. To translate these concepts into modern realities, it borrows the language of legal pluralism to describe a constitutionalized strong legal pluralism that begins with a bifurcation of *fiqh* and *siyasa* legal realms. The resulting constitutional theory provides a powerful example of constitutionalism that is not dominated by legal centralism and provides a new approach to thinking about decolonized understandings of the state.[46]

It is hoped that the proposed Islamic constitutional theory will open up new possibilities for those thinking about crafting Islamic constitutions for Muslim-majority countries. More poignantly, it demonstrates that Islamic constitutionalism deserves to have a place as a valuable participant in the global conversation about comparative constitutionalism, and especially the discourse on decolonizing ourselves from the nation-state. Given the extent and depth of Muslim experiences with colonial power, it is about time that Muslims took a seat at this table.

> Islamic Law was regarded as of speculative rather than of practical interest and received attention from a relatively few specialists and scholars. But a review of the reasons we have deemed such knowledge too alien but useful to us

show the reasons why we should abandon the smug belief that the Muslim experience has nothing to teach us.

Jackson, 1955: vi

Notes

1 I use the term "Islamic state" as the phrase used by Muslim political activists in the mid-twentieth century and popularized by thinkers such as Pakistan's Maududi and revolutionaries in Iran in 1979. I do not mean in any way to refer ISIS/Da'esh, the violent movement in Iraq and Syria currently (and, according to most of the world's Muslims, illegitimately) using the title "Islamic State."
2 Speaking specifically of "weak" legal pluralism.
3 See also Buskens (2014: 214).
4 "The idea of legal pluralism was an extension from the analysis of dualism/pluralism in colonial societies where it indicated asymmetrical power (and race) relationships between the white minority and the indigenous majority" (Benda-Beckmann, 2002: 37).
5 For more detail, see Buskens (2014).
6 As Griffiths explains, "It is the factual power of the state which is the keystone of an otherwise normative system, which affords the empirical condition for the actual existence of 'law'" (Griffith, 1986: 3). See also Van Niekerk (2001: 349, 351).
7 Buskens argues that the very term and concept of "Islamic law" is a colonial invention (Buskens, 2014: 211).
8 For more detail, see Quraishi (2012: 63–73).
9 "Some of what is seen as part of the law in Islam cannot really be imposed by anybody other than those who apply it to themselves (e.g., the duty of fasting in the month of Ramadan)" (Ahmad, 2005: 45).
10 Part of this new appreciation for legal pluralism in the west is the phenomenon of minority religious and ethnic communities living in western lands and seeking to apply their own laws within their diaspora communities. This controversial subject has become an academic field in itself, addressing complex questions of group rights, human rights, legal uniformity and predictability, diversity, and religious freedom. Public discourse on the subject pushes sensitive buttons of community identity, racism, xenophobia, and the meaning of secularism. Muslims, again, are front and center in these debates. The question of "sharia tribunals" offering sharia-based resolution of Muslim conflicts in secular western societies is perhaps the most important legal flashpoint for this subject, but there are many other examples. The debate is important, having generated violence on both sides. But it is not the subject of this chapter. The question of legal pluralism as it relates to Muslim minorities in secular western countries is a western-focused topic. My subject is not Europe or America; it is Islamic governance in Muslim-majority countries. Legal pluralism is the framework for my presentation not because I am interested in group rights or even legal pluralism per se, but rather because I believe that legal pluralism offers the best lens through which western minds can understand sharia as an Islamic rule of law.
11 See Merry (1988), Forsyth (2007: 1–12), and Galanter (1981).
12 See Vogel (2000: 31, 52, 171–73).
13 "The whole basis and foundation of sharia is to serve the welfare of God's servants in this world and in the hereafter" (Vogel, 2000: 529).
14 "As understood by [*fiqh* scholars] the ruler possesses authority under siyasa doctrine to act freely to pursue the welfare of the [community] as he understands it" (Vogel, 2000: 529).
15 See Mnookin and Kornhause (1979).

16 There are far too many examples to go into here, but for some, see Stilt (2012) describing the mixed *fiqh-siyasa* role of the *muhtasib*.
17 See, for example, Calder (2010: 54) discussing Kasani's works.
18 See, also, Calder (2010): that Islamic law books had an impractical or idealistic bias was noticed, usually with distaste, by Western scholars up to and including Joseph Schacht.
19 There are numerous examples of this mismatch by western scholars observing Muslim legal behavior. Here is one of them: in her article "Legal Pluralism," Sally Engle Merry comments that "in Islamic legal sensibility . . . facts are normative; there is no fact/law dichotomy" (Merry, 1988: 871). In support, she cites well-known anthropologists of Islam who have been critiqued for using an orientalist and narrow lens when viewing their subject. I find it absurd to suggest that there is no "fact/law" dichotomy in Islamic legal thinking, but one has to appreciate the nuanced relationship of *fiqh* and *siyasa*, and their respective operation in everyday Muslim life, to understand this. With lenses that see sharia as only *fiqh*, one is likely to make these sorts of mistakes.
20 For details on Malaysia as just one example, "between the beginning of British colonial rule in 1874 and the late twentieth century, Islamic law was transformed almost beyond recognition in Malaysia" (Moustafa, 2013: 178).
21 See Hallaq (2009: 85–114).
22 Frank Vogel comments that this is apparent

> when Islamic thinkers assume that to return to sharia one should just amend here and there the existing positive-law constitutions and statutes; or assert that a modern state is Islamic if its legislature pays respect to general Islamic legal precepts, such as bans on prostitution or gambling.
>
> *Vogel, 2000: 219*

23 For a discussion of constitutional clauses setting up sharia as a/the source of legislation in several Muslim-majority countries, see Clark B. Lombardi (2013). On the history and rise of sharia-based constitutional "repugnancy" clauses, see Ahmed and Ginsburg (2014).
24 See also Mohammad Hashim Kamali:

> The government and its legislative branch tend to act as the sole repository of legislative power . . . The advent of constitutionalism and government under the rule of law brought the hegemony of statutory legislation that has largely dominated legal and judicial practice in Muslim societies.
>
> *Kamali, 1996: 9*

25 See, e.g., Pew Research Center (2013).
26 Question asked at the end of Section 2.2.
27 These two pillars are not the only pillars I believe necessary to a contempoary model of Islamic constitutionalism. There is at least one more, namely, a way to check the public good state lawmaking so that it does not violate the purposes of sharia. But I do not have space to elaborate that pillar here. For further details, see Asifa Quraishi-Landes (2015b: 553–79), and my forthcoming publications on the subject.
28 Today, *siyasa* power is often divided into legislative, executive, and judicial power, with complex and different arrangements between them depending upon the given country. But altogether, all government power today could be called the contemporary manifestations of classical *siyasa* power.
29 See, e.g., Pew Research Center (2013).
30 The question of how to reach consensus in the public sphere—especially between religious and secular voices—is a subject of much attention these days. See, e.g., Mohammad H. Fadel (2007); Andrew F. March (2009); Abdullahi Ahmed An-Na'im (1996). My proposal does not take a position on this question because it is not its purpose. It is not crucial to my model to decide how a given society decides to identify

what is in its public interest, maslaha. My point is only to show that maslaha should be the basis of state lawmaking (however a given society decides to figure that out). My proposal does not seek to present a particular theory of political science ordering, identifying how best to determine the public good for a given polity. Rather it seeks only to identify the building blocks of Islamic constitutionalism (identifying *siyasa* based on the public good as one of those blocks) that can then be worked out in detail later as each Muslim country builds their own house on this foundation.

31 Support for *sharia* legislation is often fueled by identity politics such that it has come to symbolize what it is to be a religious Muslim, as against secularism as an extension of cultural imperialism and the politics of Christians. See Anver M. Emon (2008: 258–85).

32 See John Esposito and Dalia Mogahed (2008: 35) documenting that large majorities of Muslims around the world support democracy and also support sharia.

33 See Moustafa (2013) describing how codification and institutionalization has transformed Islamic jurisprudence—once flexible and pluralistic to fixed, singular, and state-controlled system; also documenting how this transformation has reshaped people's fundamental understanding of the nature of Islamic law itself.

34 The constitutional framework proposed here imagines a fluidity of movement inside the *fiqh* realm: Muslims choosing to access it could easily choose among the many different *fiqh* interpretations available and would not be forced to stick with one school. This differentiates the present framework not only from the millet system but also from contemporary theories of multicultural accommodation which tend to assume only one doctrinal option for a given religious community. See, for example, Ayelet Schachar (2001).

35 I am describing the *fiqh* realm as "diverse" and not one of "legal pluralism" because I follow the definition of legal pluralism as the existence of multiple legal systems or layers of law, usually with different sources of legitimacy, that coexist within a single state or social field. For more, see Griffiths (1986). The academic discourse on legal pluralism defines it not as a diversity of interpretations of the same source material (as in different justices' opinions on the meaning of constitutional text) but, rather, where different laws originating from different sources exist simultaneously in the same space. Applying these definitions, *fiqh* diversity is not legal pluralism under this definition but a legal system composed of *fiqh* and *siyasa*.

36 I realize that there are many pros and cons to non-state tribunals. The field is ripe with analysis and commentary and much debate, far too much to detail here. But my proposal here does not take a position in that discourse. As with the nuances of the public lawmaking systems in Pillar One, the details of what the parallel *fiqh* realm would look like are not my subject. I imagine many possible ways for this to be organized, each having pros and cons. Selecting among these is something to be left to each Muslim-majority society undertaking this constitutional project. My job here is only to articulate the principle behind the institution as part of the core foundation of a modern Islamic constitutional theory.

37 The importance of choice also means that there should be freedom to *not* utilize the *fiqh* realm at all. In this, the Islamic constitutional system proposed here diverges from classical Muslim systems. In pre-modern Muslim systems, *siyasa* laws were typically limited to logistical and administrative needs of society and generally did not overlap with the topics covered by *fiqh*. Thus, pre-modern Muslims could have their legal issues decided according to their chosen *fiqh* school, but they could not choose to follow no *fiqh* school at all, because there was no state law covering the topics of *fiqh*. (This arrangement is well-known as the Ottoman "millet" system, which has been borrowed by in edited variations by some colonial powers and contemporary states such as Israel and India. The framework proposed here differs significantly from the millet system because of the inclusion of a fully formed body of state law parallel to

fiqh law in all major topic areas.) In light of the changed circumstances of modernity in which many people do not directly identify with a *fiqh* school (or indeed any religion), the proposed constitutional framework imagines a much more robust *siyasa* field covering a wider range of legal issues, thus offering a tangible alternative to the *fiqh* realm for those that do have a strong *fiqh* affiliation. (For example, if both the *fiqh* and *siyasa* realms have rules regulating divorce, individuals will have a fully realized opportunity to choose which legal realm best suits them if a marriage ends.) This would help ensure that those opting in to the *fiqh* realm are affirmatively exercising this option, rather than being forced into *fiqh* by default. This also would ensure that the bifurcation of *fiqh* and *siyasa* legal realms is not a split between public and private law, nor is it a strict assignment of separate legal jurisdictions based on religious affiliation.

38 This is true even of countries committed to multicultural social and political ordering. Take, for example, South Africa, with a commitment to pluralism and to accommodating unofficial laws in its legal order. The South African Law Commission's task to harmonize indigenous law and the common law, in the words of Ryan Hill, has leaned toward "a forced convergence of state law and 'the other laws', a blending of the various systems of law into a new unified law, within a framework of Western values" (2010: 132).

39

> Just as health is not found primarily in hospitals or knowledge in schools, so justice is not primarily to be found in official justice-dispensing institutions. People experience justice (and injustice) not only (or usually) in forums sponsored by the state but at the primary institutional locations of their activity—home, neighborhood, workplace, business deal and so on (including a variety of specialized remedial settings embedded in these locations).
>
> *Galanter, 1981: 17*

40 "Freeman concludes, pluralism, just as deconstruction, ultimately ends in immobilization, since if everything is complex and variable, just as if everything is a matter of interpretation, how can one say anything?" (Merry, 1988: 885).

41 For just one of many examples, see the Center of Study and Investigation of Decolonial Dialogues www.dialogoglobal.com, which has a well-known Muslim program titled "Critical Muslim Studies" www.dialogoglobal.com/granada.

42 "Legal centralism is one style of response to this generic question of legal ordering, and its exhaustion suggests the need for reflection on other models" (Galanter, 1981: 29); Boaventura de Sousa Santos (1987) asserts that legal pluralism is the key concept in a postmodern view of law.

43 See, for example, Salman Sayyid (2014).

44 One note about the nature of legal pluralism proposed here. This is not motivated by the "group rights" discourse. It does not seek to create or protect plural legal communities in order to preserve groups and group identity within those orders. It does not adopt legal pluralism because it values legal pluralism per se. Rather, this is a pluralist constitutionalism because legal pluralism is the best way to understand the sharia-based systems from which it takes its inspiration. Those systems adopted a pluralist approach not because it sought to preserve minority cultures or groups, but because that structure was demanded by the epistemological realities of Islamic legal thought.

45 See, for example, Alexis Galán and Dennis Paterson summarizing the critique as: "whatever the explanatory merits of pluralism might be, there is no direct translation of those efforts into the normative sphere" (2013: 785).

46 It is important to note that in my proposal there is still a state; it is just not a nation-state. As Walker has noted,

> The post-Westphalian order may be one which moves beyond the state in important ways in its vesting of legal and political authority, but the state—however modified

> and however diminished—continues to be a player in the emerging multi-dimensional, multi-level order.
>
> *2002: 334*

Rather, the proposed state is one that respects both state and non-state legal experiences.

References

Ahmad, Ahmad Atif (2005), "Structural Interrelations of Theory and Practice in Islamic Law: A Study of Takhrij Al-Furu 'Ala Al-Usul Literature". PhD Thesis, Cambridge, MA: Harvard University.

Ahmad, Ahmad Atif (2006), *Structural Interrelations of Theory and Practice in Islamic Law: A Study of Six Works of Medieval Islamic Jurisprudence*. Leiden: Brill.

Ahmed, Dawood I.; Ginsburg, Tom (2014), "Constitutional Islamization and Human Rights: The Surprising Origin and Spread of Islamic Supremacy in Constitutions", *Virginia Journal of International Law*, 54(3), 615–695. Available at www.researchgate.net/publication/274636400_Constitutional_Islamization_and_Human_Rights_The_Surprising_Origin_and_Spread_of_Islamic_Supremacy_in_Constitutions.

An-Na'im, Abdullahi Ahmed (1996), *Toward an Islamic Reformation: Civil Liberties, Human Rights, and International Law*. Syracuse, NY: Syracuse University Press.

Benda-Beckmann, Franz von (2002), "Who's Afraid of Legal Pluralism", *The Journal of Legal Pluralism and Unofficial Law*, 34(47), 37–82. DOI: https://doi.org/10.1080/07329113.2002.10756563.

Buskens, Leon (2014), "Sharia and the Colonial State", in Rudolph Peters and Peri Bearman (eds.), *Ashgate Research Companion to Islamic Law*. Surrey: Ashgate, 209–222.

Calder, Norman (1996), "Law", in S. H. Nasr and O. Leaman (eds.), *History of Islamic Philosophy*. London: Routledge, 979–998.

Calder, Norman (2010), *Islamic Jurisprudence in the Classical Era*. Cambridge: Cambridge University Press.

Emon, Anver M. (2004), "Human Legislative Authority in Islamic Law", *Yale Critical Islamic Reflections Conference*, Yale University, New Haven.

Emon, Anver M. (2008), "The Limits of Constitutionalism in the Muslim World: History and Identity in Islamic Law", in Sujit Choudhry (ed.), *Constitutional Design for Divided Societies: Integration or Accommodation?* Oxford: Oxford University Press, 258–285.

Esposito, John; Mogahed, Dalia (2008), *Who Speaks for Islam: What a Billion Muslims Really Think*. New York: Gallup Press.

Fadel, Mohammad H. (2007), "Public Reason as a Strategy for Principled Reconciliation: The Case of Islamic Law and International Human Rights Law", *Chicago Journal of International Law*, 8(1), 1–20. Available at http://chicagounbound.uchicago.edu/cjil/vol8/iss1/3.

Fadel, Mohammad H. (2008), "The Challenge of Human Rights", *Seasons: the Journal of the Zaytuna Institute*, 5(1), 59–80.

Forsyth, Miranda (2007), "How to 'Do' Legal Pluralism", 1–12. DOI: https://doi.org/10.2139/ssrn.993617.

Galán, Alexis; Patterson, Dennis (2013), "The Limits of Normative Legal Pluralism: Review of Paul Schiff Berman, Global Legal Pluralism: A Jurisprudence of Law beyond Borders", *International Journal of Constitutional Law*, 11(3): 783–800. DOI: https://doi.org/10.1093/icon/mot029.

Galanter, Marc (1981), "Justice in Many Rooms: Courts, Private Ordering and Indigenous Law", *Journal of Legal Pluralism*, 13(19), 1–47. DOI: https://doi.org/10.1080/07329113.1981.10756257.

Griffiths, John (1986), "What Is Legal Pluralism?" *Journal of Legal Pluralism*, 18(24), 1–55. DOI: https://doi.org/10.1080/07329113.1986.10756387.

Hallaq, Wael B. (2009), "Colonizing the Muslim World and its Shari'a", in *An Introduction to Islamic Law*. Cambridge: Cambridge University Press, 85–114.

Hill, Ryan W. (2010), "Legal Pluralism in the Liberal State: A Defence of the Archbishop of Canterbury or a Human Rights Impasse?" *Law & Justice—Christian Law Review*, 165, 124–143.

Imber, Colin (1997), *Ebu's-Su'ud: The Islamic Legal Tradition*. Stanford: Stanford University Press.

Jackson, Robert H. (1955), "Foreword", in Majid Khadduri and Herbert J. Liebesny (eds.), *Law in the Middle East*. Washington, DC: The Middle East Institute, v–ix.

Jackson, Sherman A. (1996), *Islamic Law and the State: The Constitutional Jurisprudence of Shihab Al-Din Al-Qarafi*. Leiden: Brill.

Jackson, Sherman A. (2003), "Shari'ah, Democracy, and the Modern Nation-State: Some Reflections on Islam, Popular Rule, and Pluralism", *Fordham International Law Journal*, 27(1), 88–107. Available at https://ir.lawnet.fordham.edu/ilj/vol27/iss1/5.

Jackson, Sherman A. (2013), "Islamic Reform between Islamic Law and the Nation-State", in John L. Esposito and Emad El-Din Shahin (eds.), *Oxford Handbook of Islam and Politics*. Oxford: Oxford University Press.

Kamali, Mohammad Hashim (1996), "Methodological Issues in Islamic Jurisprudence", *Arab Law Quarterly*, 11(1), 3–33. DOI: https://doi.org/10.2307/3381731.

Stilt, Kristen (2012), *Islamic Law in Action: Authority, Discretion, and Everyday Experiences in Mamluk Egypt*. Oxford: Oxford University Press.

Lombardi, Clark B. (2013), "Constitutional Provisions Making Sharia 'A' or 'The' Chief Source of Legislation: Where Did They Come From? What Do They Mean? Do They Matter?" *American University International Law Review*, 28(3), 733–774. Available at https://digitalcommons.wcl.american.edu/auilr/vol28/iss3/3.

March, Andrew F. (2009), *Islam and Liberal Citizenship: The Search for an Overlapping Consensus*. Oxford: Oxford University Press.

Merry, Sally Engle (1988), "Legal Pluralism", *Law & Society Review*, 22(5), 869–896. DOI: https://doi.org/10.2307/3053638.

Mnookin Robert H.; Kornhause, Lewis (1979), "Bargaining in the Shadow of the Law: The Case of Divorce", *The Yale Law Journal*, 88(5), 950–997. Available at https://digitalcommons.law.yale.edu/ylj/vol88/iss5/4.

Moustafa, Tamir (2013), "Islamic Law, Women's Rights, and Popular Legal Consciousness in Malaysia", *Law and Social Inquiry*, 38(1), 168–188. DOI: https://doi.org/10.1111/j.1747-4469.2012.01298.x.

Pew Research Center—Religion & Public Life (2013), "The World's Muslims: Religion, Politics and Society", *Pewforum.org*, April 30. Available at www.pewforum.org/the-worlds-muslims-2013.

Quraishi, Asifa (2012), "The Separation of Powers in the Tradition of Muslim Governments", in Rainer Grote and Tilmann Röder (eds.), *Constitutionalism in Islamic Countries: Between Upheaval and Continuity*. New York: Oxford University Press, 63–73.

Quraishi-Landes, Asifa (2015a), "The Sharia Problem with Sharia Legislation", *Ohio Northern University Law Review*, 41, 545–566. Available at https://ssrn.com/abstract=2652896.

Quraishi-Landes, Asifa (2015b), "Islamic Constitutionalism: Not Secular. Not Theocratic. Not Impossible", *Rutgers Journal of Law & Religion*, 16, 553–579.

Reza, Sadiq (2007), "Torture and Islamic Law", *Chicago Journal of International Law*, 8(1), 21–41. Available at https://chicagounbound.uchicago.edu/cjil/vol8/iss1/4.

Santos, Boaventura de Sousa (1987), "Law: A Map of Misreading: Toward a Postmodern Conception of Law", *Journal of Law and Society*, 14(3), 279–302. DOI: https://doi.org/10.2307/1410186.

Sayyid, Salman (2014), *Recalling the Caliphate: Decolonisation and the World Order*. London: Hurst.

Schachar, Ayelet (2001), *Multicultural Jurisdictions: Cultural Differences and Women's' Rights*. Cambridge: Cambridge University Press.

Van Niekerk, Gardiol (2001), "State Initiatives to Incorporate Non-State Laws into the Official Legal Order: A Denial of Legal Pluralism?" *Comparative and International Law Journal of Southern Africa*, 34(3), 349–361. Available at https://hdl.handle.net/10520/AJA00104051_206.

Viellechner, Lars (2012), "Constitutionalism as a Cipher: On the Convergence of Constitutionalist and Pluralist Approaches to the Globalization of Law", *Goettingen Journal of International Law*, 4(2), 599–623. Available at www.gojil.eu/42-abstract-viel lechner.

Vogel, Frank E. (2000), *Islamic Law and Legal System: Studies of Saudi Arabia*, vol. 8. Leiden: Brill.

Walker, Neil (2002), "The Idea of Constitutional Pluralism", *Modern Law Review*, 65(3), 317–359. DOI: https://doi.org/10.1111/1468-2230.00383.

Weiss, Bernard G. (1978), "Interpretation in Islamic Law: The Theory of Ijtihad", *American Journal of Comparative Law*, 26(2), 199–212. DOI: https://doi.org/10.2307/839668.

Weiss, Bernard G. (2010), *The Search for God's Law: Islamic Jurisprudence in Writings of Sayf Al-Din Al-Amidi*. Salt Lake City: University of Utah Press.

3

NIHILISMS, CONTRADICTIONS, AND ANOMIE IN NEW CONSTITUTIONALISMS

A View from India

Upendra Baxi

3.1 Introduction

It is easy enough to study constitutionalisms on a world scale from an Olympian liberal or a bicentennial Eurocentric perspective, but very difficult to explore these from a subaltern, or worm's eye, standpoint. To analyse constitutions put to work in the Global South is an itinerary with several stops. As the Global South itself is changeful, how does one's doing of global social change theory affect acts of living and ideologies of a good life? (Young, 2001; Prasad, 2008, 2014; Therborn, 2013; Baxi, 2016a). Does the space for constitutional development and experience affect millions of human beings living at the margins of economic development? In what ways does what Boaventura de Sousa Santos names 'abyssal/post abyssal thought' (2007, 2014, 2015)[1] relate to an understanding of constitutional law and interpretation, or any theory of and about constitutionalism? Do constitutions matter at all for the marginalized or the 'wretched of the earth' as Franz Fanon called them? Or are they seen as merely a ruse of governance or an intellectual conceit of constitutional lawpersons and other knowledge specialists? Even as one ploughs the fields of a nascent branch of comparative constitutional studies (which I have named COCOS, for short), one should decode and ponder such questions.

Being anxious about these questions does not render routine the COCOS tasks of description, explanation, justification, and evaluation of constitutional arrangements; these are not easy and especially complex on a COCOS scale. There is no agreement on the comparative method that provides even a common scale of comparison (description), and no such agreement exists on how one may historically explain the emergence and evolution of constitutional arrangements, their justification (in terms of the history of a particular country and culture), and external (objective, third party) evaluation of their impact[2] whether on

DOI: 10.4324/9781003391920-5

governance, development, rights, or justice.[3] The COCOS tasks consist in comparing the *incomparable* rather than comparative law exercises understood as exercises in comparing the *comparable*.

One may distinguish among many forms of southern and subaltern constitutions—such as early, middle, and late colonial constitutionalisms. Similarly, from a global hegemonic perspective, one may distinguish similar phases and itineraries of Cold War, or one may focus primarily on constitutions and developments post-1980s in terms of a globalizing contemporary constitutionalism. If one were to study constitutions post-1980s, severe difficulties arise around these axes. The post-1980s are times of the so-called transitional post-socialist constitutions which furnish one large example, but there are also times of post-apartheid (South Africa), post-ethnic (Fiji, 2013), globalized (Viet Nam, South Africa), militarily imposed democratic and illiberal (post 9/11—Iraq, Afghanistan), severely divided societies (former Yugoslavia), belated postcolonial (Eritrea, Ethiopia, Mali, Tanzania, Fiji), post-monarchy (Nepal), and frankly theological (Iran, Afghanistan, Iraq) constitutionalisms. The postmodern EU federation (as Daniel Elazar calls this[4]) hovers uncertainly as a unique case of supranational, multicultural constitutionalism.

Beyond chronological time, marked even with the bicentennial constitutionalisms, there exist no unifying descriptors for these new constitutionalisms, unless the riot of 'postisms' may afford a unifying rubric! To be sure, these are all postliberal constitutions in the sense that these go beyond classical liberal doctrines and are post-Universal Declaration of Human Rights and International Bill of Human Rights. Beyond this, any agreement is hard to discern.

It is tempting to recourse to some conceptual shortcuts like 'military constitutionalisms'[5] or even 'constitutions without constitutionalism'.[6] It is even more tempting to deploy the jurisprudential distinction between 'jurisgenetic' (the old word for that was 'jurisgenerative') and 'jurispathic': the former is the creative and the latter a destructive element. In any account, these elements are best considered as in play and war with each other rather than either/or type dichotomy; Robert Cover even suggests (or can be read as suggesting) their coexistence in the same legal jural field. For example, his famous observation about legal interpretation occurring over 'the plane of pain and death'[7] may be extended to all legal and constitutional interpretation (about death penalty and power to wage wars, for example). Indeed, to extend Cover a bit, interpretation never devoid of summoning force is at once jurispathic and jurisgenerative. If so, all law is both and so are constitutions; these always entail a moral gain and a moral loss; no constitution *as such* may be described wholly as jurisgenerative or jurispathic; at best and at worst any constitution in itself and its development displays elements of both.

If we take an essentialist view of the constitutions as in the view that all constitutions are Western or liberal, the problem becomes simpler, one of measuring the deviation from the mean. Thus, we may adjudge 'constitutions without constitutionalism'—socialist, postcolonial post-socialist, and host of others, as 'jurispathic'. The harder problem, in my opinion, is one of description rather than one of judgement. That is at least what we learn from Georges Canguilhem who invented the distinction between the 'normal' and 'pathological' which was dealt with very differently by Sigmund Freud and Jacques Lacan. Canguilhem taught us that: 'Every preference for a possible order is accompanied, most often implicitly, by the aversion for the opposite possible order' (1991: 240). If constitutionalism is all about what I call 'desired social order' (Baxi, 1967), we may not ignore the politics of desire—which Jacques Lacan calls the 'lack of lack'.[8]

Here one stands confronted (to adapt Jacques Derrida) with an aporia: the constitutions, at one end, adopt a new normative culture which furnishes criteria of validity to all legislations yet the new normal cohabits the space of the old. Put differently, the new constitutional order remains normatively aspirational but, in reality, continues to mystify power relations and structures. There is thus a marked difference in the visions of a society enunciated by a constitution and the constitution-to-come. I hope that some of the resultant tension reverberates in what follows.

3.2 Contradiction and Anomie

Instead of the contrast between jurisgenerative/jurispathic, I deploy the paired notions of anomie and contradiction to study new constitutionalisms. One requires an adaptive understanding of Durkheim-Dada (Bhai) and 'Uncle' Marx to grasp these notions. We need an adequate theory of contradictions and anomie that does not set as a benchmark the Westphalian state, civil society, and its anomie. Although neither theorization comes easy, anomie and contradiction are near-permanent orders of constitutional development and experience (subjectification/subjectification).[9]

The contradiction and the anomie of the 1950 constitution of India were well articulated by Dr Bhim Rao Ambedkar, the chief architect of the Indian Constitution who had this to say on the eve of its adoption:

> On the 26th January, 1950, we are going to enter into a life of contradictions. In politics, we shall be recognizing the principle of one man one vote one value. In our social and economic life, we shall, by reason of economic structure continue to deny [this principle.] How long shall we continue to live this life of contradiction? If we continue to deny it for long, we will do so by putting our democracy in peril.
>
> *Ambedkar, 1949: 979*

Jawaharlal Nehru strove to combine the best (creative) elements that will somehow fuse into an 'organic whole' some forms of 'nationalism and political freedom' and 'social freedom as represented by socialism', which will promote a 'classless society'; the removal of 'all invidious social and customary barriers which come in the way of the full development of the individual as well as of any group' constituted the leitmotif of Indian Constitutionalism. Yet, Dr Bhim Rao Ambedkar summates (in the quote above) constitutionalism as a series of contradictions; life under constitution is for him a 'life of contradictions'.

In underscoring the contradictions of Indian Constitutionalism, D. Ambedkar, in a sense, helps us to understand the contradictions of all 'new' constitutions, even of the very form of constitutionalism itself. The grasp of constitutionalism entails a theory of contradictions, as yet not fully in COCOS sight. The contradictions of any constitution can be studied on several planes: the aspirational/institutional, normative/institutional, civilizational/cultural, material/symbolic, or performative (Rai and Reinelt, 2015) (all contradictions are 'material' in the Marxian genre as arising from the economic structure). No doubt as Ambedkar said to 'deny' these for 'long' will periclitate 'democracy'. But what is liberal (and now postliberal) democracy if not a series of structural contradictions that are lived and embodied by each and every citizen, party, and leader?

I may here only instance the immortal phrase of Jawaharlal Nehru which conceives the birth of a free India and its constitutional order in terms of a '*tryst with destiny*'. The histories of popular struggles and even insurgent reason that marked the birthing of a new constitutional order illustrate for 'South Asia' at least an impassioned quest of what Mohandas Gandhi inimitably named as '*Swaraj* in Ideas'—a principle, practice, and a process of epistemic self-determination.[10]

Yet, constitutional 'experience' also invokes the memory of a rickshaw puller named Mangu Ram (in an epigrammatic story of Saddat Hasan Manto) who was abruptly elevated to the status of citizenship, a being with rights, and decided that as a free and equal citizen, even as a *tongawala* (a horse carriage rider in Lahore, Pakistan), he can choose his clients and refuse his services to the free riders who conscripted his labour for the ends of the localized sovereign administration. Mangu Ram's exuberance also resulted in a minor altercation. When arrested by the police, he proudly proclaimed that under the newly proclaimed Constitution, he had fundamental rights to do his business as he wanted, only to learn that it still remained the old one (as Hans Kelsen would say the historically given first constitution!). The uncomprehending police beat him up and paradigmatically exclaimed: '*What rubbish are you talking? What new constitution? It is the same old constitution you fool! Then they locked him up*!'[11]

Several generations of 'South Asian' Mangu Rams continue to perform what Emmanuel Levinas once described as a virtue of 'foolish excellence'[12]—the parlances that take constitutional promises and change far too seriously for their own 'good!' However, if we were to notice the kinship with another term: 'rational fools' (Sen, 1977), their practices triumph over that of the practitioners of foolish excellence. Elsewhere, I name these practices as 'subaltern constitutionalism', reconstituted judicial Mangu Ram-type beings practice this 'foolish excellence' virtue as well! (Baxi, 2009a).

3.3 Post-1980s Constitutions: Digging a Little Deeper

For purposes of communicational clarity, and not always for good conceptual reasons or arguments, I take 'new constitutionalisms' as signifying those that came into being since the late 1980s; these are 'new' only in the sense that they are written in, and since, 1990s although they may borrow heavily from the 'old'.

The term 'new constitutionalism' has a long history, because many a Third World polity was considered a new 'nation'; it had 'new' constitutionalism (as if the large colonized countries were neither nations nor states); the postcolonial constitutionalism was termed 'transitional constitutionalisms' (as if constitutionalism had a permanent or fixed essence); and the term now is extended to global economic constitutionalism itself! In other words, the liberal West (US and most of Europe) alone had a 'modern' conception of constitutional state and law.[13] The notion of 'new constitutionalism' is puzzling as if all constitutions derive their logical or epistemic validity from a universal Westphalian essence, whereas as Hans Kelsen famously stated, 'the historically given first constitution' is the only terminus for the question: 'Why ought I follow, or obey, the Constitution?'. If so, the question can only be answered, if at all, in acts of reading history both as a past and as a future. On an allied front, we need to study the relation between mimesis and originality in terms of a recursive time.[14]

The 'old' constitutional essence—or, as John Rawls (1993) puts it, the 'constitutional essentials'—has changed in many ways. By the 'old' we no longer mean the ancient, although that was the contrast which gave the sense to the 'new'. Only the European West (led by the American and French revolutions), it was explicitly stated, was capable of constitutional innovation; their civilizing mission led to the spread of four Cs—conquest, Christianity, commerce, and civilization.[15]

Today, the four 'Cs' emerge in a different guise. The 'old' today, moreover, represents no longer socialist or actually existing socialist histories or conceptions, and the concept of the 'postcolonial' does not make any immediate and coherent sense as it used to even as late as the 1990s. The 1990s refer to two universalizations within which alone constitutionalisms make any 'sense': the constitution of late capitalism with the travails of a resilient neoliberal post-Westphalian political order and the notion of human rights-based governance. How these may have impacted the progressive new constitutionalism in Global South remains an important empirical question.

However, the idea of a constitution is a very 'old' one, and it plays a long role in health sciences, medicine, and law. We ought to take its genealogy seriously if we are to realize that at its core it is not a typically Euro-American notion. I here look at legal constitutions in terms of the eight 'Cs' (it makes a deadly cocktail to speak alongside the other four Cs!)

In my previous work, I have identified three 'Cs': 'constitutionalism' (C3) in the conventional sense invites attention to the normative theory or ideological core or even the 'spirit' of constitutions; constitutional law is the official interpretation (C2) of the text of the constitution (C1). The three 'Cs' constitute the dialectics of constitutionalism—that is, these pose a number of ideological, normative, and institutional contradictions.

C1 presupposes the idea of a constitutional text (written or unwritten, and the latter is often at play and war with the former) as the basic law which provides for the validity of all other norms in the legal order. For the idea of a constitution to exist, varieties of C3 imagined as an ideological core are already in place (certain foundational beliefs). In contrast, normative theory speaks to C3 quite differently in terms of 'constitutional essentials', although implicitly arising from some foundational liberal beliefs concerning a morally decent state and society. At any rate, the explicit ideological core C3 'justifies'/'mystifies' the idea of constitution variously.

The colonial C3 celebrated a Divine Right to Empire—forms of globally affirmed constituent and constituted power abjectly dominating the non-Euromerican others. The socialist C3 contradicted fully the liberal sacrosanctity of the right to property as a foundation of human freedom and progress, replacing this by vesting ownership of the means of production in the state. The paradigm warriors of the 'Cold War' ideological formations dared to articulate a nearly thirty-year long, and nearly permanent, divide between contending claims of 'making world safe for democracy' on the one hand and on the other fomented the 'wars of national liberation'. Many a form of postcolonial C3 stands enwombed in the killing fields marked by the two superpower formations. These forms now stated as post-ideological C3 assume an entirely different form as governance machines in an era of hyperglobalization with the escalation of 'second coming' of the primitive accumulation of global capital, in contradiction with the famed advent of a new 'Age of Human Rights'. Further, now emerge, even resiliently, multiple Shari'a-based postcolonial constitutionalism which today stand confronted with an endless variety of 'embedded liberalisms'.

Hans Kelsen offered us a very different way of thinking about the three 'Cs' proposed here. His famed and endlessly still misunderstood utterance that the Basic Norm may have any content was designed to alert us to the reality that for any constitutional legal order to exist, justices, lawyers, and officials need to presuppose the Grundnorm as being 'by and large efficacious'. This act of juristic presupposition is used to ascertain the validity of all other constitutional norms, acts of legislation, and executive decisions.

During the enormous privilege of my mid-1960s three-year-long Berkeley conversations, Professor Kelsen explained to me, over and over again, reasons why the distinction between 'validity' and 'legitimation' remained crucial. If the task of a jurist was to demonstrate the normative existence of a constitutional and legal order, there was no choice but to postulate the Grundnorm; this did not mean that the questions concerning its justice or legitimacy were thus foreclosed but rather that these had best be addressed by ethics or political philosophy. C3 is important, but more decisive remains C2 for the everyday existence and operation of any legal order. Professor Kelsen will reproach me from 'the starry heavens above' (with apologies for using this Kantian expression) and for the further complicated addition of some other 'Cs'.

Understanding the 'transformative' in COCOS contexts entails further division of C2 beyond the official (or authoritative) interpretation by others. Via C4, I designate practices of nonofficial interpretation from the learned professions, including public intellectuals and social and human rights movements. C5 designates all persons in a dominant position—'corporate', 'financial', 'market', and 'consumer' citizens—who especially contest C2 to advance their own strategic interests. C6 comprises interpretive praxes emanating from the voices of human and social suffering of the rightless or the worst-off citizens and persons who claim (in Hannah Arendt's words) the human 'right to have rights'. C6 often stands articulated by communities of resistance—for short here, on the power of social movements and human rights struggles. For C6 interpretive praxes to have any substantial impact on constitutional law (C2), the hospitable figuration of activist justices remains necessary; perhaps, this is best named as a distinctive C7.

At the same time, we also need to reckon C8—the constituted powers to suspend constitutions in a state of within-nation emergency often named as 'armed rebellions', or external threats most poignantly manifest in the contemporary grammars and rhetoric of 'wars on terror'.[16] Cognoscenti may well recall the theory of 'state of exception' as enunciated by Carl Schmitt and creatively deconstructed in *Homo Sacer* by Giorgio Agamben.[17] But in actual practice, some of which we consider in the context of the Third World (or rather third worldism—a state of mind rather than mere geographical placement), not all emergencies are commissariat dictatorships where suspension of constitutions stands justified by the plea of making these better.

I need not add that the relations between the several Cs are not *linear* but *dialectical*; that is, they crisscross and overlap making for constitutional *bricolage* rather than a *system*; the various elements in the Cs are at play as well as war with each other.

3.4 Constitutional Nihilisms

Rather, they both from the top and the bottom usher in constitutional nihilism; verily, the latter in a Nietzschean sense what we have is 'con-law' (constitutional law) and 'con-theory' (constitutional theory). The prefix 'con' is used severally. Con-theory and con-law at times appear to be gigantic con-tricks! The prefix also indicates forms of calculative rationality, in the languages of 'pros' and 'cons'. Further, in its Latin roots, the prefix further suggests ideas of working with or together. Putting to work these notions of the prefix 'con', may I suggest, remains a task of considerable importance.

In South Asia–specific contexts—but assuredly not only on that site—'con-theory' is often regarded by many as a kind of con-trick. There are several ways of describing this—in terms of 'alien' nature of con-theory, alienation of large masses of people from constitutional arrangements and the wielders of constitutional power, conflicted relationships between constitutional and societal cultures, and the crisis of legitimacy of the state. I prefer to speak here about the varieties of constitutional nihilism. And with much narrative risk, I eclectically adapt here Nietzsche's exposition of nihilism as entailing the 'devaluation of the uppermost values' ('passive nihilism') and their replacement by new ones ('active nihilism') (Heidegger, 1982: 55–56). By values, put shortly, Nietzsche signifies 'constructs of domination' and as Heidegger explains this value is 'essentially the viewpoint of the increase or decrease of these centers of domination' (Heidegger, 1982: 66). I believe that the still to be written histories of constitutionalism may benefit from a close study of Nietzsche, even when he was not much overtly concerned with constitutions and laws.[18]

An elaboration of constitutional nihilism will do better as a descriptive and evaluative category than a 'state of exception' or 'commissariat' dictatorship; it will also better equip us to grasp better the forms of nihilism that accompany the acts of usurpation, political de-subjectification, and insurgent reason that catalyses or presages violent national breakdowns. Indeed, constitutional nihilism becomes the pervasive order of belief in the extraordinary powers thus already acquired (powers of establishment or of insurgent reason).

The eight 'Cs' in their multiplex relationships help, I believe, us to chase the complexity and contradiction of the 'transformative' potential of some modern (contemporary) constitutionalism. How may then these multitudinous 'Cs' may quest the ineffable 'spirit' of constitutions beyond spectral reminders of the promises of freedom, justice, and rights articulated initially by constitutional insurgencies? How may we understand, more specifically put, some contemporary versions of the 'cargo cult' of constitutional preambles which resplendently continue to offer us a rich Thesaurus-type menu of what it may mean to say 'human' and 'having rights', 'the rule of law', 'people', 'progress', and the 'nation'? To grasp this, we need to return to some elements of 'nostalgia' and 'amnesia' in the making/unmaking, and the interregnum, of constitutions.

3.5 Constitutional Reason as the New Normal

In a sense, all unreconstructed forms of C3 'normalize' the 'new normal'. The linkage between normal and the pathological is tolerably clear to students of Georges Canguilhem and Michel Foucault. The varieties of C2, especially citizen interpretation, constantly put to question that 'new' normal. If what the justices finally say is the constitutional law, what they may say finally (and what they say is final, in the nature of things, is final for the time being) depends considerably on the power of unofficial law-saying. How may then constitutional justicing innovate law-saying?[19]

Utopian constitutional theory has always been with us, yet the 'Arab Spring' movement or the 'Occupy Now' seems now to be the harbingers of constitutionalisms[20] 'to come'.[21] That power yet remains to be studied. Do they provide a new C3? Is it a new phenomenon or perhaps a new name (or politics of naming) beyond the 'constituent' power of the 'people'? In what senses is a movement-oriented or based constitutionalism anti-politics 'politics'? In what senses does it make progressively the state more ethical, governance more just, and power in all its (not-so-hidden) habitats more accountable? Does the movement constitutionalism always endorse the remarkable adjudicatory leadership provided by the old and not-so-old South constitutionalisms? And does it provide any effective answer to global economic constitutionalism or is 'juristocracy' always to be haunted by the exceptional and therefore undemocratic (on some conceptions of it) character of judicial review as per the US Supreme Court? (Hirschl, 2000, 2004; Hirschl, Tate and Ginsburg, 2003). Where do we place insurgent reason in the unfolding of constitutions, particularly in the moments of their making and unmaking? And what role do we assign to demosprudence—democracy reinforcing adjudicative leadership—in the development of forms, generally, of C3?[22]

Yet, in so far as the aspirational constitution seeks to bring in the new normal, it minimizes the distance between new social movements and the state. The question of questions in reading constitutions, old or new, pertains to the notion of the normal and its relation to the normative. That which is 'normal' can be very *normless* and *oppressive*: and even when normative, it can impose very flawed political subjectification; this much we surely know from the stories of the 'failed states' in the Global North (although its failed states excelled in de-subjectification) or rather and more accurately the states made to fail by the Global North[23] that make the news.

And that which is normative—as the very idea of human rights and human rights law—can also justify a human right to do a moral wrong. How do we construct and construe the constitutional normal as *just*? Or as the Global South non-military constitutionalisms, and their 'liberal' democracies, have sought to recently accomplish, the constitutional normal may only be achieved by staying with the contradictions and anomie explicitly foregrounding competing and conflicting conceptions of constitutionalisms as comprising development, rights, governance, and justice.

3.6 COCOS and Post-1990s Constitutions

How might a comparative constitutional lawyer, or law person, study new constitutions/constitutionalism? This is a question not just of pedagogic but of disciplinary importance. One might even say that it is a question of epistemological and ontological orders. These types of questions are not certainly raised when we speak somewhat lazily of old and new, postcolonial, transitional, postliberal, or globalizing constitutions. These descriptors do not exhaust the experience of life under or outside the constitutions. In fact, the labels might mislead thought.

Take the qualifier 'transitional': I do not know of any form of constitution that is *not* transitional if we take the theory of contradiction and change seriously! If 'transitional' is meant a transition to a full-market society, then one is already boxed into that idea of constitutionalism where a *terminus quid* is market-liberalism, embedded or not![24]

Take the qualifier 'postcolonial'. My good American friends remind me almost constantly that theirs is the first postcolonial constitution, and so it is. Yet, it is also the world's most hegemonic constitutionalism, littered with diverse exceptionalisms.

Postcolonial takes a different turn in the Calvo Clause of the Mexican Constitution (a 150-year constitutional tradition now abrogated by NAFTA).[25] The 1923 Afghan Constitution was the first ever written constitution of South Asia, yet it began a formal history of gender and religion-based discrimination. The two great constitutions—the Indian (1950) and South African (1993)—narrate postcolonial very differently. The Indian constitution marked the beginning of the end of the Empire and was composed at a time when the Universal Declaration of Human Rights was being drafted. The South African constitution constituted the end of the system of apartheid and was the child of early contemporary globalization. A host of African and Asian Constitutions in between were gestated, and bore the effects of, the practices of Cold War. Latin American constitutions were of an older vintage in comparison, yet their itineraries were affected by the Cold War in some intense ways. The postcolonial took a different meaning, and future history, in smaller Polynesian and small island states.

This much we, COCOS folks, know well; but we do not know how to characterize the postcolonial constitutional theory, movement, development, and experience. The question is: is there a quintessence of the 'colonial'? And if so, how do we meaningfully differentiate the neo-colonial? Is the latter best understood in Kwame Nkrumah's saying that the neo-colonial consists of 'power without responsibility' and 'exploitation without redress'? How are (and here to pinch a phrase of Peter Fitzpatrick) the 'laws of the postcolonial' to be framed? In other words, how are we to grasp the varieties of postcolonial experience?

Talking about Fiji (the 2013 constitution) is a good example. How do we square Yash Ghai's (2000) comments about the second-rate mimesis of European constitutionalism in the 1980s constitutional change to the abolition of ethnicity by its replacement in 2013 (Frankenberg, 2013)? If everyone is Fijian is no one so? If ethnicity is a political construct above all (as Donald Horowitz tirelessly reminds us) is politics of identity and difference now constitutionally outlawed socially otiose in Fiji? The wider question concerns elements of originality and mimesis: are the constitutionalisms of non-Euro-American others always mimetic and never otherwise? Where may we place some astonishing judicial creativity in Global South? There are simply no constitutional precedents in the Global North for some of the adjudicative wonders performed in the Global South (some of which are noted here): a variant of COCOS is the constitutional theory of 'transplants' now.

How may we conceive of 'originality' in constitutions is a related important rendered less controversial as 'transfers'? Gunter Frankenberg (2013) has recently developed an IKEA model of constitutional transfers: may we then conceive of the world as a Western shopping mall or arcade from which countries of the non-West assemble their constitutions? Do history and context matter and if so how? Can anomie and contradiction be transplanted, transferred, or compared? Or, are these historically unique?

Very few movements *led* are movement-*based* constitutionalisms; this poses the question of the understanding of the nature and careers of social movements. The historic distance that separates the Czech from the Arab Spring movements is only partially understood by the practices of the Cold War. Yet, both the 'springs' were anti-establishment in character; these involved the joint effort of the political opposition and popular uprising. If in terms of human rights, the Czech Spring was largely about civil and political human rights; the Arab Spring is largely understood as an articulation of social, economic, and cultural rights. The 'occupy' movement bequeathed us with no constitutional thought or theory; it was not anti-politics politics but apolitical in the most profound sense.[26] What do we learn by way of constitutional theory and human rights conceptualization, from old and new social movements? What kinds of constitutionalism does a movement-led struggle bring? Can we understand it fully in terms either of human rights law or a return to human and social diversity? More concretely, how best do we understand the differing role of religious traditions in forming the constitution (differently in Tunisia and Egypt, for example)? Theocratic constitutionalism is often what the regime in power and the people's movement demand and even achieve: how do we reconcile the imperatives of the global market with that of religion as elite or mass conceived? Is constitutional secularism the best possible answer? We return again to the complexity and contradiction that form the history of insurgent reason.

3.7 Disciplinary Neoliberalism

Perhaps, one can tell the story of new constitutionalism in two words: 'disciplinary neoliberalism'[27] which also tells us a singular story about contemporary economic 'globalization'. What is the DNA of disciplinary globalization? It consists of near-total domination by the international market over state and civil society.[28] That control is described by the neo-Gramscians of today as 'hegemony' and its avatars of 'crisis' which in turn are met by the forces of 'free' market, its agents, and its forces and managers, various as they are such as cartels of capitalist states, the World Bank, the IMF and its regional affiliates, the various multinational corporations, and a variety of the community of investors. We are told that state failures will be redressed by the free market, and the free-market failures will be addressed by the state (Amartya Sen, 2000). But recent events, as well as much of history, have shown constitutionally sincere citizens are affected by both, and often at once.[29] Typically, the state–market combination produces C5 'super'-citizens who also impact the official interpretation of constitutions. Human rights become market-friendly, trade-related rights, and the 'host' state becomes a 'hostage' state.[30] How new constitutionalism may be peoples' resource against both an authoritarian state and a secular theology of free markets?

The story of neoliberalism (and Foucault preferred to tell it via the histories of bio-politics as we know) may be narrated via a combinatory of consent and coercion in disciplining the management of constitutional power by political actors in ways that endow the separation of powers doctrine some new, and menacing, meanings. It may also comprise in power over organized and systematically disorganized labour; the runway security apparatus; means of gathering information, the dissemination of news and views, and the general immunity and impunity enjoyed (by national, regional, and supranational) political and the prowess of business actors. These powers, immunities, and impunities can be cribbed and confined by constitutional courts but whether this may be done episodically or structurally in neoliberal times is an open question, although much debated. So is the question: how far may the constitutional courts impose their *demosprudence* over their *jurisprudence*?[31]

A deeper question awaits the COCOS labours. Is neoliberalism a smooth surface or a mode of production (social formation) or is it like all modes subject to contradictions? If so, where do these contradictions dwell? Do these find their abode in the distinction between *markets* as contrasted with *free markets*? Or, in the changing relations of production—capital and labour? How is one to read the crisis of finance capital in the global meltdown and its various aftermaths? How indeed are the European justices to read austerity plans and programs in their national and the EU constitutionalisms? Are the unwritten constitutions or the constitutional customs re-emerging to avenge that which gets written?

3.8 In Lieu of a Conclusion

Antonio Negri (2009) (who has done more than any thinker to de-mystify the 'constituent' power) said this at one stage of his analysis:

> The political is the horizon of the revolution, not terminated but always continued, by *the love of time*. Every human drive in search of the political consists in this: in living an *ethics of transformation* through a yearning for participation that is revealed as love for the time to constitute … *The dynamic, creative, continual, and procedural constitution of strength is the political … the expression of the multitude and the continual creation of a new world of life remains its fundamental*

> *element*. To take away this element from the political means to take away everything from it; it means to reduce it to pure administrative and diplomatic mediation, to bureaucratic and police activity—that is, exactly to that against which constituent power, as the origin of the political, continually struggles to emerge in order to emerge as strength … *[T]he routine of unchanged repetition [constitute] … the effects of dead labor, perverse inversions of constituent power, and cannot be used [to] define the political.*
>
> … Between 1968 and 1979, our generation has seen the love for time oppose any and all manifestations of being for death. The movement of the multitude has expressed its strength everywhere, with that extraordinary massive force that does not indicate its possible exceptionality but its ontological necessity.
>
> Is what is awaiting us a history of freedom? It would be foolish to say so, confronted as we are by the horrid mutilations that constituted power continues to inflict on the ontological body of human freedoms and by perpetuating negation that the unbreakable series of freedom, equality, and strength, of the multitude posed in contrast … It is our task to accelerate this strength and recognize its necessity in the love of time.
>
> *Negri, 2009. Italics added*

The italicized phrases require deep meditation, but they do tell a story. For Antonio Negri, the 'ethic' of constitutional insurgencies is also 'ethics of transformation': 'The political is the horizon of the revolution, not terminated but always continued, by the love of time'. The political signifies the power, strength, and movement of the multitudes. It also signifies 'the love of', and if we may add, *for* time.

What matters, then, perhaps is not the way the constitutions are written but the contradictions of constitutionalism and most crucially the forms of 'insurgencies' that characterize life under constitutions. Insurgencies designate constituent power—the making (and remaking) of constitutions. Constitutions as the grammars of the constituted power often tend towards the reduction of the constituent power, thus diminishing the range of the political. If we were to regard constituent power as 'the origin of the political', then the negation of the political by the constituted power invites continual 'struggles' in order to emerge as 'strength'. Negri frames these struggles in terms of the 'massive' and exceptional force of the movement of constituent power which has as its 'fundamental element' the 'continual creation of a new world of life'.

Negri writes exclusively in the registers of Euromerican thought ways; yet, his narrative would be far more enriched in the experiences of the making of postcolonial/imperial (and now post-socialist) constitutions. The transformative element here goes beyond two kinds of the Holy Trinity and the thousand gifted expositors and epigones—that forever continues to define 'politics' and the 'political'—on the one hand Hobbes, Locke, and Rousseau and on the other hand Freud, Marx and Nietzsche.

Anti-colonial and anti-empire constitutional insurgencies enact for example a radical principle of self-determination which confronted colonialism/imperialism/apartheid via a quest for the 'continual creation of a new world of life'. Insurgencies thus invented this principle and inaugurated a new Age of Human Rights, contrary to all the strange talk which still continues to insist on the sole authorship by the 'Western' world of contemporary human rights. Yet, to speak of the transformative element solely in terms of the rhetoric of 'the recognition of human rights, democracy and peaceful co-existence and development opportunities' (as does Justice Pius Langa of the South African Constitutional Court) deprives us of context-sensitive reading.[32]

Such acts of reading will forever conflate the history of these phrases with some extraordinary and mythical Euro-American claims of authorship of human rights, freedom, rule of law, and good governance because all these 'values' stood harnessed, as a matter of history, to the tasks of colonial, imperialistic, and racist subjection of the 'non-European' peoples. Yet, all this fully said, it also remains the case that postcolonial constitutional elites may also use this rhetoric to mask constitutional regression. This regression (my co-conception to distinguish this position from Negri) occurs, as Negri says, in 'the horrid mutilations … that constituted power continues to inflict on the ontological body of human freedoms and by perpetuating negation that the unbreakable series of freedom, equality, and strength, of the multitude posed in contrast'.

Far from being entirely mimetic of the European Enlightenment, the new constitutionalism also articulates differential modernity. As the Comaroff rightly observe 'modernity in the south is not adequately understood as a derivative or a *doppelganger*, a callow copy or a counterfeit, of the Euro-American "original". To the contrary: it demands to be apprehended and addressed in its own right' (Comaroff and Comaroff, 2013). Simultaneously, this differential modernity as articulated in constitutions and their interpretation encourages the belief that 'evince features of the future of Euro-America in other ways' (2013: 17).[33] What may be the future constitutional promise and peril of this different modernity?

We know enough about the perils and the promise of constitutionalism, at least in the second decade of the 21st century AD. But we do not know whether that 'ontological body' is mere work of fiction or that the 'multitude posed in contrast' remains the best hope to save us from the 'horrid mutations' of the constituent power. Or should we look to constitutionalism in the 22nd century CE to define the tasks or characteristics of the 21st century as Chibli Mallat does in 'depoliticization' of a constitutionally well-lived life? Depoliticization, he says,

> is the ultimate horizon of comparative constitutionalism, that moment in history when it matters little what politics and politicians say, because they

> have become by-and-large irrelevant to the happiness of the citizen. But this is better left to constitution-making in the 22nd century.
>
> *Mallat, 2009: 62*

Perhaps, the future history of Global South constitutionalisms is best written in terms of *depoliticization* rather than *repoliticization*.

Notes

1 See also Barreto (2014).
2 See, for example, Hart (2003), Parlevliet (2002, 2010), Samuels (2006), Babbitt and Lutz (2009).
3 Not that all constitutional texts pursue this objective but the early postcolonial constitutions born out of struggle against racism, colonization, and imperialism do.
4 See Elazar (1998a, 1998b).
5 See Katz (2006).
6 I think the phrase was invented by Professor H. W. O. Okoth-Ogando: see Okoth-Ogendo (1993).
7 See Minow, Ryan and Sarat (1995).
8 Lacan says:

> The domain of the Freudian experience is established within a very different register of relations. Desire is a relation of being to lack. This lack is the lack of being properly speaking. It isn't the lack of this or that, but lack of being whereby the being exists. This lack is beyond anything which can represent it. It is only ever represented as a reflection on a veil. The libido, but now no longer as used theoretically as a quantitative quantity, is the name of what animates the deep-seated conflict at the heart of human action ... Desire, a function central to all human experience, is the desire for nothing nameable. And at the same time this desire lies at the origin of every variety of animation. If being were only what it is, there wouldn't even be room to talk about it. Being comes into existence as an exact function of this lack. Being attains a sense of self in relation to being as a function of this lack, in the experience of desire.
>
> *Lacan, 1991: 223–224*

9 I do not here extend Arturo Escobar's searching, and enriching, analysis of the 'postcolonial': see Escobar (1992). His imagery of developing world's 'revolution' as a 'suspended caught in mid-air as they strove toward their zenith and, like fragile bubbles exploded, leaving a scrambled trace of their glorious path behind' is though accurate is perhaps too vivid as it seems to ignore the social ontology of constitutions and constitutional interpretations.
10 This dynamic principle was first sounded by Mohandas and later elaborated by philosopher Krishna Chandra Bhattacharya in October 1931 under Sir Asutosh Memorial Lectures series (Bhattacharya, 1954: 103–114). Professors K. T. Shah (who established a journal by that name) and Daya Krishna elaborated this notion further in understanding the role of public and campus intellectuals and philosophers in India.
11 See Manto (2008, 206–215). Compare the more recent work and the results from a subaltern view—and if we were to generalize in all societies of the Global South—are not much different: see Siddiqui (2013).
12 See Diamantides (2007) and Baxi (2009b).
13 See Tully (2004, 2008); see also Walker (2002).
14 See, on the importance of notions of adjudicative time as integral to constitutional time, Baxi (2014).

15 See, for a general discussion of many types of globalization, particularly conquest globalization, Baxi (2008).
16 Modern day constitutional emergencies of course relate to the 'war' on 'terror'; see, for example, Ackerman (2004). But there are other forms dealing with the failure of the leadership and administration to manage political dissent and movement: examples of constitutional dictatorship abound in the Global South constitutions when constitutions are often suspended for the convenience or the habit of the ruling elite. See, for a most recent analysis, Zitter (2014). See also Mindus (2010).
17 See, for example, Marchart (2007).
18 See also Hemming, Costea and Amiridis (2011) and Vattimo (2004).
19 This notion was richly developed by Pound (1960).
20 See, e.g., Lubin (2012); see also note 26, infra.
21 In the Derridean sense, see Derrida (1986); see also Fitzpatrick (2006).
22 On the notion of demosprudence, see Baxi (2015, 2016b).
23 See Dixit (2006).
24 See, however, Teitel (2000).
25 See Ramírez Martínez (2009); see also Schneiderman (2008, 2013). More generally, see Teubner (2015).
26 See Mitchell, Harcourt and Taussig (2013) and Mulqueen and Tataryn (2012).
27 The term is that of Stephen Gill: see Gill and Law (1989), edited and reprinted in Gill (1993); and Gill (1995). See, also, Schneiderman (2004, 2006).
28 See Supiot (2008), Leys (2008).
29 See Ortiz and Cummins (2013), Salomon (2015), and Albo and Fanelli (2014).
30 See Baxi (2013, chapters 8 and 9) and Barrow (2005).
31 See, for the distinction and its implications, Baxi (2014 and 2011). See also Hirschl (2000, 2004) and Hirschl, Tate and Ginsburg (2003).
32 See, as to this notion in the contexts of Brazil, South Africa, and India, Baxi (2013), originally presented at BISA (Brazil, India, South Africa) Conference, Courting Justice—11 April 27–29, 2009.
33 See also, Baxi (2016), specially for references concerning 'South Theory'.

References

Ackerman, Bruce (2004), "The Emergency Constitution", *The Yale Law Journal*, 113(5), 1029–1091. DOI: https://doi.org/10.2307/4135710.

Ambedkar, Bhim Rao (1949), "Speech to the Constituent Assembly on November 25, 1949", *Constituent Assembly Debates* (India), vol. XI, 972–981. Available at www.constitutionofindia.net/constitution_assembly_debates/volume/11/1949-11-25.

Babbitt, Eileen F.; Lutz, Ellen (eds.) (2009), *Human Rights and Conflict Resolution in Context: Colombia, Sierra Leone, and Northern Ireland*. Syracuse, NY: Syracuse University Press. JSTOR: www.jstor.org/stable/j.ctt1j2n95m.

Barreto, José-Manuel (2014), "Epistemologies of the South and Human Rights: Santos and the Quest for Global and Cognitive Justice", *Indiana Journal of Global Legal Studies*, 21(2), 395–422. JSTOR: www.jstor.org/stable/10.2979/indjglolegstu.21.2.395.

Barrow, Clyde W. (2005), "The Return of the State: Globalization, State Theory, and the New Imperialism", *New Political Science*, 27(2), 123–145. DOI: https://doi.org/10.1080/07393140500098235.

Baxi, Upendra (1967), "'The Little Done, The Vast Undone': Reflections on Reading Granville Austin's The Indian Constitution: Cornerstone of the Nation", *Journal of Indian Law Institute*, 9(3), 323–430. JSTOR: www.jstor.org/stable/43949944.

Baxi, Upendra (2008), "Renascent Access Notion", in Ayesha Kadwani Dias and Gita Honwana Welch (eds.), *Justice for the Poor: Perspectives on Accelerating Access*. Delhi: Oxford University Press/UNDP, 72–122.

Baxi, Upendra (2009a), "The Promise and Peril of Transcendental Jurisprudence: Justice Krishna Iyer's Combat with the Production of Rightlessness in India", in C. Raj Kumar and Chockligam (eds.), *Human Rights, Justice, and Empowerment*. Delhi: Oxford University Press, 3–25.

Baxi, Upendra (2009b), "Judging Emmanuel Levinas? Some Reflections on Reading *Levinas, Law, Politics*", *The Modern Law Review*, 72(1), 116–129. JSTOR: www.jstor.org/stable/20533227.

Baxi, Upendra (2013), "Preliminary Notes on Transformative Constitutionalism", in Oscar Vilhena, Upendra Baxi and Francois Viljon (eds.), *Transformative Constitutionalism*. Pretoria: Pretoria University Press, 19–47.

Baxi, Upendra (2014), "Preface", in Mayur Suresh and Siddharth Narrain (eds.), *The Shifting Scales of Justice: The Indian Supreme Court in Neoliberal India*. Delhi: Orient Blackswan.

Baxi, Upendra (2015), "Demosprudence versus Jurisprudence: The Indian Judicial Experience in the Context of Comparative Constitutional Studies", *Macquarie Law Journal*, 14, 3–23. Available at www5.austlii.edu.au/au/journals/MqLawJl/2014/13.htm.

Baxi, Upendra (2016a), "Some Newly Emergent Geographies of Injustice: Boundaries and Borders in International Law", *Indiana Journal of Global Studies*, 23(1), 15–37. JSTOR: www.jstor.org/stable/10.2979/indjglolegstu.23.1.15.

Baxi, Upendra (2016b), "Demosprudence and Socially Responsible/Response-able Criticism: The NJAC Decision and Beyond", *NUJS Law Review*, 9(3–4), 153–172. Available at http://14.139.214.185/handle/123456789/273.

Bhattacharya, Krishna Chandra (1954 [1931]), "Swaraj in Ideas", *Visvabharati Quarterly*, 20, 103–114.

Canguilhem, George (1991), *The Normal and the Pathological*. New York: Zone Books.

Comaroff, Jean; Comaroff, John L. (2013), "Writing Theory from the South: The Global Order from an African Perspective", *The World Financial Review*, Sept.–Oct. 2013: 17–20. Available at https://worldfinancialreview.com/writing-theory-south-global-order-african-perspective.

Derrida, Jacques (1986), "Declarations of Independence", *New Political Science*, 7(1), 7–15. DOI: https://doi.org/10.1080/07393148608429608.

Diamantides, Marinos (2007), "Levinas and Critical Legal Thought: Imbroglio, Opera Buffa, Divine Comedy?", in Marino Diamantides (ed.), *Levinas, Law, and Politics*. Abingdon: Routledge-Cavendish. DOI: https://doi.org/10.4324/9780203945087.

Dixit, Avinash (2006), "Predatory and Failed States: An Agency Perspective", *CEPS Working Paper* No 131. Available at https://gceps.princeton.edu/wp-content/uploads/2017/01/131dixit.pdf.

Elazar, Daniel Judah (1998a), *Constituting Globalization: The Postmodern Revival of Confederal Arrangements*. New York: Rowman and Littlefield.

Elazar, Daniel Judah (1998b), *Covenant and Civil Society: The Constitutional Matrix of Modern Democracy*. New York: Transactional Press.

Escobar, Arturo (1992), "Imagining a Post-Development Era? Critical Thought, Development and Social Movements", *Social Text*, 31/32, 20–56. JSTOR: www.jstor.org/stable/466217.

Fitzpatrick, Peter (2006), "'The New Constitutionalism': The Global, the Post-Colonial and the Constitution of Nations", *Law, Democracy & Development*, 10(2), 1–20. Available at www.ajol.info/index.php/ldd/article/view/138332.

Frankenberg, Günter (ed.) (2013), *Order from Transfer: Comparative Constitutional Design and Legal Culture*. Cheltenham: Edward Elgar.

Ghai, Yash (2000), "Universalism and Relativism: Human Rights as Framework for Negotiating Interethnic Claims", *Cardozo Law Review*, 21, 1095–1102. Available at https://heinonline.org/HOL/LandingPage?handle=hein.journals/cdozo21&div=45&id=&page=.

Gill, Stephen (1995), "Globalization, Market Civilisation, and Disciplinary Neoliberalism", *Millennium: Journal of International Studies*, 24(3), 399–423. DOI: https://doi.org/10.1177/03058298950240030801.

Gill, Stephen; Law, David (1989), "Global Hegemony and the Structural Power of Capital", *International Studies Quarterly*, 33(4), 475–499. DOI: https://doi.org/10.2307/2600523.

Gill, Stephen; Law, David (1993), "Global Hegemony and the Structural Power of Capital", in S. Gill (ed.), *Gramsci, Historical Materialism and International Relations*, Cambridge: Cambridge University Press. 93–124. DOI: https://doi.org/10.1017/CBO9780511558993.005.

Greg Albo, Greg; Fanelli, Carlo (2014), *Austerity Against Democracy: An Authoritarian Phase of Neoliberalism?* Toronto: The Centre for Social Justice. Available at www.socialjustice.org/publication/austerity-against-democracy.

Hart, Vivien (2003), "Democratic Constitution Making", *United States Institute of Peace Special Report 107*. Washington, DC: USIP. Available at www.usip.org/publications/2003/07/democratic-constitution-making.

Heidegger, Martin (1982), *Nietzsche Volume IV: Nihilism*. New York: Harper & Row. Translated by Frank A. Capuzzi.

Hemming, Laurence Paul; Costea, Bogdan; Amiridis, Kostas (eds.) (2011), *The Movement of Nihilism: Heidegger's Thinking After Nietzsche*. London: Continuum.

Hirschl, Ran (2000), "The Political Origins of Judicial Empowerment through Constitutionalization: Lessons from Four Constitutional Revolutions", *Law & Social Inquiry*, 25(1), 91–149. DOI: https://doi.org/10.1111/j.1747-4469.2000.tb00152.x.

Hirschl, Ran (2004), *Towards Juristocracy—the Origins and Consequences of the New Constitutionalism*. Cambridge, MA: Harvard University Press.

Hirschl, Ran; Tate, Neal; Ginsburg (2003), *Tom Judicial Review in New Democracies—Constitutional Courts in Asian Cases*. Cambridge: Cambridge University Press.

Katz, Stanley Nider (2006), "Democratic Constitutionalism after Military Occupation: Reflections on the United States' Experience in Japan, Germany, Afghanistan and Iraq", *Common Knowledge*, 12(2), 181–196. DOI: https://doi.org/10.1215/0961754X-2005-001.

Lacan, Jacques (1991), *The Seminar of Jacques Lacan. Book II. The Ego in Freud's Theory and in the Technique of Psychoanalysis, 1954–1955*. New York: W. W. Norton.

Leys, Colin (2008), *Total Capitalism: Market Politics, Market State*. London: Merlin Press.

Lubin, Judy (2012), "The 'Occupy Movement': Emerging Protest Forms and Contested Urban Spaces", *Berkeley Planning Journal*, 25(1), 184–197. DOI: https://doi.org/10.5070/BP325111760.

Mallat, Chibli (2009), "Constitutions for the 21st Century: Emerging Patterns—the EU, Iraq, Afghanistan ...", *Center for International & Comparative Law Occasional Papers*, 1, 41–62. Available at https://scholarship.law.duke.edu/faculty_scholarship/1940.

Manto, Sahib Singh (2008), "*The New Constitution" in Bitter Fruit*. Delhi: Penguin Books. Translated by Khalid Hasan.

Marchart, Oliver (2007), *Post-Foundational Political Thought: Political Difference in Nancy, Lefort, Badiou and Laclau*. Edinburgh: Edinburgh University Press.

Mindus, Patricia (2010), "Sorting out Modern Constitutional Emergencies: A Taxonomic Framework", *Redescriptions: Political Thought, Conceptual History and Feminist Theory*, 14(1), 107–132. DOI: https://doi.org/10.7227/R.14.1.7.

Minow, Martha; Ryan, Michel; Sarat, Austin (eds.) (1995), *Narrative, Violence and the Law: The Essays of Robert Cover*. Ann Arbor, MI: The University of Michigan Press.

Mitchell, W. J. T.; Harcourt, Bernard E.; Taussig, Michael (2013), *Occupy: Three Enquires in Disobedience*. Chicago: University of Chicago Press. DOI: https://doi.org/10.7208/chicago/9780226042886.001.0001.

Mulqueen, Tara; Tataryn, Anastasia (2012), "Don't Occupy This Movement: Thinking Law in Social Movements", *Law and Critique*, 23, 283–298. DOI: https://doi.org/10.1007/s10978-012-9103-z.

Negri, Antonio (2009), *Insurgencies: Constituent Power and the Modern State*. Minneapolis, MN: University of Minnesota Press. Translated by Maurzia Boscagli.

Okoth-Ogendo, H. W. O. (1993), "Constitutions without Constitutionalism: Reflections on an African Political Paradox", in Douglas Greenberg, Stanley N. Katz, Melanie Beth Oliviero and Steven C. Wheatley (eds.), *Constitutionalism and Democracy: Transitions in the Contemporary World*. New York: Oxford University Press, 65–82.

Ortiz, Isabel; Cummins, Matthew (2013), "The Age of Austerity: A Review of Public Expenditures and Adjustment Measures in 181 Countries", *Initiative for Policy Dialogue and the South Centre Working Paper*. DOI: https://doi.org/10.2139/ssrn.2260771.

Parlevliet, Michelle (2002), "Bridging the Divide—Exploring the Relationship between Human Rights and Conflict Management", *Track Two*, 11(1), 8–43. Available at https://hdl.handle.net/10520/EJC111535.

Parlevliet, Michelle (2010), "Rethinking Conflict Transformation from a Human Rights Perspective", in Véronique Dudouet and Beatrix Schmelzle (eds.), *Human Rights and Conflict Transformation: The Challenges of Just Peace*. Berlin: Berghof Conflict Research, 15–46. Available at https://berghof-foundation.org/library/human-rights-and-conflict-transformation-the-challenges-of-just-peace.

Pound, Roscoe (1960), *Law Finding Through Experience and Reason: Three Lectures*. Athens, GA: University of Georgia Press.

Prasad, Vijay (2008), *The Darker Nations: A People's History of the Third World*. New York: The New Press [reprint].

Prasad, Vijay (2014), *The Poorer Nations: A Possible History of the Global South*. London: Verso.

Rai, Shirin; Reinelt, Janelle (eds.) (2015), *The Grammar of Politics and Performance*. London: Routledge.

Ramírez Martínez, Álvaro (2009), "The Mexican Constitution and its Safeguards against Foreign Investments", *Cornell Law School Inter-University Graduate Student Conference Papers 39*. Available at https://scholarship.law.cornell.edu/lps_clacp/39.

Rawls, John (1993), *Political Liberalism*. New York: Columbia University Press.

Salomon, Margot E. (2015), "Of Austerity, Human Rights and International Institutions", *LSE Law, Society and Economy Working Papers*, 2, 2–29. DOI: https://doi.org/10.2139/ssrn.2551428.

Samuels, Kirsti (2006), "Post-Conflict Peace-Building and Constitution-Making", *Chicago Journal of International Law*, 6(2), 663–683. Available at https://chicagounbound.uchicago.edu/cjil/vol6/iss2/10/.

Santos, Boaventura de Sousa (2007), "Beyond Abyssal Thinking: From Global Lines to Ecologies of Knowledges", *Review (Fernand Braudel Center)*, 30(1), 45–89. JSTOR: www.jstor.org/stable/40241677.

Santos, Boaventura de Sousa (2014), *Epistemologies of the South: Justice Against Epistemicide*. London: Routledge. DOI: https://doi.org/10.4324/9781315634876.

Santos, Boaventura de Sousa (2015), *If God Were a Human Rights Activist*. Redwood City, CA: Stanford University Press. DOI: https://doi.org/10.1515/9780804795036.

Schneiderman, David (2004) "Habermas, Market-Friendly Human Rights, and the Revisibility of Economic Globalization", *Citizenship Studies*, 8(4), 419–436. DOI: https://doi.org/10.1080/1362102052000316007.

Schneiderman, David (2006), "Investment Rules and the New Constitutionalism", *Law & Social Inquiry*, 25, 757–787. JSTOR: www.jstor.org/stable/829135.

Schneiderman, David (2008), *Constitutionalizing Economic Globalization: Investment Rules and Democracy's Promise*. Cambridge: Cambridge University Press.

Schneiderman, David (2013), *Resisting Economic Globalization: Critical Theory and International Investment Law*. Basingstoke: Palgrave Macmillan. DOI: https://doi.org/10.1057/9781137004062.

Sen, Amartya K. (1977), "Rational Fools: A Critique of the Behavioural Foundations of Economic Theory", *Philosophy & Public Affairs*, 6(4), 317–344. JSTOR: www.jstor.org/stable/2264946.

Sen, Amartya (2000), *Development as Freedom*. New York: Anchor.

Siddiqui, Osama (2013), *Pakistan's Experience with Formal Law: An Alien Justice*. Cambridge: Cambridge University Press. DOI: https://doi.org/10.1017/CBO9781139814508.

Supiot, Alain (2008), *The Spirit of Philadelphia: Social Justice vs the Total Market*. London: Verso. Translated by Saskia Brown.

Teitel, Ruti G. (2000), *Transitional Justice*. New York: Oxford University Press.

Teubner, Gunther (2015), "Transnational Economic Constitutionalism in the Varieties of Capitalism", *The Italian Law Journal*, 1(2), 219–248. Available at www.theitalianlawjournal.it.

Therborn, Göran (2013), *The Killing Fields of Inequality*. Cambridge: Polity Press.

Tully, James (2004), *Strange Multiplicity: Constitutionalism in an Age of Diversity*. Cambridge: Cambridge University Press [5th reprint].

Tully, James (2008), *Public Philosophy in a New Key*. Cambridge: Cambridge University Press. DOI: https://doi.org/10.1017/CBO9780511790744.

Vattimo, Gianni (2004), *Nihilism & Emancipation: Ethics, Politics, & Law*. New York: Columbia University Press. Translated by William McCuaig.

Walker, Neil (2002), "The Idea of Constitutional Pluralism", *The Modern Law Review*, 65(3), 317–359. JSTOR: www.jstor.org/stable/1097577.

Young, Robert (2001), *Postcolonialism: An Introduction*. London: Blackwell.

Zitter, Andrej (2014), "Arab Spring—State of Emergency and Constitutional Reform", *Air and Space Power Journal*, 5(2), 48–65. Available at http://hdl.handle.net/11370/e7f71a4a-047e-4996-9fdb-2d889fdfdb83.

4

INDIGENOUS WOMEN

Towards a New Transformative Constitutionalism?*[1]

Rosalva Aída Hernández Castillo

4.1 Introduction

The various constitutional reforms undertaken in the continent in the last three decades have in common a recognition of the cultural diversity of the Latin American nations and, in most cases, have led to the recognition of indigenous law and/or local spaces for enacting justice. In some cases, these reforms have involved a strengthening of political autonomy, embodied in the recognition of indigenous jurisdictions (Sánchez Botero, 1998), while others reveal processes for the reconstitution or reinvention of community justice (Sierra *et al.*, 2013; Sieder, 2017). There are also experiences which reveal a weakening of the autonomy that existed prior to the constitutional reforms, in the form of new indigenous tribunals created by the state which overlap with the local judicial institutions.[2]

This chapter aims to contribute to the debates presented in this book on the so-called *transformative constitutionalism* via different experiences of legal pluralism, which include processes for reconstituting the law by including the feelings and thinking of indigenous women. I am inclined to support those who argue that indigenous justices have their own constitutions, which are the product of political pacts that establish their own institutions, and legal and political mechanisms intended to defend those pacts. These perspectives[3] engage with the concept of *transformative constitutionalism*, not only in referring to experiences in countries such as Bolivia and Ecuador, where claims emerging from indigenous struggles have been included in the national constitutions, thus creating a rupture with many of their Eurocentric principles,[4] but also with reference to the legal regulations, institutions and practices that have been developed in some indigenous regions elsewhere on the continent. In analysing two specific experiences of indigenous community justice in Mexico, I seek to demonstrate that many of these indigenous

DOI: 10.4324/9781003391920-6

constitutions are also the product of internal struggles for the reconceptualization of culture and rights from the perspective of women.

Legal pluralism, recognized in recent decades by the Latin American constitutions, has a long history that is closely linked to colonial and neocolonial processes in the continent. The coexistence of parallel spaces for government and indigenous justice has been a reality since colonial times, when the Indian Laws recognized indigenous jurisdictions as subordinate to the Spanish Crown.[5] These so-called 'indigenous justices' have undergone several processes of reconstitution through ongoing dialogue with the justices of the postcolonial nation states. More than simply ancestral justices, they are the historical end results of the principles and epistemologies of indigenous peoples, Catholic moral and religious principles resulting from five hundred years of occupation, and legal proceedings based on state law. Although the liberal reforms of the nineteenth century imposed legal monism in most Latin American countries, these parallel systems continued to function *de facto* and, in many contexts, were tolerated due to the inability of the state to respond to the needs of justice in the indigenous regions.

The discourses and practices surrounding monocultural and exclusionary liberal citizenship began to be questioned directly by a growing continental indigenous movement that denounced the validity of internal colonialism and laid claim not only to cultural recognition but also their autonomous and territorial rights. The commemoration, in 1992, of five hundred years of the erroneously named 'Meeting of Two Worlds' created a rallying point for indigenous representatives from all over the continent, whose voices were united in denouncing the racism and exclusion which continued to characterize attempts to integrate indigenous peoples into Latin American national projects.

In the 1980s, influenced by this cultural climate and partly in response to the demands of indigenous organizations, a legislative reform process was launched in various Latin American countries with the aim of achieving recognition for the multicultural character of the states, replacing the discourse on equality with a new rhetoric focused on cultural diversity and the need to develop multicultural public policies. These reforms vary widely from one country to another but most include recognition of the multicultural nature of the nation, the collective rights of indigenous peoples and recognition of their regulatory systems and forms of self-government, as well as the right to use and preserve their own indigenous languages.[6] Based on these reforms, government censuses have acknowledged the existence of 40 million men and women who identify themselves as indigenous, approximately 10% of the inhabitants of Latin America.[7]

In this new political context, the defenders of universal citizenship have made their voices heard in rejecting or limiting the scope of multicultural reforms aiming to isolate the cultural dimension from the territorial or political dimension. Latin American neoliberal states have deployed a strategy of separating a politics of recognition from a politics of redistribution in order to reduce the radical nature of indigenous demands. Many academics committed to the struggles of indigenous peoples have condemned the new obstacles which these reforms present for indigenous autonomy (Hernández *et al.*, 2004).

However, voices have also been questioning the limitations of the struggles for indigenous rights from other political positions, pointing out the constraints imposed by indigenous identity as a space for political mobilization or denouncing the way it has been used by neoliberal governments as a new strategy for control and regulation.

These perspectives consider multicultural constitutionalism to be a new form of neoliberal governance that has resulted in the hegemony of discourses on rights as a way of 'narrating or coding' indigenous identities, which often serve as the basis for constructing essentialist discourses for indigenous cultures, displacing other discourses on social justice such as those referring to internal colonialism or economic exploitation.[8]

These perspectives suggest that, by placing responsibilities held by the state in the hands of indigenous peoples and communities, multicultural reforms respond to the needs of the neoliberal agenda for decentralizing and promoting a more participatory civil society, encouraging the construction of what has been defined as neoliberal regimes of citizenship (Yashar, 2005). The social regulation required by the neoliberal model includes the construction of a pluralist state in which everyone participates, and which coincides with the political agenda of indigenous peoples who demand greater autonomy and more extensive spaces for participation. In the context of these perspectives, Charles Hale (2002, 2005) popularized the concept of *neoliberal multiculturalism* to refer to the uses that neoliberal states have made of multicultural recognition policies as a strategy for silencing or displacing more radical demands from the indigenous movement.

Even in states that have tried to move beyond multicultural reforms by recognizing the existence of plurinational states, as was the case with both Ecuador and Bolivia, giving rise to the term *transformative constitutionalism*, considerable setbacks have been observed. The inclusion of indigenous epistemologies as a way of recognizing the rights of nature was not sufficient to guarantee rights to territory and prior consultation in the case of government projects which, in the name of 'national interests', are depriving the indigenous peoples of resources, polluting their lands and rivers and destroying their forests.

Paradoxically, the new Ecuadorean Constitution, adopted in 2008, was the first Latin American Constitution to incorporate terms from indigenous epistemologies in its text by including the *principios del buen viver* and *Sumak Kawsay* – principles for a harmonious way of living – in Articles 275 to 278 (Title VI: Development Structure). Article 275 specifies that: '*buen vivir* shall imply that individuals, communities, peoples and nationalities effectively exercise their rights and fulfill their responsibilities within the framework of interculturality, respect for their diversity and harmonious coexistence with nature' (Ecuador, 2008: 49). At the same time, this Constitution also pioneered recognition of the rights of nature, thus breaking with the anthropocentrism of the liberal philosophical and juridical tradition which considers that these rights only pertain to individual or legal corporate entities entitled to manage and exploit nature.[9]

These legislative reforms, largely celebrated by academics and activists, became a hollow exercise from the moment President Rafael Correa broke one of his main campaign promises in sanctioning the exploration of the Ishpingo, Tambococha and Tiputini (ITT) oil fields located in the Yasuní National Park, in the middle of the Ecuadorean Amazon. The Yasuní Biosphere Reserve, comprising the Yasuní National Park and the Huaorani Reserve, is considered one of the most biodiverse areas on the planet. It is also home to the Huaorani, Tagaeri and Taromenane indigenous peoples, who had remained in relative isolation until the beginning of the twentieth century. The Yasuní-ITT environmental project was launched by Ecuador in 2006 with the intention of raising 3.6 billion dollars via the international community over a thirteen-year period as compensation for the non-exploitation of around 846 million barrels of oil. Three years after a trust fund had been created through the United Nations to receive contributions, the initiative resulted in just 13.3 million dollars in concrete deposits, while another 116 million remained as pledges. Although Decree 1572 of February 2009 established an indefinite period for this initiative, in August 2013 the Ecuadoran president requested that the National Assembly should open the Yasuní region to oil exploration, arguing that it had become a matter of 'national interest'.

This decision was strongly rejected by the Ecuadoran indigenous organizations, who mobilized in protest, demanding their right to prior consultation. Indigenous organizations and ecologists argue that the creation of a petroleum hub in Yasuní will have a heavy environmental impact, resulting in contamination, deforestation and changes to the ecological balance in a unique ecosystem. It would also mean opening the region up to colonization, with all that this implies, including the decimation of forests and the arrival of drug trafficking. *Sumak kawsay* has simply become government rhetoric when confronted by the interests of big business and the developmentalism of President Rafael Correa.

Nowadays, something similar is happening with the principles of 'harmonious life' and 'land without evil' promoted by *Suma Qamaña* in Bolivia. Following the footsteps of Ecuador, the Bolivian *Magna Carta*, which was reformed in 2009, incorporated concepts from Aymara epistemologies in the constitutional text, establishing in Article 8(1) that:

> The state assumes and promotes as ethical-moral principles of a plural society: *Ama qhilla, ama llulla, ama suwa* (not being weak, not being a liar, not being a thief), *suma qamaña* (living well), *ñandereko* (living harmoniously), *teko kavi* (a good life), *ivi maraei* (a land without evil) and *qhapaj ñan* (a noble path or life).
>
> *Bolivia, 2009*

Moreover, the preamble to the Constitution states that 'we have left the colonial, republican and neoliberal State in the past. We take on the historic challenge of collectively constructing a Unified Social State of Plurinational Community Law' (Bolivia, 2009). In this case, it is the construction of a road project linking Bolivia to Brazil, destroying an important part of the Amazonian forest in the process and adversely affecting the habitat of the indigenous peoples of the region, which has resulted in President Evo Morales and his government losing sight of the principles of *Suma Qamaña*. This road development project affects the *Territorio Indígena del Parque Nacional Isiboro Sécure* (Tipnis), which has an area of 1.2 million hectares. It is located between the departments of Beni and Cochabamba in the provinces of Mojos and Marbán (Beni) and Chapare (Cochabamba). The Amazonian indigenous populations who mobilized against the project have been criminalized and their leaders arrested, involving the use of strategies very similar to those deployed by the government of Gonzalez Sanchez de Lozada (2002–2003) against the indigenous peoples of the *Movimiento Al Socialismo*. Paradoxically, many of the indigenous peoples who supported changes to the Plurinational Constitution and participated in the historic March for Territory and Dignity that began on 15 August 1990 had to confront the government of Evo Morales and the incumbent detention orders placed on them.

The reason I have chosen to focus on the cases of Ecuador and Bolivia is not because the expropriation and violence directed against indigenous peoples in the name of a 'developmentalist utopia' is more serious than in the rest of Latin America, but the fact that expectations that it would be different in these countries were greater. The idea that these were to be 'post-neoliberal regimes' with transformative constitutions, in which the 'well-being' of society took priority over the interests of big business, together with the use of indigenous rhetoric calling for '*Buen Vivir*' in a broader sense to include the rights of nature, served to arouse great expectations, not only among the indigenous Ecuadorans and Bolivians but all the indigenous peoples of the continent who saw the plurinational constitutional reforms as an example.

The issue of indigenous justice and its legal structure has occupied a central place in this political context, both in terms of the political demands of indigenous movements and the analytical concerns of Latin American legal anthropology. Was recognition of plurinational constitutionalism part of the neoliberal administrative reforms aimed at reducing the costs of the judiciary? Was it only about complementary justice, with no recognition for its own jurisdiction or political autonomy? Was it about prioritizing recognition of the essentialist perspectives of indigenous law that had become fossilized, thus removing its history? Did this represent a step backward for the rights of indigenous women?

For the past ten years, I have been involved in three collective research projects[10] that have proposed to address some of these issues, in permanent dialogue with indigenous organizations which have appropriated the discourse on rights as part of their political struggles and claim indigenous justice (*justicia propia*) as part of their autonomic rights. These collective projects have set out to explore the contradictions that emerge within the new forms of neoliberal governance, through discourses and legal reforms and the counter-hegemonic uses of the law by indigenous men and women in their daily practices.[11]

These experiences have shown that state hegemony is always an unfinished process and hence the agenda of neoliberal multiculturalism is not entirely successful, while the need to strengthen civil society and promote decentralization has, in turn, opened up new opportunities for indigenous peoples wishing to expand their spaces for autonomy and self-determination.

The analysis of these experiences, and similar ones in other geographical and cultural contexts, has left me with reservations regarding analytical perspectives that emphasize the productive capacity of state discourses on *indigeneity* and rights, while failing to recognize the ability of social actors to reject or resist these constructs.

The impact of multicultural reforms on spaces for justice is as diverse as the peoples inhabiting the continent: their 'regulatory' or 'emancipatory' character depends on multiple factors. The objective of this chapter is not to present a thorough analysis of the impact of these reforms, but rather to address certain concrete experiences in which indigenous women have participated in processes for the 'reconstitution' of their own law, drawing on their critical perspectives on the 'traditions and customs' which exclude them to reformulate community regulations or rethink local legal practices. This could be considered being in the presence of a reformulation of an indigenous *transformative constitutionalism* in which women are able to include their voices in the new political pacts that govern indigenous communities. This is the case with the Women's Revolutionary Laws under the Good Governance Boards in the Zapatista regions of Chiapas, as well as the Communitarian Statute of Tlahuitoltepec, supported by the active participation of Ayuujk women.

In this chapter, I propose to address the experiences of indigenous women in the Mexican states of Chiapas and Oaxaca, specifically their use of spaces for community justice as spaces for the cultural production of new indigenous and gender identities. Beyond the limitations that multicultural reforms have presented, this has also entailed negotiating how concepts of 'culture' and 'justice' are understood within the indigenous communities themselves. When practices previously viewed as 'life itself' are labelled 'culture' and ways of resolving community conflicts are called 'indigenous law' (*derecho propio*) and their internal regulations are 'indigenous constitutions', new spaces for enunciation are created which are also being occupied by the counter-hegemonic discourses of indigenous women. These renewed perspectives on culture are part of the new communitarian regulations, thus formulating a new *transformative constitutionalism* that includes the specific needs of indigenous women.

4.2 Naming Culture and Justice from Women's Perspectives

In several regions of Latin America, indigenous women are appropriating the global discourses surrounding women's rights, while at the same time defending the right of their peoples to maintain their own spaces for community justice and, in a broader sense, their rights to political and territorial autonomy.[12]

These are different experiences in which indigenous women have appropriated new multicultural spaces in order to debate or rethink the way in which culture and tradition are understood. The new context for recognizing the 'multicultural character of the nation' has led to an increasing tendency among indigenous peoples, especially the organic intellectuals of their movements, to reflect on their practices and systematize, theorize and philosophize on these issues.[13]

In the process of 'giving a name' to the culture, negotiations are taking place between the genders with a view to defining it. These processes of 'political creativity' appear to confront feminist criticisms of the politics of cultural recognition.

A vast amount of literature based on feminist theory emphasizes that both official and ethnic nationalisms tend to use women's bodies as raw materials in the construction of their political projects.[14] This perspective has highlighted the fact that the emphasis on the politics of recognition has led to a strengthening of cultural essentialisms that often serve patriarchal interests within the collective identities. Ahistorical representations of cultures as homogenous entities with shared values and customs, regardless of power relations, give rise to cultural fundamentalisms that view any attempt by women to transform practices affecting their lives as a threat to the collective identity of the group. Faced with these essentialist positions, there is a need to historicize cultural practices in order to demonstrate that many of the 'traditional' practices that affect and violate women's lives, often originating in colonial contexts, have changed over time, and their modification or disappearance does not affect the continuity of the group identity.

Over time I have discovered that arguments surrounding the dangers of 'cultural integrity' arise when transformations of certain traditions affect the interests of the sectors in power. This has led me to rethink indigenous cultures from analytical perspectives that include the dialogues of power that constitute them. Deconstructing the way in which certain traits (rather than others) are selected as representative of a culture or integral to an identity can reveal the power networks hidden behind the representation of difference. The historical perspective on indigenous identities allows us to appreciate how certain cultural traits change with the passage of time without this being viewed as endangering cultural integrity (e.g., the incorporation of automobiles, agricultural technology, the media, etc.), while other changes are selectively seen as constituting a cultural loss.

In the Latin American context, some academic advocates of indigenous rights have contributed towards producing idealized representations of these peoples which offer no scope for voices and questions emanating from women within the groups themselves. These representations have been used by power groups within the collectives to legitimize their privileges. At the other extreme, there is the perspective of those who, due to their colonial origins, dismiss all indigenous institutions and practices, also stereotyping their cultures by means of a 'selective labelling' process.

This is a debate in which I have become politically involved since, for several decades, I have positioned myself among the voices critical of the essentialism of the continental indigenous movement, which has refused to address the issue of gender exclusions and domestic violence within indigenous communities.

My dual identity as an academic and activist in a feminist organization that actively campaigns against sexual and domestic violence through a support centre for women and minors in San Cristóbal de las Casas, Chiapas – where a high percentage of those attending were indigenous women – has forced me to confront both the idealizing discourses of indigenous culture derived from an important sector of Latin American anthropology and the ethnocentrism of a key sector of liberal feminism.[15] In a polarized context in which women's rights have been presented in opposition to the collective rights of peoples, it has been difficult to lay claim to more nuanced perspectives on indigenous cultures that are able to recognize the power dialogues that constitute them, while at the same time supporting the indigenous peoples' right to their own culture and self-determination.

In the Mexican context, the polarization of feminist and Indianist positions has deepened in the last two decades as a result of the need, affirmed by the Zapatista movement, for constitutional reform that recognizes the autonomous rights of indigenous peoples.[16] In this context, a key sector of Mexican liberal feminism has allied itself with the liberal anti-autonomy sectors as a means of denouncing the danger that recognition of the collective rights of their peoples would represent for indigenous women. Suddenly, a number of academics who had failed to write one line in favour of indigenous women began to 'worry' about their rights and even cite out-of-context works by certain feminist scholars who had written about violence in indigenous regions. This altered the context of the academic exchanges in which I participated, imposing the need to contextualize reflections on domestic violence beyond cultural analysis to include the analysis of state violence and highlight the importance of the structural context in which this violence presents itself.

At this political crossroads, it has been the organized indigenous women themselves who have provided us with clues on how to rethink indigenous demands from a non-essentialist perspective. Their theorizations of culture, tradition and gender equality are reflected in political documents, memories of meetings, public speeches and so on. Indigenous women have never asked for this liberal intellectual or state 'protection' which sets out to limit the autonomy of their peoples. On the contrary, they claim the right to self-determination and to their own culture, while fighting within the indigenous movement to redefine the terms in which tradition and custom are understood, and to actively participate in the construction of autonomous projects.

4.3 Women Facing up to Indigenous Transformative Constitutionalism

In Mexico, this rethinking of 'traditions and customs' by women takes place in the space dedicated to communitarian regulations governing indigenous justice. In various parts of the country, indigenous women's organizational processes have led them to focus on and, in some cases, participate directly in areas of community justice. These are incipient experiences whose analysis cannot be applied generally to all the indigenous regions of Mexico, although their symbolic importance is reflected in the new discourses and imaginaries surrounding indigenous law and what has been termed new indigenous *transformative constitutionalism* from women's perspectives.

The two experiences specifically addressed in this section are the Zapatista spaces for justice within the Good Governance Boards in Chiapas, in the Tseltal, Tsotsil and Tojolabal territories, and the case of the Communitarian Statute of Tlahuitoltepec, Oaxaca, in the Ayuujk (Mixe) area. These are two very different experiences in terms of community justice: the first case involves a fully autonomous space not recognized by the state, in which the Zapatista grassroot structures are exercising their own justice without intervention from state institutions; the second case concerns a space for integrating indigenous justice that has been recognized by the constitutional reforms which have taken place in Oaxaca over the last decade.

Since the public appearance of the *Ejército Zapatista de Liberación Nacional*, on 1 January 1994, the numerical and political significance of indigenous women within this political-military organization has attracted attention. Several have played a leading role in taking control of municipal presidencies. However, it was the inclusion of gender claims within its platform for struggle, through the so-called Women's Revolutionary Law, that differentiated Zapatism from other guerrilla movements in Latin America. Although not all indigenous women are familiar with the details of this law, its existence has become a symbol of the possibilities for a fairer life for women.[17]

The Women's Revolutionary Law has been fundamental to reconstructing Zapatista justice. The new structures and normativities of Zapatista justice have been consolidated into an autonomous justice system from 1996 onwards, when the Mexican government ignored the agreements which its own representatives had reached with the Zapatista leadership. The so-called 'San Andrés Accords' laid the foundations for indigenous autonomy and established the foundations for the creation of *de facto* autonomous regions which are not legally recognized by the Mexican state but have been tolerated, ignored or repressed by various governments over the last two decades. In 2001, the Congress of the Union approved a new constitutional reform known as the 'Law on Indigenous Rights and Culture' (Mexico, 1998) which, in a very diluted form, restored some aspects of the San Andrés agreements but in essence violated the agreement on rights to territorial autonomy and management of natural resources established between the Zapatista Army and the federal government on 16 February 1996.[18]

After an intense political struggle for the recognition of indigenous rights, involving marches, forums and national meetings, coinciding with the disenchantment associated with a limited indigenous law that was considered a betrayal on the part of the Mexican political class, the Zapatistas opted for building their own autonomous project on the margins of the state, basing their law on the San Andrés Accords. Zapatista autonomous regions are political-administrative divisions located in the geographical territory under the influence of the rebel army, where forms of self-government and various social and production programs have been introduced, including education, health and organic farming. These autonomous regions include several communities established on land recovered by the Zapatistas since 1994 by expropriating large livestock estates that constituted the basis of a latifundium system maintained through the exploitation of the indigenous workforce.

Zapatista autonomy has also implied the rejection of the presence of governmental institutions and official education, health and social development programs. Autonomous education, health, justice and sustainable development systems have been created, operating through committees in which men and women from the Zapatista communities participate through a system of rotating positions.[19] As an integral part of these committees, the Commission for Honor and Justice was created, which has responsibility for the administration of justice at the municipal level.

From 2003 onwards, Zapatista autonomy was restructured with the aim of separating the military authorities from the civil authorities and improving coordination between the different regions by creating five *Caracoles*. These are broader administrative units covering the autonomous municipalities, in which the highest authority is the Good Governance Boards. In her analysis of the scope of Zapatista justice, Mariana Mora provides an account of how the Zapatistas managed to challenge state power, administering justice not only for the Zapatista community-based support system but also for the non-Zapatista population who use it.[20]

This new autonomous system, applied through the Commission for Honor and Justice, would supplement the spaces for community justice that continued to function in the Zapatista communities, in which the elders play a very important role as counsellors in intra-community conflicts, although the assembly remains the higher authority. If problems cannot be resolved at the community level, they are transferred to the Commission for Honor and Justice in the *Caracoles*, composed of men and women from the Zapatista grassroots support base.

The fact that women participate in the Commission for Honor and Justice already implies a change in relation to the previous dynamics of community justice. This has represented a challenge for many women who are not accustomed to speaking in public, but it has been assumed as part of the new communitarian commitments. Emiliana, a member of the Commission for Honor and Justice in *Caracole* IV, *Whirlwind of our Words*, describes the challenges to learning that are involved in participating in these new spaces for government and also gives an account of a new political consciousness which rejects racism and exclusion:

> At first, I did not want to take this position. I didn't think I could do it, but little by little they managed to convince me. I told them I don't know how to count, read or speak well in Castilian. But cocomrades told me that of course I could do well, that the only thing necessary is the will and the enthusiasm, because here you learn everything. [...] I saw that it is here where I can learn more things and support my village more. I had been wrong; I had thought that knowledge was in the city and that my village could not learn anything new. But to be a good government, we have to learn and teach. It is much harder. That is why I am here to serve my people. I have my position on the Good Governance Board so that no outsider will ever call out 'Squaw-legged Indian' to a young woman like me.
>
> *apud Mora Bayo, 2014*

Despite the fact that spaces for community justice are still marked by generic sex ideologies that exclude women from many of the political decision-making spaces, new generations of Zapatista women have appropriated the Women's Revolutionary Law to struggle for greater participation and other types of conciliatory processes in which their voices can be heard. The work of the Commission for Honor and Justice also involves the empowerment and training of other young women in understanding their rights:

> The work of honor and justice is also similar to that of the collectives. There, it is about encouraging female comrades and explaining their rights. Although sometimes, when we explain their rights to women, they do not always understand them ... In my village we talked about this. If your husband treats you badly, it's not because of the gossip or because God wants it. They have no right to treat you like this. That is why women are also given talks.
>
> *apud Mora Bayo, 2014*

The work of Márgara Millán (2008) and Violeta Zylberberg (2008) in the Zapatista regions of Tojolabal and Seltal, respectively, as part of our first collective project[21] and the work of Mariana Mora (2013) in the second project reveal the contradictions that this rethinking of community justice is presenting to those authorities whose perspectives are still marked by generic and exclusionary sex ideologies.

Violeta Zylberberg (2008) describes the case of María Angélica, one of the members of the women's commission, who wanted a divorce because of constant ill-treatment by her husband and his family due to her political work. Her frequent trips to regional meetings made her the focus of community gossip, which her husband responded to with jealousy and harassment. Faced with the request for a divorce, the community authorities resorted to conciliation and asked the two parties to reconsider their positions. María Angélica was certain she did not wish to continue with the relationship, but community pressure forced her to accept a conciliation that failed to improve her relationship with her husband.

Mariana Mora, in turn, discusses a rape case for which the Commission for Honor and Justice delivered a sentence that comprised 'clearing 15 hectares of pasture' (Mora, 2013: 214). Commenting on the sentence, the author notes that:

> This case raises a number of key issues linking Zapatista justice to a gender approach. How can a collective operating in the public spaces of the municipality repair the damage caused by a violent assault directed at a woman's body? How does this penalty ensure that the culprit does not commit a similar offense again? How does the woman who suffers the grievance participate in defining what constitutes a reparation for harm or an act of justice?
>
> *Mora, 2013: 214*

These cases exemplify the persistence of ethical-moral perspectives influenced by the Catholic tradition, which is opposed to divorce and continues to see the autonomy of indigenous women as a threat to 'family integration'. It is a very complex context in which different visions of the world overlap and confrontations between generations revolve around 'must be feminine and masculine'.

Relations between men and women in the Zapatista communities are being impacted by the effects of a new transformative constitutionality which, in many respects, is opposed to 'custom'. For many of the women, Zapatism represents a rupture with a context of violence that was justified in the name of tradition:

> Before, women were sometimes beaten at home. The comrades did not know our rights. Now, we share the task of bathing the children with comrades who previously never did what was the work of the woman.
>
> *apud Mora, 2014*

Community justice is being reformulated in many Chiapas communities in dialogue with new Zapatista laws, as well as national and international law. These processes are difficult and full of contradictions, yet they tell us about the flexibility and historicity of community justice and confront any essentialist perspective on indigenous law.

Moreover, this phenomenon of rethinking community justice is not exclusive to the Zapatista autonomous regions. In the Mixe, or Ayuujk, municipality of Santa María Tlahuitoltepec where there has been great organizational enthusiasm for indigenous rights and communitarian autonomy since the 1970s, women have not been marginalized in political debates on so-called 'uses and customs'.

The long history of struggles against the Revolutionary Institutional Party chiefdoms and in favour of indigenous rights has defined the political dynamics of this region, with mixed intellectuals proving to be pioneers in theorizing community justice and indigenous autonomy. Anticipating the debates on autonomy which the indigenous movement would develop on a national level in the 1990s, the mixed intellectual Floriberto Díaz had been writing about communitarian autonomy since the 1970s, as the main theoretician for a political current which claims *communality* as one of the principal values of indigenous democracy.[22]

Influenced by this line of thought, the *Comité de Defensa de los Recursos Humanos y Culturales Mixes* (CODREMI) was formed during this period. The committee would be involved in the *Asamblea de Autoridades Mixes* and the founding of the Civil Association of Services for the Mixe People in 1988, serving as a support, advisory and management body for the municipal and communal authorities and for organized groups of producers who would later combine to form the *Asamblea de Productores Mixes* (ASAPROM).

All of these organizations have also provided training for Ayuujk women activists who have been directly involved in the political struggles of the municipality and have begun to question the gender exclusions that occur within the community. As a result of this struggle, Ayuujk women were incorporated into the musical orchestras of the municipality and nowadays are trained alongside men in the most important indigenous conservatory in the country, the *Centro de Capacitación y Musica Mixe* (CECAM), which has its headquarters in Tlahuitoltepec and is also an example of the achievements of the indigenous movement in the region.

In this region, community justice has always been in the hands of the indigenous authorities and has functioned relatively independently of state law. The Community Assembly has served as the highest advisory body for the application of justice, and the administrator, supported by officers and advised by the Council of Elders, is in charge of routine community conflict resolution (Vianey Vargas, 2011). Paradoxically, the relative autonomy of community justice has been considerably restricted by constitutional reforms dedicated to recognizing the so-called 'system of uses and customs'.[23]

The series of modifications to local legislation, which commenced in the state of Oaxaca in 1990 with recognition of its 'plural ethnic composition' (Article 16) and were consolidated in 1998 in the Law on the Rights of Indigenous Peoples and Communities of the State of Oaxaca (Mexico, 1998), recognize the right of communities to their own normative systems and ways of electing local governments. This recognition has had contradictory effects since, on the one hand, it has strengthened the mechanisms for state control of community justice, increasing the presence of state-controlled human rights organizations responsible for 'monitoring' community justice to ensure it does not violate individual rights,[24] while, at the same time, the issue of indigenous law has begun to be thematized and is becoming a topic for political discussion within the community.

In this new political context, Mixe women have started to reflect on elements of community justice which they consider to have an effect on their lives. In 2011, a dedicated space opened up for these reflections when the municipal government proposed to develop a Communitarian Statute to systematize the principal norms and values of Mixe Justice. Despite the potential contradictions involved in elaborating on the procedural laws of an eminently oral nature, the collective discussion spaces opening up around the Communitarian Statute have enabled different perspectives on Mixe culture and traditions to be expressed and negotiated in public forums.

Liliana Vianey, a Mixe anthropologist and member of our research team who has studied and participated in these processes of reflection, describes this new *cultural climate* in Tlahuitoltepec, stressing that

> The voices of indigenous women, whose protagonism has been increasing since the Zapatista uprising, have indicated that indigenous community justice and state justice have serious limitations in promoting the equitable development of originary women due to social, cultural and gender inequalities. Now, the importance of the indigenous women's movements is that they come to question the internal system on the one hand, but at the same time try to rethink the dynamics with a view to collective development, dignifying and re-signifying human life.
>
> *Vianey Vargas, 2011:5*

These proposals for 'rethinking community justice' have come, on the one hand, from Mixe women organized through the *Network of Mixe Women* and the *Group of Women in Action with Ayuujk Word and Thought*, who began to organize spaces for collective reflection with women from the communities in order to discuss their rights and experiences of Mixe Justice, and, on the other hand, from unorganized women in the municipality who have participated in workshops on the Communitarian Statute and have emphasized, through these spaces, that

> If the woman does not begin to participate jointly in the Community Assembly, there will be many empty spaces [...] As indigenous, we must see real things; if things have been happening for years in the sense of not recognizing the importance of women, we have to change them today.
>
> *apud Vianey Vargas, 2011*

This is an incipient process that has neither the institutional structure of the Good Governance Boards nor the legitimation of a Revolutionary Women's Law to support the demands of organized women in the Ayuujk region. However, it is an experience which is paving the way for conceiving and discussing Ayuujk *communality*, broadening the meanings of communitarian citizenship through the increased participation of women in politics and justice.

4.4 Final Thoughts

The 'juridification of politics' has implied that the struggles for rights and legality have come to occupy a central place in the campaigns of indigenous peoples. It may be said that these political initiatives have established the language through which resistance can operate. Adopting the definition of hegemony provided by William Roseberry, it can also be said that reforms of multicultural constitutionalism can be analysed as a new hegemony which has built 'a common language or a way of speaking about social relations that established the terms around which resistance and struggle would take place' (Roseberry, 1994: 360–361).

The language of rights is being appropriated and vernacularized by indigenous men and women in Latin America with the aim of fighting for new societal agreements with the nation states and within the communities themselves. The simultaneous denunciation of the use of violence and the exclusion of indigenous peoples resulting from Latin American national projects, which is also directed against women through ethno-nationalist projects emanating from indigenous movements, highlight the complexity of the struggles for justice taking place in the continent. *Transformative constitutionalism*, which has been proposed by the indigenous people themselves in many regions of the continent, has served to reshape their internal regulations with the active participation of women.

Discussing cultural rights, autonomic rights and women's rights implies a new language of resistance that, in many cases, has replaced more radical political discourses, such as the discourses on internal colonialism, sovereignty and revolution. However, through this process of vernacularizing discourses on rights,[25] which has involved constructing subaltern cosmopolitan legalities (Santos and Rodríguez-Garavito, 2007), new meanings have also been created to address what is meant by culture, justice and tradition and, in a broader sense, what it means to be an indigenous woman or man in the contemporary world. Legislative reforms aimed at cultural recognition or the restoration of indigenous justice have been accompanied by processes of collective reflection and political creativity in which indigenous women have played a fundamental role.

Over the past ten years, we have learned from the practices and discourses of these women, who have led us to rethink many of our theoretical paradigms and our own feminist practices. The voices that speak for culture have diversified, and this has led to confronting and destabilizing purist and ahistorical perspectives associated with indigenous cultures. We have also witnessed the construction of new spaces for dialogue, negotiation and confrontation through the reconstitution of indigenous justice. These are processes marked by intra-community hierarchies and power relations which, as such, have represented many challenges for women who have chosen to transform their spaces for justice while defending indigenous autonomy.

In the field of justice, we have learned through our academic work that demanding respect for indigenous jurisdictions does not imply denying or silencing diverse voices within the communities themselves that are engaged in rethinking the way in which justice and their own law should be understood.

Recognizing the productive capacity of academic knowledge has led me to position myself politically as a part of the voices demanding a broad and non-exclusive definition of indigenous identity which recognizes the multiplicity of experiences and political genealogies that define the sense of belonging to the imaginary of this community. I therefore reject the temptation to reify indigenous identities and their spaces for justice, either involuntarily or strategically, on the basis of criteria for authenticity, since I believe that this can contribute towards creating new exclusions. Listening to and echoing the diversity of voices that speak from the indigenous being and seek to strengthen indigenous justice is a political responsibility for those of us in academic circles who support the recognition of so-called 'indigenous rights'.

Notes

* Translation by Neil Walker.

1 An extended version of this text, which includes the experiences of Guatemala and Colombia, was published under the title *Indigenous Justices: New Spaces of Struggle for Women*, in Hernández Castillo (2016).

2 See Buenrostro (2013).

3 See the chapter by Orlando Aragón Andrade in this book (Chapter 13).

4 See Santos (2012).

5 In the so-called 'Indian Laws', Book 5 sets out legislation on various aspects of public law, jurisdiction, functions, competences and the powers of mayors, magistrates and other minor indigenous officials.

6 Several authors have analysed these legislative reforms and the multicultural public policies promoted by Latin American States. See Assies *et al.* (2000), Van Cott (2000) and Sieder (2002).

7 This is inaccurate data, since different countries have very different criteria for defining who is and is not indigenous. For an analysis of the demographic data for the indigenous population on the continent, see González (1994).

8 See Sierra (1997) and Sieder and Witchell (2001: 201).

9 See Santos and Grijalva (2012).

10 The '*Viejos y Nuevos Espacios de Poder: Mujeres Indígenas, Organización Colectiva y Resistencia Cotidiana*' project co-ordinated by the author, which included case studies on Mexico, Guatemala and Colombia; the '*Globalización, Justicia y Derechos desde una Perspectiva de Género y Poder*' project, which included case studies on Mexico and Guatemala, co-ordinated by Maria Teresa Sierra and the author; the '*Mujeres y Derecho en América Latina: Justicia, Seguridad y Pluralismo Legal*' project co-ordinated by Rachel Sieder, which included case studies on Bolivia, Guatemala, Ecuador, Colombia and Mexico.

11 See Hernández Castillo (2007, 2008, 2016), Sierra *et al.* (2013), Hernández Castillo and Terven, Venezuela (2017) and Sieder (2017).
12 See Sierra (2004) and Hernández Castillo (2016).
13 See the works of Chirix and Delfina (2003), Gabriel Xiquín (2004), Álvarez (2005), Sánchez (2005), Cumes (2007a, 2007b), the books of the Kaqla Mayan Women's Group (2000, 2004), López (2005), Painemal (2005), Vianey Vargas (2011), Villa (2012) and Méndez (2013).
14 See Yuval Davis (1997) and Gutiérrez Chong (2004).
15 See Hernández Castillo and Caligaris (1995.
16 See Hernández Castillo *et al.* (2004).
17 See Speed *et al.* (2006) and Mora Bayo (2008).
18 See Hernández Castillo *et al.* (2004).
19 For an analysis of the functioning of the various Zapatista autonomous areas, see Baronnet *et al.* (2011).
20 See Mora Bayo (2008, 2013).
21 See Hernández Castillo (2008).
22 Floriberto Díaz had been invited by the Zapatista movement to act as an advisor in discussions with the government prior to his untimely death in 1994. His complete work on communality was published in 2007 by UNAM under the title *Floriberto Diaz. Escrita. Comunalidad Energía Viva del Pensamiento Mixe* (Robles and Cardoso, 2007).
23 Article 25 of the Constitution of the State of Oaxaca establishes that: 'The law will protect the traditions and democratic practices of indigenous communities that have so far been used for the election of their municipalities'.
24 In his case study, included in our collective project, Juan Carlos Martínez examines the way in which governmental human rights bodies have acted in opposition to the communitarian authorities of Tlahuitoltepec, reversing the decisions of their community justice system and violating indigenous autonomy. Martínez states that this represents a setback for the recognition of indigenous rights in Oaxaca and observes that:

> The pluralistic state model that was acceptable to the political economy of the Oaxaca State until the late twentieth century encounters serious issues with implementation through a system that has opened itself up to structural, political and economic reforms requiring a state model based on the real concentration of political power and the opening of the entity's resources to the market and to large investments.
>
> *Martínez, 2013:127*

25 See Engle (2006).

References

Álvarez, Carmen (2005), 'Cosmovisión Maya y Feminismo. Caminos que se unen?' Ponencia Presentada en la Mesa 'Mayanismos y Feminismos', *Congreso de Estudios Mayas*, Guatemala, August.

Assies, Willem; Van Der Haar, Gemma; Hoekema, André J. (eds.) (2000), *The Challenge of Diversity: Indigenous Peoples and Reform of the State in Latin America.* Amsterdam: Thela Thesis.

Barnet, Bruno; Mora, Mariana; Stahler-Sholk, Richard (2011), *Luchas 'Muy Otras': Zapatismo y Autonomía en las Comunidades Indígenos de Chiapas.* Mexico City: UAM/CIESAS.

Bolivia (2009), 'Constitución Política del Estado', *Gaceta oficial del Estado Plurinacional de Bolivia*, February 7th. Available at www.contraloria.gob.bo/portal/Uploads/PDFportal/20121217_318.pdf

Buenrostro, Manuel (2013), 'Reformas Legales, Espacios y Modalidades de la Justicia Indígena de los Mayas en Quintana Roo', *in* Teresa Sierra, R. Aída Hernández and Rachel Sieder (eds.), *Justicias Indígenas y Estado. Violencias Contemporáneas*. Mexico: FLACSO-Ciesas, 89–121.

Chirix García; Delfina, Emma (2003), *'Alas y Raíces, Affectividad de las Mujeres Mayas. Rik'in Ruxik ' y Ruxe ' il, Ronojel Kajowab'al Ri Mayab ' Taq Ixoqi'*. Guatemala City: Grupo de Mujeres Mayas Kaqla, Nawal Wuj.

Cumes, Aura (2007a), 'Las Mujeres son 'Más Indias': Género, Multiculturalismo y Mayanización. Esquivando o Retando Opresiones?' *in* Santiago Bastos and Aura Cumes (eds.), *Mayanización y Vida Cotidiana. La Ideología Multicultural en la Sociedad Guatemalteca*, Vol 1. Guatemala: FLACSO-CIRMA-Cholsamaj, 155–185. Available at http://glefas.org/download/biblioteca/estudios-descoloniales/Aura-Cumes.-Las_mujeres_son_mas_indias_de_Cumes.pdf.

Cumes, Aura (2007b), 'Multiculturalismo y Unidad Nacional en Guatemala: Dinamic de Mayanización en un Contexto Turbulento e Ideologizado'. Release presented at the Coloquio Internacional *Multiculturales de América. Migraciones, Relaciones Interétnicas y Etnicidad*, Monterrey, Nuevo León, Mexico, October 29th to 31st.

Ecuador (2008), 'Constitución de la República de Ecuador', *Official Records*, No. 449, October 20. Available at www.asambleanacional.gob.ec/sites/default/files/documents/old/constitucion_de_bolsillo.pdf.

Engle Merry, Sally (2006), *Human Rights and Gender Violence: Translating International Law into Local Justice*. Chicago: University of Chicago Press.

Gabriel Xiquín, Calixta (2004), 'Liderazgo de las Mujeres Mayas en las Leyendas y Mitologías según su Cosmovisión' (unpublished manuscript). City of Guatemala.

González, Mary Lisbeth (1994), 'How Many Indigenous People?' *in* George Psacharopoulos and Harry Anthony Patrinos (eds.), *Indigenous People and Poverty in Latin America: An Empirical Analysis*. Washington, D.C.: World Bank. DOI: https://doi.org/10.1596/0-8213-2958-8.

Grupo de Mujeres Mayas Kaqla (2000), 'Algunos Colores del Arco Iris, Realidad de las Mujeres Mayas', debate paper. City of Guatemala: Grupo de Mujeres Mayas Kaqla.

Grupo de Mujeres Mayas Kaqla (2004), *La Palabra y el Sentir de las Mujeres Mayas de Kaqla*. City of Guatemala: Cholsamaj.

Gutiérrez Chong, Natividad (ed.) (2004), *Mujeres y Nationalismos en América Latina. De la Independencia a la Nación del Nuevo Milenio*. Mexico: Universidad Nacional Autonoma de México.

Hale, Charles (2002), 'Does Multiculturalism Menace? Governance, Cultural Rights and the Politics of Identity in Guatemala', *Journal of Latin American Studies*, 34 (3), 485–524. JSTOR: www.jstor.org/stable/3875459.

Hale, Charles (2005), 'Neoliberal Multiculturalism: The Remaking of Cultural Rights and Racial Dominance in Central America', *Political and Legal Anthropology Review*, 28 (1), 10–28.DOI: https://doi.org/10.1525/pol.2005.28.1.10.

Hernández Castillo, Rosalva Aída (ed.) (2007), *Historias a Dos Voces: Testimonios de Luchas y Resistencias de Mujeres Indígenas*. Mexico: IMC/CDI.

Hernández Castillo, Rosalva Aída (ed.) (2008), *Etnografías e Historias de Resistencia. Mujeres Indígenas, Procesos Organizativos y Nuevas Identitades Políticas*. Mexico: CIESAS-PUEG.

Hernández Castillo, Rosalva Aída (2016), *Multiple Injustices. Indigenous Women, Law and Political Struggle*. Tucson, AZ: University of Arizona Press.

Hernández Castillo, Rosalva Aída; Caligaris, Anna Garza (1995), 'En Torno a la Ley y la Costumbre: Problemas de Antropología Legal y Género en los Altos de Chiapas',

in *Traditiones y Costumbres Jurídicas en las Comunidades Indígenas de México*. Mexico, D.F.: CNDH, 217–227.
Hernández Castillo, Rosalva Aída; Sierra, Teresa; Peace, Sarela (eds.) (2004), *El Estado y los Indígenas en Tiempos del PAN: Neoindigenismo, Legalidad e Identidad*. Mexico: CIESAS-Porrúa.
Hernández Castillo, Rosalva Aída; Terven, Adriana (2017), 'Methodological Routes: Towards a Critical and Collaborative Legal Anthropology', *in* Rachel Sieder (ed.), *Demanding Justice and Security. Indigenous Women and Legal Pluralities in Latin America*. New Brunswick: Rutgers University Press, 265–288.
López, Alma (2005), 'Aciertos y Desaciertos de la Participación Política de las Mujeres Mayas Kichés: Un Reto Histórico de Nosotras', *in* Marta Sánchez (ed.), *La Doble Mirada: Luchas y Experiencias de las Mujeres Indígenas de América Latina*. Mexico City: UNIFEM/ILSB, 23–31.
Martínez, Juan Carlos (2013), 'Oaxaca: Un Paso Atrás: Reforma Neoliberal y Regresión en el Reconocimiento de Derechos Autonómicos de los Pueblos Indígenas; El Caso de Tlahuitoltepec', *in* María Teresa Sierra, Rosalva Aída Hernández Castillo and Rachel Sieder (eds.), *Justicias Indígenas y Estado: Violencias Contemporáneas*. Mexico: FLACSO-CIESAS, 123–153.
Méndez, Georgina (2013), 'Mujeres Mayas-*Kichwas* en la Apuesta por la Descolonización de los Pensamientos y Corazones', *in* Georgina Méndez, Juan López Itzin, Sylvia Marcos and Carmen Osorio (eds.), *Senti-pensar el Género. Perspectivas desde los Pueblos Indígenas*. Mexico: Editorial Casa del Mago/Red INPIIM A.C./Red de Feminismos Descoloniales, 27–63.
Mexico (1998), 'Ley de Derechos de los Pueblos y Comunidades Indígenas del Estado de Oaxaca', *Official Journal of the State of Oaxaca*, June 19. Available at www.osfeoaxaca.gob.mx/documentos/marcolegal/estatal/19LeyDerechosPueblos.pdf.
Millán, Margara (2008), 'Nuevos Spatios, Nuevas Actoras. Neozapatismo y su Significado para la Mujeres Indígenas', *in* R. Aída Hernández (ed.), *Etnografías e Historias de Resistencia. Mujeres Indígenas, Procesos Organizativos y Nuevas Identidades Políticas*. Mexico: CIESAS-PUEG/UNAM, 217–248.
Mora Bayo, Mariana (2008), *Decolonizing Politics: Zapatista Indigenous Autonomy in an Era of Neoliberal Governance and Low Intensity Warfare*. Master's thesis, University of Texas, Austin. Available at http://hdl.handle.net/2152/18194
Mora Bayo, Mariana (2013), 'La politización de la Justicia Zapatista Frente a la Guerra de Baja Intensidad', *in* María Teresa Sierra, Rosalvo Aída Hernández Castillo and Rachel Sieder (eds.), *Justicias Indígenas y Estado. Violencias Contemporáneas*. Mexico: FLACSO/CIESAS, 195–224.
Mora Bayo, Mariana (2014), 'Repensado la Política y la Decolonización en Minúscula: Reflexiones sobre la Praxis Feminista desde el Zapatismo', *in* Márgara Millán (ed.), *Más allá del Feminismo: Caminos para Andar*. Mexico: Pez en el Agua/Red de Feminismos Descoloniales, 155–182. Available at www.academia.edu/8620234/Repensando_la_pol%C3%ADtica_y_la_descolonizaci%C3%B3n_en_min%C3%BAscula_Reflexiones_sobre_la_praxis_feminista_desde_el_zapatismo?auto=download.
Painemal, Millaray (2005), 'La Experiência de las Organizaciones de Mujeres Mapuche: Resistencias y Desaphíos Ante una Doble Discriminación', *in* Marta Sánchez (ed.), *La Doble Mirada: Luchas y Experiencias de las Mujeres Indígenas de América Latina*. Mexico City: UNIFEM/ILSB, 77–87.

Robles, Sofia; Cardoso Jiménez, Rafael (comp.) (2007), *Floriberto Diaz. Comunalidad Energía Viva del Pensamiento Mixe*. Mexico: UNAM.

Roseberry, Williams (1994), 'Hegemony and the Language of Contention', *in* James Scott, Gilbert M. Joseph and Daniel Nugent (eds.), *Everyday Forms of State Formation: Revolution and the Negotiation of Rule in Modern Mexico*. Durham, NC: Duke University Press, 355–366. DOI: https://doi.org/10.1215/9780822396666-012.

Sánchez, Martha (ed.) (2005), *La Doble Mirada: Luchas y Experiencias de las Mujeres Indígenas de América Latina* . Mexico: UNIFEM/ILSB.

Sánchez Botero, Esther (1998), *Justicia y Pueblos Indígenas de Colombia. La Tutela como Medio para la Construcción del Entendimiento Intercultural*. Bogota: Unijus.

Santos, Boaventura de Sousa (2012), 'Cuando los Excluidos Tienen Derecho: Justicia Indígena, Plurinacionalidad e Interculturalidad', *in* Boaventura de Sousa Santos and Agustín Grijalva Jiménez (eds.), *Justicia Indígena, Plurinacionalidad e Interculturalidad en Ecuador*. Quito: Abya Yala, 13–50.

Santos, Boaventura de Sousa; Grijalva Jiménez, Agustín (eds.) (2012), *Justicia Indígena, Plurinacionalidad e Interculturalidad en Ecuador*. Quito: Abya Yala.

Santos, Boaventura de Sousa; Rodríguez-Garavito, César (2007), 'El Derecho, la Política y lo Subalterno en la Globalización Contrahegemónica', *in* Boaventura de Sousa Santos and Cesar Rodríguez Garavito (eds.), *El Derecho y la Globalización desde Abajo. Hacia una Legalidad Cosmopolita*. Barcelona: Anthropos, 7–28.

Sieder, Rachel (ed.) (2002), *Multiculturalism in Latin America: Indigenous Rights, Diversity and Democracy*. London: Palgrave Press.

Sieder, Rachel (org.) (2017), *Demanding Justice and Security. Indigenous Women and Legal Pluralities in Latin America*. New Brunswick: Rutgers University Press.

Sieder, Rachel; Witchell, Jessica (2001), 'Impulsando las Demandas Indígenas a Través de la Ley: Reflexiones sobre el Proceso de Paz en Guatemala', *in* Pedro Pitarch Ramon and Julián López García (eds.), *Los Derechos Humanos en Tierras Mayas: Política, Representaciones y Moralidad*. Madrid: Sociedad Española de Estudios Maya, 55–82. Available at https://dialnet.unirioja.es/servlet/articulo?codigo=2775724.

Sierra, María Teresa (1997), 'Esencialismo y Autonomía: Paradojas de la Reivindicaciones Indígenas', *Alteridades*, 7 (14), 131–143. Available at https://alteridades.izt.uam.mx/index.php/Alte/article/view/517.

Sierra, María Teresa (2004), 'Diálogos y Prácticas Interculturales. Derechos Humanos, Derechos de las Mujeres y Políticas de Identidad', *Desacatos*, 15–16, 126–147. DOI: https://doi.org/10.29340/16.1075.

Sierra, Maria Teresa; Hernández Castillo, R. Aída; Sieder, Rachel (2013), *Justicias Indígenas y Estado. Violencias Contemporáneas*. Mexico: FLACSO-CIESAS.

Speed, Shannon; Hernández Castillo, R. Aída; Stephen, Lynn (2006), *Dissident Women. Gender and Cultural Politics in Chiapas*. Austin, TX: University of Texas Press.

Van Cott, Donna (2000), *The Friendly Liquidation of the Past: The Politics of Diversity in Latin America*. Pittsburgh, PA: University of Pittsburgh Press.

Vianey Vargas, Liliana (2011), *Las Mujeres de Tlahuitoltepec Mixe, Frente a la Impartición de Justicia y el Uso del Derecho Internacional 2000–2008*. Mexico: INMUJERES.

Villa, Rufina (2012), 'Las Mujeres Nahuas y su Experiência del Juzgado Indígena de Cuetzalan, Puebla', *in* Rosalva Aída Hernández Castillo and Andrew Canessa (eds.), *Género, Complementariedades y Exclusiones en Mesoamérica y los Andes*. Lima: International Work Group for Indigenous Affairs (IWGIA)/Abya Yala Press/The British Academy of Science, 346–352.

Yashar, Deborah (2005), *Contesting Citizenship in Latin America: The Rise of Indigenous Movements and the Postliberal Challenge*. New York: Cambridge University Press. DOI: https://doi.org/10.1017/cbo9780511790966.

Yuval Davis, Nira (1997), *Gender and Nation*. London: Sage Press.

Zylberberg Panebianco, Violet (2008), 'Queriendo se Puede Cambiar Todo?: Un Acercamiento al Proceso de Discusión y Cambio que se Vive al Interior de una Comunidad Zapatista', *in* R. Aída Hernández Castillo (ed.), *Etnografías e Historias de Resistencia. Mujeres Indígenas, Procesos Organizativos y Nuevas Identidades Políticas*. Mexico: CIESAS-PUEG/UNAM, 287–330.

5

MODERN CONSTITUTIONALISM, LEGAL PLURALISM AND THE WASTE OF EXPERIENCE*

Sara Araújo

5.1 Introduction

Modern constitutionalism is based on the ideas of unity, uniformity and homogeneity: one state, one nation, one law. As mentioned in the introduction of the book, the history of the relationship between subjects and the nation state, although shrouded in a fictional narrative of inclusion, encompasses the denial of citizenship to many social groups, as well as the fallacy of an alleged monocultural understanding that conceals a past of marginalization or destruction of other models of social organization, nations and legal orders. The imposition of the modern state, as an exclusive unit of social intelligibility, required law to be naturalized as state law, wasting much of the legal experience in the world (Santos, 2002, 2014; Araújo, 2016). This chapter addresses the possibilities and limits of the concept of legal pluralism in expanding the recognized legal reality and the possibilities of political imagination within the modern constitutional paradigm.

The reduction of law to the norms created and administered by the state, or those which are formally sanctioned, was ensured by scientifically legitimized processes of codification. In accordance with modern epistemology, founded exclusively on the basis of the Eurocentric canon, forms of organization and legal regulation emanating from colonial territories have been ignored or classified as primitive. The transformation of private property into an indicator of the presence of civilization facilitated the classification of *terra nullius*, the legal concept that upheld the 'diffusionist myth of emptiness',[1] legitimized the invasion and occupation of indigenous territories and ensured that other forms of relationships between people and land remained invisible (Darian-Smith, 2001; Roy, 2008; Maldonado-Torres, 2009; Santos, 2014). The myth of the universality and neutrality of modern law is embedded in the colonial construction of otherness (the universal as opposed

DOI: 10.4324/9781003391920-7

to the particular, order as opposed to disorder) (Fitzpatrick, 1992). Supported by monocultural scientific reason, state law acquired the status of irrefutability and immunity to context and politics (Santos, 2002, 2014).

The modern constitutional paradigm has survived the national independence processes and, framed within the developmental rhetoric of the rule of law, has been presented as a neutral device, the universal archetype of a linear evolution project (Roy, 2008; Mattei and Morpurgo, 2010; Madlingozi, 2010; Araújo, 2016). It is therefore a 'globalized localism' (Santos, 2002), built up as a 'European enterprise' which celebrates the Eurocentric cultural experience and contributes to its hegemony (Nunn, 1997: 351). The modern state is thus constitutive of the abyssal lines responsible for making the diversity of the world invisible and, as such, responsible for modern epistemicide and juricide (Santos, 2011, 2014, 2018).

The abyssal line, as a key concept in the epistemological, pedagogical and political proposal of the 'epistemologies of the South', is a metaphor for the exclusionary foundations of modernity, representing an ontological and epistemological division (Santos, 2014, 2018). On this side of the line, inequalities are non-abyssal, that is, oppression is visible, and resistance can be expressed in validated legal and scientific language. Social struggles are therefore recognized as legitimate. On the other side, the social contract has no value, and inequalities are abyssal. Subjects whose claims are not expressed in categories defined and accepted by the modern canon are ignored, their knowledge is disregarded and the violence they suffer is invisible. Their ideas for a different society can be formulated but must contend with the naturalization of language and principles based on the modern constitutional paradigm and hence remain inaudible on this side of the line (Santos, 2014, 2018). When Gayatri Spivak discussed whether the subaltern has the capacity to speak, she did not question the competence of the latter to express herself – as she clarified in an interview – but the impossibility of doing so on her own terms and being heard (*apud* De Kock, 1992). The abyssal line, which complements the concept of the 'bifurcated state' identified by Mamhood Mamdani (1996) with reference to the African continent, establishes a hierarchy for modern law and customary law and legitimizes the distinction between the civilized and the savage, denying the latter the possibility of self-representation (Santos, 2014). However, the same division has taken place in other areas. In Europe, for example, the modern project has been based on the elimination of its 'Souths' or, in other words, non-recognition of the violence imposed on the 'ungrievable lives' (Butler, 2016) of those that inhabit the zone of non-being (Fanon, 2008 [1952]) and the denial of the types of knowledge and legal systems which they produce.

At the beginning of the twentieth century, the concept of 'living law' (Ehrlich, 2002 [1913]) contradicted the myth of legal centralism (Griffiths, 1986: 3) on which the modern constitutional paradigm is based. Subsequently, the concept of legal pluralism and the scientific works that defined and identified it empirically began to offer a more systematic challenge to the hegemonic narrative and encourage different recognition policies with different political meanings. The objective of this chapter is to critically discuss the extent to which the theories and empirical studies of legal pluralism, as well as the different recognition policies, have contributed to decolonizing the Eurocentric legal canon and challenging the legal abyssal lines of the modern constitutional paradigm.

The chapter first presents the concept of legal pluralism and the epistemological instruments that drive reflection, while also clarifying the specific objectives of the study. The argument is then developed through an analysis of different approaches to legal pluralism in terms of scientific theories, but also the policies that have addressed it. Using Sally Engle Merry's widely accepted classification (1988), I begin by discussing theories and studies of legal pluralism in the classical period and in the new legal pluralism. The focus then shifts to global legal pluralism. Two other approaches are also identified: instrumental legal pluralism and intercultural legal pluralism. Unlike Sally Engle Merry, I have not chosen to define these approaches chronologically since, even if they start at a certain time and determine a specific period, they are not always replaced and therefore the emergence of a new design does not necessarily eliminate the previous one. A sociology of absences (Santos, 2014) is applied to this analysis, identifying the extent to which each approach has served to reproduce the abyssal line, even when it is challenged or displaced. I will also attempt to identify the emergences that have resulted from the various studies and are now available to think which explores a post-abyssal future. It is an incomplete exercise which aims to contribute towards a discussion that requires multiple viewpoints and varied sensibilities, both from within and outside the academic community.

5.2 Legal Pluralism and the Challenges of 'Epistemologies of the South'

The coining of the concept of legal pluralism is often attributed to a collection of essays published in the early 1970s (Gilissen, 1971), but its origins date back to the work of George Gurvitch a few decades earlier (Gurvitch, 1935). The dissemination of the idea and the recognition it gained within the scientific community owe much to the anthropology and sociology of law, which ensured sustained reflection on the empirical dimension by identifying in practice the coexistence and interaction of multiple legal systems. Initially restricted to the study of colonial and postcolonial societies, the concept was later applied to societies in the global North and, in recent decades, the analysis of legal complexity in the face of neoliberal globalization, as well as the different recognition processes within local legal systems. Today, there are countless scientific articles and books, ethnographies and theoretical controversies which address the idea of legal pluralism. Given the extent of the scientific production and the depth of the debates, is it still relevant to discuss this concept and the theoretical and empirical possibilities it entails?

Almost two decades ago, Boaventura de Sousa Santos classified the discussion on legal pluralism as one of the core debates in the sociology and anthropology of law. In his view, there were four metatheoretical conditions which supported this claim: the flexibility that enabled it to include new dimensions; the vagueness of its borders; the possibility of making connections between theoretical and empirical work; and its openness to interdisciplinary debates (Santos, 2002: 91–92). With the identification of the abyssal line, as well as the dichotomic thinking it sustains, the 'epistemologies of the South' challenge us to observe and interrogate the absences produced by conventional questions in order to provide visibility for disregarded theoretical dimensions, establish dialogues with postcolonial theories in their diversity, build new indicators to broaden the observed reality and foster unexpected interdisciplinary links.

Recognizing the existence of multiple legal orders that have survived attempts at legal centralization does not necessarily imply a broadening of the legal canon or a disposition to learn from diversity. State law has invariably occupied the positive pole of the recurring modern dichotomies: modern, formal, state and official. Local legal forms are grouped into artificial categories occupying the negative pole and are seen as part of the uncivilized world, remnants of the past to be eliminated through development or accepted with condescension if they are insurmountable but do not conflict with good constitutional order. Regardless of the designation – local, traditional, non-state, informal, customary, popular, indigenous – the classification is expressed in terms of absence or defect in comparison to the modern canon.

The question of the potential of legal pluralism in promoting access to justice – an area in which I worked for several years, in various contexts (Araújo, 2008, 2010, 2012, 2016; Meneses *et al.*, 2017) – appears to operate on the other side of the line but does not always escape the modern frame of reference which dictates the concepts, variables and indicators on this side, nor the internal hierarchies of academia which, although open to the exotic, scarcely admit the possibility that it might be capable of challenging the canon. Questioning the emancipatory nature of legal pluralism is also not sufficient to build a post-abyssal legal mindset. When Boaventura de Sousa Santos defined the concept of the abyssal line, he recognized that the regulation/emancipation dichotomy is only relevant where the social contract is valid (Santos, 2014). On the other side of the line, the same dichotomy takes the form of appropriation and violence. Building a post-abyssal mindset is not just about shifting the abyssal line and making this side more inclusive. The terms of the social contract must be questioned, taking the legal plurality of the world into consideration. I suggest the use of two key epistemological instruments: the sociology of absences and the sociology of emergences (Santos, 2014, 2018). The legal sociology of absences denaturalizes the Eurocentric prescription and promotes a position of suspicion with regard to the alleged neutrality and technical superiority of the modern constitutional paradigm, situating it within a colonial, capitalist and heteropatriarchal civilizational project. The legal sociology of emergences operates in the field of social transformation, paving the way for new utopias emerging from the world's legal experiences, built within and outside the modern framework and, to a greater or lesser extent, hybrid, consolidated or embryonic, whether completed or partially developed.

Without entering into the endless debate on the concept of law, it is understood in this chapter as a map of imagination, social representation and description of reality (Santos, 1987). Like maps, the law inevitably distorts reality by means of three mechanisms that are not neutral: scale, projection and symbolization. The choices on which they are based promote certain interests and disputes while suppressing others (Santos, 1987: 297). Legal maps not only configure our representation of the present, but also our imagined notions of future possibilities. As with other maps, it is not the distortion that configures the problem, but rather the recognition of a single cartographic process. I would therefore pose the following question: can theories and empirical studies of legal pluralism, as well as the different recognition policies, contribute to the provincialization of modern law and the construction of post-abyssal legal thinking? In the following pages, five different scientific and political approaches to legal pluralism will be analysed.

5.3 [Approach I] Classical Legal Pluralism

The first legal ethnographies – developed in societies in Africa, Asia and the Pacific – provided the social sciences with a variety of examples of 'social control, social pressure, custom, customary law, and judicial procedures' showing that colonized populations maintained indigenous law alongside European law (Merry, 1988: 869). Bronislaw Malinowski (1926), who studied 'primitive law' in the Trobriand Islands, was one of the first authors to develop this type of research and reach a wider audience. The question of contact between the different legal systems and the hybridism that resulted from this was still overlooked, but Malinowski's work made it possible to denaturalize modern assumptions, such as the idea that law is a construct exclusive to Western societies. The legal anthropology and ethnographic work of this first period revealed that the judicial void was, in fact, filled with legal systems, although they were different from those recognized by the West. Yet, despite shedding light on what existed on the other side of the line, it still failed to question the hierarchy. Conditioned by the five monocultures of modern thought (Santos, 2014) – knowledge and the rigor of knowledge, the universal and the global, capitalist productivity, the naturalization of differences and linear time – the work continued to observe legal systems and subjects on the other side as unqualified, local, primitive, savage and unproductive.

On the African continent, some of the initial work on legal pluralism was carried out by anthropologists and ethnographers in close collaboration with the colonial powers, promoting what Raquel Yrigoyen Fajardo would call colonial or subordinate legal pluralism, that is, a recognition policy subjected to the economic interests and cultural values of colonial power and its requirements for local administration (Yrigoyen Fajardo, 2017: 12). The colonial model of indirect rule anchored itself in this type of relationship with legal pluralism, upholding the bifurcated state analysed by Mamhood Mamdani (1996). Recognition of diversity did not constitute a celebration of difference. On the contrary, it formally established an abyssal line (Santos, 2014) which distinguished between citizens and subjects, humans and those considered less than human, modern law and custom, religion and pagan belief, culture and rituals, art and crafts, linguistic discourse and vernacular communication, and the civilized and the savage (Mamdani, 1996: 61).

Within the model of indirect rule, citizens responded to the law of the metropolis and modern institutions, while the indigenous people were subjected to customary rights and traditional chiefs, (re)created according to the requisites of the project for domination. Flexibility, plurality and normative conflict were ignored or interpreted as yet another sign of the local and the primitive. Tribes were demarcated, norms were codified and a reality that had never been rigid was formally crystalized (Mamdani, 1996: 118–119; Chanock, 1998: 9–10). The design for a deeply conservative society functioned as an instrument for the reproduction of a backward continent that was reluctant to modernize, facilitating a type of capitalist exploitation that benefited the Europeans alone (Ranger, 1994). The non-privatization of land, codified as part of customary law, prevented Africans from entering the capitalist world and kept them strictly dependent on the traditional chiefs whose entitlements, based on a guarantee of loyalty to the government, included the distribution of land (Chanock, 1991).

The authorities and political and legal institutions in the African continent were transformed into 'traditional chiefs', legal plurality and living law into 'customary law', and cultural diversity into 'traditional culture', the 'exotic' and the 'primitive'. The innovation did not lie in the interpretation or recreation of the customary law by those who controlled the traditional institutions, but rather in the privilege enjoyed by the institution of traditional leaders as the only customary authority (Mamdani, 1996). Before European colonization, most Africans moved between multiple identities, alternating between defining themselves as the subject of the chief, a cult, a clan or a group (Ranger, 1994: 248). Ending the forms of popular control to which the chiefs were traditionally subjected constituted a major change. Thus, one of the main instruments of the colonial social sciences was implemented: denial of the possibility of people self-nominating, self-identifying and explaining themselves on their own terms. Hence, claims about the direction of the future and the meaning of progress were silenced.

Max Gluckman (1955) was one of the first academics to initiate a turning point in the anthropology of law in Africa. Although influenced by the colonial period in which he lived and accused of viewing local law as traditional, thereby failing to see it as a result of the encounter with colonialism (Chanock, 1998), he showed that the study of customary law had to extend beyond conversations with groups of elders and move towards analysing adjudicating processes and the context in which they occurred. For Sally Falk Moore, Gluckman was the key author in studies of the anthropology of law in the mid-twentieth century and the first anthropologist to systematically study the functioning of an African court by listening carefully to the stories of the complainants and the arguments they presented. Moore concluded that he could be considered responsible for a methodological revolution (Moore, 2001: 97–98).

In the 1960s, Gluckman was a leading figure in one of the most interesting debates on the epistemological status of the concept of law in anthropology. The controversy concerned whether the use of folk concepts from the anthropologist's culture was legitimate (Gluckman) or illegitimate (Bohannan) in the analysis of other societies. Gluckman's argument is based on the idea that Western cultural concepts are not used in anthropology without being subjected to an analytical reduction that frees them from the main ethnocentric (ideological) connotations, thus avoiding the danger of Westernizing and thereby distorting empirical observations (Gluckman, 1997 [1969]). On the other hand, for Bohannan, this analytical endeavour, although meritorious, can never be pursued to the point of eliminating all traces of ethnocentrism and cultural imperialism, hence there was no alternative other than to use the native concepts and categories of the societies being studied (Bohannan, 1997 [1969]).

Beyond the results of the controversy or unwavering convictions, it is important to be aware of the difficulty of eradicating the ethnocentrism of scientific knowledge processes even when opting for the use of native concepts. If, on the one hand, the centralist view promotes the abyssal line and the dehumanization of subjects by denying the existence of legal knowledge on the other side of the line, the recognition of legal pluralism, as we have seen, can be used to strengthen abyssal inequalities. Hence, classifying the plurality of normative orders as law does not mean that hierarchies are necessarily broken. At the same time, refusing to employ the modern concept – law – can result in a lack of validation and the impossibility of including these realities in sociolegal debates.

5.4 [Approach II] New Legal Pluralism

From the 1970s onwards, authors such as Boaventura de Sousa Santos, Sally Falk Moore and Marc Galanter have shown that legal pluralism is not a phenomenon exclusive to colonial and postcolonial societies, but a condition existing in virtually any society.[2] A 'new legal pluralism' (Merry, 1988) was therefore added to the classical approach. The wider geographical coverage of ethnographic subjects has enabled legal pluralism to reduce the connotations of exoticism and marginality, demonstrating that this is not an indicator of underdevelopment. The theory has acquired complexity, since the distinction between external imposed law and local laws is no longer clear, and legal orders are beginning to be observed in their interactive and shifting dimensions (Merry, 1988; Santos, 2009). In the 1970s, one of the greatest contributions in this area came from

Sally Falk Moore. With the innovative concept of the 'semi-autonomous social field', the author questions the perception that fundamental social change can be immediately realized through legal means. Using examples taken from the clothing industry in New York and the Chagga in Tanzania, she shows that foreign legislation does not produce the expected effects precisely because of the semi-autonomous nature of the social field in which it has to operate, given that the internal bonds of mutual obligations are often stronger than external law (Moore, 2000 [1978]). This is a particularly relevant contribution to overcoming abyssal thinking. By showing that modern law does not always have the capacity to eradicate customary laws, the concept of a semi-autonomous social field challenges the image of a natural hierarchy of power in which modern state law dominates.

The fundamental distinction between 'weak legal pluralism' and 'strong legal pluralism' also defines this approach (Griffiths, 1986). From the perspective of weak legal pluralism, a legal system is plural when the state recognizes the different legal orders placed under its dependence. This is a commitment which the ideology of legal centralism is obliged to make with the recalcitrant social reality, at least until the heterogeneous, primitive populations of the former colonial states engaged in the process of building the nation state become homogeneous populations in the image of the modern state. The concept of strong legal pluralism accounts for the multiple legal systems that coexist in society, regardless of whether they are recognized by the state or not. In addition to challenging the hierarchy between modern and traditional law by recognizing a relationship, albeit unequal, between the said forces, this distinction validates the argument that formally recognizing legal pluralism does not mean valuing the maps of political imagination included in this diversity.

The identification of legal pluralism in Northern global societies during this period was accompanied by a wave of enthusiasm for the processes of informalizing justice and a focus on alternative dispute resolution mechanisms (ADR), including conciliation, mediation and arbitration. The academic debate on informal or popular justice has problematized a number of interesting issues concerning the challenges to overcoming legal abyssal lines. The discussion makes it clear that the legalization or creation of informal mechanisms does not necessarily result in broadening the modern constitutional paradigm. On the one hand, various authors have identified a tendency for informal justice to mimic the behaviours of the state and also for the state to colonize informal justice (Merry and Milner, 1993). The metaphor of the Trojan horse (Krieken, 2001: 9) has been used to illustrate concerns about the expansion of the formal regulation of the state into spheres that tend to evade its areas of influence (Abel, 1982; Fitzpatrick, 1992). Moreover, democratizing access to justice is not always the main motive for investing in informal justice. In Northern countries, reforms that have led to the informalization of justice have been largely motivated by the number of pending court cases, thus providing a repository for the 'less serious "junk" cases' and offering a second-class justice that can undermine the informal bargaining spaces on the fringes of the law (Mathews, 1988: 10–12).

5.5 [Approach III] Global Legal Pluralism

The legal sphere has been challenged by the processes of globalization. The movement of people across borders has been facilitated; technological transformations have changed the way we relate to each other, allowing us to communicate, work collectively and receive information from different geographies; and global markets have financed themselves and gained increasing power in society. The scale of the nation state has meant that it has ceased to respond to most contemporary problems:

> the globalization of capital, the movement of people and goods across borders, the reach of global corporate activity, the impact of worldwide NGOs, and the development, in recent decades, of over a hundred international or transnational tribunals all make it far more likely that local communities will be affected by activities and entities with no local presence.
>
> *Berman, 2007: 1182*

In 2002, Boaventura de Sousa Santos claimed that we had entered the phase of global legal pluralism, which incorporates infra-state, state and supra-state legal orders (Santos, 2002). William Twining presents an analytical framework with eight levels of law to account for the diversity within global legal pluralism: global, international, regional, transnational, inter-communal, territorial state, sub-state and non-state (Twining, 2010: 505–506).

The relationship between the state and globalization, and in particular the issues associated with sovereignty, has occupied a relevant space in academic debates. Does this mean the myth of legal centralism is effectively being questioned? It seems clear that the sovereignty of the state is being transformed. Can global legal pluralism, in its complexity, question the Eurocentric premises on which modern legal thinking is based and pave the way for non-abyssal legal thinking? In other words, can global legal pluralism destabilize the hierarchies between the law on this side of the line and the laws on the other side of the line? Observing reality does not leave much scope for epistemological optimism.

The literature on legal pluralism draws attention to what distinguishes supra-state from infra-state law. As Ralph Michaels maintains, 'many studies of nonstate law in globalization share the emphasis on functional coupling and institutional foundation over social embeddedness' (Michaels, 2009: 7). This is true of the approaches to *lex mercatoria, lex sportive, lex constructionis, lex digitalis* and other non-state legal systems. Although, as the author notes, this perspective is not restricted to Teubner and systems theory; Teubner's analysis of *lex mercatoria* – 'the alleged self-created transnational law of global commerce' (Michaels, 2009: 6) – is a very clear formulation of this approach, which is based on a technocratic argument in relation to legislative production.

The financialization of the world has resulted in the importance of financial markets in people's lives and the increasing complexification of these markets, which cross borders and jurisdictions (Carruthers, 2020: 152). In this increasingly complex and neoliberal type of society, technical legitimacy tends to overtake democratic legitimacy. For Teubner,

> the focus in lawmaking is shifting to private regimes, that is, to agreements among global players, to private market regulation through multinational enterprises, internal rulemaking within international organizations, interorganizational negotiating systems, and world-wide standardization.
>
> *Teubner, 2004: 3*

This kind of 'spontaneous' global law is not a 'hypermodern variant of traditional customary law'. Both have social origins and some common characteristics, such as the fact that they do not result from a positivist process originating in a sovereign state. However, customary law stems from 'long-term processes of diffuse communication and recursive interaction', while the new private regimes 'are a typical product of social differentiation'. The latter emerge 'not on the basis of informal co-ordination of conduct in a gradual process of repeated interactions, but through positive lawmaking in organized decision-making processes in specialized fora organizations' (Teubner, 2004: 4). For Teubner, there is no transfer of power from government actors to the economy. According to the author, globalization is an opportunity for law to create a dual Constitution in autonomous social spheres, such as research, education, the health system, the media and the arts. In order to achieve this, the internal differentiation of each subsystem must dynamically combine a formally organized rationality and informal spontaneity. This combination has been partially achieved only in economics and politics. Thus, Teubner classifies the activities of protest movements as 'only irritations' with 'little potential to solve the problems they raise' (Teubner, 2004: 10). This is what Teubner calls the 'motivation–competence–dilemma' which, as he explains in an interview, boils down to the following: business actors have no motivation for self-limitation, while social movements, public opinion and political actors have no competence (Teubner *apud* Valenzuela Gascón, 2019).

By subjecting the concept of competence to a sociology of absences, the ideology behind its alleged neutrality and universality emerges. The hegemony of neoliberalism, enshrined in the Washington Consensus, created a political atmosphere that considers good governance to be the language and processes of (de)regulation that favour financial markets and present political choices as rational, neutral and universal solutions. The 'monoculture of knowledge and the rigor of knowledge' (Santos, 2014) is not the result of a higher rationality, but of the proclamation of a canon which imposes the terms of efficiency and the possibilities for transformation and progress, and defines who has the authority to sit at the negotiating table. This monoculture strengthens the abyssal line that renders invisible knowledge and rights that contemplate possibilities for social transformation beyond the limits imposed by Eurocentric modernity. In a deeply critical reading, Mattei and Morpurgo denounce the primacy of imperial law as the dominant layer for the worldwide legal systems, arguing that

> law has been constructively turned into a technology and a mere component of an economic system of capitalism, thus hiding its intrinsic political nature, and annulling the relevance of local political systems, now impotent in front of the dynamics of global law.
>
> *Mattei and Morpurgo, 2010: 18*

For Boaventura de Sousa Santos, the concept of 'dual law' has a very different meaning from the one used by Teubner. In a recent publication, the author states that official state law has been occupied by the elites in power, the oppressors, and this occupation operates through 'a radical division between two legal systems: the law of the 1% and the law of the 99%, the law of the oppressors and the law of the oppressed' (Santos, 2017: 366). In this context, the oppressed are subjected to abyssal and non-abyssal inequalities, and it is important here to go back to Santos' concept of the three circles of civil society in order not to lose sight of the different types of inequalities: intimate, strange and uncivil (Santos, 2002). Intimate civil society is the sphere of hyper-inclusion, of citizens connected with state power who enjoy full rights and have access to public resources far beyond those guaranteed by the policy of rights. Strange civil society is the intermediate circle composed of people who enjoy moderate inclusion, where citizens can more or less freely exercise their civic and political rights but have little access to social, economic and cultural rights. Uncivil civil society is the outer circle, composed of citizens excluded from the social contract who inhabit the zone of invisibility (Santos, 2002). For the intimate circle, legal pluralism has been highly advantageous, while for the strange circle, in the context of neoliberal globalization, state law tends to lose its emancipatory potential because the social state gives way to the neoliberal state. The uncivil civil society, which has always lived beyond the abyssal line, experiences a reinforcement of the logic of exclusion.

It is now widely recognized that the state is an actor in its own apparent erosion and that the creation of a neoliberal market has required a strong and reconfigured state (Santos, 2002; Knox, 2017). Markets depend on public authorities, while 'financial market actors continue to anchor their rules and institutions in public law, and they repeatedly seek the authority of the state to undergird and privilege their private arrangements' (Carruthers, 2020: 153). State concerns have been redirected away from social justice to the positive functioning of the financial markets (Brabazon, 2017: 132), and public law has been modelled according to the principles of the market and private law to the point where public and private have merged into the concept of *governance* (Tzouvala, 2017: 132).

In the context of global legal pluralism, the 'porosity' of legal orders becomes increasingly intense and complex. The concept of interlegality (Santos, 2002) points to the contact and porosity of the laws in circulation, both at the macro and micro level, and accentuates the tendency of the new legal pluralism to understand this from a dynamic perspective. The intensification of global legal pluralism coexists with the growing heterogeneity of the state. Not only do different sectors of activity develop at different paces and sometimes in opposite directions, but state action is marked by inconsistencies, making it difficult to identify a coherent model (Santos, 2002). Hence, processes of state decentralization and centralization may be simultaneously observed. In this context, different modes of legal regulation emerge, each politically anchored in a microstate (Santos, 2009: 70). The concept of the state of exception has become central to analysing modern societies (Agamben, 2005; Ferreira, 2016). Constitutions that enshrine the right to life and legally ensure universal access to health, education, housing and employment coexist with regulations that dismantle social security and favour the needs of the market.

The abyssal lines that extend from this do not only divide the global North from the South, crossing countries and creating deep internal disparities. It is also clear that there are inequalities in terms of military and economic power between countries. A recent study on the implementation of austerity policies in Europe published in 2010 shows that the measures which were imposed reinforced inequalities between countries, while also intensifying the abyssal and non-abyssal divisions in each country, with certain groups – such as women, young people and racialized populations – suffering the impacts much more intensely than others, leading to even greater differentiation (Meneses *et al.*, 2020).

The emancipatory power of state law has been precarious in this context. Other legalities are needed to dispute power. Antônio Carlos Wolkmer, familiar with the tradition of the 'law found on the street',[3] proposes a participatory community type, in response to neoliberal legal pluralism. This paradigm of an open and democratic model of legal pluralism sets out to expand an underground reality as a response to the injustice, ineffectiveness and exhaustion of the individualist liberal legalist model. The author observes 'law as a phenomenon resulting from desired social relations and values' and defends the necessity of 'establishing another legality from the multiplicity of normative, non-obligatory statist resources', promoting 'legitimacy based on the "just" fundamental demands of social actors' and 'viewing the institution of society as a decentralized, pluralistic and participatory structure' (Wolkmer, 1994: 69).

As Boaventura Sousa Santos argues, 'reconfigurative law' – the state law mobilized by social movements – has less and less emancipatory potential. Hence, theories of legal pluralism need to include subaltern legalities, that is, forms of 'prefigurative law' which emerge from the diversity of social struggles, ranging from the *Indignados* Movement to indigenous struggles for an intercultural society. This is the legality of those who refuse the terms of the social contract that legalizes the abyssal lines and do not accept being classified as residual, inferior, ignorant, unproductive and local, identifying neoliberal capitalism, colonialism and patriarchy as the main sources of oppression (Santos, 2017). This law seeks not only to make the social contract more inclusive but also to renegotiate its terms. It is a law so plural in form that it easily escapes the indicators defined in projects for legal pluralism. For Boaventura de Sousa Santos, 'it is prefigurative in the sense that, both in its conception and in its exercise, it witnesses a foresight or anticipation of an alternative society in which democracy, justice and equality are truly lived' (Santos, 2017: 376).

To sum up, global legal pluralism, today is an umbrella concept that accommodates heterogeneous entities and extremely diverse legal systems associated with a complex legal and political arena, permeated by very unequal relations (Benda-Beckmann and Turner, 2018: 265).

5.6 [Approach IV] Instrumental Legal Pluralism

Investment in the 1980s and 1990s to promote the rule of law in designated developing or post-conflict countries has not delivered proportionate results. Among donors, one of the most popular ideas for explaining the failure of reforms is the fact that they have focused exclusively on state legal systems (Janse, 2013). Thus, after decades of trying to impose a universal model of rule of law based on a centralist legal design, the World Bank came to include legal pluralism in its reports. This does not mean that the need to decolonize the development processes was recognized. However, it was impossible to continue to ignore the failure of universalist policies that do not respect the contexts in which they are implemented. Conferences and sponsored publications have invited experts with recognized academic merit to establish productive dialogues with development officials (Isser, 2011; Tamanaha *et al.*, 2013). The United Nations, through its agencies and bodies such as UNICEF, UNDP or UN Women, has also acknowledged the inadequacy of *one-size-fits-all* approach, opening up the potential of local authorities and their ability to provide cheaper, faster and culturally relevant solutions (Wojkowska, 2006; UN Women, UNDP, UNICEF, 2012).

The concepts of legal pluralism and informal justice have been linked to a set of terms compatible with the Eurocentric design of progress, such as development policies, effectiveness, donor agencies, sector reform, capacity building, impact measurement and poverty. This pluralist approach has become central under the World Bank's 'Justice for the Poor' program. If the concept of poverty is, from the point of view of post-abyssal thinking, particularly problematic and debatable, evoking a logic of linear development within the paradigm defined by the North, the concept of justice for the poor refers to the idea of a bifurcated state which differentiates citizens from subjects.

Roland Janse classifies this donors' view as 'weak or mild legal pluralism' and lists a number of concerns. To begin with, it is not clear how the relationship between non-state systems and the state system is developed. The acknowledged models have their origins in the colonial period and are based mainly on the codification of customary law or the incorporation of local institutions into state institutions. Moreover, the tendency to consider that formal and non-formal systems are compatible and similar and that the state legal system is ultimately superior still remains (Janse, 2013).

The instrumental approach uses a weak conception of legal pluralism and supports monocultural development projects, since the colonial recognition of customary law promotes a subordinate legal pluralism (Yrigoyen Fajardo, 2017). In addition to failing to challenge Eurocentric hierarchies, it produces knowledge that facilitates the manipulation of local structures. Formal justice systems can therefore be used as the administrative arm of the central state and put at the service of 'good governance' by resolving what are considered to be minor conflicts – hence freeing the judicial courts and ensuring social peace – and presenting universal prescriptions in vernacular terms to make them more effective.

Thus, the officialization of legal pluralism does not necessarily involve an appreciation of the richness it entails or any real investment in the institutions from which it emerges. Constitutional recognition may coincide with an absence of regulation or essential support for the functioning of local legal structures (Araújo, 2016). The modern legal system is based on a set of assumptions that have been naturalized but remains highly ideological, such as private property, individualism and competitiveness or monogamous marriage, which suits the demands of the capitalist market and social reproduction. Since donors do not seem willing to build integrated systems, legal pluralism is understood here only from the point of view of conflict resolution bodies, not as a multiplicity of legal maps. The latest approach to legal pluralism [Approach V] takes the processes of decolonizing the modern constitutional paradigm much further.

5.7 [Approach V] Intercultural Legal Pluralism

Not all processes for recognizing legal pluralism were driven from above and developed as described in the previous section. The most striking examples of recognition of legal pluralism from below are the constitutional reforms of Ecuador and Bolivia in 2008 and 2009. Both comprise the third cycle in a series of constitutional reforms based on the social struggles of those excluded from modern law. These struggles have questioned the central elements of the configuration and definition of the Latin American republican states established in the nineteenth century, as well as the colonial heritage: multicultural constitutionalism (1982–1988), pluricultural constitutionalism (1989–2005) and plurinational constitutionalism (2006–2009) (Yrigoyen Fajardo, 2011: 140). In the plurinational model, the monocultural nation state–state law equation is significantly challenged.

On a continent particularly marked by the extractivism which began during colonization and was subsequently legitimized by a Eurocentric model for the rule of law, together with the imperialist logic of neoliberal global law (Mattei and Morpurgo, 2010), the social struggles that emerged in the 1990s, calling for social rights and a state which actively protects territories and their populations from the activities of multinational companies, succeeded in achieving constitutional recognition in the two aforementioned countries (Yrigoyen Fajardo, 2011: 149). New rights were institutionalized, such as the right to water and to *Sumak Kawsay* or *Sumak Qamaña* ('*buen vivir*', 'the good way of living' in Quechuan and Aymaran, respectively).

The matrix characteristics of the modern paradigm include the perception of nature as a machine which can be studied, understood and dominated by humans. Modern science has ensured technological development, while law has provided the legal mechanisms for transforming nature into capital (Capra and Mattei, 2015). As previously mentioned, the absence of any concept of private property among colonized peoples helped legitimize appropriation and violence. The conception of nature as Pachamama, or Mother Earth and therefore not objectifiable – contrary to the anthropocentric conception that legitimizes extractivist practices – is one of the greatest achievements of this transformative constitutional process.

The transformative constitutionalism of Ecuador and Bolivia established the basis of the paradigm shift in the modern state (Santos, 2010). Recognition of legal pluralism was not based on weak or instrumental approaches but resulted from the work of constituent assemblies which incorporated a strong legal pluralist view. Indigenous collectives asserted themselves as constituent subjects and, together with other peoples, defined a new model for the state and relations between its peoples (Yrigoyen Fajardo, 2011: 149) which extends beyond affirmation of social rights, recognition of social diversity or the modern formalization of institutions that resolve the minor conflicts of second-class citizens. The millennial roots of indigenous peoples were explicitly recognized and their world views, disregarded in the construction of the state, were now valued. A 'biocentric spin' has accompanied this recognition of indigenous justice as an important part of a political project with a decolonizing and anti-capitalist mission (Santos, 2010; Yrigoyen Fajardo, 2011; Wolkmer, 2013).

The constitutional reforms of Bolivia and Ecuador were not only intended to protect indigenous populations but also to promote reciprocal learning processes among peoples that would enable a better country to be built for all. The need to combat climate change – one of the greatest contemporary global challenges – requires a relationship with nature that is not compatible with the Western instrumental conception that was imposed on the world as part of an allegedly neutral scientific and legal paradigm. Indigenous world views and their legal systems have proved that they have the potential to constitute themselves as a subaltern legality, a prefigurative law which supports struggles against the global colonial and capitalist structure by seeking to promote a more inclusive social contract and protect the world against self-destruction.

Applying the sociology of absences to these processes of constitutional transformation enables multiple continuities of the abyssal lines to be identified. The initial optimism that accompanied the processes gave way to a disenchanted vision less than a decade later. Once the Constitution was transformed and approved, the Constituent Assembly's power came to an end and power was placed in the hands of the modern political elites. Though intercultural, the Constitution remains a Eurocentric instrument and is subject to guidelines issued in international regulations. The modern constitutional paradigm has not been overcome. Extractivism remains an integral part of reality in both countries, and the protection of nature and lives requires constant struggle.[4]

Although the advances were less significant than the initial enthusiasm had suggested, the legal maps on the other side of the line were included in the debate on the future of democracy, with several voices denouncing the abyssal lines of the modern constitutional paradigm, advancing the discussion on decolonization, demercantilization and depatriarchalization. The reflections emerging from these processes of struggle and legal transformation have enabled a clearer distinction to be made between neoliberal multiculturalism (Walsh, 2014), which is compatible with subordinate legal pluralism (Yrigoyen Fajardo, 2017) and critical interculturality (Walsh, 2014), which demands an egalitarian legal pluralism (Yrigoyen Fajardo, 2017). The latter requires even greater efforts on the path towards cognitive justice. Raquel Yrigoyen Fajardo evokes five premises to characterize a policy of egalitarian legal pluralism: (1) the end of cultural hierarchies, the end of the submission of one culture to another, equal dignity between peoples and cultures; (2) the decolonization of relations based on equality/inferiority between peoples and cultures and between the state and indigenous peoples; (3) indigenous peoples exercising control over their ways of life and institutions; (4) the impossibility of imposing neocolonial limits, including constitutional limits, on indigenous jurisdictions, which will act in accordance with their own law and their social and cultural needs; and (5) egalitarian legal pluralism based on a Pact between peoples and intercultural dialogue aimed at defining human and other forms of rights (such as the rights of nature) that respect all peoples and the state (Yrigoyen Fajardo, 2017: 13).

5.8 Conclusion

Recognition of legal pluralism does not always challenge the centralist view of the modern constitutional paradigm and does not necessarily call into question the hegemony of the Eurocentric canon and the hierarchies this entails which, in effect, are compatible with legal imperialism. When, in the late 1990s, Boaventura de Sousa Santos asked 'Why is it so difficult to construct a critical theory?', he was drawing attention to the fact that the weaknesses of modern critical theory begin with the failure to grasp that a critique of reason cannot be promoted on the basis of the same type of reason. Thus, beyond simply describing legal plurality, it is important to foreground the potential for criticism and the possibilities of legal and political imagination contained in this plurality.

This objective requires, on the one hand, an exercise in the legal sociology of absences that denaturalizes the Eurocentric prescription and the alleged technical superiority of state law and global financial law, placing them firmly within a colonial capitalist and heteropatriarchal civilizational project. It is also necessary to develop exercises based on the legal sociology of emergences, identifying alternatives from the great diversity of legal maps of the world that reside within and outside the modern framework. These maps may be hybrid to a greater or lesser extent, consolidated or embryonic and complete or partially developed and can pave the way for the construction of new utopias supported by real experiences and knowledge, considered and constructed by those who have personally suffered the effects of structural violence and fought against oppression in its various forms (Santos, 2014, 2018).

The way forward from the traditional proposals of legal pluralism is epistemological. Legal pluralism will only challenge the abyssal line if it is formulated in terms of the ecology of knowledge, as an ecology of legal maps, including the 'law found on the street' and rights sustained by ancestral world views, as in the case of egalitarian legal pluralism. This does not mean discarding the possibilities that exist in modern law, but instead holding it up to strange mirrors, namely prefigurative subaltern legalities. It is not a simple exercise, but one which requires research projects to be designed as rearguard projects with no closed definitions or inflexible sets of indicators, hence allowing them to be redefined while progressing through deep listening exercises (Santos, 2018) that extend beyond the limits of modern categories. Given that most of our analytical tools have been built by Northern epistemologies, this is a highly challenging exercise which needs to focus on the decolonization of epistemological instruments and methodologies and the production of knowledge with the 'South', not about the 'South'.

Rather than remaining a central debate within studies on the sociology of law, post-abyssal legal pluralism needs to occupy other debates in which the rules of modern law are presented as neutral and universally valid, and Eurocentric technocratic criteria support political choices that promote inequalities. It must cross disciplinary boundaries, fostering dialogues not only within anthropology and sociology but also within other disciplines, such as political economy, history and biology. This chapter aims to support an empirical and interdisciplinary approach that can be used to identify wasted legal experience made invisible by the abyssal line.

This is not only a challenge for the societies of the geographical South. It is also fundamental to think about the future of Europe. Different social groups cannot be integrated on the basis of granting citizenship to those who are forced to repress their identity to fit Eurocentric legal maps, but rather by recognizing the diversity of the legal maps that make up Europe and the world as a whole and by deconstructing the colonial hierarchies. An expanded legal and political imagination can emerge from horizontal and reciprocal learning.

Notes

* Translation by Neil Walker.

1 J.M. Blaunt's concept is used by Nelson Maldonado-Torres (2009) in the discussion of the coloniality of being. The recognition of non-European regions as empty or virtually uninhabited and unfamiliar with private property and rationality legitimated the appropriation of the territories.

2 From the extensive work of each of these authors, see, for example, Santos (1977), Moore (2000 [1978]) and Galanter (1981).

3 The 'law found on the street' is an approach developed from the theory of Roberto Lyra Filho which reflects on law through the claims and actions of social movements, assuming that it is made in the course of the historical process of liberation, while also unveiling the obstacles facing non-harmful freedom to others (Sousa Júnior, 2019).

4 See the chapter by Rosalva Aída Hernández Castillo in this book (Chapter 4).

References

Abel, Richard (1982), 'Introduction', in Richard Abel (ed.), *The Politics of Informal Justice. Vol.1: The American Experience*. New York: Academic Press, 1–13.

Agamben, G. (2005), *State of Exception*. Chicago: The University of Chicago Press.

Araújo, Sara (2008), 'Pluralismo Jurídico em África. Ficção ou Realidade?', *Revista Critica de Ciências Sociais*, 83: 121–139.

Araújo, Sara (2010), 'Legal Pluralism and Interlegality: The Role of Community Justices in Mozambique', in Manfred O. Hinz; Mapaure Clever (eds.), *In Search of Justice and Peace. Traditional and Informal Justice in Africa*. Windhoek: Namibia Scientific Society.

Araújo, Sara (2012), 'Toward an Ecology of Justices: An Urban and Rural Study of Mozambican Plurality', in Kyed Helene; Coelho João; Paulo Borges; Souto Amélia; Sara Araújo (eds.), *The Dynamics of Legal Pluralism in Mozambique*. Maputo: Kapicua.

Araújo, Sara (2016), 'O Primado do Direito e as Exclusões Abissais: Reconstruir Velhos Conceitos, Desafiar o Cânone', *Sociologias*, 43(18): 88–115. DOI: https://doi.org/10.1590/15174522-018004304.

Benda-Beckmann, Keebet; Turner, Bertram (2018), 'Legal Pluralism, Social Theory, and the State', *The Journal of Legal Pluralism and Unofficial Law*, 50(3): 255–274. DOI: https://doi.org/10.1080/07329113.2018.1532674.

Berman, Paul Schiff (2007), 'Global Legal Pluralism', *Southern California Law Review*, 80(6): 1155–1238. Available at: https://southerncalifornialawreview.com/2007/09/04/global-legal-pluralism-article-by-paul-berman.

Bohannan, Paul (1997), 'Ethnography and Comparison in Legal Anthropology', in Laura Nader (ed.), *Law in Culture and Society*. Berkeley, CA: University of California Press, 401–418 [2.ª ed.; orig. 1969]. DOI: https://doi.org/10.1525/9780520341807-023.

Brabazon, Honor (2017), 'Introduction. Understanding Neoliberal Legality', in Honor Brabazon (ed.), *Neoliberal Legality. Understanding the Role of Law in the Neoliberal Project*. Abingdon: Routledge, 1–21.

Butler, Judith (2016), *Frames of War. When Is Life Grievable?* London: Verso.

Capra, Fritjof; Mattei, Ugo (2015), *The Ecology of Law. Toward a Legal System in Tune with Nature and Community*. Oakland: Berrett-Koehler Publishers.

Carruthers, Bruce G. (2020), 'Law, Governance, and Finance: Introduction to the *Theory and Society* Special Issue', *Theory and Society*, 49: 151–164. DOI: https://doi.org/10.1007/s11186-020-09390-5.

Chanock, Martin (1991), 'Paradigms, Policies and Property: A Review of the Customary Law of Land Tenure', in Roberts Richard; Mann Kristin (eds.), *Law in Colonial Africa*. Portsmouth: Heinemann Educational Books.

Chanock, Martin (1998), *Law, Custom and Social Order. The Colonial Experience in Malawi and Zambia*. Portsmouth: Heinemann.

Darian-Smith, E. (2001), 'Postcolonial Law', in Neil J. Smelser; Paul B. Baltes (eds.), *International Encyclopedia of Social & Behavioral Sciences*. Oxford: Pergamon, 11841–11844.

De Kock, Leon (1992), 'Interview with Gayatri Chakravorty Spivak: New Nation Writers Conference in South Africa', *ARIEL: A Review of International English Literature*, 23(3): 29–47. Available at: https://journalhosting.ucalgary.ca/index.php/ariel/article/view/33464.

Ehrlich, Eugen (2002 [1913]), *Fundamental Principles of the Sociology of Law*. New Brunswick, NJ: Transaction Publishers.

Fanon, Frantz (2008 [1952]), *Black Skin. White Masks*. New York: Grove Press.

Ferreira, António Casimiro (2016), *Política e Sociedade. Teoria Social em Tempo de Austeridade*. Porto: Vida Económica.

Fitzpatrick, Peter (1992), 'The Impossibility of Popular Justice', *Social & Legal Studies*, 1(2): 99–215. DOI: https://doi.org/10.1177/096466399200100205.

Galanter, Marc (1981), 'Justice in Many Rooms: Courts, Private Ordering and Indigenous Law', *Journal of Legal Pluralism and Unofficial Law*, 13(19): 1–47. DOI: https://doi.org/10.1080/07329113.1981.10756257.

Gilissen, Jaques (org.) (1971), *Le Pluralisme Juridique*. Brussels: The Free University of Brussels.

Gluckman, Max (1955), *The Judicial Process among the Barotse of Northern Rhodesia*. Manchester: University Press.

Gluckman, Max (1997) [1969], 'Concepts in the Comparative Study of Tribal Law', in Laura Nader (org.), *Law in Culture and Society*. Berkeley: University of California Press [2.ª ed.], 349–373.

Griffiths, John (1986), 'What is Legal Pluralism?', *Journal of Legal Pluralism*, 18(24): 1–55. DOI: https://doi.org/10.1080/07329113.1986.10756387.

Gurvitch, George (1935), *L'Expérience Juridique et la Philosophie Pluraliste du Droit*. Paris: Éditions A. Pedone.

Isser, Deborah H. (ed.) (2011), *Customary Justice and the Rule of Law in War-Torn Societies*. Washington, D.C.: USIP Press Books.

Janse, Ronald A (2013), 'Turn to Legal Pluralism in Rule of Law Promotion?', *Erasmus Law Review*, 6(3/4): 181–190. DOI: https://doi.org/10.5553/ELR.000010.

Knox, Robert (2017), 'Law, Neoliberalism and the Constitution of Political Subjectivity. The Case of Organised Labour', in Honor Brabazon (ed.), *Neoliberal Legality. Understanding the Role of Law in the Neoliberal Project*. Abingdon: Routledge, 92–118.

Krieken, Robert (2001), 'Legal Informalism, Power and Liberal Governance', *Social & Legal Studies*, 10(1): 5–22. DOI: https://doi.org/10.1177/a016320.

Madlingozi, Tshepo (2010), 'On Transitional Justice Entrepreneurs and the Production of Victims', *Journal of Human Rights Practice*, 2(2): 208–228. DOI: https://doi.org/10.1093/jhuman/huq005.

Maldonado-Torres, Nelson (2009), '*A Topologia do Ser e a Geopolítica do Conhecimento: Modernidade, Império e Colonialidade*', in Boaventura de Sousa Santos; Maria Paula Meneses (eds.), *Epistemologias do Sul*. Coimbra: Almedina, 337–381.

Malinowski, Bronislaw (1926), *Crime and Custom in Savage Society*. London: Kegan Paul.

Mamdani, Mamhood (1996), *Citizen and Subject. Contemporary Africa and the Legacy of Late Colonialism*. Princeton, NJ: Princeton University Press.

Mathews, Roger (1988), 'Reassessing Informal Justice', in Roger Mathews (ed.), *Informal Justice?* London: SAGE, 1–24.

Mattei, Ugo; Morpurgo, Marco (2010), 'Global Law and Plunder: The Dark Side of the Rule of Law', *Bocconi School of Law, Student-Edited Papers*, No. 2009-03/EN: 1–19. Consulted on 08.07.2018, at https://doi.org/10.2139/ssrn.1437530.

Meneses, Maria Paula; Araújo, Sara; Ferreira, Sílvia (2020), 'Welfare, Labour and Austerity: Resistances and Alternatives through Women's Gaze', in Trudie Knijn; Dorota Lepianka (eds.), *Justice and Vulnerability in Europe: An Interdisciplinary Approach*. Cheltenham: Edward Elgar, 178–196. DOI: https://doi.org/10.4337/9781839108488.00018.

Meneses, Maria Paula; Araújo, Sara; Ramos Gonçalves, Marisa; Carvalho, Beatriz (2017), *Para uma Justiça de Matriz Timorense: O Contributo das Justiças Comunitárias*. Dili: CES and CRL.

Merry, Sally Engle (1988), 'Legal Pluralism', *Law and Society Review*, 22(5): 869–896. DOI: https://doi.org/10.2307/3053638.

Merry, Sally Engle; Milner, Neal (1993), 'Introduction', in Sally Engle Merry; Neal Milner (eds.), *The Possibility of Popular Justice*. Ann Arbor, MI: University of Michigan Press, 3–30.

Michaels, Ralph (2009), 'Global Legal Pluralism', *Duke Law School Public Law & Legal Theory, Research Paper No. 259*. Available at: https://ssrn.com/abstract=1430395.

Moore, Sally Falk (2000) [1978], *Law as a Process. An Anthropological Approach*. Hamburg: LIT.

Moore, Sally Falk (2001), 'Certainties Undone: Fifty Turbulent Years of Legal Anthropology, 1949–1999', *The Journal of the Royal Anthropological Institute*, 7(1), 95–116. DOI: https://doi.org/10.1111/1467-9655.00052.

Nunn, Kenneth, B. (1997), 'Law as a Eurocentric Enterprise', *Law & Inequality: A Journal of Theory and Practice*, 15(2): 323–371.

Ranger, Terence (1994 [1983]), 'The Invention of Tradition in Colonial Africa', in Eric Hobsbawm; Terence Ranger (eds.), *The Invention of Tradition*. Cambridge: Cambridge University Press, 211–262 [2. ª ed.].

Roy, Alpana (2008), 'Postcolonial Theory and Law: A Critical Introduction', *Adelaide Law Review*, 315–357. Available at SSRN: https://ssrn.com/abstract=2620107

Santos, Boaventura de Sousa (1977), 'The Law of the Oppressed: The Construction and Reproduction of Legality in Pasargada', *Law & Society Review*, 12(1): 5–126. DOI: https://doi.org/10.2307/3053321.

Santos, Boaventura de Sousa (1987), 'Law: A Map of Misreading. Toward a Postmodern Conception of Law', *Journal of Law and Society*, 14(3): 279–302. DOI: https://doi.org/10.2307/1410186.

Santos, Boaventura de Sousa (2002), *Toward a New Legal Common Sense*. London: Butterwords.

Santos, Boaventura de Sousa (2009), *Sociología Jurídica Crítica*. Madrid: Trotta.

Santos, Boaventura de Sousa (2010), *Refundación del Estado en América Latina. Perspectivas desde una Epistemología del Sur*. Quito: Abya Yala.

Santos, Boaventura de Sousa (2011), *Para uma Revolução Democrática da Justiça*. São Paulo: Cortez.

Santos, Boaventura de Sousa (2014), *Epistemologies of the South*. Boulder, CO: Paradigm.

Santos, Boaventura de Sousa (2017), *As Bifurcações da Ordem. Revolução, Cidade, Campo e Indignação*. Coimbra: Almedina.

Santos, Boaventura de Sousa (2018), *The End of the Cognitive Empire. The Coming of Age of Epistemologies of the South*. Durham, NC: Duke University Press.

Sousa Júnior, José Geraldo (2019), 'O Direito Achado na Rua: Condições Socias e Fundamentos Teóricos', *Revista Direito e Práxis*, 10(4): 2776–2817. DOI: https://doi.org/10.1590/2179-8966/2019/45688.

Tamanaha, Brian Z.; Sage, Caroline; Woolcock, Michael (eds.) (2013), *Legal Pluralism and Development. Scholars and Practitioners in Dialogue*. Cambridge: Cambridge University Press.

Teubner, Gunther (2004), 'Global Private Regimes: Neo-spontaneous Law and Dual Constitution of Autonomous Sectors in World Society', *Globalization and Public Governance*. Ashgate: Aldershot, 71–87.

Twinning, William (2010), Normative and Legal Pluralism: A Global Perspective, 20 *Duke Journal of Comparative & International Law*, 473–518. Available at: http://scholarship.law.duke.edu/djcil/vol20/iss3/8.

Tzouvala, Ntina (2017), 'Continuity and Rupture in Restraining the Right to the Strike', in Honor Brabazon (ed.), *Neoliberal Legality. Understanding the Role of Law in the Neoliberal Project*. Abingdon: Routledge, 119–139.

UN Women, PNUD, UNICEF (2012), *Informal Justice Systems. Charting a Course for Human Rights-based Engagement*. UN Women, PNUD, UNICEF.

Valenzuela Gascón, Ricardo (2019), 'Constitutional Sociology and Corporations. A Conversation with Gunther Teubner', *Tempo Social*, 31(1): 323–334. DOI: https://doi.org/10.11606/0103-2070.ts.2019.146006.

Walsh, Catherine (2014), 'Interculturalidad Critica y Pedagogía Decolonial', *Red de Interculturalidad Network*. Available at: https://redinterculturalidad.files.wordpress.com/2014/02/interculturalidad-crc3adtica-y-pedagogc3ada-decolonial-walsh.pdf.

Wojkowska, Ewa (2006), *Doing Justice: How Informal Justice Systems Can Contribute*. United Nations Development Programme, Oslo Governance Centre. Available at: www.un.org/ruleoflaw/files/UNDP%20DoingJusticeEwaWojkowska130307.pdf.

Wolkmer, Antônio Carlos (1994), *Pluralismo Jurídico. Fundamentos de uma Nova Cultura do Direito*. São Paulo: Editora Alfa Omega.

Wolkmer, Antônio Carlos (2013), 'Pluralismo Crítico e Perspectivas para uma Novo Constitucionalismo na América Latina', in Antônio Carlos Wolkmer and Milea Petters Melo (eds.), *Constitucionalismo Latino-americano. Tendências Contemporâneas*. Curitiba: Juruá, 19–42.

Yrigoyen Fajardo, Raquel (2011), 'El Horizonte del Constitucionalismo Pluralista: Del Multiculturalismo a la Descolonización', in César Rodríguez Garavito (ed.), *El Derecho en América Latina. Un Mapa para el Pensamiento Jurídico del Siglo XXI*. Buenos Aires: Siglo Veintiuno Editores,139–159.

Yrigoyen Fajardo, Raquel (2017), 'Qué es el Pluralismo Jurídico Igualitario?', *Revista Alertanet*, 10–25. Available at: www.derechoysociedad.org/revista-alertanet.

PART II

Post-Colonial Transitions: The Case of South Africa

6

LEGACIES AND LATITUDES

Past, Present and Future in South Africa's Post-colonial Legal Order

Heinz Klug

6.1 Introduction

Critical debate over South Africa's post-colonial legal order has increasingly devolved into two broad camps. On the one hand, there is anxiety over what is perceived to be increasing threats to a "liberal" legal order that was the celebrated outcome of the 1994 "miracle" credited with saving the country from what many political analysts predicted would be a "blood bath" or as Mahmood Mamdani noted, "if Rwanda was the genocide that happened, then South Africa was the genocide that didn't" (Mamdani, 2001: 185). On the other hand, there is increasing criticism of what is perceived to be a "liberal" legal order created by the historic transition from apartheid and now blamed for its failure to address the legacies of racism and economic inequality that survived the democratic transition. These latter concerns are reflected both in discussion within the ruling African National Congress (ANC) about the need for a "second transition" and in the patterns of increasing political protest and conflict that erupt across the South African landscape—from Parliament and social media to the streets of towns and cities across the land. The goal of this chapter is to contextualize these arguments in order to understand the legacies of apartheid and colonialism and the impact of these legacies on the evolution of a post-apartheid legal order.

Central to these divergent views of South Africa's post-colonial legal order is a questioning of the "negotiated revolution" that enabled the democratic transition in South Africa. Speaking to the Oxford Union in late November 2015, Julius Malema, former President of the ANC Youth League and now leader of the opposition Economic Freedom Front (EFF) in South Africa's Parliament, criticized the legacy of Nelson Mandela stating that "the Nelson we celebrate now is a stage-managed Mandela who compromised the principles of the revolution, which are

DOI: 10.4324/9781003391920-9

captured in the Freedom Charter" (Malema *apud* Meintjies, 2015). Explaining this characterization of Mandela and his assertion that "the deviation from the freedom charter was the beginning of selling out of the revolution", Malema argued that while "perhaps it was necessary to have a cooling off period … we cooled off for too long—21 years" and that the EFF is "not going to compromise like Madiba did" (Malema *apud* Meintjies, 2015). Less rhetorical but perhaps more threatening, given that the ANC remains the dominant political party in South Africa, have been the persistent attacks on the judiciary from within the ruling party as well as growing tensions: over failure to follow the laws governing state procurement; to respond to court orders meant to remedy government failures; or simple intransigence in the face of challenges to government malfeasance—such as the resistance to properly address the findings of the Public Protector in the cases of Nkandla (the spending of public resources on the President's private homestead) and Hlaudi Motseneng (questioning his appointment as a chief operating officer of the state broadcaster, the SABC). It is in these contexts that concerns over the "rule of law" extend beyond individual legal challenges and begin to raise questions about the very nature of legal culture and the post-colonial state in South Africa.

In his extraordinary book on the making of South African legal culture, Martin Chanock asks a question that remains a central challenge to students of law in South Africa: "how can South Africa develop a democratic legal culture which is open to dialogue yet retains the distinctive characteristics of a 'rule of law'?" (Chanock, 2001: 512). In taking up this challenge I will begin by distinguishing two different visions that are prominent in the politics and literature of post-apartheid South Africa and then suggest an alternative understanding that might offer an approach that may go some way towards responding to Martin Chanock's challenge. First, there is the claim that a liberal legal order—one which protects individual interests and focuses on constraining state power—emerged out of the "miracle" of the democratic transition (Dugard, 1998) and is a legacy of South Africa's long legal tradition (Ellmann, 1992; Meierhenrich, 2008). Second, there is a critique of this same legal order as one created by an historic compromise but also one that through the interpretative work of the judiciary and the Constitutional Court in particular holds the promise of a "transformative constitutionalism". From this perspective "the critical task is to force open the interpretative politics of legal formalism in order to reshape the hidden politics of interpretation into an open site of democratic contestation and transformation" (Van Marle and Le Roux, 2007: xii). While both these perspectives focus on the role of the judiciary and the task of constitutional interpretation, I believe that a fuller understanding of South Africa's post-apartheid legal order requires us to view the post-1994 transformation of law through the lens of state reconstruction and the legacies of institutional and legal continuity inherent to this process.

From this vantage point, the legal order and doctrinal change in particular must be understood not only as the product of legal challenges and interpretative politics but also within the context of institutional development and state capacity—including the function and dysfunction of bureaucratic and political institutions at all levels of government. A significant aspect of this approach is reflected in recent scholarship that reconstructs the jurisprudence of the Constitutional Court as a process of constitution-building in which the court has been attempting to implement the constitutional order created by the constitutional assembly (Fowkes, 2016). In order to further pursue this approach to understanding the post-apartheid legal order, it is essential that we reconsider the idea of path dependency to include not only the long history of law and legal culture but also the more recent legacies of the struggle against apartheid and the democratic transition that began in 1990 and continues through the process of constitution-making and the Truth and Reconciliation Commission and remains contested and unfinished in struggles over economic power, land and democratic governance in rural South Africa. Before exploring this third perspective, it is important to situate this conception of the place of post-colonial law in the context of the state, and post-colonial states in Africa more generally.

6.2 States and Constitutionalism in Africa

Over the last quarter century, constitutional change has swept Africa. Of Africa's fifty-five internationally recognized states, all but nine adopted completely new constitutions in the years following the end of the cold war in 1989. All but one of these nine outliers, Liberia, made significant revisions to their constitutions in the same period. Although Africa was not unique in its embrace of constitutional change in the post-cold war era, the depth and breadth of change are matched only by the states which emerged from the collapse of state socialism and the breakup of the Soviet Union in this period. While Afro-pessimism (Mandani, 1996: 285) may lead many to question the salience of constitutional developments in Africa—given the sad history of military dictatorships, corruption and state failure that characterized the first decades of the post-colonial era—the dramatic constitutional changes that have swept the continent require us to place any discussion of the post-apartheid era within this broader context to avoid the dangers of analytical exceptionalism that so often taints discussions of South Africa.

Martin Chanock recently characterized the dominant analysis and practice of constitution-making in Africa as top-down, resulting in

> the writing of increasingly complex constitutions, with increasingly sophisticated institutions and rights guarantees, which have, as has been shown time and time again, floated meaninglessly above the societies for which they have been designated, until the bubble bursts in outbreaks of violence.
>
> *Chanock, 2016: 14*

This critical, yet clear-eyed view of Africa's post-colonial constitutional experience poses a direct challenge to us—how do we bring our commitments to a better future into a more effective engagement with the patterns of historical experience and society in Africa? Chanock suggests that

> constitutionalism must be based on a rule of law that builds from the bottom up rather than a bill of rights handed down … [and that] African constitutionalism must be based on a common law with which people identify.
>
> *Chanock, 2016: 14*

To meet this challenge, our analysis of constitutionalism in Africa must be rooted in an understanding of the state in Africa, and we must embrace a contextualized and comparative approach to the history of post-colonial constitutionalism in Africa more generally.

Before proceeding, however, it is necessary to clarify two preliminary issues. First, Africa is a vast and diverse continent, and any notion of a singular culture, historical trajectory or constitutional form would, on its face, be a gross and unjustifiable simplification. Even if it is possible to identify a number of broad historical patterns and alternatives etched into the political landscape of Africa by the colonial experience and nationalist struggles that saw the emergence of independent African states from 1957 until the formal end of apartheid in South Africa in 1994, these commonalities overlay vast cultural, economic, ethnic, language and political differences. Furthermore, the emergence of post-colonial independent states spans a period of nearly half a century, and while the cold war was a common element through most of this period, it was the end of the cold war in 1989 that both allowed the decolonization of Namibia and the democratic transition from apartheid, while simultaneously fragmenting the established post-colonial order throughout Africa, leading to a second, more autochthonous, wave of state reconstruction in sub-Saharan Africa. While heralded as a wave of democratization in which single-party and military-dominated states witnessed multi-party elections and the installation of new democratic governments that it was hoped could address what the World Bank had identified in 1989 as Africa's governance problem (World Bank, 1989), the subsequent civil and military conflicts, as well as state failure, genocide and international interventions, make it clear that the malaise lies deeper than the simple design of democratic constitutions. The recent Arab spring in North Africa added yet another dimension to this constitutional foment.

Second, not only did Africans share a variety of colonial experiences—depending on the identity of the colonial power and the extent of colonial settlement—they also shared an important factor in the process of decolonization, a process of constitution-making in which the key element was the transfer of power to those struggling to be free from colonization. Thus, the first post-colonial constitutions were largely negotiated instruments in which the nationalist parties were centrally concerned with their ability to exercise power as representatives of a new nation and thus accepted many specific constitutional formulations largely designed by the retreating colonial authorities. Even if these constitutions sought, in a variety of creative ways, to address what their designers thought were the underlying problems facing the newly independent states—such as ethnic diversity and legal pluralism—their foreshortened lives reflect the fact that they were not embraced by either those who were to govern through the institutions and structures they created or the governed, who often rejoiced at their demise, rather than defending them as reflecting their own social and political aspirations. While South Africa's interim 1993 Constitution was also designed to ensure the transfer of power to a democratically elected government, its inclusion of a process of further constitution-making has clearly prolonged the sense of legitimacy often denied other post-colonial African constitutions.

Chanock's challenge is of course only the latest in a series of analyses that have questioned the place of constitutions in Africa. While Okoth-Ogendo eloquently critiqued the first wave of post-colonial constitutions as producing "constitutions without constitutionalism" (1991). Other participants in a conference on "State and Constitutionalism in Africa", held in Harare, Zimbabwe, in May 1989—on the verge of the second wave of post-colonial constitution-making—heralded the possibility of a new, popular democratic constitutionalism, described by Issa Shivji as a "new concept of constitutionalism [that] should rest on [an] accountable/responsive state and collective rights/freedoms" (1991a: 39–40). Other African voices—including Muna Ndulo (2001), who sees constitution-making in Africa as essential to the establishment of good governance necessary for economic development, and Yash Ghai, who, as both an analyst and practitioner of constitution-making in Africa, has sought to promote popular participation in the constitution-making process (Ghai and Galli, 2006)—have seen constitution-making as a means to build effective government and a culture of human rights in Africa. In my own work on South Africa, I have reflected on the process of constitution-making and how it took place within a global context which framed the opportunities for local innovation as well as a national history and culture that shaped alternatives and imposed a certain path dependency on the options that were embraced (Klug, 2000, 2010). Taking up Chanock's challenge requires a deeper analysis of the processes and impacts of constitutionalism in Africa and demonstrates why South Africa's post-colonial legal order must be located within a broader, comparative view of the post-colonial state in Africa.

Constitutions have been classically understood and normatively embraced as reflections of the society they constitute. The late Chief Justice of South Africa Ismail Mohammed stated that

> The Constitution of a nation is not simply a statute which mechanically defines the structures of government and the relations between the government and

> the governed, it is a "mirror reflecting the national soul", the identification of the ideals and aspirations of a nation.
>
> *apud Ndulo, 2001: 108*

While this popular and symbolic notion of a constitution is central to the legitimating function of constitutionalism and is regularly embraced by constitution-makers, judicial interpreters of constitutional meaning and advocates of constitutional patriotism, or those who perceive constitutionalism in the United States as civic religion, I believe we need to embrace a more sociological conception of constitutions as social phenomena that serve the essential role of organizing, establishing and conserving public and social power in society. Drawing from Chris Thornhill's recent book *A Sociology of Constitutions* in which he concludes "that constitutions are functional preconditions for the positive abstraction of political power and, as such, they are also, over longer periods of time, highly probable preconditions of institutions using power: that is states" (Thornhill, 2011: 372), I argue that we must locate our analysis of the post-apartheid legal order within the context of the post-colonial state and specifically its genealogy in colonialism and decolonization.

One explanation for the phenomena of thin constitutionalism in Africa, reflected in both the Harare discussions in 1989 and Martin Chanock's characterization of the products of constitution-making "floating meaninglessly above the societies for which they have been designated", is that there is a fundamental incongruence between the new institutional architecture they offer and the institutional legacies that remain dominant within those societies. If state reconstruction fails to address the particular institutional and historical form of governance that dominates a society, it should not be a surprise that past legacies may frustrate the aspirations of new constitutional orders. In the literature on the state in Africa, there are two key perspectives that I believe are of direct significance to the task of identifying and conceptualizing issues important to our understanding of post-colonial constitutionalism. First, there is the view that the colonial state in Africa has a particular form and that the common features of this form define patterns of governance despite the vast diversity of African societies. Second, the history of constitutionalism in post-colonial Africa reflects the continued influence of both, this colonial legacy and the common history of decolonization, or what Crawford Young (2012) describes as the code of decolonization.

In his earlier book, Crawford Young argued that although the colonial state in Africa is not unique among colonial states, "when we assemble its traits, examine its trajectory, and weave together the determinants of its structure and behavior, a singular historical personality looms before us" (Young, 1994: 281). In his conclusion to this work, Young identifies seven key characteristics of what he terms "Bula Matari" (he who crushes rocks), colonialist Henry Stanley's nickname and a telling metaphor for capturing "the crushing, relentless force of the emerging colonial state in Africa" (Young, 1994: 1). These characteristics include the late nineteenth-century division of Africa under the emergent international doctrine of "effective occupation" which compelled an immediate "requirement of confirming propriety title by forcible demonstration of dominance" (Young, 1994: 279); ruthless extractive action; an active role in forcing rural Africans into labour service; advanced technologies of dominance reflected in sheer military supremacy; spheres of policy thought permeated by a virulent racism that constructed Africans as savage; unsparing efforts to "monopolize the production of meaning and thus the construction of culture"; and, finally, a "syndrome of citizen attitudes and expectations" produced by the particular "sequencing of decolonization" and the reliance by the late colonial state on developmentalism and a paternalistic bestowal of state welfare in its attempt to gain legitimacy, while remaining an "alien and predatory other" (Young, 1994: 279–281). Similarly, for Mahmood Mamdani the colonial state has a particular essence that lies in its institutional segregation, creating what he terms a "bifurcated state" reflecting the dynamics of direct and indirect rule (Mamdani, 1996: 16–18). The apartheid state in South Africa is in Mamdani's analysis not exceptional but rather reflects the fundamental logic of the colonial state in Africa.

The second perspective highlights the process of decolonization as a source of explanation of the form taken by the post-colonial state in Africa. For Crawford Young the "code of decolonization" was set by the United Nations General Assembly resolution on the Granting of Independence to Colonial Territories and Peoples in 1960, which produced a focus on territoriality, representative institutions, universal suffrage, the centrality of political parties, sovereignty and "finally speed became of the essence" (Young, 2012: 89–96). As Issa Shivji argued in his conclusion to the edited collection of papers that came out of the 1989 Harare conference:

> From civilian to military regimes and from one-party "socialist" to one-party "capitalist" states, the role of constitutions [in Africa] has lain in constituting the sovereignty of the states (Okoth-Ogendo) or in simply effecting the transfer (Nolutshungu) or re-ordering (Hutchful) of political power.
>
> *Shivji, 1991b: 253*

Describing the limited notion of constitutionalism that dominated the process of decolonization, Sam Nolutshungu argues that the idea of "constitutional function"—what the constitution was supposed to do—was fragmentary and undeveloped, while the idea of "constitutional moment"—focused on the transfer of power—meant that constitutional debate was "dominated by the need for a settlement between parties to a political dispute" (Nolutshungu, 1991: 92–93). Summarizing this perspective, Issa Shivji concludes that,

> while we have had great use, if not reverence, for the documents called constitutions, there has been little regards for constitutional principles or

> constitutionalism. Constitutional documents have neither been an outcome of a clash of principles nor are they seen as embodying a political commitment to a global societal vision.
>
> *Shivji, 1991b: 254*

The post-colonial state, from these perspectives, is embedded in the legacies of colonialism and whether it is through the specific process of decolonization or broader processes of path dependency and legal continuity, the impact has produced a fundamental disconnect between the formal constitutional product and the nature of the state and institutions of governance that have emerged in the post-colonial period. Evaluating the literature on the post-colonial state in Africa, Crawford Young argues that the "postcolonial state was thus a hybrid creature" which took three forms. The first combines "residues of the colonial state ... [and] practices of ruling group management of power that drew on customary repertoires" (Young, 2012: 70). Second, a "neopatrimonial practice permeated the political realm" producing a "predatory extraction of public resources and severely compromising state capacity to function according to normative state precepts" (2012: 70–71). Third is a form of hybridity that "privileges the blend of democratic norms ostensibly embraced by the state and the reality of a range of authoritarian practices that limit their scope" (2012: 71). Mahmood Mamdani extends his analysis of the bifurcated nature of the colonial state to argue that the post-colonial state in Africa rests on a specific mode of rule reflected in the continued division between state and traditional authority and the interaction of a rural–urban division which is both geographic and institutional—producing a decentralized despotism in the colonial era and requiring for the project of democratization a transcendence of the "dualism of power around which the bifurcated state is organized" (Mamdani, 1996: 301).

Another perspective on the state in Africa is presented by Jean-François Bayart who concludes that the "State in Africa rests upon autochthonous foundations and a process of reappropriation of institutions of colonial origin which give it its own historicity" (Bayart, 1993: 260) and as such cannot be seen as "a purely exogenous structure" (1993: 260). Bayart's conception of the state in Africa as a "rhizome state" is seen by Pierre Englebert (1997) to be similar in approach to that taken by Mamadou Dia (1996), who describes the state in Africa as "disconnected", and William Reno (1995), whose focus on corruption leads him to describe the state in Africa as a "shadow state". Englebert acknowledges that there are differences in these approaches, but he sees a stark contrast in Bayart's minimizing of "imported statehood" and Mahmood Mamdani's placing of the colonial state at the "core of his theory" (Englebert, 1997: 773). While Bayart's notion of "reciprocal assimilation of elites" through which the various governing structures in Africa, including single-party states, military regimes and dominant party democracies all allow some space for political practices conducive to the unification of elites and the creation of dominant ruling classes, may seem to be at odds with approaches that focus on colonial legacies and path dependency, this is not necessarily the case. Instead of focusing on contrasting Bertrand Badie's conception of the imported state and Mahmood Mamdani's "bifurcated state" based on colonial legacies, with Bayart's notion of an autochthonous state, it might be more productive to trace the relationship between these legacies and what Bayart describes as the "failure to achieve an integral ...well policed State" (Bayart, 1993: 261). As Bayart acknowledges, the "postcolonial State is not dissimilar from its colonial and precolonial predecessors" and while Mamdani focuses on the "bifurcation" that produces citizens and subjects in the post-colonial era, Bayart focuses more on the overall effect, a state that "functions as a rhizome of personal networks and assures the centralization of power through agencies of family, alliance and friendship" (1993: 261). From this perspective, it is possible to acknowledge both the historical legacies that shape to form the post-colonial state and the "vibrant complexity" of the modern African state, in which each country has a specific history that is reflected in the particularities of institutional forms and politics in the twenty-first century.

While this literature on the post-colonial state produces a clear picture of the historical linkages between the colonial period and the history of independent Africa, it also enables us to understand how the joint legacies of colonialism and the process of decolonization effectively displace the design of constitution-makers in the process of decolonization. There is however another literature that views a number of alternative legacies, of the traditional rule of law in the one instance and in more recent judicial biography to argue that judicial independence and the daily operation of the law may provide a basis for building the rule of law and respect for constitutionalism in Africa. On the one hand, Jennifer Widner explores the biography of Justice Francis Nyalali of Tanzania to detail the construction of a new institutional order through struggles to "establish the separation of powers, the independence of the judiciary, and the rule of law in common law Africa" (Widner, 2001: 24). Widner's work provides a valuable perspective on the ways in which the judiciary, in at least one post-colonial state, was able to build legal institutions and respect for the formal rule of law despite the structural limitations and politics of the one-party state and legal pluralism.

If Widner's approach emphasizes the slow task of institution building and incremental constitutional change, there are a number of academics who have argued that even if law served the colonial project, its institutional practices provide the basis for constitutionalism in the post-colonial era. Both Stephen Ellmann (1992) and Jens Meierhenrich (2008) have argued that the tradition of the judiciary as well as the depth of legal tradition in the country since the arrival of settlers at the Cape in 1652 respectively provides a path-dependent legacy of legitimacy and law upon which South Africa's post-apartheid rule of law and constitutionalism may be rooted. While Ellmann has acknowledged, based on Chanock's work, that "race was at the heart of the entire enterprise of South African judging", prior to 1994 (Ellmann, 2010: 76), Meierhenrich's conception of the legacy of law in colonial South Africa and under apartheid providing a basis for a post-apartheid rule of law stands in contrast to Martin Chanock's more pessimistic argument that if

> law is seen as the means through which solutions to conflicts, which the political processes may have failed to compromise, are to be found … the idealizing language of law conceals not only the ambitions of the State, but also its incapacities, which are the major threat to a "rule of law".
>
> *Chanock, 2001: 538*

The danger of legal idealization is that it obscures the fact that law is embedded within institutions, and if these institutions are hollowed out through patronage and political dysfunction the law in all its majesty will, as Chanock states, merely float above society.

The link between the promise of the rule of law and constitutionalism is further highlighted in post-colonial Africa by the question of legal pluralism and the accommodation of traditional authority. Muna Ndulo notes that "[i]n a typical African state a large percentage of the people remain outside the formal structures of the state … within a traditional social and cultural context" (2001: 109) and calls for the incorporation of traditional authority into the new constitutional orders as a means of enhancing the legitimacy of local government. While Mahmood Mamdani warns that this recognition is a basic element of the inherited, bifurcated state, Martin Chanock recognizes that "culture is a dialogue between aspirations and sedimented traditions" and argues that it "is from this dialogue, including a dialogue with the imported individualizing discourse and centralizing ambitions of bills of rights, that we might find the basis for a rule of law, and, ultimately, a constitutional democracy" (2010: 141). In South Africa, this dialogue between a constitutionally recognized "customary law" and the post-apartheid legal order is ongoing while the evolution of "customary law" through processes of development, legislative alteration and incorporation, invalidation and harmonization is being increasingly documented and recognized (Sloth-Nielsen and Mwambene, 2010). Given the impact of colonialism and decolonization on the creation and emergence of a post-colonial state, as well as the impact of these legacies on the constitution-making processes that swept Africa after 1989, it becomes important that we explore and understand the specific legacies and latitudes that shape the prospects of constitutionalism and the rule of law in South Africa today.

The puzzle then is to explain the similarities in Africa's post-colonial constitutional experience—weak administrations, patrimonial forms of leadership and governance, coups and authoritarianism—despite repeated adoptions of formal democratic constitutions. While Martin Chanock's point that "working constitutionalist democracies are rare" and that "failure to establish democratic constitutionalist states is not a peculiarly African failure" (2010: 127) is well taken, any attempt to understand constitutionalism in Africa must begin by seeking to understand both the sources of commonality and possible sources of variation. It is in this spirit that we will focus on the legacies of colonialism and apartheid in South Africa as well as the nature of legal continuity in order to understand the present conjuncture of increased resistance and yet continued loyalty to the liberation movement.

6.3 Legal Continuity and South Africa's Democratic Transition

With the adoption of the United Nations Declaration on Apartheid (UN, 1989) in late 1989, the international community embraced the principles and process for a transition from apartheid adopted earlier that year by the Organization for African Unity and presented as the minimum conditions for international re-acceptance of South Africa into full membership of the community of nations (OAU, 1989). A core element of this scheme was the requirement that there be an interim government to oversee the transition to democracy. While the ANC would continue to argue for the establishment of an interim government through the collapse of the first round of formal negotiations at CODESA in May 1992, the apartheid regime had no intention of giving up power until there was some basic agreement on the future constitutional structure of the country. Furthermore, the government insisted that any new dispensation would have to be brought into existence by the apartheid legislature in terms of the existing 1983 Constitution. This demand was made in the name of legal continuity and the notion that there could not be a break between the existing and future legal systems.

For the National Party government, any suggestion that there should be a legal break with the apartheid past raised issues of the sovereignty of the South African state and the legitimacy of its position as a de jure government and was thus non-negotiable. As a holder of state power for over forty years (O'Meara, 1996), the National Party was determined to project its power into the future, if not to control the outcome, at least to ensure certain basic property and social interests through the insulation of private power in the post-apartheid order.[1] The ANC responded to these demands at first by proposing a Transition to Democracy Act, in terms of which the tri-cameral apartheid Parliament would pass extensive amendments to the 1983 Constitution so as to provide for an interim government that would prepare the country for elections and the creation of a democratically elected constituent assembly. However, the apartheid regime continued to reject this approach and continued to insist that any new constitution would have to be first negotiated, federal in character and adopted either by consensus or by a 75 per cent majority of participants in a multi-party forum, including among representatives of the proposed federal units of the new state. This conflict was manifested not only in the process of negotiations but most significantly in the rising wave of violence that began to consume the country after the release of Nelson Mandela in March 1990. Understanding the consequences of this violence as well as the inability of either the apartheid regime or the liberation movement to take the upper hand in this confrontation is the key to any explanation of the negotiated "miracle" that was achieved in South Africa.

As Raymond Suttner cogently argued in his response to Julius Malema's claim that Mandela sold out the revolution, the conditions during the democratic transition did not meet the expectations of those who expected "to smash the apartheid state and establish a state of 'people's power'". Instead, it was a time of random and indiscriminate violence directed at "terrorizing entire communities that were seen as the support base of the ANC" (Suttner, 2016). As Songezo Zibi wrote in response to the same claim, "you must remember that we did not defeat the apartheid regime" despite the ANC's successive electoral victories and its insinuation "that it 'defeated apartheid', a proposition that raises the natural question of why a victor would negotiate" (Zibi, 2015). Instead, we need to understand that given the international context—the collapse of the Soviet Union—as well as repression in South Africa, the ANC's victory, as Zibi argues, was "always strategic, and depended more on the effectiveness of its diplomats, propaganda and negotiators than any military threat it posed to the apartheid regime" (2015). At the same time, we must also acknowledge that the apartheid regime was also forced to the negotiating table once it realized that despite its military superiority "it could not render South Africa 'governable' in the long term" (Suttner, 2016). South Africa's democratic transition was thus initiated by the realization in both major parties that there was a stalemate in which the country would slowly degenerate, resulting in increasing political violence and economic chaos. At the same time, both parties sought to impose their own authority and vision on the process of transition. It was this contestation that produced a death toll from political violence during the 1990–1994 transition that was greater than the whole decade of the 1980s in which the internal struggle against apartheid, involving both mass resistance and armed struggle, had reached its peak.

The year following F. W. de Klerk's unilateral announcement that he would free Nelson Mandela and unban all the political parties and organizations that had been proscribed by the apartheid regime did not produce peace, nor an even political playing field. Instead, it ushered in a period of talks about talks—which mainly focused on the suspension of political trials, release of political prisoners and the return of exiles—as well as mounting violence. The intensity of this "third force" violence as well as the pattern it took coincided with each attempt by the ANC to advance its demands for either an interim government or an elected constitutional assembly. As Raymond Suttner described this period, "it was a time of death and it was not the 'enemy' or 'settlers' who were dying. There were few such deaths. It was ordinary black people, young and old, who were being killed" (1996). It was in this context that the leadership of the ANC was confronted by delegates demanding access to Umkhonto we Sizwe arms caches at its first "National Consultative Conference" in Soweto in December 1990. While Nelson Mandela publicly refuted these calls, repeatedly calling upon the regime to stop the violence, it was "[i]n the light of the extensive bloodshed" that the leadership of the ANC came to the conclusion "that a way had to be found to end the killings, while simultaneously unblocking the route to democratic rule" (Suttner, 2016).

While the collapse of the Codesa negotiations in May 1992 marked the outer limits of the National Party government's ability to assert a purely elite constitution-making process, the gunning down of ANC protestors marching outside the Ciskei Bantustan's capital of Bisho in September 1992 highlighted the limits of the ANC's strategy of mass action aimed at forcing the regime to accept an unfettered constituent assembly. While the Record of Understanding signed between the regime and the ANC following the Boipatong and Bisho massacres restarted formal negotiations, it was the assassination of communist party general secretary and senior ANC leader Chis Hani in April 1993 that finally forced the regime to accept the need to set a date for elections. The key element of the negotiated transition was the "sunset clause" proposals publicly advanced by ANC leader Joe Slovo and adopted by the ANC National Executive Committee in February 1993 (Keller, 1993: 1). While in form, these proposals represented the epitome of an elite pact, the proposals laid the groundwork for the two-stage constitution-making process that first provided the negotiated guarantees demanded by the regime and then allowed for a genuinely democratic constitutional assembly to produce a "final" constitution. The essential feature of the "sunset" proposal was the offer of a constitutionally entrenched system of executive power sharing that was to be guaranteed for five years after the first democratic election.

While initially criticized within the ANC and rejected by other parties, such as the Pan African Congress, these proposals provided the linchpin that enabled the political transition to continue. Overcoming the stalemate required concessions from both sides; however, it was the post-cold war international consensus on the parameters of democratic transitions which enabled the ANC to withstand both the National Party's and Inkatha Freedom Party's demands to avoid the establishment of a democratically elected constitution-making body. The National Party's concession of an elected constituent assembly and the ANC's acceptance of a Government of National Unity under a transitional constitution provided the key elements of the agreement in South Africa's democratic transition. By accepting a democratic constitution-making process, the National Party made it possible for the ANC to agree to the adoption of a negotiated "interim" Constitution which would entrench a Government of National Unity for five years and ensure the legal continuity the National Party government required. The architecture of this agreement, reflecting continuity and change, negotiation and participation, allowed the multi-party negotiations to resume at the World Trade Center outside Johannesburg concluding with the adoption of an "interim" Constitution by the South African Parliament in December 1993. This "interim" Constitution came into force on 27 April 1994, the eve of South Africa's first democratic elections.

6.4 Legacies of Colonialism and Apartheid

Once we understand the constraints implicit in South Africa's democratic transition, it becomes important to identify the specific legacies that emerge from this context and which characterize the terrain upon which the new South Africa is being built. Identifying and understanding these legacies is the first step towards both appreciating the latitudes within which the present legal system operates and the terrain upon which legal and political struggles for a more sustainable future are being waged. As Karl Marx argued, "men make their own history, but not of their own free will; not under circumstances they themselves have chosen but under the given and inherited circumstances with which they are directly confronted" (1973 [1852]: 146). It is in this way that path dependency becomes a way to understand the parameters of change that shape the choices and understandings of participants and institutions engaged in the reconstruction of South Africa. While South African society is burdened with multiple legacies, this section will focus on a set of conditions that have framed to first twenty years of post-apartheid governance: social inequality; the incorporation of the existing apartheid civil service; the extended non-democratic transition in local government; the recognition of traditional authorities; and the limited role of the Truth and Reconciliation Commission.

Stark economic inequality continues to be a hallmark of South Africa's social structure. While this reality may be recognized as a clear legacy of apartheid, especially as a result of the disparate impact apartheid policies had on land ownership, job opportunities and education, it is important to also understand how these different legacies have been exacerbated in the post-apartheid era. Given the military and strategic stalemate that heralded South Africa's democratic transition, the ANC recognized that a negotiated transition would preclude simply dispossessing the ancient regime and an early proposal to adopt a wealth tax similar to the post-war equalization tax in Germany was quickly abandoned when it came under intense attack. Instead, the ANC sought less direct means to address the economic legacies of apartheid. Apart from developmental plans, such as the Reconstruction and Development Plan (RDP) which aimed to redistribute resources by addressing the unequal distribution of infrastructural and social resources—including housing, health, education, pensions and other government entitlements or programs—the ANC adopted the idea of affirmative action as a means to benefit those who had been historically excluded.

Even before democratic elections were held, business recognized that it needed to quickly incorporate black leaders so as to ensure continuing links with those with political power. As a result, there was a concerted effort to recruit individuals onto the boards of corporations with deals that included loans to enable individuals to gain equity while paying off their loans through service on the boards. These opportunities were of course only extended to a few individuals who would later emerge as significant members of the new black middle class; however, the government soon recognized that it could use government authority and procurement to increase black access to the economy. On the one hand, the new Black Economic Empowerment policy included the negotiation of various sector agreements in which whole sectors of the economy agreed to ensure the integration of their workforces, to provide opportunities to black business and to integrate their ownership and management structures. On the other hand, the government sought to extend economic opportunity by weighing decision-making in government tender processes towards emerging black entrepreneurs—allocating points based on the participation of black businesses and partners in any tender process. While subject in theory to strict legal conditions, the opportunity was soon grasped by those with access to the state so that civil servants and politicians soon found themselves connected to many of these wealth-generating deals.

Apart from individuals, political parties and especially the ruling ANC used these new opportunities to fund their election and party coffers. While not illegal, the effect over time has been to produce a system of nepotism as well as ultimately corruption and political contestation based on access to these resources. In an effort to ensure greater access to government procurement by ordinary citizens, the government introduced the idea of broad-based Black Economic Empowerment; however, these changes do not seem to have had much impact on what has become a fairly entrenched system of patronage based on access to government resources. As an important study conducted for the Mapungubwe Institute for Strategic Reflection—a think tank of former ANC government officials—noted, popular distrust in state institutions which reflects the country's history of discrimination and oppression means that ordinary citizens do not trust public institutions to deliver and since "they do not have any other means or alternate sources of income … patronage politics [is left] as the primary source of livelihood or material advancement" (Ndletyana, Makhalemele and Mathekga, 2013: 18).

A key element of the agreement allowing the democratic transition to proceed was a guarantee that all civil servants would be guaranteed their positions for at least five years. The Government of National Unity did not last much beyond the adoption of the final Constitution in 1996 and never involved the degree of consensus and thus political influence that the old regime, and former President de Klerk in particular, assumed they would enjoy; however, the consequences of absorbing the old apartheid bureaucracy had an enduring and profound impact on the post-apartheid State. This impact was immediate. While the Mandela government deliberately created a new Ministry to implement the ANC's election manifesto the RDP, it soon discovered that announcing policy and even allocating funds would not ensure that the line departments in charge of implementation would actually perform their tasks. The abandonment of the RDP and the adoption of a neo-liberal macro-economic policy labelled the Growth, Employment and Redistribution (Gear) policy were the result of a number of political and economic changes; however, the inability to secure active support from the civil service is one of the important legacies of this period.

Early demands by the National Party for the protection of local community decision-making were criticized as attempts to privatize apartheid, yet the very spatial reality created by apartheid severely complicated the planning for local-level democracy—distinct from the racially constituted character of local communities. As a result, the future of local government, imagined by most as the location where the government is closest to the people, was sandwiched between the conditions created by local struggles and demands for effective governance. On the one hand, the negotiations over the future form of local government were left to those who had been at the forefront of the local struggles of the late 1980s. On the other hand, local government was tasked with resolving three of the most intractable issues facing the country: the delivery of public services, local economic development and democratic participation.

The state's attempt to impose local authorities was the trigger for the 1984 uprising, which led to continuing states of emergency and the ultimate demise of the apartheid state. Yet it was also local politics that first turned to negotiations as a means to manage and eventually resolve intractable conflict (Pieterse, 2002). Although it is true that the trade union movement, which had fought for recognition in the late 1970s, laid the basis for the later embrace of negotiations as a means of resolving South Africa's racial conflict, the local negotiations that began in response to local struggles—including rent boycotts and consumer boycotts against white business owners launched by township dwellers in towns across South Africa—served as a parallel track in the process of negotiations that led to democratic national elections in April 1994. These local negotiations and their subsequent coming together in the Local Government Negotiating Forum (LGNF) in 1993 empowered local participation in the negotiations for a democratic future. The negotiations also reflected the more restricted options available when conservative white authorities continued to exercise local state power—even if the townships had become ungovernable—as street committees and people's courts sought to establish alternative forms of governance.

The results of these negotiations were both local and constrained. The LGNF reached an early agreement on a three-phase process of transformation at its second plenary meeting on 30 June 1993, well before the national negotiators had reached an agreement on the future of the country. However, this agreement embraced consensual decision-making and explicitly delayed the establishment of truly democratic local authorities until some undetermined time in the future. First, there would be a pre-interim phase in which members of local authorities would be appointed in equal numbers from what were termed the statutory and non-statutory sectors—that is, from those who were part of old government structures and those who were in opposition, usually activists from the local civic associations that residents had established. Second, there would be an interim phase, beginning after the first national elections, in which transitional local councils would be created throughout South Africa according to the provisions of the Local Government Transition Act (LGTA). These provisions were agreed upon at the LGNF; enacted into law by the undemocratic "tricameral" Parliament; and incorporated unchanged into the 1993 interim Constitution. In addition to the LGTA, the negotiating forum produced a constitutional outline for local government that was later incorporated directly as Chapter 10 of the interim Constitution. Finally, there would be the establishment of truly democratic local government in the final phase of the transformation, the details of which were left, in mid-1993, to a future constitution-making process.

By keeping local government out of the national negotiations, the LGNF enabled local participants to engage in local bargaining and allowed them to formulate specific processes that reflected local patterns of conflict and relations of power. Yet it also constrained the pace of local transformation by requiring a greater degree of co-operation than was possible to sustain at the national level. National negotiations were propelled by dramatic events—such as the slaying of ANC and Communist Party leader Chris Hani. However, the mid-1993 agreements on local government set in place a more gradual transition, which was adopted into law and incorporated directly into Chapter 10 of the interim Constitution. The key element of this compromise was the acceptance of a form of consociationalism at the local government level, a form of governance the National Party demanded at the national level but was ultimately rejected by the ANC. This consociationalism was manifested in the agreement to adopt forms of representation and decision-making that ensured that the white minority would have a veto when it came to decisions that would affect the distribution of resources among different parts of cities and towns. The result would ensure that the formerly white areas would continue to receive superior levels of municipal services. Tied together with the national agreement that guaranteed civil servants their existing positions for five years, it meant that there would be little redistribution of local government resources and services to the historically black and underdeveloped townships in the immediate post-apartheid era.

While the ANC won the majority of elected local government seats in the 1995–1996 local government elections, the pace of transformation was slowed by the structure of municipal decision-making, which was divided between management and elected officials. In addition, the requirement of super-majorities for budget decisions forced the contending sides to negotiate all major issues. Even though the national negotiators rejected the National Party's attempt to give voting rights to corporate entities that owned property at the local level (Spitz and Chaskalson, 2000: 189–190), they acquiesced to include constitutional provisions that required the following: a two-thirds majority to pass the budget of a local government;[2] an absolute majority for the adoption of town planning decisions;[3] and, when such decisions were delegated to an executive committee, the requirement that any failure to reach consensus be decided by a two-thirds majority of the proportionally appointed executive.[4] Finally, the interim Constitution also guaranteed the distribution of local government representatives in such a way as to ensure that "irrespective of their numbers 30% of ward-representation belong to these voters [white coloured and Indian]", thus extending the legacy of the apartheid Group Areas Act despite its formal abolishment (Basson, 1995: 333).[5]

Truly democratic local governments were only established in South Africa after the local government election in 2000, which marked the end of the interim phases and the beginning of local government organized under the framework of the final 1996 Constitution. However, in tandem with the emergence of democratic local government there has been a resurgence of traditional authority in the approximately 10,000 chieftaincies across six of the nine provinces (Letsholo, 2006: 4). During the colonial and apartheid periods, traditional authorities constituted local government in areas of the country under tribal authority. However, the expansion of municipalities under the 1993 LGTA and the 1996 Constitution's requirement that democratic local government be extended to all parts of South Africa effectively displaced chiefly control over local government. Meanwhile, traditional authorities continue to "exercise a substantial influence and material patronage over communal tribal land" (2006: 4). The demarcation of municipal boundaries that, at times, cut directly "across traditional tribal land … led to accusations that traditional leaders are never consulted on issues specifically relating to the well-being of their communities" (2006: 4). While the roles of traditional leaders are explicitly recognized in Chapter 12 of the 1996 Constitution, customary law, as well as the institution, status and role of traditional leadership, is made subject to the Constitution. The Constitution does, however, explicitly provide that national legislation may provide "for a role for traditional leadership as an institution at local level"[6] and states that in order to address issues relating to traditional authorities, "customary law and the customs of communities observing a system of customary law",[7] legislation may provide for the establishment of houses of traditional leaders at both the national and provincial levels.

The transformation of local government has been profound, yet the extraordinary levels of inequality between and within municipalities (Makgetla, 2007) have produced an uneven landscape in which contestation over resources, unfulfilled expectations and governance failures are reflected in ongoing—and at times violent—service delivery and other protests. Local protests increased after the 2004 national elections, grew to a crescendo of around 6,000 in 2006 (Letsholo, 2006: 6) and have continued sporadically since then. While these forms of public resistance are clear evidence of local anger and disenchantment with ineffective delivery or unpopular government decisions—such as the redrawing of municipal and provincial boundaries—the vast majority of municipalities have been engaged in a protracted process of transformation with decidedly mixed results. Analysts have identified three underlying problems that they argue are the main causes of public anger: "ineffectiveness in service delivery, the poor responsiveness of municipalities to citizen's grievances, and the conspicuous consumption entailed by a culture of self-enrichment on the part of municipal councillors and staff" (Atkinson, 2007: 53).

In addition to the civil service, which included over 600,000 former Bantustan officials, the post-apartheid state incorporated the existing traditional authorities whose future was guaranteed in the Constitutional Principles negotiated as part of the transition and listed in Schedule 4 of the "interim" Constitution. Recognition of indigenous law as well as traditional authorities—including a constitutional provision enabling both regional and national governments to establish either houses of traditional leaders or a Council of Traditional leaders, respectively—has enhanced the status of these institutions. While the political consequences of this recognition were less partisan—in that many traditional leaders quickly shifted allegiance from the former Bantustans to the ANC if they were not already aligned with the liberation movement—the social and constitutional implications run much deeper. On the one hand, there has been a swift multiplication of the number of Kings and Queens and other traditional leaders following the constitutional recognition and government support for these institutions. On the other hand, the long overdue formal recognition of indigenous laws and institutions as being of equal status provides a significant response to the centuries of colonial interference and dictates over these areas of African culture and communal life. However, even if there is cause to celebrate the embrace of genuine legal pluralism and recognition, it must also be acknowledged that many of the existing "customary laws and institutions" have been deeply shaped by colonialism. Even in those cases where they resisted apartheid and colonial intrusion, there are still significant levels of conservatism that pose a direct challenge to the Constitution's guarantees of equality and democratic participation which all laws—including indigenous law and traditional authorities—are formally subject.

The passage of the Promotion of National Unity and Reconciliation Act 75 in 1995 and the establishment of the Truth and Reconciliation Commission projected the process of transition and the role of transitional law into the democratic era (Du Bois and Du Bois-Pedain, 2008). Although the TRC sought to achieve some level of national reconciliation through its three separate branches—the victims' hearings, amnesty process and reparations committee—the TRC's focus on the political conflicts of the past produced a process of limited amnesty, accountability and forgiveness but failed to address many of the fundamental injustices that the apartheid system produced (Mamdani, 2002: 33). The refusal to address the harms of apartheid policies—including forced removals and the migrant labour system—may have facilitated the political transition, but it has fundamentally undermined the legitimacy of the process in the eyes of many who recognize that the legacies of those policies continue to harm the future of millions of South African citizens. In this context, the recognition of socio-economic rights and the emphasis on restitution, employment equity and affirmative action as means to address these legacies gained greater political attention in the making and implementation of the final Constitution but coexisted with a growing sense of impunity fostered by the failure to take responsibility for the crime of apartheid—especially by senior officials of the former regime, including the last apartheid President F. W. de Klerk.

6.5 Conclusion

While there are many good reasons to be critical of the government and the ANC, particularly the failure to address the extraordinary inequalities created by apartheid and colonialism, it is not possible to understand these failures without taking cognizance of the legacies of both this history and the particular conditions of South Africa's democratic transition. This understanding is especially important at a time when some political leaders are finding it easier to lay the blame for present conditions on the choice to find a negotiated solution in the early 1990s rather than acknowledging the limits of that transition and seeking ways to address the continuing legacies today. The "miracle" of South Africa's transition lies in the fact that leaders from all sides recognized that they could negotiate beyond the military and political stalemate of that era. Today, it is vitally important that the promise of the Constitution, adopted as the crowning achievement of that historic moment, is fulfilled as it provides the space and opportunity for social transformation through legally mediated processes. By challenging nepotism and corruption while using the political authority contained in the Constitution, the South African government has the opportunity to challenge the present failures to address the country's many daunting legacies.

Notes

1 See, generally, Friedman (1993: 26–27).
2 Section 176(a) of the 1993 "interim" Constitution (Constitution of the Republic of South Africa, 1993).
3 Section 176(b) (Constitution of the Republic of South Africa, 1993).
4 Section 177(c) (Constitution of the Republic of South Africa, 1993).
5 See also section 245(3) (Constitution of the Republic of South Africa, 1993).
6 Section 212(1) (Constitution of the Republic of South Africa, 1996).
7 Section 212(2) (Constitution of the Republic of South Africa, 1996).

References

Atkinson, Doreen (2007), "Taking to the streets: has developmental local government failed in South Africa?" in Sakhela Buhlungu, John Daniel, Roger Southall and Jessica Lutchman (eds.), *State of the Nation: South Africa 2007*. Cape Town: HSRC Press, 53–77. Available at www.hsrcpress.ac.za/books/state-of-the-nation-south-africa-2007.

Basson, Dion (1995), *South Africa's Interim Constitution: Text and Notes*. Kenwyn: Juta [rev. ed.].

Bayart, Jean-Francois (1993), *The State in Africa: The Politics of the Belly*. London: Longman.

Chanock, Martin (2001), *The Making of South African Legal Culture 1902–1936: Fear, Favour and Prejudice*. Cambridge: Cambridge University Press.

Chanock, Martin (2010), "Constitutionalism, Democracy and Africa: Constitutionalism Upside Down", *Law in Context*, 28(2): 126–144. Available at https://search.informit.org/doi/10.3316/agispt.20124155.

Chanock, Martin (2016), "African Constitutionalism from the Bottom Up", in Heinz Klug and Sally Engle Merry (eds.), *The New Legal Realism: Studying Law Globally*. Cambridge: Cambridge University Press, 13–31. DOI: https://doi.org/10.1017/CBO9781139683432.003.

Constitution of the Republic of South Africa (1993), *Constitution of the Republic of South Africa Act 200 of 1993*. Available at www.gov.za/documents/constitution/constitution-republic-south-africa-act-200-1993.

Constitution of the Republic of South Africa (1996), *Constitution of the Republic of South Africa No. 108 of 1996*. Available at www.gov.za/sites/default/files/images/a108-96.pdf.

Dia, Mamadou (1996), *Africa's Management in the 1990s and Beyond: Reconciling Indigenous and Transplanted Institutions*. Washington, D.C.: World Bank. DOI: https://doi.org/10.1596/0-8213-3431-X.

Du Bois, Francois; Du Bois-Pedain, Antje (eds.) (2008), *Justice and Reconciliation in Post-Apartheid South Africa*. Cambridge: Cambridge University Press.

Dugard, John (1998), "The new constitution: a triumph for liberalism? A positive view", in R. W. Johnson and David Welsh (eds.), *Ironic Victory: Liberalism in Post-Liberation South Africa*. Cape Town: Oxford University Press, 23–29.

Ellmann, Stephen (1992), *In a Time of Trouble: Law and Liberty in South Africa's State of Emergency*. Oxford: Clarendon Press.

Ellmann, Stephen (2010), "A Bittersweet Heritage: Learning from The Making of South African Legal Culture", *Law in Context*, 28(2): 76–94. Available at https://search.informit.org/doi/10.3316/agispt.20124152.

Englebert, Pierre (1997), "The Contemporary African State: Neither African nor State", *Third World Quarterly*, 18(4): 767–775. DOI: https://doi.org/10.1080/01436599714759.

Fowkes, James (2016), *Building the Constitution: The Practice of Constitutional Interpretation in Post-Apartheid South Africa*. Cambridge: Cambridge University Press.

Friedman, Steven (ed.) (1993), *The Long Journey: South Africa's Quest for a Negotiated Settlement*. Johannesburg: Ravan Press.

Ghai Yash; Galli, Guido 2006), *Constitution Building Processes and Democratization*. Stockholm: International IDEA. Available at: www.idea.int/sites/default/files/publications/constitution-building-processes-and-democratization.pdf.

Keller, Bill (1993), "Mandela's Group Accepts 5 Years of Power-Sharing", *New York Times*, February 19. Available at www.nytimes.com/1993/02/19/world/mandela-s-group-accepts-5-years-of-power-sharing.html.

Klug, Heinz (2000), *Constituting Democracy: Law, Globalism and South Africa's Political Reconstruction*. Cambridge: Cambridge University Press.

Klug, Heinz (2010), *Constitution of South Africa: A Contextual Analysis*. Oxford: Hart Publishing.

Letsholo, Sydney (2006), "Democratic Local Government Elections in South Africa: A Critical Review", *EISA Occasional Paper Number 42*. Available at www.eisa.org/pdf/OP42.pdf.

Makgetla, Neva Seidman (2007), "Local government budgets and development: a tale of two towns", Sakhela Buhlungu, John Daniel, Roger Southall and Jessica Lutchman (eds.), *State of the Nation*. Cape Town: HSRC Press, 146–167. Available at www.sahistory.org.za/archive/state-nation-south-africa-2007-edited-sakhela-buhlungu-john-daniel-roger-southall-jessica.

Mamdani, Mahmood (1996), *Citizen and Subject: Contemporary Africa and the Legacy of Late Colonialism*. Princeton, NJ: Princeton University Press,

Mamdani, Mahmood (2001), *When Victims Become Killers: Colonialism, Nativism, and the Genocide in Rwanda*. Princeton, NJ: Princeton University Press.

Mamdani, Mahmood (2002), "Amnesty or Impunity? A Preliminary Critique of the Report of the Truth and Reconciliation Commission of South Africa (TRC)", *Diacritics*, 32(3–4): 32–59. JSTOR: www.jstor.org/stable/1566444.

Marx, Karl (1973), "The eighteenth brumaire of Louis Bonaparte", in David Fernbach (ed.), *Karl Marx. Surveys from Exile. Political Writings*, Vol. 2. London: Allen Lane [orig. 1852].

Meierhenrich, Jens (2008), *The Legacies of Law: Long-Run Consequences of Legal Development in South Africa, 1652–2000*. Cambridge: Cambridge University Press.

Meintjies, Marvin (2015), "Motsepe, Ramaphosa 'sold their black skin' to become rich: Malema", *Times Live*, November 26. Available at www.timeslive.co.za/politics/2015-11-26-motsepe-ramaphosa-sold-their-black-skin-tobecome-rich-malema.

Ndletyana, Mcebisi; Makhalemele, Philiana Oupa; Mathekga, Ralph (2013), *Patronage Politics Divides Us: A Study of Poverty, Patronage and Inequality in South Africa*. Johannesburg: Mapungubwe Institute for Strategic Reflection (MISTRA). DOI: doi.org/10.2307/j.ctv13qfwfh.

Ndulo, Muna (2001), "Constitution-making in Africa: Assessing Both the Process and the Content", *Public Administration and Development*, 21(2): 101–117. Available at https://scholarship.law.cornell.edu/facpub/57.

Nolutshungu, Sam (1991), "The constitutional question in South Africa", in Issa Shivji (ed.), *State and Constitutionalism: An African Debate on Democracy*. Harare: SAPES Trust, 91–100.

OAU—Organization for African Unity (1989), *Declaration of the OAU AD-HOC Committee on Southern Africa on the Question of South Africa*. Harare: OAU. Available at https://archives.au.int/handle/123456789/6823.

Okoth-Ogendo, H. W. O. (1991), "Constitutions without constitutionalism: reflections on an African political paradox", in Issa Shivji (ed.), *State and Constitutionalism: An African Debate on Democracy*. Harare: SAPES Trust, 3–25.

O'Meara, Dan (1996), *Forty Lost Years: The Apartheid State and the Politics of the National Party, 1948–1994*. Johannesburg: Ravan Press.

Pieterse, Edgar (2002), "From Divided to Integrated City? Critical Overview of the Emerging Metropolitan Governance System in Cape Town", *Urban Forum*, 13(1): 3–37. DOI: https://doi.org/10.1007/s12132-002-0001-6.

Reno, William (1995), *Corruption and State Politics in Sierra Leone*. Cambridge: Cambridge University Press.

Shivji, Issa (1991a), "State and constitutionalism: a new democratic perspective", in Issa Shivji (ed.), *State and Constitutionalism: An African Debate on Democracy*. Harare: SAPES Trust, 27–54.

Shivji, Issa (1991b), "Contradictory class perspectives in the debate on democracy", in Issa Shivji (ed.), *State and Constitutionalism: An African Debate on Democracy*. Harare: SAPES Trust, 253–260.

Sloth-Nielsen, Julia; Mwambene, Lea (2010), "Talking the Talk and Walking the Walk: How Can the Development of African Customary Law Be Understood?" *Law in Context*, 28(2): 27–46. Available at https://search.informit.org/doi/10.3316/ielapa.753115674053276.

Spitz, Richard; Chaskalson, Matthew (2000), *The Politics of Transition: A Hidden History of South Africa's Negotiated Settlement*. London: Hart Publishing.

Suttner, Raymond (2016), "Did Mandela 'Sell Out' the Struggle for Freedom?" *Polity*, March 8. Available at http://m.polity.org.za/article/did-mandela-sell-out-the-struggle-for-freedom-2016-03-08.

Thornhill, Chris (2011), *A Sociology of Constitutions: Constitutions and State Legitimacy in Historical-Sociological Perspective*. Cambridge: Cambridge University Press. DOI: https://doi.org/10.1017/CBO9780511895067.

UN—United Nations (1989), "Declaration on Apartheid and Its Destructive Consequences in Southern Africa", *UN General Assembly A/RES/S-16/1*, 14 December 1989. Available at https://digitallibrary.un.org/record/84666.

Van Marle, Karin; Le Roux, Wessel (2007), "Introduction", in Karin van Marle and Wessel le Roux (eds.), *Post-Apartheid Fragments: Law, Politics and Critique*. Pretoria: University of South Africa Press.

Widner, Jennifer (2001), *Building the Rule of Law: Francis Nyalali and the Road to Judicial Independence in Africa*. London: W.W. Norton.

World Bank (1989), *Sub-Saharan Africa: From Crisis to Sustainability*. Washington, D.C.: World Bank Group. Available at https://documents.worldbank.org/en/publication/documents-reports/documentdetail/498241468742846138/from-crisis-to-sustainable-growth-sub-saharan-africa-a-long-term-perspective-study.

Young, Crawford (1994), *The African Colonial States in Comparative Perspective*. New Haven, CT: Yale University Press.

Young, Crawford (2012), *The Postcolonial State in Africa: Fifty Years of Independence, 1960–2010*. Madison, WI: University of Wisconsin Press.

Zibi, Songezo (2015), "Unembargoed: Claim Mandela Sold Out Is Easy but Ahistorical", *BDlive*, December 7. Available at https://historymatters.co.za/content/unembargoed-claim-mandela-sold-out-easy-ahistorical-songezo-zibi-bdlive-07-december-2015.

7

SHARED EXPERIENCES FROM SOUTH AFRICA CONSTITUTIONAL COURT[1]

Albie Sachs

7.1 Introduction

It is strange how sometimes music suddenly comes from nowhere into your head. When I was being driven to Coimbra from the airport at Oporto, the words from a Portuguese revolutionary song popped into my consciousness: *Não há machado que corte a raiz ao pensamento* [No hatchet will ever chop off the root of thought].[2] I have not remembered these melodies for maybe forty years, but I was now going to meet Boaventura and intellectual, political and musical emotions surged within me. Boa and I met at the time of this song, at the time of *Grândola*,[3] the time of the revolution in Portugal, the Carnation Revolution (1974), which had so much impact not only on our spirit of hope in South Africa but even on certain aspects of our constitutional development. I am thinking about where he is today and where I am today and a phrase comes to my mind: the epistemology of critical hope. Our paths in some way have diverged. Boaventura is still there, he is still critical, he is still hopeful, and he is still reaching out to people on all continents who are critical and hopeful. And I, who was a critical law professor then, have in the meantime become the great legitimiser of law in my society, in the mainstream of the mainstream, even directing the course of the mainstream, a Constitutional Court judge defending our new constitutional order. Is anything left in me and my experience of the critical vision we shared at the time of "Grândola"?

7.2 Transformative Constitutional Jurisprudence and the Enforcement of Economic and Social Rights

Thinking back on my fifteen years on the Constitutional Court of South Africa, I remember one moment with great specificity. It was a moment of crisis for

DOI: 10.4324/9781003391920-10

me when I wondered: can I continue to be a judge? The case, which we refer to as *The Port Elizabeth Municipality Case*,[4] dealt with an eviction order against about thirty poor black African families living in simple shelters they had constructed on vacant land next to a wealthy and overwhelming white suburb. And the owners of the land living in their beautiful homes in this up-market suburb went to the Port Elizabeth Council, which happened to be a council of overwhelmingly black people democratically elected by the overwhelmingly black population of the city, and said, "This is our land, please exercise your municipal responsibilities and get them out". And the city went to the High Court, and the High Court gave an order of eviction. The order was taken to the Supreme Court of Appeal which overturned it but on technical grounds that seemed to be rather tenuous. The Council then asked the Constitutional Court to restore the eviction order. And to my consternation, the Chief Justice says: "Albie will you write the first judgment [the lead judgment for our Court] in this matter?"

And I'm thinking to myself "Oh no, why me?" We have a Constitution, we live under the rule of law, people can't just come and put up their shacks on somebody else's land and defy the rights of the owners to vacant possession. We don't want our hard-won non-racial democracy to be associated with chaos, where people just help themselves and the laws passed by the black majority in Parliament are simply ignored. I as a judge have sworn an oath to uphold the law without fear, favour or prejudice.

But beyond being a judge, I'm also Albie, whose consciousness was forged in the freedom struggle. I was amongst the people who had denounced the injustices of Apartheid. We had pointed out that 87% of the surface area of our country had by law been expressly reserved for whites only, including all the beautiful and well-developed areas; that black people could only come to the towns if they had passes permitting them to work and live there; and that black people had by law been rendered landless and homeless, compelled to be destitute migrant workers in the land of their birth. How could I, Albie, who had fought for the new constitutional dispensation offering hope to the majority for the first time, be the author of a decision in the name of justice, in the name of our new Constitution, that told the families that they have to leave? The land would remain vacant while the white owners continued to live in comfort nearby.

The situation was serious. If I can't carry out my obligation under the Constitution to uphold the law without fear, favour or prejudice, then, I must resign as a judge. I loved the work on the Court. It was honourable or it was nothing. I remained an idealist, coining the phrase: while always sceptical of law's pretensions, I would never become cynical about law's potential. Our lives and dreams had gone into the Constitution. When taking my oath of office, I had deliberately done so by raising the arm that had been shortened by an apartheid bomb, in memory of those who had died for our freedom. I could not violate my oath. But neither could I order the eviction of these families.

Years later I was to have a debate with my colleagues about the extent to which intuition guides a judge's hard legal reasoning. Writing as a participant observer rather than as a pure theorist, I had argued for acknowledging the role that intuitive responses play in shaping the landscape of values within which judges go on to do the reasoning. These intuitions are highly tutored, having been shaped by years of engagement with people, concepts and words in the pursuit of justice. And happily for me, at least, I was able to convert what seemed to be a purely personal clash between my intuition for justice, on the one hand, and my oath to uphold the law, on the other, into an objective constitutional tension. The issue was no longer one of constitutional conscience but of constitutional consciousness. Hooray, I would not have to resign!

At a formal level, the competing principles were contained in two neighbouring sections of the Constitution. While Section 25, the Property Clause in the Bill of Rights, did not expressly protect the right to private property, it did stipulate that no one shall be arbitrarily deprived of their property. Accordingly, if the state allowed private individuals to come and camp on your land and did nothing about it, that could be seen as a form of permitting arbitrary deprivation of your property. Section 26, the Housing Rights Clause, on the other hand, declared that everyone has the right to adequate housing and provided further that no one should be removed from their home without a Court order that takes account of all relevant circumstances.

These last words—"all relevant circumstances"—are not very helpful. What do they mean? Some degree of specificity was given in one of the first statutes to be adopted under the new Constitution, the Prevention of Illegal Eviction and Unlawful Occupation of Land Act.[5] Under Apartheid, the state had used the criminal law to lock up black people who had had the effrontery to occupy land without the permission of the owners. Private law and public law worked hand in hand to maintain racial exclusiveness. The bulldozer, the baton and the prison van became the symbols of apartheid justice. Now the law was being turned on its head or, rather, put back on its feet. The new Act forbade the use of criminal law to advance private property interests and created protections against arbitrary eviction from one's home.

A key provision of the Act stated that an eviction order could only be made if it was "just and equitable" to do so. Yet once more, the words were not very helpful. What is just and equitable to the owners of the property is to get the people out. Yet what is just and equitable to the occupiers is to ensure they have a home where they can rest their heads. We had to find a way of making the law and the Constitution respond meaningfully to these competing interests. It soon became clear that simply applying the traditional principles of land law based on protecting title and the rights of the owner couldn't provide a constitutionally satisfactory answer. Equally unsatisfactory would be simply to ignore the rights of the landowner altogether. Only a contextual transformative vision of our Constitution, including a transformative vision of property and the meaning of property in our country, would enable us to get a result that would take account of all circumstances and be just and equitable.

Before proceeding with the story of the case, I need to say something about the importance of constitutionalism in our new democracy. The narrative goes back to February 1995. We were in a room smaller than the platform in this hall, with a very low ceiling, jam-packed with dignitaries who were unusually excited. Nelson Mandela takes the microphone:

> The last time I appeared in court was to hear whether or not I was going to be sentenced to death. Fortunately for myself and my colleagues we were not. Today I rise not as an accused but, on behalf of the people of South Africa, to inaugurate a court South Africa has never had, a court on which hinges the future of our democracy.

We were the eleven judges being sworn in to defend the Constitution and the law. We were thrilled, and it was especially meaningful that it was Nelson Mandela who was presiding over that occasion. How does a new young Court with a new mission express its members' appreciation for Nelson Mandela? Twenty-six years in jail, some of us had worked with him in the underground or defended him when on trial for his life, we had all been appointed by him and all admired him enormously. Well, six months later we struck down two important measures adopted by him as President at the request of our first democratically elected Parliament. Now, that is gratitude for you! With a single blow, one arm of government, the Court, invalidated both the Proclamations of the President and the Act of Parliament that had authorised him to adopt them. To compound the matter even further, the Proclamations were manifestly democratic in their substance, dealing with the structures and rules necessary for the holding of South Africa's first democratic local government elections. Yet, in our view, an exceptionally meaningful constitutional principle left us with no alternative. Because of a shortage of parliamentary time, Parliament had asked the President to use his presidential powers to speedily create the necessary legal framework for the holding of the elections. By a large majority, our Court decided that the Constitution entrusted primary legislative authority to Parliament and to Parliament alone. In this case, Parliament had abdicated its responsibility by entrusting basic law-making authority to the President. Pressure of time and the manifestly democratic objectives could not justify this abdication of responsibility. In my judgement, if I remember correctly, I referred to the tragic consequences for Germany and the world of the Reichstag giving Hitler supreme powers to bypass Parliament and issue decrees in his own name.

How did Nelson Mandela respond? Not only had the decision been trumpeted as a victory for the opposition to the African National Congress (ANC), but the Members of Parliament had to be flown in from all over the country to attend an emergency session to ensure the elections could go ahead as planned. Mandela went on television very quickly to give his answer. He said:

> When I adopted these measures, I acted on legal advice and I accept that that legal advice was wrong, and I, as President, must be the first person to show respect for the Constitution, as interpreted by the Constitutional Court.[6]

For me, that was a magnificent day. I am sure that many people in this room have seen pictures of the marvellous day twenty years ago when we first voted together as equals in South Africa, black and white—our day of democracy, 27th April. But to me, no less important was the day on which President Mandela accepted that he was bound by the Constitution and graciously accepted the rulings of the Constitutional Court. That was the day we firmly proclaimed ourselves not just as a democracy but as a constitutional democracy. From then on, once Mandela had accepted the supremacy of the Constitution as interpreted by the Constitutional Court, no one in government, high or low, would feel personally offended if a ruling went against them.

I tell this story to show how profound and important the Constitution and constitutionalism became in our country. This was not just another document. It was the document that constituted us as a nation. The process of getting it, the institutions created by it and the values it espoused completely redefined the nature of the country. It was a peace pact, an act of internal decolonisation and a basic law wrapped up in one. At a time when the world felt it would be impossible for black and white to live together as equals in one country, it was through constitutionalism that we found the way forward. Central to the project that enabled black and white to live together under democratic rule, with a democratically elected Parliament based on majority rule—one person one vote—was to have a strongly entrenched Bill of Rights. This protected the rights of everybody—not as whites, not as blacks, but as human beings.

The word "apartheid" meant separateness. The whole apartheid ideology was based on notions of separate sovereignties. Fragmentation had been used to maintain racial domination by the white minority. When I was a child, oppressors talk was about the need to uphold white western Christian civilisation. Then, in responding to the world condemnation of apartheid, the key term used was pluralism. The argument had been that black and white, with their different histories, cultures and languages, could not live together as equals in a united country, so whites would live in their separate domain enjoying the democratic forms of government appropriate to their culture and black people would continue to live under the control of their traditional authorities in their own separate areas. To each their own. In the eyes of the great majority in South Africa, connecting political rights with ethnic identity was designed to frustrate true self-determination and maintain a white supremacist policy of divide and rule. In this context, unity was not seen as the enemy of diversity, but rather as its guarantor. The motto of the new constitutional order in fact became unity in diversity. The right to be the same became the foundation for the right to be different. Equality meant accepting people as they were across differences, not the suppression of differences or the division of the country into separate zones of authority.

The terrain of how minority rights should be protected in fact became the central battleground in our constitutional negotiations. The paradox in South Africa was that the minority had behaved as a majority and treated the majority in a way that minorities were treated in other countries. Leaders of the white government argued insistently in favour of protecting minority rights, and referred to them as group rights. They relied extensively on the writings of Lijphart on consociational democracy. They argued that in deeply divided societies, democracy was best served by states being structured on notions of separate sovereignties or else of power-sharing between segmented communities, each having exclusive control over its own special interests. Yet, balkanising South Africa would have been disastrous. Racial divisions would have been entrenched. Freedom of association would have been used to permit the creation of constitutionally protected racially based communes. Apartheid would have been privatised. Government would have been dysfunctional; the marginalisation of the majority would have been consolidated; and the huge disparities in wealth would have been entrenched. The clash of visions led to a serious breakdown in the negotiations. Events outside the negotiating chambers had a huge influence on the process. There were massacres by secret "third force" groups followed by rolling mass action in response. In the end, huge and well-controlled demonstrations throughout the country in favour of peace and non-racial democracy, coupled with a two-stage process of constitution-making, got the negotiations back on track. The concept of a united South Africa with a common voters' roll and equal rights for all protected by an entrenched Bill of Rights triumphed. The Constitution, as finally adopted by the democratically elected Parliament with a 90% majority, did not protect the community interests of whites as such. On the contrary, it protected the rights of all people to associate in terms of language, culture and religion. It also provided safeguards against people being abused, discriminated against and driven from their homes simply on the grounds of their origin, ethnicity, appearance or political allegiance.

This approach had significant consequences for the nature of the debate that continues to this day in our country concerning unity and diversity. To say that we have a united South Africa based on principles of equal citizenship and to emphasise that non-discrimination runs right through the nature of our society and institutions are not to presuppose that we must all be the same. Our Constitution acknowledges that the right to be the same does not exclude the right to be different and, as will be seen, the issue of harmonising the principle of equality with the principle of diversity in fact became central to the Court's decisions in a number of matters.

The new Constitution ended up with a system of wall-to-wall democracy in South Africa. At a political level, there were no enclaves that could function in a manner that would be immune to the broad democratic sweep of the Constitution. Sovereignty was divided to the extent that certain exclusive powers were given to local and regional governments operating in their respective spheres. But the whole of South Africa was to be governed by democratically accountable officials.

The status, institution and role of traditional leaders were recognised by the new Constitution, and customary law was recognised as an original source of law. This meant that customary law would now function in the same way that Roman Dutch common law and aspects of the English common law had long done as primary sources of law in South Africa. It must be stressed that customary law was quite different from the way in which custom had been used in the English common law system, namely, referring to the customs of merchants and others to fill in gaps. Indigenous customary law dealt with the way in which indigenous communities organised their affairs, constituted their families, dealt with issues of land, succession and so on. However, the Constitution made it clear that indigenous customary law would be subject to the Bill of Rights so the compatibility of patriarchy—which was central to the way customary law had been enunciated until then—with equality, a core element of the Bill of Rights, became an issue in a number of matters which reached the Constitutional Court.

Before dealing with these cases, I would like to return now to *The Port Elizabeth Municipality Case*. I have mentioned earlier how my existential crisis was converted into a constitutional dilemma. Resolving that constitutional dilemma was in fact to have a considerable impact on the manner in which the Court understood its role in an evolving democratic society characterised by great disparities largely associated with origin. The technical question was to decide what was just and equitable in the circumstances. We held that there are some cases where you could not say there was a right answer. This was one of them. Not all legal questions have the right answer. I got that notion from the German Constitutional Court. A dissenting position in the Second Senate in the abortion case said there is no right answer to certain deep fundamental human situations of competing claims.[7] You give the best answer you can, the most principled one, that is, the one that is most compatible with the goals of the Constitution and the society envisaged by that Constitution. In *The Port Elizabeth Municipality Case*, the answer could not be simply looking at land law and without more enforcing the traditional property rights of the owner. Nor, on the other hand, could it be found by simply upholding the right of access to housing of the occupants and ignoring the property rights of the owner. The best possible outcome would be obtained by reconciling these two clashing principles as harmoniously as possible.

Furthermore, it was necessary to put human dignity rather than human freedom at the centre of the debate. If freedom is correlated with and subsumed into the rights to own property and to do what you like with it, then the answer would have been, as in the old days, to get them out. But human dignity meant we had to acknowledge the dignity of people who had nowhere to lay their heads, nowhere to put up their homes. A home wasn't just a shelter, protection from the elements. Home is the place where you're with your family, where you express your most intimate thoughts and develop your most personal relationships with others. Your home is a little shared space of protection from an invasive and frequently hostile world. That is where you sleep, where you dream, where you make love, where you study, where you write, where you read, where you are together with people who are close to you. What was being claimed by these homeless families, as I said then, wasn't just protection from the wind and rain, it was to have a home as a place of permanence and intimacy in a country where the law had converted the great majority into eternal wanderers.

These occupants were descendants of generations of homeless South Africans, ever since the conquest, ever since the dispossession, ever since the state was used to drive people from the land, to convert millions of people into migrant workers, to deprive them of ordinary family relationships. Justice and equity required taking account of that. But the judgement went on further to say that it was not just the dignity of the occupants that was being assaulted by the fact that they had nowhere to live. It was an affront to the dignity of all South Africans that in a country with the richness that our country had, any human being should be living like that.

This made it necessary to bring into our legal discourse the principle of Ubuntu. Ubuntu is a deep African philosophical principle based on the idea that "I am a human being, because you are a human being". I can't separate my humanity from an acknowledgement of your humanity. I enrich my autonomy, I enrich my independence by recognising the autonomy and independence of my fellow human beings, and we strengthen each other through our interdependence. We found the conceptual seam of Ubuntu to be deeply enriching for our jurisprudence. It underlined the interconnectedness of all our people and the deep error of isolating particular legal questions from the context in which they cropped up and had to be resolved.

It was impossible, then, to come up with a purely technical legal answer, using pure legal logic, as to which of the two colliding rights should prevail. The best response in the circumstances required showing an appropriate degree of respect to each of the competing notions. Yet the requisite give-and-take could not be found simply by syllogistic juggling in the judicial mind. The parties themselves had to be brought directly into the equation. They were literally on the ground, able to contribute practical proposals to help manage the tricky balancing required. In methodological terms, it implied achieving a response not through formal classification but through empathetic mediation. Justice and equity required a process that was inclusive as well as a result that was fair. In the matter before the Court, the use of mediation would have introduced a needed dialogical and procedural dimension into the search for a balanced outcome. The element of citizenship became vital. The occupiers would have had a meaningful voice at a crucial time, and the city officials would have been required to fulfil their responsibilities with appropriate regard for the interests not just of wealthy ratepayers but of all the inhabitants of the city.

The Court decided, then, that the original eviction order should not have been issued because it would not have been just and equitable to order the removal if the parties had not been given a meaningful opportunity to engage with each other through mediation. The Court emphasised that it saw its role as being not simply to decide on technicalities that had the law on their side in a particular matter, but to manage a socially stressful situation in a manner that took the best account of the constitutional principles involved.

In a subsequent case, my colleague Zac Yacoob said to me: "Albie, mediation is too technical and precise; the theme of meaningful engagement is the one that we have got to use". The case where he had been asked to write the lead opinion was one where poor people were packed into a derelict building in the centre of Johannesburg. The water had been cut off, the electricity stopped, the rubbish hadn't been collected and an eviction order was eventually sought against them because the building was said to constitute a dangerous fire trap and health hazard. The Court's answer was that it had become a health hazard because the Council had cut off the water and was refusing to collect the rubbish. The occupiers were human beings who had a right to a home somewhere. If, for the sake of development, they had to leave that building, then the Council that sought to remove them had a responsibility to them at least as powerful as it had to protecting the interests of the developers. We did not want stinking buildings that were fire traps and unhealthy in the centre of our city. At a more generalised level, we did not want black majority rule in our country to be associated with blight in derelict cities that were without beauty, without dignity and without appropriate urban style. But why should the poor carry the burden of development? Why should social sustainability be equated with bureaucratically enhanced richness for some, and intensified indigence for others? Meaningful engagement[8] has in fact become an important element in the way we enforce social and economic rights. In cases of this kind, the local authorities and the people facing eviction have to engage in a meaningful way and report back to the Court by a certain date. The Court will indicate issues that should receive particular attention, a central one always being the availability of alternative accommodation in areas reasonably close to the places of work of the family breadwinners. The Court has insisted that the poor should not be looked at as an anonymous mass to be shifted around this way or that or thrown onto the streets and left to their own devices. Each individual and each family was particular. Some of the occupiers had been living in the building for twenty years, others had only arrived weeks before. Each person had rights under the Constitution. At the same time, the poor show extreme creativity in developing means of survival in what would seem to be impossible circumstances, and the Court requires that they display the same proactive spirit in contributing to just solutions to the potential eviction situations.

We have found that the notion of meaningful engagement, which involves a combination of both substantive and procedural elements, encourages a form of dialogue that strongly promotes active citizenship. The function of the Court becomes the broader one of promoting principled interaction between the litigating parties in a manner that best furthers the achievement of the rights set out in the Constitution. As another of my colleagues on the Court, Sandile Ngcobo often said: "In a constitutional democracy the hands of justice are never tied". By this, he meant that if the application of formal rules in the traditional way leads to unjust outcomes that are manifestly in conflict with the letter and spirit of the Constitution, then the traditional forms of reasoning need to be reconfigured.

The Courts cannot say that the result of the order which we are giving is clearly unjust, but unfortunately that's the law, someone else must deal with it, and our hands are tied. The Court is obliged to rethink the "givens" of the standard legal discourse so as to bring them into line with constitutional requirements. The Constitution, then, cannot be seen simply as a repository of tried and tested norms that serve as a benchmark of the constitutionality of state action. It is an active font of norms and standards that flow into every area of our law, including the common law and customary law. It also serves as a key instrument for determining how statutes have to be interpreted. In addition, it establishes a springboard for the taking of proactive measures by the public authorities to enable people to achieve in their daily life the rights it guarantees. Its foundational premise is not that we are living in a good society that must be protected from undue interference from the government. On the contrary, its point of departure is that we are living in a profoundly unjust society that requires deep and meaningful transformation to be initiated by democratically chosen institutions. At the same time, the processes of change must themselves comply with constitutional standards so that one form of arbitrariness and injustice is not replaced with another. It follows, then, that the Constitution has played a central role in determining the way that issues concerned with interculturality are dealt with.

7.3 Constitutional Court and Interculturality

The term interculturality is not found in our legal discourse, but the issues raised under the rubric of interculturality are certainly well-known to us. I will deal with two areas in which the Court dealt with themes of diversity in an unequal society. The first concerned the development of a transformative and accommodatory approach to equality. The second related to applying a transformative vision to the application of customary law. In both areas, the ubiquity of the foundational principles of non-racism and non-sexism, coupled with the egalitarian nature of the Bill of Rights, proved to be decisive and the idea of seeking justice either through forced assimilation or through enforced structural separation was rejected.

7.3.1 Equality in the Difference

One of the last cases of my term on the Court dealt (as my colleague Pius Langa, the Chief Justice, neatly observed) with a tiny object that had huge ramifications: a little nose stud. Sunali Pillay, a girl of Tamil origin, wanted to wear a tiny jewel when attending Durban Girls High School to mark her Tamil identity. Her mother gave her forceful support.[9] The school had a policy on dress that forbade the wearing of jewellery of any kind. The motive was said to be to prevent the rich girls from flaunting their flashy jewellery. In any event, a rule was a rule, and the Headmistress ordered Sunali to obey the general prohibition in the same way as the other girls did: no nose stud on the school premises, if you don't mind. The Pillays did mind. They took the matter through various legal structures and eventually the case came on appeal to the Constitutional Court.

No one in the Constitutional Court argued for the application of the principle *de minimis non curat lex* [the law is not concerned with trifles]. Everyone accepted that the law should indeed care about this miniscule object. The question was how to do so. The unanimous answer of the Court was that the approach of the school had been wrong. What was needed in cases like this was not the application of a uniform rule that suppressed difference, but rather the implementation of a policy of reasonable accommodation that accommodated cultural/religious diversity in a principle and manageable way. The fact that Sunali could wear that little jewel while the other girls could not wear jewellery of any kind didn't mean that there would be unfair discrimination against the other girls. Sunali was expressing an important part of her identity, an identity that had been denied to members of her community through generations of racial and religious marginalisation in South Africa. She was affirming a right through a detail of her appearance to identify herself with a well-established cultural and religious community. If there was a lack of understanding on the part of the other girls (and many of their teachers) of why it was that she could wear a jewel and they could not, this created a great educational opportunity for the school to have serious discussion about the meaning of equal citizenship in a multi-cultural, multi-faith society.

At the technical level, the Chief Justice said it was not central to the case to decide whether the wearing of the nose stud was a cultural or a religious practice, though the evidence suggested it was a mixture of both. Similarly, it was not vital to determine whether the wearing of the nose stud was obligatory or voluntary. What mattered was that it had a deep intrinsic meaning to Sunali as a symbol of her identity. Respect for diversity was constitutive rather than destructive of national unity.

In fact, the notion of unity in diversity as highlighted in the Preamble to the Constitution implied that equality did not require treating everybody in identical fashion. Rather, it meant treating everybody with equal concern and respect. This in turn necessitated acknowledgement of two key ingredients of our equality law. The first was to locate the search for equality not in formal propositions about treating like persons alike, but to look through historical, social and experiential lenses at the manner in which the measures concerned either affirmed or else undermined the dignity of the people affected. The second was to acknowledge that the right to be the same in terms of civil, political and socio-economic rights was not at all in conflict with the right to be different in terms of belief, culture, sexual orientation and self-identification. On the contrary, the right to be the same and the right to be different were joined symbiotically at the hip. Each needed and complemented the other. Equality was not to be achieved through the suppression of difference but rather through the furnishing of equal treatment across difference.

7.3.2 Customary Law

I now turn to the manner in which the Court dealt with customary law (often referred to as indigenous law) as an original source of law. The issue became important in a matter dealing with the restitution claims of the nomadic Richtersveld community that had been pushed off a semi-desert piece of land to make way for whites when diamonds had been discovered there. The new Constitution provided for restitution if they could show that they had been deprived of property rights because of their race. The area had been so dry and dusty that the British colonial authorities hadn't bothered to survey it or put up fences and grant title to anybody. The state argued that it was therefore *res nullius*, land belonging to nobody. The Court rejected this argument, accepting rather that the community that had lived there could claim the aboriginal title. The fact that they moved their grazing to wherever there might have been a few plants growing from time to time didn't mean they didn't, as a community, have rights to the land.[10]

The *Bhe* case raised a completely different issue. It revolved around the tension between the way in which customary law had been presented in the textbooks as being inherently patriarchal in character and the requirements of gender equality in the Bill of Rights. The particular issue in this case was the constitutionality of the principle of primogeniture. An African woman lived in a poor area with the father of her two daughters in a house worth the equivalent of about $500. When the man died, a cousin of the deceased came along and said: "In terms of our traditional customary law, the oldest male surviving descendant inherits the propriety. I happen to be that person and I'm going to sell the house to pay for the funeral expenses". And he sought to have them evicted. This was a shocking case. The idea that somehow in our new democratic South Africa customary law can be used in a way that's going to render the mother and the two children homeless couldn't be right.[11] Yet until then, the general attitude of South African courts had been that because our Constitution both recognised customary law as an independent source of law and allowed people freedom to develop their own cultures, it followed that central tenets of customary law such as patriarchy and primogeniture should be regarded as constitutionally protected. The Constitutional Court rejected this approach. To begin with, we said, customary law is living law. It is organic. It develops; it grows to take account of changing circumstances and evolving values. The textbook rules have become ossified. The vitality of customary law comes from its congruence with the lives of the people who live under it. The idea that customary law now means that a boy child can inherit and a girl child can't violates profound notions of our new constitutional order. In that specific sense, and to that extent, we declared that customary law was unconstitutional and in need of development. We left it to Parliament to decide precisely how the estates of deceased persons from the African community should be dealt with in the case of persons who regulated their lives according to customary law. In the meanwhile, the general principles of intestate succession should apply and the two daughters recognised as the heirs. The point was that where rules said to be part of customary law discriminated on grounds of gender and were clearly in conflict with the foundational principle of non-sexism, they could not be enforced by a court of law. They had to be struck down as unconstitutional and replaced with rules that were developed in a way that was consistent with the Constitution.

It was not only African customary law that had to be developed in keeping with the Constitution, but the common law as well. Thus, in the *Sodomy* case, the Court declared that the common law offence of sodomy, inherited from the Netherlands as part of the common law, was unconstitutional and had to be expunged from the criminal law. This was because it denied people their rights to dignity, equality and privacy; it was oppressive to a section of our society.[12] Similarly, in the case of *Fourie*, we declared that the common law definition of marriage as being between one man and one woman was unconstitutional because it was under-inclusive. It denied same-sex couples the same right to publicly express their love and intimacy and accept marital responsibilities as heterosexual couples could do.[13]

Thus, in the same way that we developed the common law to make it compatible with the Constitution, we upheld the need for customary law to be developed in keeping with the Constitution. The people themselves were adapting customary law notions to keep pace with the changing nature of their lives. The rules of patriarchy might have been meaningful in traditional African society at a time when people lived, produced and consumed on one piece of land, making it convenient in patrilineal societies at least for the male head of the family to represent the household in dealings with outsiders. Now people work in factories, schools and hospitals far from home. Production is separate from the home, property itself is different, people have bank accounts, use credit cards and ATMs and buy goods on credit. In practice, a huge number of households are headed by women. If customary law was to be meaningful in these circumstances, it had to evolve, otherwise it would ossify and die.

This was the issue in the case of *Shilubana*, where the Constitutional Court had to decide whether it was permissible for an African community to choose a woman to be their traditional leader. The Hosi (traditional leader) of the Baloyi community was very ill and the rest of the Royal Family met with him to discuss who should succeed him when he passed. Their decision was that the next Hosi should be his cousin, Ms Shilubana, whose lineage would have entitled her to succeed to the position that he now held had it not been accepted in apartheid South Africa that only men could occupy the position. He was a party to her being chosen. The decision of the Royal Family was later supported by a general meeting of the community. Shortly before he died, however, he changed his mind and said that his son should in fact take over. On his death, however, the national government said it was recognising Ms Shilubana as the Hosi. The son objected and took the matter to court. In the High Court and the Supreme Court of Appeal, the judges upheld the son's contention that under customary law traditional leaders were born and could not be elected. Furthermore, if I remember correctly, the judges declared that according to customary law only men could succeed. Ms Shilubana, who happened to be a Member of Parliament, appealed to the Constitutional Court. Two busloads of rural women travelled through the darkness to attend the hearing, one filling the public seating until the tea break, the other taking over in the session that followed. This was a case where the people themselves wanted a woman to be their leader; that was their choice.[14] It was moving for us. At the end of the day's rather technical debates, Chief Justice Pius Langa got his law clerk, who spoke the language of that particular community, to thank them for listening so patiently to proceedings in a language that wasn't their first language. He didn't say we would give judgement in their favour. He just thanked them for being there.

The judgement in fact turned out to be in their favour, and Ms Shilubana to this day is the king or, rather, the queen of the Baloyi people. The Court underlined the fact that customary law was living law. The community overwhelmingly regarded her as their true traditional leader. The government was not using the Constitution as a battering ram to compel the community to accept a woman as their traditional leader in order to uphold the principle of gender equality. On the contrary, the government was acknowledging that gender equality was being voluntarily incorporated by the rural community themselves into their way of constituting their traditional leadership. It had in fact been University-trained judges functioning in the national courts who, citing rigid formulations made by colonial magistrates a century before in league with elderly male traditionalists, had imposed ossified patriarchal rules in defiance of what the local community had sought for themselves. The rural community was evolving and demanding change and participating actively in the processes of transformation. The Constitutional Court was not going to halt the evolution of customary law. On the contrary, it sought to affirm the manner in which the members of the community, both men and women, had embodied constitutional values in their thinking.

At the beginning of this presentation, I mentioned that Portuguese constitutional development had entered into and made a positive contribution towards the jurisprudence of the South African Constitutional Court. The context was a debate, which in fact divided our Court, about how best to balance participatory democracy with representative democracy. By a large majority, the Court held that a failure by the legislature to consult the broad public in a manner it had promised to do rendered the legislation invalid, even though it had been adopted with the requisite majorities. The consequences of the decision can be felt to this day.

These consequences became evident when the government tried to get through Parliament a measure called the Traditional Courts Bill.[15] The proposed law dealt with establishing Traditional Courts in areas of the country that had formerly been demarcated as Bantustans and then empowering them to apply customary law to resolve disputes. The Bill was vigorously opposed by a group called the Rural Women's Action Research Unit. The women saw the Bill as portending a double disaster. In the first place, it would congeal and give legitimacy to the old territorial boundaries created by the Apartheid state in pursuance of its policy of ethnic divide and rule. Secondly, it would entrench patriarchal domination in the rural areas, reversing significant progress that women had made. It would allow the male traditional leaders (with maybe one or two subaltern women) to sit on Courts under their control, reasserting male domination in areas where women were the main farmers, looked after the cattle, cared for the children, built the homesteads and generally managed most aspects of family life, often while the menfolk were away in the towns. They saw this as foreshadowing a great setback to what they had achieved through years of struggle on the ground backed by the principles of the new Constitution. Meanwhile the Government, for which they had in fact voted, was pushing ahead with the Bill. Then, an interesting thing happened, and this is where the Portuguese connection eventually came in: the second Chamber of Parliament, entitled the National Council of Provinces (NCOP), decided to consult widely in the Provinces on the terms of the Bill. The result was a wave of opposition so powerful and so extensive that the Bill was dropped completely.

In embarking on public consultation, the NCOP was acting in terms of a ruling by the Constitutional Court in an earlier case called *Doctors for Life* (DFL).[16] DFL, an anti-abortion family-oriented Catholic group, had tried to persuade Parliament not to amend the Termination of Pregnancy Act in a way that would allow senior nurses as well as doctors to perform terminations. After failing to persuade the National Assembly, DFL sought a hearing in the NCOP. The NCOP replied that it would not be necessary to come down to Parliament in Cape Town to make representations, because the NCOP would in fact be holding public hearings throughout the country on three medically related Bills, including the one at issue.[17]

When the time for the proposed hearings was close, however, the NCOP sent out notices saying that because of extreme pressure of time in Parliament the public consultations would not be held. DFL then came to our Court to argue that

Parliament had violated a constitutional provision that said that legislatures were obliged to take reasonable steps to involve the public in the adoption of legislation. Until the case was brought, the tacit understanding had been that it would be reasonable simply to do the following: you publish a draft of the proposed law in advance together with a white paper expressing what its aims and objects are; you later allow the public to make representations on the text directly to members of the Portfolio Committee handling the Bill in Parliament; and the public and the Press are given facilities for attending Parliamentary proceedings. The question raised in the Court was whether these steps were sufficient to meet the standard of reasonableness. As I recall, three of my colleagues said they were. The remaining eight members of the Court, however, said they were not.

The main judgement of the Court was written by Sandile Ngcobo, who said that what was reasonable would depend on the circumstances of each case. In this case, the legislature had in fact itself thought that it had been reasonable to take the Bills to the public. Its decision to renege on its commitment simply because of internal logistical problems was not reasonable. As a result, the Constitution had been violated. The question for the Court then was what the remedy for the breach should be. Should it in effect be a polite reprimand followed by an expectation of non-repetition? Sandile Ngcobo's judgement was firm: a constitutional requirement had been breached and the law had to be declared invalid.

Central to the reasoning was the weight the majority gave to the importance our Constitution gave to participatory democracy. The point was made that we had got our Constitution through participatory democracy. Involvement of the public was not something that should only take place through elections, important though they were; the people were not like Sleeping Beauty kissed into life once every five years. We looked through the world to see examples of other countries and constitutions that required participative democracy. While the rhetoric in favour of participatory democracy was becoming almost universal, it was only from Portugal that we found a clear example of legislation which had otherwise been validly adopted being invalidated because of a failure to engage in extra-Parliamentary consultation of a kind required by the Constitution. Thus, decisions by the Portuguese Constitutional Court invalidating labour legislation that had been adopted without the degree of consultation with organised labour stipulated for in the Portuguese Constitution assisted our Court in arriving at its own pronouncements.

Not for the first time, I should add, our Court was acting largely as a pioneer in the jurisprudential sense. We declared that dialogue was particularly important in a country as diverse as ours and one with so many cleavages. We pointed out that our Constitution envisaged a Parliament that listened not only when elections were looming, but all the time; and one that acknowledged that it was especially important to give voice to groups that might not be well represented in the powerful political formations of the country. In a concurring judgement,

I referred to the importance of meaningful democracy of having a consultation on the ground with traditional healers in the areas where they lived and where they worked with local leaves, barks, roots, animal relics and waters. Parliament would be seen as being on the spot and concerned and, furthermore, involving itself in a local discourse using a language familiar and meaningful to the people concerned. Without using the word interculturality, I was emphasising the extent to which democratic accountability should be seen as something ongoing, not periodic, qualitative and not just numerical, and responsive to the pluralism of our society, not just hegemonic.

So it came to pass that when the Council of Provinces decided in relation to the Traditional Courts Bill to go out and consult in the Provinces, they found that the people on the ground were indeed very ready to speak. In one Province after the other, the rural women made their opinions very clear: "How can we go back?" they declared,

> How can we restore power to traditional leaders, many of whom collaborated with Apartheid, who didn't fight in the freedom struggle, who are patriarchal in their very bones and who don't recognize women as full human beings, as full citizens in their own right? They'll be deciding over the land, where people can put up their homes, where they can graze their cattle, where they can plant. They'll be handling family disputes with a bias towards the men, deciding criminal cases in a manner that supports favoured families, even seeking to reintroduce corporal punishment which our Constitution has declared to be unconstitutional.

The uproar was great, and it strengthened the hands of those inside the Government and the ANC who saw the Bill as a profoundly retrogressive measure. The NCOP decided not to go ahead with it.

This was an outstanding example of productive work having been done by a socially conscious and legally creative body based at the University of Cape Town. Liaising closely with organised rural women, as well as with other social movements, they encouraged optimal use by the rural women of the opportunities that had resulted from the Constitutional Court's requirement that public participation in the legislative process be taken seriously. The consequence of the public involvement in the adoption of legislation was the avoidance of legislation supported by strong political figures that could have been extremely disempowering to the great majority of people living in the poorest and least developed parts of the country. Rural Women's Action and Research Unit is a warning of new legal battles ahead. They state that the traditional leaders are claiming the right without consulting local communities to sign contracts with mining houses that would destroy communal tenure, degrade the environment and enrich senior families while leaving the majority of commoners destitute and insecure.

The moral of the story is that the concept of interculturality itself needs to be subjected to intercultural interrogation. One person's maize is another person's poison, and, more happily, vice versa!

Notes

1 Revised transcription of a lecture delivered at the Colloquium Epistemologies of the South, Coimbra, Portugal on 12 July 2014.

2 This lyrics, from Carlos de Oliveira, are part of a Portuguese revolutionary song from Manuel Freire called "Livre (não há machado que corte)" www.youtube.com/watch?v=cJ1oYirmOpo.

3 "Grândola, Vila Morena" is another Portuguese revolutionary song, from Zeca Afonso, chosen to be one the signalling passwords of the Carnation Revolution in 1974 www.youtube.com/watch?v=gaLWqy4e7ls.

4 *Port Elizabeth Municipality v Various Occupiers* (CCT 53/03) [2004] ZACC 7; 2005 (1) SA 217 (CC); 2004 (12) BCLR 1268 (CC) (1 October 2004).

5 Act 19 of 1998. Available at: www.gov.za/sites/default/files/gcis_document/201409/a19-98.pdf.

6 To the Associated Press, the President stated:

> Preparations for local government elections must continue so that these elections take place as planned. The Court's judgement does not create any crisis whatsoever. I should emphasise that the judgement of the Constitutional Court confirms that our new democracy is taking firm root and that nobody is above the law.

Available at: www.aparchive.com/metadata/SOUTH-AFRICA-CONSTITUTIONAL-COURT-RULING-ON-ELECTION-BOUNDARIES/947a2c78b7a720e97783b4cb47c32026.

7 Judgement of 28 May 1993, BverfG, 88 BVerfGE 203–205.

8 In the Olivia Road Case (*Occupiers of 51 Olivia Road, Berea Township and 197 Main Street Johannesburg v City of Johannesburg and Others* (24/07) [2008] ZACC 1; 2008 (3) SA 208 (CC); 2008 (5) BCLR 475 (CC), 19 February 2008), the Court states the meaningful engagement as the following: [14] Engagement is a two-way process in which the City and those about to become homeless would talk to each other meaningfully in order to achieve certain objectives [...].

9 *MEC for Education: Kwazulu-Natal and Others v Pillay* (CCT 51/06) [2007] ZACC 21; 2008 (1) SA 474 (CC); 2008 (2) BCLR 99 (CC) (5 October 2007). On 20 and 21 February, the Constitutional Court heard an appeal from the KwaZulu-Natal High Court concerning the right of a learner to wear a nose stud to school. In 2004, Sunali Pillay returned to Durban Girls' High School from the spring holiday with a small nose stud. After a period of correspondence between the school and Sunali Pillay's mother, Ms Pillay, the school decided that Sunali Pillay should not be allowed to wear the stud. Ms Pillay took the school and the KwaZulu-Natal MEC for Education to the Equality Court alleging that they had unfairly discriminated against Sunali Pillay and had violated her religious and cultural rights. The Equality Court found that the school had not unfairly discriminated against Sunali Pillay. On appeal, the High Court overturned the decision, finding that the school had discriminated against Sunali Pillay and that the discrimination was unfair. The High Court declared the decision prohibiting the wearing of a nose stud in school by Hindu/Indian learners to be null and void. Both the school and the Department appealed directly to this Court. After the appeal was lodged, Sunali Pillay completed her matric and left the school. Chief Justice Langa wrote the majority judgement, concurred in by Moseneke DCJ, Madala J, Mokgoro J, Navsa AJ, Ngcobo J, Nkabinde J, Sachs J, Skweyiya J and Van

der Westhuizen J, which dismissed the appeal. He found that it was in the interests of justice for the Court to consider the matter because of the impact the decision would have on schools across the country. He held that the rule prohibiting the wearing of jewellery had the potential for indirect discrimination because it allowed certain groups of learners to express their religious and cultural identity freely, while denying that right to others. The evidence before the Court showed that the wearing of a nose stud was a voluntary practice that formed part of Sunali Pillay's South Indian Tamil Hindu culture, which itself was inseparably intertwined with Hindu religion. He emphasised that both obligatory and voluntary practices qualified for protection under the Equality Act. The school had therefore interfered with Sunali Pillay's religion and culture. As that burden was not imposed on others, the school's interference amounted to discrimination against Sunali Pillay. What was relevant was not whether the practice was characterised as religious or cultural, but the importance it held for the individual in question. Nor was it sufficient to state that Sunali Pillay could attend another school. Our Constitution requires the community to affirm and reasonably accommodate difference, not merely to tolerate it as a last resort. Langa CJ observed that the school had taken meaningful steps to accommodate diversity in its community and that uniforms and school rules served an important purpose in education. However, this case was not about uniforms in general, but about a specific exemption to a uniform. There was no evidence that permitting this particular exemption would imperil uniformity or school discipline in general. The fact that granting an exemption to Sunali Pillay might encourage more learners to express their religion or culture was to be celebrated, not feared. Accordingly, the Chief Justice concluded that the school's discrimination against Sunali Pillay was unfair. He granted an order declaring that the refusal by the school to grant her an exemption from the Code unfairly discriminated against her. In addition, he ordered that the school, in consultation with learners, parents and staff, amend the Code to provide for a procedure to reasonably accommodate religious and cultural practices. The Department was ordered to pay Ms Pillay's costs, while the other parties had to bear their own costs (Media Summary, SACC).

10 *Alexkor Ltd and Another v Richtersveld Community and Others* (CCT19/03) [2003] ZACC 18; 2004 (5) SA 460 (CC); 2003 (12) BCLR 1301 (CC) (14 October 2003).

11 *Bhe and Others v Khayelitsha Magistrate and Others* (CCT 49/03) [2004] ZACC 17; 2005 (1) SA 580 (CC); 2005 (1) BCLR 1 (CC) (15 October 2004).

12 *National Coalition for Gay and Lesbian Equality and Another v Minister of Justice and Others* (CCT11/98) [1998] ZACC 15; 1999 (1) SA 6; 1998 (12) BCLR 1517 (9 October 1998). In this case, the Constitutional Court was asked to confirm an order made by the Witwatersrand High Court that the following laws are unconstitutional and invalid: the common law offence of sodomy, the inclusion of sodomy in schedules to certain Acts of Parliament and a section of the Sexual Offences Act which prohibits sexual conduct between men in certain circumstances.

13 *Minister of Home Affairs and Another v Fourie and Another* (CCT 60/04) [2005] ZACC 19; 2006 (3) BCLR 355 (CC); 2006 (1) SA 524 (CC) (1 December 2005). Writing for a Court that was unanimous on all matters except in relation to the remedy, Sachs J held that it was clearly in the interests of justice that the *Fourie* and the Equality Project matters be heard together. He observed that this Court had in five consecutive decisions highlighted that South Africa has a multitude of family formations that are evolving rapidly as our society develops, so that it is inappropriate to entrench any particular form as the only socially and legally acceptable one; there was an imperative constitutional need to acknowledge the long history in our country and abroad of marginalisation and persecution of gays and lesbians although a number of breakthroughs have been made in particular areas; there is no comprehensive legal regulation of the family law rights of gays and lesbians; and finally, our Constitution represents a radical rupture with the past based on intolerance and exclusion, and

the movement forward to the acceptance of the need to develop a society based on equality and respect by all for all. He pointed out that at issue was the need to affirm the character of our society as one based on tolerance and mutual respect. The test of tolerance is not how one finds space for people with whom, and practices with which, one feels comfortable, but how one accommodates the expression of what is discomforting. The exclusion of same-sex couples from the benefits and responsibilities of marriage was not a small and tangential inconvenience resulting from a few surviving relics of societal prejudice destined to evaporate like the morning dew. It represented a harsh if oblique statement by the law that same-sex couples are outsiders and that their need for affirmation and protection of their intimate relations as human beings is somehow less than that of heterosexual couples. It signifies that their capacity for love, commitment and accepting responsibility is by definition less worthy of regard than that of heterosexual couples. The intangible damage to same-sex couples is as severe as the material deprivation. They are not entitled to celebrate their commitment to each other in a joyous public event recognised by the law. They are obliged to live in a state of legal blankness in which their unions remain unmarked by the showering of presents and the commemoration of anniversaries so celebrated in our culture. If heterosexual couples have the option of deciding whether to marry or not, the judgement continued, so should same-sex couples have the choice as to whether to seek to achieve a status and a set of entitlements and responsibilities on a par with those enjoyed by heterosexual couples. By both drawing on and reinforcing discriminatory social practices, the law has failed to secure for same-sex couples the dignity, status, benefits and responsibilities that it accords to heterosexual couples. Although considerable progress has been made in specific cases through constitutional interpretation and by means of legislative intervention, the default position of gays and lesbians is still one of exclusion and marginalisation (Media Summary, SACC).

14 *Shilubana and Others v Nwamitwa* (CCT 03/07) [2008] ZACC 9; 2008 (9) BCLR 914 (CC); 2009 (2) SA 66 (CC) (4 June 2008).

15 B 1—2012. Available at www.justice.gov.za/legislation/bills/2012-b01tradcourts.pdf.

16 *Doctors for Life International v Speaker of the National Assembly and Others* (CCT12/05) [2006] ZACC 11; 2006 (12) BCLR 1399 (CC); 2006 (6) SA 416 (CC) (17 August 2006).

17 A second one dealt with technical aspects of the organisation of dentists and a third was the Traditional Healers Bill, which for the first time would be granting traditional healers in South Africa a degree of acknowledgement and protection under the law.

8

ON SETTLER COLONIALISM AND POST-CONQUEST *CONSTITUTIONNESS*

The Decolonising Constitutional Vision of African Nationalists of Azania/South Africa

Tshepo Madlingozi

The fact of conquest … has been excluded from the universe of juristic facts.
Ramose, 2003a: 543

8.1 Introduction

This chapter aims to contribute to the ecology of constitutional theories and praxes by suggesting that the heuristic metaphor of the 'abyssal line' (the Line) put forth by Boaventura de Sousa Santos (2007: 45) is a productive metaphor for constitutional analysis and praxis. More specifically, I seek to show how Mogobe Ramose's proposal of the exigency of a 'post-conquest Constitution' seeks to dismantle the Line and instantiate a quest towards the constitution of a polity and a society based on African humanness. I locate Ramose's manifesto in the decolonising constitutional tradition of African nationalists to demonstrate a long lineage of concerns with and serious attempts to posit constitutional visions and political jurisprudences that overcome the constitutive Line. I juxtapose the latter constitutional tradition with hegemonic constitutional theory and praxis in South Africa, which, I argue, reconfigure but ultimately reiterate the Line.

Santos' metaphor of the Line is of special significance when it comes to constitutional re-arrangements and constitutional analyses of historically settler colonial states. These states are constituted by and constitute an abyssal line on the basis of visible and invisible distinctions between settler-invaders and the indigenes with the latter pushed to the 'other side' of the Line, the sub-human side (Santos, 2007: 45). Having violently positioned themselves at the centre of the 'new world' through the extermination and/or peripheralisation and 'invisibilisation' of the conquered peoples, the conquering group declared that the conquered do not

DOI: 10.4324/9781003391920-11

possess rationality, a normative system and a jurisprudence; or at best, that these are pre-modern. In these societies and polities of apartness, settlers attempt to internally re-draw the amity lines to ensure that only the settlers' way of being in the world is valorised, violently enforced and ultimately constitutionalised.

Ultimately, and to borrow an official designation from colonial South Africa, settlers transform the indigenes into 'foreign natives'—the disinherited, denationalised, 'invisibilised' and dispensable Others *of* the settler-created polity. More so than colonialism, therefore, 'settler colonialism mobilises peoples in the teleological expectation of irreversible transformation' (Veracini, 2010: 99). Constitutional law, written or unwritten, is a fundamental constitutive apparatus in these processes of conquest, dispossession, internal and external alienation of 'the native' as well as socio-political projects of indigenising the settler and naturalising the fact of conquest.

The premise of this chapter is that the historical uniqueness and socio-political specificity of settler colonialism demand a different set of constitutional enquiries and remedies to the ones posed and rehashed when dealing with colonialism, authoritarianism and/or low-intensity democracy. As I show in the next section, the failure to appreciate, or rather a tendency to elide, this specificity has resulted in mimetic constitutional theories and praxes that at best fail to provide solutions to the bequeathals of settler colonialism or at worst entrench their realisation. With a focus on South Africa, the main objective of this chapter is to put forward Mogobe Ramose's constitutional philo-praxis for dislodging what I term neo-apartheid constitutionalism. This latter dispensation is an outcome of post-1994 constitutional re-arrangements that have shifted but recast the Line in a way that ultimately facilitates a transition from settler domination to settler hegemony.

Two main questions animate my critical offering of Ramose's manifesto. First, to what extent can a Constitution embody within itself the decolonising project and its sensibilities? Second, and more precisely, to what extent is the essential horizon of Ramose's post-conquest constitutional dispensation—complete and unencumbered restoration of indigenous sovereignties together with the normative structures and being-in-the-worldliness they constitute—realisable and even desirable? Or does the hyphen in 'post-conquest' already hint at the fact that this constitutional vision of redemptive returns—a horizon that finds encapsulation in the rallying cry *Mayibuye iAfrika!* [Return Africa!]—gestures at an African*ist* world that is not the anteriority of settler colonisation?

These two central enquiries inspire the discussion in the next section on the paradox of post-settler colonialism constitution-making, namely the concurrent de-constitutionalising and constitutionalising paradox. In Section 8.3, I will demonstrate that the failure to face this paradox head-on in South Africa has resulted in five interrelated crises of constitution and consequentially a neo-apartheid constitutionalism. The Pan-African Congress (PAC) of Azania's constitutional vision was a direct pre-emption of such a neo-settler colonial constitutionalism. More specifically, this vision was a direct confrontation with what, from a constitutional perspective, I regard as the three main legacies of settler colonialism, namely: (i) the colonial state form, and conversely the eternal subjugation of indigenous sovereignties; (ii) the entrenchment of a world of apartness and the deliberate failure to resolve the National Question; and (iii) the continuing subordination of African life ways and their epistemology and jurisprudence. I argue that responses to these bequeathals constitute the three main pillars of a decolonising constitutional vision and praxis.

In Section 8.4, I explore this African nationalist constitutional vision and contrast it with that of the triumphant ruling African National Congress (ANC). In particular, I argue that in contradistinction to the Africanists' vision, the ANC's constitutional vision was, finally, consonant with the imperatives of settler hegemonic preservation since in its teleological linearity it was biased towards African elite inclusion into 'this side' of the Line. My subtext is that the dominant constitutional theory and praxis are in broad accord with this constitutional vision. Finally, taking the aforementioned main legacies of settler colonialism in turn and demonstrating how the triumph of the ANC's liberal multiracial constitutional vision failed to address these legacies, I critically discuss Ramose's counter-hegemonic constitutional manifesto, its main tenets and show that it holds hope to de-constitution neo-settler colonial constitutionalism in South Africa and in respect of other historically settler societies.

8.2 The Paradox of Post-Colonial Constitution-Making

The two enquiries at the heart of this chapter and the miserable reality of neo-colonial constitutional dispensations in many parts of Africa and neo-apartheid constitutionalism in South Africa—more on the latter shortly—have to do with the paradox that I detect to be at the heart of post-colonial constitution-making endeavours. Post-settler colonialism constitution-making projects seek to pursue, simultaneously, de-constitutionalising and constitutionalising objectives. On the one hand, post-settler colonialism constitutionalists aim to constitute both a sovereign state and a new society. However, as has been observed in many post-independence African scenarios (Mandaza, 1991: 86), a danger always lurks that hurried constitutionalising efforts and processes might facilitate the onset of neo-settler colonialism or embody what Latin American theorists term 'coloniality' in the sense of perpetuating the institutional, socio-economic and cultural arrangements sedimented during settler colonialism. In this scenario, the main edifice of the politically, culturally and psychically alienating settler-created house remains and no indigenous-inspired home is built. More pertinently, settler hegemony, as with any 'elite preservation' efforts via constitutional transformations (Hirschl, 2004: 89), is guaranteed through the claw-back mechanisms of constituted power.

If post-settler colonialism's foundational law and its accompanying processes are to be genuinely constitutive enterprises, rather than being a grafting onto the rotten and 'invisibilising' foundations of the settler-created house, they must at the same time aim to de-constitutionalise the settler-created world, its state form and the underwriting normative structures. What precisely needs to be de-constitutionalised? In the decolonial vision of Frantz Fanon (1963 [1961]: 100), 'everything' is liable to this de-constitutionalising undertaking.

A decolonising Constitution can only be cosmogenic, instantiate a re-birth of the indigenes' world and give primacy to the invisibilised indigenous people when it ensures that 'the last shall be the first and the first last', suggests Fanon (1963 [1961]: 37) in his most apocalyptic moment. The paradox here is that such a seemingly post-settler constitutional dispensation would then still be structured by a Manichean worldview. This world is not the posterity of the settler colonial world and its invisible frontiers because it continues to be moored in the epistemological-ontological praxis of apartness. The problem here is twofold. First, the anti-humanness economy of racial classification and hierarchical existences is seemingly inverted but remains current. Second, instead of being bifocal in the sense of being both backward-looking and forward-looking, such a constitutional vision is entombed in an attitude that David Scott (2004) decries as 'anti-colonial longing'. Such emancipation then does not become a resumption of the self-determining history of the indigenes and an enactment of liberation as a forward march.

Fortunately, anti-settler colonialism activists, scholars and constitutionalists are well-attuned to these pitfalls. As Ato Sekyi-Otu brilliantly demonstrates (1996: 103–104), Fanon himself counselled against this kind of emancipation. The 'first will be the last' is the reaction that immediately presents itself in reaction to settler colonialism's Manichaeism. Fanon (1963 [1961]: chapter 3) then goes on to show that this reaction is the nationalist bourgeoisie's reaction which will simply lead to disaster moving from racialism, to xenophobia, to ethnic chauvinism, social injustice and ultimately to full-blown neo-colonialism. To the aforementioned twofold pitfall of such decolonising constitutional vision, we can add another one which is that it leads to elite nationalism and a constitutional dispensation in which, as H.W.O. Okoth-Ogendo (1991: 6–21) has shown, 'the first' are the nationalist bourgeoisie. Stated differently, the seeds of counter-revolution lie in the failure to transcend the colonial discourse and its anti-humanness worldview. The springboard to such transcendence involves dipping into the well of modern indigenous life worlds.

If conquest and settler colonialism are acts of temporal interruption and a never wholly successful attempt to ossify indigenous life worlds and their norms and structures, decolonisation ought to enable the colonised nation, 'to reassume its history and assert its sovereignty' (Fanon, 1967 [1964] 83–84). Such resumption enables the ex-conquered to assume their authorial responsibility and (re)continue their messy historical march together (Sekyi-Otu, 1996: 48–50). The claim here is not that things were pristine before colonialism. The claim is rather that African modes of dispute resolution, norms of co-existence and social ordering—and indeed unwritten constitutional law—were displaced and that decolonisation is an occasion to retrieve and valorise them.

This gesture of a 'return to the source' (Cabral, 1973: 59–61) enables a remembering of subjugated indigenous ethics and epistemologies and a re-membering of the fractured triadic community of the living-the living dead-the yet-to-be born under the banner of African humanness (Ngũgĩ, 2009). Since African humanness, as elaborated by Ramose, decrees a non-ending quest towards cosmic harmony, wholeness and national being-becoming, it is proper to refer to this quest as a quest of post-conquest constitution*ness* in contrast to the linear and rigid order of post-colonial constitutional*ism*.

8.3 The Crises of Constitution

The main aim of this chapter is to tease out the key tenets of post-conquest constitutionness as framed by African nationalists before 1994 and as proposed by Ramose today. As the epigraph to this chapter makes clear, Ramose's constitutional vision is a counter-hegemonic vision in that he moves from the premise that the territory baptised as South Africa is still a conquered territory. A characteristic constitutional analysis, both liberal and leftist, takes it as a given that South Africa's problem and history of conquest and colonisation have been resolved. The hegemonic constitutional project is then how to integrate the 'formerly' oppressed and excluded into the 'new' South African polity and state through universal enfranchisement, extension of human rights to all, equitable distribution of (mainly) state goods and de-racialisation of the spheres of civil society and the economy. The consensus is that all of these can be, and are being achieved, through South Africa's peculiar brand of 'transformative constitutionalism' (Klare, 1998: 150). And yet, from the perspective of historical victims of settler colonialism, transformative constitutionalism neither realised the aforementioned de-constitutionalising exigency nor the constitutionalising imperative. It is from this perspective that we should apprehend the following intersecting crises of 'post-Apartheid' constitutionalism.

8.3.1 The Crisis of Ongoing Racial Dehumanisation and Social Invisibility

The first crisis is evidenced by the fact that impoverished black communities and black-led trade unions stage over 2000 protests every year (Alexander *et al.*, 2015). Every single day one or other impoverished black community engages in a community insurrection to protest against the nonexistence of democracy, their permanent state of marginalisation and invisibility, and to demand basic social good. These extra-institutional insurrections are the result of the fact that the majority of black South Africa believe, in the words of *Abahlali baseMjondolo*[1] (2014), that post-1994 constitutional re-arrangements have actually imprisoned them in a liminal state of 'unfreedom'. A state of 'unfreedom' because this sector of society still suffers from systemic invisibility, structural impoverishment, gender oppression and racial subordination. It is from this perspective that in spite of the lauded constitutional provisions for socio-economic rights and deafening praises of jurisprudence flowing from these, a study by the state-funded Human Science Research Council effectively concluded that the lives of many (nominally) South African citizens 'remain constituted as bare life, disempowered and … "marginal" to society …' (Barolsky, 2012: 137).

8.3.2 The Crisis of Re-nativisation

The second manifestation of a state of anti-black bifurcation is the fact that the post-1994 constitutional dispensation has failed to fundamentally transform the situation in which many black South Africans do not have a sense of full belonging as South Africans. In *Citizen and Subject*, Mahmood Mamdani (1996: 16–18) demonstrated that post-1994 constitutional and state transformation processes have failed to deal with the late colonialism-created 'bifurcated state' form. In this state, 'some' (if we bear in mind the first crisis above) urban-based dwellers are governed through a system of civil law and are thus citizens, whereas rural-based dwellers continue to be governed through a system of traditional leaders-inspired, and thus self-serving, 'customary law' (Oomen, 2005: 115–122). Thus, in spite of the fact that the urban and the rural spheres are not hermeneutically sealed from each other, rural dwellers are generally interpellated not as citizens but as subjects.

Today, state elites are constantly appealing to the rural electoral fodder presumably controlled by traditional leaders by seeking to reconfigure the regime of rural land governance or by granting more surrogate executive and judicial powers to traditional authorities. The effect of these placation manoeuvres is to reiterate the colonial agenda of ethnic fragmentation and spatiotemporal ossification—in a word, an agenda of 're-nativisation'. Therefore, rural dwellers—some 18 million people—are precluded from claiming *for themselves* a dynamic sense of double belonging to both the indigenous moral order and the order of the modern state.

8.3.3 The Crisis of Subservient Legality and Subjugation of Indigenous Lifeways

This situation of bifurcated statehood constitutes and is constituted by the failure to develop and valorise a state of productive legal pluralism. The third 'post-Apartheid' constitution crisis is, therefore, the fact that despite on constitutional paper African law being placed on an equal footing with Eurocentric common law, African law remains subservient to Eurocentric law. The argument that jurisprudential parity has been achieved because African law, like all law, has been recognised on the basis that it complies with constitutional values ignores the fact that the current Constitution, as is the nature of all constitutions, is not culturally and civilisationally neutral. As Ramose demonstrates in Section 8.4, the Constitution overwhelmingly reflects the epistemological paradigm of South Africa's historical conquerors. The continuing subalternisation of African jurisprudence is symptomatic of the fact that African lifeways, their epistemologies and norms and systems of social ordering are still deemed inferior in the 'new South Africa'.

8.3.4 The Crisis of the Subjugation of Indigenous Sovereignties

Fourthly, these two crises of privation of nation-wide jurisprudential equivalence—let alone an avowal of the lived experiential reality of 'interlegality' in the rural areas (Santos, 1995: 473)—as well as a preclusion of a sense of a belonging to multiple orders are caused and intensified by the fact that indigenous sovereignties remain subjugated to the inherited colonial state form. Along with, or because of, the recognition of 'cultural difference', the current South African Constitution recognises 'traditional authorities' subject to the Constitution and the Traditional Leadership and Governance Framework Act of 2003. Through this scheme, traditional leaders and traditional councils have been offered constitutional sanction but are granted limited powers as well as strict conditions for ongoing recognition.

This constitution crisis together with the two preceding ones suggests Barbara Oomen's wry observation that 'although the South African Department of Native Affairs was renamed Traditional Affairs after the transition to democracy, many things stayed the same' (2005: 37) is not at all hyperbolic. The ongoing subjugation of indigenous sovereignties, together with the ANC's appeasements of recognised traditional authorities, prevents democratic and organic reconstruction of autochthonous orders in a way that ensures that their reclamation is not in favour of traditional leaders and male elders.

8.3.5 The Crisis of the Entrenchment of Settler-Native Relation

The final constitution crisis goes to the core of the failure to establish a genuine post-settler dispensation. The property clause in the Constitution has effectively constitutionalised land dispossession through regimes of land redistribution and land restitution on the basis of what, *de facto*, is a system of 'willing buyer, willing seller'. The result of this is that only a puny percentage of the land has been redistributed, let alone restituted to various dispossessed peoples. The result is that the settler (dispossessing)-native (dispossessed) antithetical relation remains viscerally real.

These five cursorily outlined constitution crises are indicative of the fact that South Africa's 'transformative Constitution' has not led either to the de-constitution of the main edifice of the unhomely settler-created world or to the constitution of a united and humane post-settler colonial world. The continuing situation of anti-black bifurcation means that in South Africa the issue is not Okoth-Ogendo's brilliantly observed paradox of 'constitution[s] without constitutionalism' (1991: 6). The overwhelming constitutional drive towards the preservation of white material, psychic and cultural interests and the assimilation of black elites into 'this side' of the Line points, rather, to the fact that we are here dealing with a paradox we can call constitutionalism without 'constitution'. This is because the current Constitution has not resulted in a state of constitution in one etymological sense of *con stare* denoting 'to stand together'. In other words, the construction of what Upendra Baxi (2013: 21) calls a distinctive post-colonial constitutional and societal 'we-ness' has not taken place. Hence, I refer to these five interrelated crises as the 'crises of constitution'. These crises are indexes of the reality of neo-apartheid constitutionalism. In the next section, I will explore Ramose's submission that only a post-conquest Constitution can overcome this situation of a reconfigured abyssal line.

8.4 Against Neo-apartheid Constitutionalism: Ramose's Africanist Post-Conquest Manifesto

C. R. D. Halisi has noted that, from early on, movements of emancipation in South Africa had to confront troubling questions of citizenship and national identity such as 'how the "people" are to be defined, who belongs to the political community, and what are the criteria of inclusion and exclusion' (1999: 4). Divergent responses to these questions of Constitution account for the main and persistent historical antinomy in black emancipatory thought, and hence constitutional visions, namely the ruling ANC's liberal multiracial unionism and the PAC non-racial African nationalism. In this section, I will contrast these constitutional visions to demonstrate that the aforementioned indexes of neo-Apartheid constitutionalism were actually anticipated and pre-empted in the latter vision. Together, the PAC's apartheid-era vision and Ramose's contemporary critique offer a model of avoiding the pitfalls of post-colonial constitution-making I outlined in Section 8.2. Even more significantly, they help us to distil the following *essentialia* of a decolonising Constitution: (i) rescinding the colonial state form; (ii) resolving the National Question; and (iii) remembering and re-membering Africa.

8.4.1 De-constituting the Colonial State

Ernest Wamba-dia-Wamba (1991: 58–59) reminds us that the colonial state is a shell created out of the following threefold colonisation process: imposition of borders created out of artificial carving and consolidation during conquest; balkanisation of existing political communities; and forced integration into a newly created state that serves the interests of the metropolitan capital. A decolonising Constitution ought to undo this legacy.

In South Africa, as elsewhere, the colonial settler state was established through what Harry Smith, a historically significant colonial Lieutenant-General in South Africa, termed 'the right of conquest' (cited in Mostert, 1993: 784). Declaiming in 1836, Smith invoked this right to justify the permanent expulsion of the Xhosas from the frontier. Every defeat of the indigenous peoples in the hundred-year Frontier Wars/Wars of Dispossession and other wars inland resulted in deterritorialisation, expulsion and scattering of indigenous people, and concomitantly, the shifting of frontiers and the expansion of the territories that the disparate group of settlers had arrogated for themselves.

Settler-invaders established the Union of South Africa, through the South African Act of 1910, with the aim of facilitating 'racial cooperation' between the two sets of settlers, renouncing Africans in 'white man's country' and laying the conditions for eventually, in 1913, consigning 'native tribes' to 13% of arid and overcrowded territories known as 'tribal reserves'. In this way, conquerors constitutionalised and naturalised the 'right of conquest' (Ramose, 2003a: 543–548). The advent of apartheid in 1948 was only a latest iteration of colonialism, a latest twist in the saga of intra-settler rivalry and an attempt to find a final solution to the 'Native Problem'. The 1961 Constitution created the Republic of South Africa as an independent settler colony that could freely lord over 'the natives'. From the standpoint of the conquered, the emergence and the various transformations of the South African state were concretisations of conquest. How did emancipatory movements in South Africa respond to this state of affairs?

On the one side, ANC leaders campaigned for the incorporation of (westernised) Africans into the Union state on the basis of Cecil Rhodes's notion of 'equal rights to all civilised men' (South African Native Congress, 1972 [1903]: 16). These African elites were, at best, ambivalent about the exigency of restoring subjugated African sovereignties and their territories. The ANC, therefore, took the sovereignty of the state for granted (Motlhabi, 1984: 40–41). After a brief period in which the ANC, impelled by its young league, made a rhetorical case against 'national oppression' and for self-determination, the ANC returned to its traditional approach of self-determination-as-democratisation in the mid-1950s. This understanding found concrete expression in the ANC co-sponsored Freedom Charter. This Charter opens with the historically significant words: 'South Africa belongs to all who live in it, black and white'. Following this declaration, Charterists could only make a call for equitable sharing of the land. With this liberal but multiracialism Charter, the ANC made it clear that it upheld the legitimacy of the state, it had renounced land reclamation and that its focus was on inclusion and democratisation.

On the other side, the PAC argued, quite correctly, that the notion of a multiracial union would perpetuate the myth of race, secure white hegemony and concretise the abandonment of the original objectives of the liberation struggle: land reclamation and Africanist nation-building (PAC, 1965 [1959]: paras. H and I).

These African nationalists differentiated themselves from the ANC by declaring that, for them, the nature of the struggle is both nationalist and democratic in that

> it involves the restoration of land to its rightful owners—the Africans … At the same time, our struggle is for democracy, if we understand democracy to mean the implementation of the wishes of the majority of the inhabitants of the country.
>
> *Leballo, 1957: n.p.*

As is clear, the PAC's point of departure was that the South African state was a colonial state in that Africans were oppressed as a 'subject nation'; and not as a class as the ANC and its allies posited (Sobukwe, 1977a [1959]: 506–510).

African nationalists made it clear that they wished to reclaim 'Afrika for Africans' and not for everyone as the Charter insisted (Sobukwe, 1977b [1959]: 507). The PAC took the slogan *Mayibuye iAfrika!* [Return Africa!] to its logical conclusion by making clear that 'the struggle for national emancipation, and *the regaining of all things that were lost as a result of White conquest of Africa,* is the cornerstone of Africa's struggle for liberation' (Letlaka, cited in Gerhart, 1978: 146; original emphasis). To African nationalists, 'lost things' included land, sovereignties and what they regarded as Africans' innate quality of and an inclination towards 'Africanism'. They expounded that this quality moulds, and should mould, Africans into one nation in spite of ethnic affiliations (Lembede, 2015: 143–144). Robert Sobukwe, the first president of the PAC, went even further and often emphasised that the spirit of 'Africanism' predated colonialism and that gradually social and political pressure would have led to the creation of a federated polity of African kingdoms (Motlhabi, 1984: 74). For the PAC, therefore, a post-conquest Constitution is one that constitutes an African federal state. The final piece of the Africanist vision pertaining to state and sovereignty is that this federal, non-racial, Africanist state should have a Pan-Africanist orientation by ceding its ultimate sovereignty in service of African unity and anti-imperialism. In this way, the right of conquest is rescinded, the colonial state form is dissolved, and Africa can be returned to Africans.

The ANC and the PAC's divergent apprehension of the nature of state continued right up to the triumph of the ANC, vis-à-vis the PAC, in the late 1970s. More specifically, from its years in exile up to the 1990s when it returned to the country, the ANC continued to accept the legitimacy of the South African state and its international legality and only protested the legitimacy of the white minority government (Alexander, 2002: 46). Although rhetorically the ANC accepted its communist allies' characterisation of the South African situation as that of 'Colonialism of a Special Type' or a situation of internal colonialism, neither for the communists nor for the ANC did that characterisation commit them to campaign for self-determination understood as full land reclamation and the restoration of subjugated indigenous sovereignties (Mafeje, 1986: 98–99).

The 1990s transitional negotiations, which the PAC boycotted, were over-determined by Euro-American constitutional praxis and a liberal discourse—indexes of hurried constitution in the terms of Section 8.2 above—resulting in the reconstruction of a state into a Euro-modern state. It is this Euro-modern transformation of the state, together with the extension of civil and political rights to all, which leads many analysts (e.g. Magubane, 1996: xvii) to argue that the colonial nature of the South African state has been extinguished. Ramose disagrees and asserts that a post-conquest South Africa is yet to be born.

Ramose's constitutional vision pivots around the fact of conquest and how to dissolve Smith's 'right of conquest'. Ramose trains his unrelenting eye on this putative right because this right justifies the reification and naturalisation of the colonial state form since in the terms of this right indigenous loss of territories and sovereignties over them are permanent and irreversible (Ramose, 2003a: 551). His point of departure is that 'the right of conquest', de-territorialisation and denial of state-formation are consequences of the 16th-century drawing of the amity lines in terms of which beyond the lines were beings who do not possess rationality and were thus sub-humans (2003a: 548). The colonists thus regarded the lands on which these beings existed as 'nobody's land'. Additionally, because these beings were incapable of reason, they could not elaborate norms of social ordering and could therefore not constitute sovereignties. The PAC recounts that, in the case of South Africa, this belief justified colonisation and 'denuded Africa of Africans', leading to 'the loss of sovereignty by the indigenous peoples and the alienation of more and more of their land' (PAC, 1965 [1959]: paras. A and B). Ramose's main thesis is that post-1994, constitutional re-arrangements have not reversed these consequences.

Rather, by excluding the fact of conquest from juristic facts, the 'final Constitution' of 1994 constitutionalises the 'right of conquest' (Ramose, 2003a: 543). From a Ramosean perspective, the consequences of precluding Africans from asserting their fundamental and natural right to reclaim titles over their territories and sovereignties over them are deadly serious. The effect is to disremember and dis-member, through the recasting of the abyssal line, the re-entrenchment of the notion that Africans are below the human line and that, being the case, they are not deserving of reparations, recovery of sovereignties and restoration of titles over land.

It is Ramose's argument, then, that 1994 should be seen less as a constitutive moment of rupture but as an outcome of South Africa's history of 'evolutionary constitutionalism' with the difference that this time a multiracial democracy is installed, government succession has taken place and conversely the question of state succession is jettisoned (2012: 22). Indeed, the preamble to the 'final Constitution' repeats the Freedom Charter's integrationist and anti-decolonising constitutional vision that 'South Africa belongs to all who live **in** it …'. In the context where title over lands and sovereignties over them have not been restored, the granting of equal constitutional status to both the dispossessor and the dispossessed has resulted in the conferral of what Ramose terms 'limping sovereignty' (2003a: 557). It is this situation that informs Ramose's unequivocal post-conquest constitutional manifesto:

> the restoration of complete, unencumbered and integral sovereignty to the conquered as at conquest ... [and] ... since the concept of sovereignty without territory is empty, it follows that this exigency of restoration entails by necessity the return of the land to the indigenous people.
>
> *Ramose, 2006a: 7–8*

For all the reasons I alluded to when outlining the contemporary constitution crises, it should be clear that the fact that the Constitution makes provision for 'land redistribution' and 'land restitution' does not satisfy this anti-neocolonial constitutional manifesto. Indeed, Ramose makes the significant point that the conversion of the collective right to the title of territory into private right to ownership of land during the negotiations reduced the issue to that of land reform and not territorial sovereignty (Ramose, 2003a: 555). Similarly, the reluctant recognition of historical political authorities does not amount to the restoration of sovereignty. These authorities are not vested with 'complete original sovereignty' (Ramose, 2006b: 352). Ramose's Africanist decolonisation manifesto for complete recovery of sovereignties and recovery of titles over land aims to rescind the colonial state form. The effect of this is that 'the conquerors' South Africa would be dissolved' (Ramose, 2003a: 570). Ramose (2006b: 356) suggests that the outcome of this would be an emergence of a state composed of independent and equal autochthonous sovereignties under a system of federalism, confederalism or consociatioanalism.

8.4.2 Dislodging the Line and Enabling an Africanist Being-belonging

What is the status and belonging of 'successors of the right of conquest' in this post-conquest constitutional dispensation; this dispensation where Africa, at least as far as territories and sovereignties are concerned, has been returned to Africans? To recast Mahmood Mamdani's (1998) provocation, how would an Africanist Constitution convert settlers into natives? More to the point, how does Ramose's uncompromising de-constitution project avoid the pitfalls we discussed earlier—the pitfalls of reasserting the counter-humanness economy of racial classification and nativism and of irredentist politics becoming a cover for elite self-aggrandisement?

That the colonial settler state is never at any stage a nation-state since it exists on the basis of the national oppression of the conquered peoples means that the struggle for emancipation is often couched in nationalistic terms. In South Africa, divergent apprehensions of the nature of the state and affiliated *teloses* of the struggle for emancipation resulted in two forms of nationalism and attendant constitution visions. On the one hand, there was the ANC's 'inclusive nationalism' which envisaged that the process of building an inclusive nation-state would be predicated on Africans winning political rights in the South African state (Gerhart, 1978: 12–13). Proceeding from a perspective that recognised the legitimacy of the state, the post-apartheid (not post-colonial) constitutional ends here were to both guarantee the group rights of various 'races' and to deracialise the polity and society in order to create a conducive environment for the realisation of the liberal ideal of equality of opportunity (Alexander, 2002: 46).

The disruption of the ANC's long-held vision of multiracial nation-building by its youth wing was short-lived as the Freedom Charter swept aside an emergent discourse of African nationalism in favour of a liberal nation-building project. According to the Charter, the social contract of the new nation would be based on the equitable distribution of resources and land while its cultural identity would be reflective of the diversity of its four nations (an ANC typology). The Charter's opening declaration and the assertion that 'our people [black and white] have been robbed of their birthright to land, liberty ...' (Preamble to the Charter) made it clear that for the ANC and its allies the goals of (re)conciliation and integration took precedence over historical and structural realities as far as the National Question is concerned.

The PAC's nation-building agenda proceeded from the twin notion that South Africa is not an independent state and that one nation (European) had conquered the other nation (African). Flowing from this, Africanists insisted that multiracialism was an anathema not only because it reasserts the myth of the existence of races. The PAC argued that the Charter's multiracial unionism actually sabotaged in advance the infinite process of post-colonial nation-building because such a union would be a union of 'givers and beggers, masters and slaves' (Raboroko, 1960: 26–27). In this context, the PAC argued stringently that the ANC's campaign for 'constitutional guarantees' for both historical conquerors and the historical conquered would perpetuate white domination and thus perpetual 'tutelage of the Afrikan people' (PAC, 1965) [1959]: H). A key jurisprudential insight of African nationalists is that, in an un-decolonised context, constitutionalism and (racial) group rights are 'techniques of control' to induce voluntary enslavement and secure the ultimate triumph of settler colonialism (Sobukwe cited in Gerhart, 1978: 187). This triumph is secured by the assimilation of the Black elite into the 'new' polity while the majority of Africans remain constricted on 'the other side' of the Line (Sobukwe cited in Gerhart, 1978: 190).

If the ANC's constitution horizon was grounded on an alleged 'inclusive nationalism', the PAC's was thus an 'orthodox nationalism' based on the idea that 'South Africa' belonged to Africans by virtue of autochthony and the fact that they are the majority (Gerhart, 1978: 13). In this constitution vision, an all-inclusive nation-building project would only begin *after* the situation of conquest has been extinguished and Azania is birthed. It is, however, important to add that for these nationalists the process of returning Africa to Africans, the decolonising imperative, instigates but not overcomes the historical antagonism. Nkutsoeu Raboroko, the author of the PAC's Manifesto, stated that for the Africanists, national conciliation and equality would only become a possibility when the antithetical categories of oppressor and oppressed have battled it out and are superseded. 'The final synthesis of these [conqueror/conquered] categories', the PAC insisted, is only possible in 'Africanism' (Raboroko cited in Motlhabi, 1984: 77).

By Africanism the PAC meant to capture an ideology and a consciousness that holds that the diverse indigenous ethnic groups are all African because they share a 'domination by the same spirit'; that Africans are the rightful owners of Africa; that Africans have a history, a proud history of civilisation, statecraft, ethnic synthesis and anti-colonial struggles; that they are part of the African continent and of African peoples in the diaspora; and that socialist living and humanness are the core of their being-in-the-worldliness (Lembede, 2015: 137, 129–131). This consciousness and ideology are initially deployed to create a national consciousness amongst the conquered peoples and then it becomes the national ideology of the all-inclusive post-settler colonial state. In the PAC's nationalism, settlers would only belong in and be integrated into the post-colonial nation-state after they (i) relinquish all benefits flowing from the right of conquest; and because they have given up their conqueror identity (ii) a route is open for them to become Africans by declaring loyalty to Africa as their only home and abide by majoritarian democracy (Sobukwe, 1977b [1959]: 516). For these pre-figurative constitutionalists, Africanism was thus a liberatory humanist and unifying philosophy that should underpin the post-conquest foundational law.

What is the status of the National Question in South Africa today? To begin with, the historical discussion so far alerts us to the fact that when it comes to historically settler societies this question revolves around three main imperatives: (i) overcoming institutionalised racism and dismantling white hegemony; (ii) ensuring equitable distribution of material, cultural, epistemic and other societal resources; and (iii) building a humane and united nation or a multination state. If the crises of constitution I offered in the previous section are valid, then it is clear that this question remains stubbornly present, and more than twenty years of 'post-Apartheid' constitutionalism have simply reconfigured the Line, and those not-yet African are still at the centre of the 'new' South Africa.

For the ANC and its interlocutors, the spectacular constitution-making process together with its creature, a supreme Constitution with a Bill of Rights for all, was pivotal to creating a post-apartheid nation-state. It is from this perspective that Cyril Ramaphosa, the ANC's chief negotiator, hailed the adoption of the Constitution as 'the birthday to the South African rainbow nation. This is the day South Africa is truly born' (cited in Oswin, 2007: 96). Additionally, mindful of the need to supersede the European/settler-African/native schism, the ANC propagated the proposition that the adoption of the Constitution launched the process of African post-apartheid becoming and belonging. Thus, at the occasion of the adoption of the Constitutional Bill in 1996, Thabo Mbeki, then Deputy President, made his classic 'I am African' speech to postulate a notion of an all-inclusive Africanness and, more fundamentally, to deftly argue that autochthony and settler-invasion are now irrelevant historical factors (Mbeki, 1996). Mbeki cast the adoption of the 'final Constitution' as an act of cosmogony and proceeded to use that understanding to short-circuit the debate around the meaning of the slogan 'Africa for Africans'. In this understanding, the Constitution had converted settlers into natives and the Truth and Reconciliation Commission, which was starting a few months later, was going to unify and heal this African nation.

Two years later, however, Mbeki was to make another landmark speech bemoaning the failure of reconciliation. Mbeki decried the fact that South Africa was still a country of 'Two Nations': one white and prosperous and another black and impoverished (Mbeki, 1998). Seeming to impugn the constitutional false consciousness he helped to diffuse, Mbeki went on to lament that the black nation, 'has virtually no possibility to exercise what in reality amounts to a theoretical right to equal opportunity, with that right being equal within this black nation only to the extent that it is equally incapable of realisation' (Mbeki, 1998). By the year 2016, the National Question remained unresolved, and the reality of an abyssal society remains: 'the South African society remains divided. The privilege attached to race, class, space and gender has not yet been fully reversed', notes the National Planning Commission (NPC, 2014: 2). The NPC regretted that this is in spite of the Constitution laying down a solid foundation for the creation of a non-racial, non-sexist united society. From an African nationalist perspective, the Constitution itself is guilty of securing white hegemony and entrenching apartness.

Ramose's critique moves from the premise that the praxis of 'standing divided' endures because neo-colonialism in the form of a transmogrified situation of internal colonialism subsists in South Africa today. Ramose's contribution to the second pillar of a decolonising constitutional praxis begins with a reminder that neo-colonialism is an outcome of the stillbirth of self-determination and the resulting failure to decentre successors of the 'right of conquest' (Ramose, 1991: 27–28). Such a decentring is pivotal to the de-constitution of the abyssal society because colonisation, especially settler colonisation, is driven by an ontology of the separation of Man from the cosmos, the decision to mould the cosmos according to Man's needs and the elimination or suppression of the Other so that Man-the-conqueror's position at the centre of the world is guaranteed (Ramose, 2003a: 544; 1991: 27).

Ramose's post-conquest nation-building agenda is based on the following three multi-directional phases agenda: (i) decentring successors of the 'right of conquest' through the decolonisation agenda of Restoration-Recovery-Reparation, (ii) converting the settler's identity away from being the colonising Other, and (iii) national being-becoming through African humanness. In Ramose's approach to the National Question, one can see affinities with the PAC, in that Ramose also asserts that the process of decentring historical settlers should be followed by the latter's 'conversion' to enable their (re)admission as members of the (African) family (Ramose, 2006a: 10; 2012: 55). Such a process of conversion, as the PAC also argued, begins when historical colonisers do not hinder the decolonisation project and accept the self-determination agenda. If, for the PAC, such synthesis takes place in and through Africanism, in Ramose's Constitution vision synthesis is found in African humanness.

Ramose would assert that the reason why the goals of 'reconfiliation' and post-colonial national being-becoming have not been realised in South Africa is due to South African evolutionary constitutional order. This order not only preserves white hegemony, it also 'invisibilises' the ethical-epistemological philosophy of African humanness. The decision to overwhelmingly base the putative foundational law of the 'new South Africa' on the ethical epistemology of one sector of society adversely affects the projects of nation-building and social cohesion in at least two ways. On one level, the dominance of the Eurocentric paradigm and the exclusion of the philosophy of the majority people in South Africa, *Ubuntu*, imply that the majority peoples and their living philosophy are effectively excluded in post-1994 constitutional re-arrangements (Ramose, 2014: 122). This epistemological, and thus ontological, position can be contrasted with that found in the decolonising and indigenous peoples-valorising constitutions of Ecuador and Bolivia, which, respectively, put *sumak kawsay* and *pachamama* principles at the core of the new dispensation.

At another level, Ramose might suggest that the marginalisation of *Ubuntu* and African jurisprudence has damaged the prospects of building a united and humane society because Western jurisprudence is innately inimical to building cohesive and humane societies. This is because the latter jurisprudence is predominantly geared towards atomisation, fragmentation and abstraction. By contrast, the main aim of African jurisprudence is social cohesion (Murungi, 2004: 522–523). African jurisprudence, motored by *Ubuntu*, seeks and commands wholeness as be-ing becoming. 'Be-ing' because in this philosophy, 'motion is the principle of *be-ing*; to be is to be in, with and by motion' (Ramose, 2007: 124; emphasis in the original).

Ramose expounds that African humanness 'suggests both a condition of being and the state of becoming, of openness or ceaseless unfolding' (2009: 308). It is in this sense, then, that Ramose's constitutional vision should be characterised as that of *constitutionness* because while advocating for inclusion, cohesion and 'standing together', it is an open and never-ending quest towards wholeness; that is, towards national being-becoming.

African constitutional law is fit for the purpose of *constitutionness* because it proscribes apartness and the peripheralisation of 'the Other'. This is because *Ubuntu,* the core of this constitutional law, decrees that 'to be a human be-ing is to affirm one's humanity by recognising the humanity of others and, on that basis, establish humane relations with them' (Ramose, 1999: 52). Finally, unlike contemporary South Africa's operative monoculture of constitutional law motion, the prescription to reach out towards other persons, and thus a refusal to prescribe immutable and eternal values, invites intercultural dialogue and thus a moving away from bounded reasoning and its concomitant drawing of Lines (Ramose, 2007: 126). The fact that African humanness demands openness and that Africans are never in a 'normative coma' (Gordon, 2015: 129), even as they are under conquest, means Africans remain Africans even when they adopt norms and values from those they encounter and 'reconfilliate' with. It is this interculturality that modifies the re-membering imperative leading to the forging of an all-embracing Africanist nation that, contra Mbeki's ahistorical Afropolitanism, does not sacrifice memory, truth and justice.

8.4.3 Enabling a 'return to the source'

The two preceding pillars of post-conquest constitutioness seek to address structural legacies in the form of the colonial state form and institutionalised apartness. The final pillar attempts to confront an imperceptible but most insidious bequest of an abyssal constitutional praxis: the notion that the historically conquered are not fully human because they do not possess rationality. It is this 16th-century amity lines-concretised belief that oils and maintains contemporary subalternisation of African lifeways, institutionalised racism and habits that normalise the dehumanisation of 'the blacks'. The project of post-conquest constitutionness must valorise and centralise African knowledge systems, cosmologies and elements of 'traditional' political culture. Towards this end, a post-conquest Constitution is post-abyssal and post-conquest to the extent that it enables 'a radical break with modern Western ways of thinking and acting' (Santos, 2007: 66). In line with the simultaneous de-constitution and constitution imperative I outlined in Section 8.2 above, after epistemological break comes the 'return to the source'. For this subsection, I read Ramose to suggest that a homegrown post-conquest Constitution is the apogee of the struggle for epistemic justice and the reinstatement of the African as a human second to none. I begin by briefly contrasting the ANC's and the PAC's postures towards the idea that epistemological break and a 'return to the source' are prerequisites for the constitution of a home where Africans can feel and experience a sense of belonging.

The ruling ANC is a creation of a movement of late 19th-century African elites that self-styled themselves as 'New Africans'—'New' Africans because they were educated by Christian missionaries and were acculturated. Many of these African politicians were alienated from African customs and norms; indeed, they 'were doctrinaire cultural assimilationists' (Halisi, 1999: 48). Their constitutional critique was, thus, refracted by a 'civil imaginary'—the idea that cultural and religious conversion should lead inclusion in European/colonist civil society (de Kock, 2004: 125). These Christian liberals had imbibed the notion that the human rights discourse is the only legitimate grammar of dignity and that the bouquet of rights enjoyed by Europeans in South Africa and abroad were the most desirable. Concomitantly, the ANC accepted the Western paradigm of democracy and its institutional architecture.

As we have seen, African nationalists desired not only to return 'Africa to Africans', they wished to 'Return Africa' itself. This campaign for the homecoming of Africa meant celebrating and avowing African history, civilisation, values and way(s) of living. To realise this voyage, the PAC struggled for the 'complete overhaul of the present structure of society' (Sobukwe, cited in Gerhart, 1978: 196). This decolonisation objective could only be achieved, the PAC understood, when a 'total war (is waged) against the demi-god of white supremacy' and a 'mental revolution' is also undertaken to decolonise the mind of the conquered (Sobukwe, 1977c [1959]: 545–546). The PAC's proposed revolution was an absolute defiance of the logic of amity lines and abyssal thinking because it sought to remind Africans that 'they are not immature or irrational but that they are human' (Sobukwe, 1977c [1959]: 546).

While arguing stringently for self-pride and self-acceptance, the PAC's Africanism was not of the variant that rejected all things Western. Anton Lembede, the initiator of 20th-century Africanism in South Africa, was therefore at pains to point out that to 'Know thyself' did not preclude one from adopting worthwhile features from other cultures, it simply meant that Africans had to know the difference between 'borrowing and assimilating' and 'being borrowed and assimilated' (Lembede, 2015: 134). Thus, in their foundational critique of the colonial-apartheid constitutional order, African nationalists took a distance from Western modernity, substituted assimilation and mimicry for mental decolonisation and self-determination, embraced Africanity and on this basis sought to build an Africanist world that was faithful to African modern lifeways and incorporating of edifying elements from other civilisations.

Alas, the history of post-colonial constitution-making has too often forsaken this path. The result being that 'the independence constitutional order was therefore, as it were, an excrescence' (Shivji, 1991: 29). Writing in 2000, Bertrand Badie raised the distress that 'the years following decolonisation clearly revealed the failure of all mimicry in the constitutional area. Everything indicates, however, that mimicry has not ceased and that it has even intensified' (cited in Chanock, 2015: 21). These constitutional orders tend not to connect to the social experience of the majority of Africans and are thus 'extremely alienating' (Ake cited in Chanock, 2015: 5). In view of this alienating and petrifying reality and the fact that constitutionalism and the rule of law have little grounding in many parts of Africa, Martin Chanock argues that the issue that was avoided at decolonisation needs to be put back on the table: 'the extent to which indigenous African law, its language, ideas and in particular its processes, can become the basis for a rule of law for Africa' (2015: 16).

As far as South Africa is concerned, Issa Shivji despairingly concluded that the ANC's 1989 Constitutional Guidelines were 'squarely within a liberal-democratic paradigm' (1991: 38). With regard to the 'final' Constitution, although this Constitution was drafted through an impressive process of public consultation, ultimately, as Jeremy Sarkins points out, both the 'interim' Constitution and the 'final' Constitution are products of 'constitutional borrowings' (1998: 176). Sarkins continues, 'international and foreign experience substantially affected the process of constitutional drafting ... Areas influenced included the structure of the state, the structure of the court system, and, most prominently, the content and language of the two bills of rights' (1998: 177). The outcome is a constitutional order that is 'emphatically Eurocentric, and liberal' and that renders 'things African' subservient and invisible (Comaroff and Comaroff, 2004: 521). It is this reality that has caused most of the crises of constitution that currently bedevil South Africa leading to the majority of Africans feeling existentially and culturally as if they are once again 'foreign natives'.

Ramose's starting point is that only a homegrown 'authentic Constitution' will terminate the putative 'right of conquest' (Ramose *et al.*, 1991: 27). It is this right that is responsible for the constitutive sin of creating a polity where Africans are interpellated as pariahs and beings with defective ontology. Agitating on the eve of the post-1990 constitution-making process, Ramose and his colleagues argued that an absolute point of departure is to refuse 'mimetic constitutionalism' because the latter course would reinsert the future nation into the Euro-American colonial matrix of power and consequently legitimate the logic of the amity lines (Ramose *et al.*, 1991: 14–15).

Ramose would regard constitution-making to be a crucial territory for what he terms 'the struggle for reason' (2003b: 1). This struggle is impelled by the fact that Westerners appropriated reason itself and elevated themselves to the status of being the only animals with rationality. Casting his eyes across 'independent' Africa, he discovers that Africans do not only feel like outcasts in their countries, but they also continue to be regarded as animals without rationality 'despite democracy and the culture of human rights in our time' (Ramose, 2003b: 3). This being the case, it is the intrinsic job description of constitutionalists to either recast the Line, perpetuate epistemicide and continue 'sub-ontologising' the historically conquered, or disavow the ontology of conquest, dislodge the Line and enable quests of remembering and re-membering.

As we can expect, the Ramosean critique is that South African constitutionalists—saddled by cultural and spiritual exile, constrained by and mimicking uni-versal fads in constitutionalism—chose route one between the two routes outlined above. Accordingly, 'the dominant and exclusive voice of the "constitutional order" of South Africa is the epistemological paradigm of the successors in title to the questionable "right of conquest"', protests Ramose (2012: 32). 'Constitutional borrowings' together with the exclusion and silencing of the legal epistemological paradigm of indigenous peoples proves that despite the fact of public participation in the constitution-making process, the historically conquered were in fact excluded from constitution-making (Ramose, 2012: 32). The outcome is spiritual and cultural, 'imprisonment by a constitution with dubious home-grown credentials together with epistemicide' (Ramose, 2003c: 139). Furthermore, the redundant invocation of *Ubuntu* in constitutional judgements and its deployment as an ornament to supplement South Africa's Eurocentric law entrenches epistemicide (Ramose, 2012: 31–32). This cannibalising of *Ubuntu* is an attempt to dupe the historically conquered into accepting the South African Constitution's deceptive tagline: 'One Law, One Nation'.

The struggle and the search for a truly Azanian Constitution must continue. With respect to this final pillar, such a Constitution would be one that is genuinely a mirror of society in which everyone would see themselves reflected and valorised. For any law to be legitimate, more especially constitutional law, it must derive its authority from the active presence of *umuntu*. The current constitutional law excludes *Bantu*, and it thus makes itself felt to the *Bantu* people of South Africa as an 'excrescence' and as an alienating and oppressive cultural apparatus. In their legal consciousness, this law is still the 'law of conquerors' (Ramose, 2003c: 139). As was the case with the law of colonial apartheid, this law is often approached in the most tactical and cynical manner by the historically conquered.

Constitutional legitimacy and ownership will not be achieved through the missionary approach of 'workshopping' the historically conquered and of vernacularising concepts and symbols of this Eurocentric constitutional law. Epistemicide and the inferiorisation of African lifeworlds and institutions would only come to an end when there is a revalorisation of *Ubuntu* constitutional law. Ramose aligns himself with leading anti-neocolonialists in submitting that such a revalorisation must also mean the retrieval of principles of 'traditional' African political culture without which there can never be a truly liberated and emancipative reality in Africa. Echoing the PAC, Ramose (1992: 69) also asserts that such a retrieval need does not mean discarding everything from the alien European culture as far as some institutional design and procedures are concerned.

I will conclude this section by recalling that for Amilcar Cabral a 'return to the source' involves a double gesture of delinking from Western modernity and of 're-Africanisation' achievable by drinking in the well of those not completely ensnared in the orbit of Western modernity (Cabral, 1973: 60). It is here in the villages and other rural areas that African norms, values and institutions are continually created and recreated in response to the normal progression of life, the irruption of Western modernity, civil law and the pernicious and African law-bastardising impacts of the system of indirect rule. At the source is where 'living customary law' together with a regime of 'interlegality' resides. The final pillar involves building on this complex and creole African modern law to craft a post-conquest Constitution.

8.5 Conclusion

At the time of writing, South Africa was in the throes of an intellectual and physical decolonisation struggle instigated by black students at institutions of higher learning. Began as a struggle to decommodify access to higher education and to decolonise university curricula, this struggle has expanded to a complete disavowal of the country's lauded transitional justice process and an emergent discourse of rejecting what these students consider to be the country's liberal, cultural alienating and white supremacy-preserving Constitution. In this chapter, I employed Santos's metaphor of the Line to demonstrate that the current state of neo-apartheid constitutionalism means that the constitutive sin of apartness installed during settler colonisation has been reconfigured but not dislodged. I dipped into the constitutional and jurisprudential archive of African nationalists to recall a tradition of constitutional critique that pre-empted and rejected this neo-colonial constitutional dispensation. Mogobe Ramose's manifesto of post-conquest constitutionness represents a foundational critique that seeks to dislodge the Line and instantiate a post-abyssal line society based on principles of African humanness. This counter-hegemonic manifesto is urgently needed in South Africa today and is of relevance to all historically settler colonial societies.

Note

1 The Shack-dwellers Movement of South Africa.

References

Abahlali baseMjondolo (2014), "UnFreedom Day 2014: We Mourn Twenty Years of UnFreedom", *Abahlali.org*, April 26. Accessed on 29.4.2016 at www.abahlali.org/node/13640.

Alexander, Neville (2002), *An Ordinary Country: Issues in the Transition from Apartheid to Democracy in South Africa*. Pietermaritzburg: University of Natal Press.

Alexander, Peter; Runciman, Carin; Maruping, Boitumelo (2015), "South African Police Service (SAPS) Data on Crowd Incidents: A Preliminary Analysis", Social Change Research Unit, University of Johannesburg. Accessed on 20.9.2016 at https://africacheck.org/wp-content/uploads/2015/06/South-African-Police-Service-Data-on-Crowd-Incidents-Report.pdf.

Barolsky, Vanessa (2012), "'A better life for all', social cohesion and the governance of life in post-apartheid South Africa", *Social Dynamics*, 38(1), 134–151. DOI: https://doi.org/10.1080/02533952.2012.698951.

Baxi, Upendra (2013), "Preliminary notes on transformative constitutionalism", in Oscar Vilhena, Upendra Baxi and Frans Viljoen (eds.), *Transformative Constitutionalism: Comparing the Apex Courts of Brazil, India and South Africa*. Pretoria: PULP, 19–47.

Cabral, Amilcar (1973), *Return to the Source: Selected Speeches of Amilcar Cabral*. New York: Monthly Review Press.

Chanock, Martin (2015), "African constitutionalism from the bottom up". Accessed on 16.8.2016 at www.customcontested.co.za/wp-content/uploads/2015/04/Chanock-PublicLecture-2015.pdf.

Comaroff, John; Comaroff, Jean (2004), "Policing culture, cultural policing: Law and social order in postcolonial South Africa", *Law and Social Inquiry*, 29(3), 513–535. DOI: https://doi.org/10.1111/j.1747-4469.2004.tb00999.x.

de Kock, Leon (2004), "Sitting the civilisational test: The making(s) of a civil imaginary colonial South Africa", in Leon de Kock *et al.* (eds.), *South Africa in the Global Imaginary*. Pretoria: UNISA Press.

Fanon, Frantz (1963), *The Wretched of the Earth*. New York: Grove Press.

Fanon, Frantz (1967), *Toward the African Revolution*. New York: Grove Press.

Gerhart, Gwendolen (1978), *Black Power in South Africa: The Evolution of an Ideology*. California: University of California Press.

Gordon, Lewis (2015), *What Fanon Said: A Philosophical Introduction to His Life and Work*. New York: Fordham University Press.

Halisi, C. R. D. (1999), *Black Political Thought in the Making of South African Democracy*. Bloomington, IN: Indiana University Press.

Hirschl, Ran (2004), "Political Origins of the New Constitutionalism", *Indiana Journal of Global Legal Studies*, 11(1), 71–108. JSTOR: www.jstor.org/stable/10.2979.

Klare, Karl (1998), "Legal Culture and Transformative Constitutionalism", *South African Journal on Human Rights*, 14(1), 146–188. DOI: https://doi.org/10.1080/02587203.1998.11834974.

Leballo, Potlako (1957), "The Nature of the Struggle Today", *The Africanist*, December.

Lembede, Anton (2015), *Freedom in Our Lifetime: The Collected Writings of Anton Muziwakhe Lembede*. Cape Town: Kwela Books.

Mafeje, Archie (1986), "South Africa: The Dynamics of a Beleaguered State", *The Journal of African Political Economy*, 1(1), 95–119. JSTOR: www.jstor.org/stable/23500221.

Magubane, Bernard (1996), *The Making of a Racist State; British Imperialism and the Union of South Africa, 1875–1910*. Trenton, NJ: Africa World Press.

Mamdani, Mahmood (1996), *Citizen and Subject: Contemporary Africa and the Legacy of Late Colonialism*. London: James Currey.

Mamdani, Mahmood (1998), "When does a settler become a native: Reflection on colonial citizenship in Equatorial and South Africa". Accessed on 10.7.2016 at http://citizenshiprightsafrica.org/wp-content/uploads/1998/05/mamdani-1998-inaugural-lecture.pdf

Mandaza, Ibbo (1991), "Perspectives on Armed Struggle and Constitutionalism: The Zimbabwe Model", in Issa G. Shivji (ed.), *State and Constitutionalism: An African Debate on Democracy*. Harare: SAPES, 71–89.

Mbeki, Thabo (1996), "Speech at the Adoption of the Constitutional Bill, 8 May 1996". Accessed on 12.6.2016 at www.anc.org.za/content/i-am-african-thabo-mbekis-speech-adoption-republic-south-africa-constitution-bill.

Mbeki, Thabo (1998), "Statement of Deputy President Thabo Mbeki at the Opening of the Debate in the National Assembly on Reconciliation and Nation Building", National Assembly Cape Town, 29 May 1998.

Mostert, Noel (1993), *Frontiers: The Epic of South Africa's Creation and the Tragedy of the Xhosa People*. London: Pimlico.

Motlhabi, Mokgethi (1984), *The Theory and Practice of Black Resistance to Apartheid: A Social-ethical Analysis*. Johannesburg: Skotaville Publishers.

Murungi, John (2004), "The Question of an African Jurisprudence: Some Hermeneutic Reflections", in Kwasi Wiredu (ed.), *A Companion to African Philosophy*. Malden, MA: Blackwell, 519–526.

Ngũgĩ, wa Thing'o (2009), *Re-membering Africa*. Nairobi: East African Educational Publishers.

NPC—National Planning Commission (2014), *Medium-Term Strategic Framework 2014 to 2019—Outcome 14: National Building and Social Cohesion*. Accessed on 15.7.2016 at www.dpme.gov.za/keyfocusareas/outcomesSite/MTSF%201/Outcome%2014%20Nation%20Building%20MTSF%20Chapter.pdf.

Okoth-Ogendo, H.W.O. (1991), "Constitutions without Constitutionalism: Reflections on an African Political Paradox", in Issa G. Shivji (ed.), *State and Constitutionalism: An African Debate on Democracy*. Harare: SAPES, 3–25.

Oomen, Barbara (2005), *Chiefs in South Africa: Law, Power and Culture in the Post-Apartheid Era*. Oxford: James Curry.

Oswin, Natalie (2007), "The End of Queer (as we knew it): Globalization and the Making of Gay-friendly South Africa", *Gender, Place and Culture,* 14(1), 93–110. DOI: https://doi.org/10.1080/09663690601122358.

PAC—Pan-Africanist Congress (1965), "The PAC Manifesto", in PAC (ed.), *The Basic Documents of the Pan Africanist Congress of Azania*. Johannesburg: PAC.

Raboroko, Nkutseou (1960), "Congress and the Africanists: (I) the Africanist Case", *SAHO*, Accessed on 11.5.2016 at www.sahistory.org.za/sites/default/files/DC/asapr60.5/asapr60.5.pdf.

Ramose, Mogobe (1991), "Self-determination in Decolonisation", in William Twining (ed.), *Issues of Self-determination*. Aberdeen: Aberdeen University Press. 25–32.

Ramose, Mogobe (1992), "African Democratic Tradition: Oneness, Consensus and Openness", *Quest*, 6(2), 69–83.

Ramose, Mogobe (1999), *African Philosophy through Ubuntu*. Harare: Mond Books.

Ramose, Mogobe (2003a), "Justice and Restitution in African Political Thought", in P. H. Coetzee and A.P.J. Roux (eds.), *The African Philosophy Reader*. London: Routledge, 541–589.

Ramose, Mogobe (2003b), "The Struggle for Reason in Africa", in P. H. Coetzee and A.P.J. Roux (eds.), *The African Philosophy Reader*. London: Routledge, 1–9.

Ramose, Mogobe (2003c), "Transforming Education in South Africa: Paradigm Shift or Change?" *South African Journal of Higher Education*, 17(3), 137–143. DOI: https://doi.org/10.4314/sajhe.v17i3.25413

Ramose, Mogobe (2006a), "Philosophy and Africa's Struggle for Economic Independence", *Politeia* 25(1), 3–17.

Ramose, Mogobe (2006b), "The King as Memory and Symbol of African Customary Law", in Manfred Hinz (ed.), *The Shade of New Leaves: Governance in Traditional Authority a Southern African Perspective*. Berlin: LIT VERLAG, 351–373.

Ramose, Mogobe (2007), "African Philosophy as Bridge towards Intercultural Philosophy", *International Journal of the Humanities*, 4(9), 123–132. DOI: https://doi.org/10.18848/1447-9508/CGP/v04i09/43434.

Ramose, Mogobe (2009), "Ecology through Ubuntu", Munyaradzi F. Murove (ed.), *African Ethics: An Anthology of Comparative and Applied Ethics*. Scottsville: University of Kwazulu-Natal Press.

Ramose, Mogobe (2012), "Reconciliation and Reconfiliation in South Africa", *Journal of African Philosophy*, 5, 20–39.

Ramose, Mogobe (2014), "Ubuntu: Affirming a Right and Seeking Remedies in South Africa", in Leonhard Praeg and Siphokazi Magadla (eds.), *Ubuntu: Curating an Archive*. Scottsville: University of KwaZulu-Natal Press, 121–136.

Ramose, Mogobe; Maphala, Tshepo; Makhabane, Thabo (1991), "In Search of a Workable and Lasting Constitutional Change in South Africa", *Quest*, 5(2), 5–31.

Sarkins, Jeremy (1998), "The Effect of Constitutional Borrowings on the Drafting of South Africa's Bill of Rights and Interpretation of Human Rights Provisions", *Journal of Constitutional Law,* 1(2), 176–204.

Santos, Boaventura de Sousa (1995), *Toward a New Common Sense: Law, Sciences and Politics in a Paradigmatic Transition.* New York: Routledge.

Santos, Boaventura de Sousa (2007), "Beyond Abyssal Thinking: From Global Lines to Ecologies of Knowledges", *Review,* (1), 45–89.

Scott, David (2004), *Conscripts of Modernity: The Tragedy of Enlightenment.* Durham, NC: Duke University Press.

Sekyi-Otu, Ato (1996), *Fanon's Dialectic of Experience.* Cambridge, MA: Harvard University Press.

Shivji, Issa (1991), "State and Constitutionalims: A New Democratic Perspective", in Issa G. Shivji (ed.), *State and Constitutitutionalism: An African Debate on Democracy.* Harare: SAPES, 27–54.

Sobukwe, Robert (1977a), "Future of the Africanist Movement Questions and Answers by R. M. Sobukwe", in Thomas Karis and Gwendolen Carter (eds.), *From Protest to Challenge: A Documentary History of African Politics in South Africa 1882–1964.* Vol. 3: *Challenge and Violence, 1953–1964.* Stanford, CA: Hoover Institution Press, 506–510.

Sobukwe, Robert (1977b), "Opening Address at Inaugural Convention 4–6 April 1959", in Thomas Karis and Gwendolen Carter (eds.), *From Protest to Challenge: A Documentary History of African Politics in South Africa 1882–1964.* Vol. 3: *Challenge and Violence, 1953–1964.* Stanford, CA: Hoover Institution Press, 510–517.

Sobukwe, Robert (1977c), "The State of the Nation on National Heroes Day 2 August 1959", in Thomas Karis and Gwendolen Carter (eds.), *From Protest to Challenge: A Documentary History of African Politics in South Africa 1882–1964.* Vol. 3: *Challenge and Violence, 1953–1964.* Stanford, CA: Hoover Institution Press, 542–548.

South African Native Congress (1972), "'Questions Affecting the Natives and Coloured People Resident in British South Africa', Statement by the Executive of the South African Native Congress, 1903", in Thomas Karis and Gwendolen Carter (eds.), *From Protest to Challenge: A Documentary History of African Politics in South Africa 1882–1964.* Vol. I. Stanford, CA: Hoover Institution Press, 8–29.

Veracini, L. (2010), *Settler Colonialism: A Theoretical Overview.* New York: Palgrave Macmillan.

Wamba-dia-Wamba, Ernest (1991), "Discourse on the National Question", in Issa G. Shivji (ed.), *State and Constitutionalism: An African debate on Democracy.* Harare: SAPES, 57–69.

PART III

The Return of the Abyssally Excluded?

The Indigenous Constitutional Struggles in Latin America

9

CAN SILENCE BE A CONSTITUENT?

A Reading of the Indigenous Communitarian Constitutionalism of Bolivia

Salvador Schavelzon

9.1 Introduction

The aim of this chapter is to present certain aspects of the Bolivian constituent process which approved a new Constitution in 2009, with a particular focus on the elements of indigenous peasant politics that emerged and came to maturity through the traditions and political struggles referred to in studies of communitarian and social organization over the decades. I will deal with the difficulties these ideas and political forms have faced in creating space within alien institutions that would ultimately prevail, and the characteristics of the constitutionalism pervaded by these incursions.[1]

In July 2006, the Constituent Assembly was inaugurated in the city of Sucre. At the time, it was still not possible to measure the scope, mood and political direction of the transformations being promoted by the new government, nor the type of political experience that would characterize the MAS (*El Movimiento al Socialismo*), a peasant-based party that would lead the way to the formation of the government of Evo Morales, a coca grower and trade unionist of Aymara origin. In addition to strong opposition from the east of the country calling for regional autonomy, there was a demand from the department of Chuquisaca to return the seat of government to Sucre (the country's official capital, but for the last century limited to serving as the seat of the judiciary). It is possible that this strong opposition was an important factor in maintaining an unruptured and complex alliance—a bloc—which united the peasants, the indigenous people and the left. From this union would emerge the proposal for constituting a plurinational and communitarian state that would confront the opposition from the liberal and conservative political sectors.

DOI: 10.4324/9781003391920-13

The social and political bloc that would generate the plurinational proposal had emerged from the common path traversed by indigenous organizations, agrarian unions and the left, and through parties, NGOs and culture, a political cycle that had engaged in acts of remembrance throughout the 500 years of conquest, and the solidarity and protest organized during the period 2000–2005, a time of rebellions, roadblocks and demands presented to the state. It was from this that the Pact of Unity had emerged, as the brains behind a constituent proposal that lay beyond the control of the party that formed the new government. It was mainly composed of peasant-based organizations (essentially peasant and 'intercultural' colonizer unions), as well as indigenous highland and lowland organizations (the CIDOB and CONAMAQ) that were independent of the government. After a long journey, the electoral triumph of the MAS and the opening of the Constituent Assembly established the conditions that would pave the way for a constituent dialogue.

The establishment of common ground between the peasant and indigenous elements which gave rise to the 'peasant originary indigenous' and between the state and autonomy, or development and communitarian alternatives, would become an impossibility after the Constitution was approved. Yet, it is precisely this moment and this potential for interconnecting differences that interest me, as a productive moment when silences became public and the solidified forms of a colonial and capitalist legality were questioned. A critique of Western civilization, neoliberal capitalism and liberal republicanism was able to emerge as a political focal point which, although not dominant, was nevertheless ever-present during the discussions that gave rise to a new Constitution.

Within the dynamics of the Constituent Assembly, the mixed race and regional opposition persistently denounced the risks to the rule of law and demanded changes. These changes were carried out, yet the opposition persisted in its criticism as if the risks remained intact. On the other hand, indigenous organizations maintained their support and mobilized through the new Constitution, even when they saw their demands continually postponed, curtailed and distorted. Beyond the written text itself, the dispute seemed to be situated elsewhere. At stake was a real war between worlds or ontologies that disputed the very existence of something that did not fit into the political reality which the institutions and norms steadfastly held onto as a reference point.

Due to the characteristics of the indigenous demands, they were included in the articles of the Constitution, but their strength lay elsewhere. They may be described as 'constituent silences' because they are, in some way, invisible to state law. Obviously, the social organizations presented claims that materialized in writing, but the wording was always vague. At the same time, what was said proved insufficient, while expressing more than was apparent. Consequently, the catastrophic predictions of the opposition were revived repeatedly prior to new 'essential and fundamental' modifications being made. This happened at each stage of the Assembly: in the committees, before each version negotiated at the table with the opposition, and after the final agreement when the opposition reviewed the entire Constitution and still continued to campaign against its approval, raising the same spectres they had prided themselves on removing in Congress through amendments.

Part of the strength of these silences and spaces for ambiguity within the Constitution were detected by the opposition member of the Assembly and political scientist Jorge Lazarte who, in an opinion column in the newspaper *La Razón* shortly before the referendum, stated that the danger within the 'MAS Constitution' lay precisely in what it did not say (Lazarte, 2008). Moreover, the Cochabamba newspaper *Los Tiempos* stated that: 'We are faced with a masterpiece of political engineering which, *without explicitly saying so*, constitutes a fourth power of the state', a reference to the 'Social Power' that the MAS had constitutionalized without anyone noticing (*Los Tiempos*, 2008; my italics).

This political power of the indigenous, the communitarian and the plurinational referred to centuries of invisibility in a republic of the few and would gain a political victory with the approval of the new Constitution of Bolivia. However, this force for change would not be brought into being through the framework of the government implementing it, and its defeat would originate in its inability to involve the country in the reforms and changes inscribed in these existing worlds which had emerged, retracted by a government that had stabilized and looked to nationalism for its income transfer policies and the promise of expanding the middle class, promoting consumption and the process of industrializing economic development as a government formula.

The peasant and communitarian indigenous would leave the scene, their difficulties not reduced to the advancement of a state, a leader and the logic of representation. Yet even in their absence, they would leave their mark on a constitutionalism whose main virtue would be to open up space for arguments that had never been expounded in such a powerful way before at state level.

9.2 The Ethnography of the 'peasant originary indigenous' Constitutionalization

The first draft of the Constitution was formulated from the political space created around the Pact of Unity. Presented in 2006, it was used by the MAS as a base document in the thematic committees. According to Luis Tapia, the role of the Pact of Unity was not marginal, having established itself as a forum for connection on an ethical-political level, as it had been throughout the phase of combating neoliberalism. It did not function as a body for corporate negotiation, Tapia states, but rather as an intellectual organic collective of peasants and indigenous people for whom the introduction of the proposal for a plurinational state was due (2011: 92–95). For an analysis of the role of the Pact of Unity in the constituent process, see Garcés (2010) and Schavelzon (2013).

Within the Pact of Unity, the politics of the countryside and city majorities stood alongside minority visions emanating from the originary territories, meaning that the latter could also become protagonists in the constituent process. Without the peasant majorities, integrated into the market and now assumed to be citizens of a state in which the peasants were in power, this process would not have been set in motion. Yet, it was due to the ethnic community, the *ayllu*, and the projects for autonomous territoriality that an alternative political model could be linked to a Bolivian reality in which the indigenous community also had a presence, within trade unions, cities and migrant peasant communities.

In combining political positions from the minority and from the majorities in power, the Pact of Unity facilitated the convergence of a movement oriented toward guaranteeing and defending sovereignty over natural resources, together with those who, from a less globalized perspective, sought the possibility of envisaging life according to different conceptions of development. Through this encounter between worlds of internal dialogue and the new political majority, the indigenous proposals were *peasantized*, while certain ideas from the peasant sector were *indianized*. The work of the Communitarian Plurinational State would leave in its wake a project containing elements of civilization, silences and invisibilities, as well as mixed ideologies. Counsellors, leaders and militants were converted into alchemists who proposed and reached partial agreements that were repeatedly subjected to revision and change.

From the ethnographic records of the discussions in the Constituent Assembly, it can be seen how the indigenous elements faced several barriers. A large part of the dynamics of committee meetings with the opposition, or the drafting of articles within the MAS and with allies, was organized around the requirement for a strict definition of how the Pact of Unity proposals would be introduced. Faced with this requirement, the indigenous members and their advisors saw the work of constitutionalization, which took place throughout 2007, acquire a high level of sophistication and strategic subtlety. From then on, drafting a Constitution often became *the constitutionalization of silences* on topics that were better left out than included in a rigid or closed form that would affect their possible future scope.

Throughout the discussions, many of the proposals would end up linking to the multicultural model already in force in Bolivia, due to inertia. The 'plurinational', meanwhile, would operate as a concept that was not yet defined in an unambiguous or clear way but, even so, or precisely because of this, would still have the power to threaten, as a possibility for a different form of constitutionalism. It was from within the community—as a silence and a place for misunderstandings—that the institution of the republic could be questioned. However, from the point of view of the republic and the state, the collective territoriality, alternative forms of social organization and an economic sphere indistinguishable from politics and life were incomprehensible. The new Constitution of Bolivia departed from this *non-place*, an unknown location denied even by a Eurocentric left or a developmentalist nationalism which, although peasant-based, looked to the city, the exploitation of resources and peripheral capitalist development—as an exporter of raw materials—as the place from which to establish Bolivia in the world.

One of the discussions that clearly expressed the amorphism and the Pact of Unity's capacity for articulation focused on a definition of the composition of the Bolivian people contained in Article 3. Anti-state forces emerging from the Water War, the plateau mobilizations and the Gas War made it clear that natural resources should be in the hands of the people: a state could re-sell or redistribute these assets, as the history of colonialism in Bolivia reveals. The members of the Assembly established that the state would only be an administrator of the resources, while the people would be the true owner. Prior to this amendment, the members and the Pact of Unity had discussed how this entity should be defined.

The debate is reproduced in detail elsewhere (Schavelzon, 2012, Chapter 1), but it is worth highlighting the positions that sought to define people as indigenous or with reference to social class. It is also worth mentioning the open resolution, added without opposing class and ethnicity—inspired by the 'looking with two eyes' of Katarist Indianism of the 1970s and 1980s—and framed through the idea of viewing 'indigenous peasants' as a single political subject. This central formula would then pave the way for introducing a collective subject into the Constitution, which would be defined as 'peasant originary indigenous nations and peoples', to which would be added, in Article 3 of the Constitution, '*las bolivianas y los bolivianos*', 'intercultural' communities—the term used by the colonizer unions, including the coca growers, to define themselves—and 'Afro-Bolivians', all given equal status with the indigenous peoples in terms of rights in another article in the Constitution (Republic of Bolivia, 2009: 11).

It was not only a matter of enumerating but also of recognizing multiple and historically excluded identities that should be expressly named. The social organizations were clear in demanding that their denominations were included in this article. For the MAS members, instead of redundancy, this complemented the non-exclusionary definitions: peasants who were also indigenous; Bolivians who were also intercultural. Some actors then did not accept that the definitions proposed by each Pact of Unity organization should be separated by a comma, as in 'indigenous, originary and peasant'. Thus, the central subject of the new Constitution included the majorities (the peasants) and minorities (the indigenous), to some extent erasing this differentiation, as well as those who were only identified as '*las bolivianas y los bolivianos*'. In this definition, the categories referred to different groups but at the same time combined them in a single formula, reflecting the flexible, open and overlapping ways in which many Bolivians define themselves. It was the creative result of a combination of perspectives from minority peoples, Indianistic thinking, and horizons anchored in the national, in socialism and in left pluralism.

From 2006 onward, a large part of Bolivian politics would be built from this immense, but also non-existent, space between indigenous peoples and peasants. Instead of separating the peasant from the indigenous by a comma, there was a silence. A comma is a silence, and it was now this silence which facilitated the conceptualization and production of the meeting point for different civilizations, ontologies and political projects. What would also serve to separate the indigenous peoples from the peasants shortly afterward—for example, in the peasant blockade and subsequent police repression at an indigenous march in Chaparina during the TIPNIS conflict—materialized in the Constituent Assembly via a linguistic device facilitated by the Pact of Unity, a constituent silence; an emptiness which, in the absence of a grammatical separation, spoke volumes. It was the silence of decolonization, the possibility of a new state to be built by indigenous peasants, nations and peoples, '*las bolivianas y los bolivianos*'.[2]

In this way, the proposal that the Pact of Unity and the MAS presented to the Assembly sought to break with the idea of miscegenation advocated for decades by nationalism, an idea based on the homogeneity of the people which avoids any juxtaposition of ethnic nationalities, instead diluting them through an imagined national community. The three elements that formed the Pact of Unity were recombined to present an extremely original image of the people, in the sense of breaking their own singularity. The highland peasant, the originary peoples of the highlands and the lowland indigenous peoples have thus generated countless possibilities through a wide and diffuse definition.

However, there would be no break with the nationalist vision which allocated the people a status equivalent to that of a piece in the political jigsaw completed by the state. Via this Constitution, the people encountered their organization and representative in the state. Yet this did not act as a deterrent, at least in the construction of the constitutional text—since, it would be difficult to develop a logic opposed to that of the state from the outside—as dispersed indigenous minorities, distanced from the political centre, had the possibility of *Buen Vivir*, which had initially emerged as a proposal linked to the highland communities. In this constituent encounter, the cyclical temporality of the Andes—where 'the past is ahead', 'the future has already been seen' and the present may be an inversion of space-time—was combined with the linear temporality of a discourse on development and the nomadic and anti-productive spatiality of the lowlands.

Underlying the constitutional innovations was the political fact of the emergence of the indigenous peoples, confirmed by the 2001 Census, in which 62% of the population stated that they belonged to an indigenous ethnic group. This widespread identification as indigenous, which is not limited to rural communities but also recognizes city-based Quechuan and Aymara, was a true unifier which—without eliminating singularity—created problems for the liberal opposition, who insisted that some of those who had declared themselves as such were not, 'in reality', indigenous. Yet, above all, it allowed for interconnections between different people, who did not dilute their particularity but, while still remaining Bolivians, maintained or recovered their sense of belonging.[3]

Opponents of the MAS saw discrimination against non-indigenous people in Article 3. By not being included in the definitions other than by a reference in the generic description to '*bolivianos y bolivianas*', an indigenous state would be created, thereby damaging the republic and the push toward equality (cf. Mesa, 2012). The curious thing is that this accusation also came from the radical sectors of Indianism whose proposal was explicitly to indianize the institutions and who felt the MAS had failed to advance this goal. An open Constitution filled with things unspoken yet present meant that it could be viewed either as a Constitution for Indianism or, alternatively, one that belonged to a *blancoide* ('white') environment and served to keep coloniality intact.

The difficulties involved in the process of approving the new Constitution and the withholding of authorization for the constitutive referendum by the former Congress which, in effect, held the text drafted by the MAS hostage left the opposition able to intervene in the elaboration of the text, vetoing, correcting and blocking various elements of the version that had been approved as a definitive text in December 2007. The word 'nation' was reintroduced in the description that defines the people, while in other articles the term 'republic' reappeared after it had been eliminated but, in the final version, was only retained in a critical sense—as a continuation of colonialism—in the preamble: 'We have left the colonial, republican and neoliberal State in the past' (Republic of Bolivia, 2009: 7). Once the Constitution was approved, Evo Morales signed a decree in which he changed 'Republic' to the 'Plurinational State of Bolivia', even though all the republican institutions would be preserved.[4]

During one of the intense conflicts that were resolved with explicit contradictions, the Constituent Assembly experienced a real battle between the community and the liberal state on the subject of the constitutionalization of indigenous justice, which was in widespread use throughout the Andes and even in urban localities, as has been discussed elsewhere (Schavelzon, 2016a). The definitive relationship between the two systems was not resolved in the Constitution: this would only be accomplished through a post-constitutional implementation which rendered indigenous justice subordinate to ordinary justice. Discussions on community justice questioned the limitations of a system that was closed to pluralism yet failed to clearly define whether it would result in a new intercultural system or a multicultural segment of state justice as a whole. Thus, it remained an open question whether indigenous justice would be established as a parallel system on an equal footing with the ordinary system, whether it would be introduced via the state, thereby affecting all national justice or whether it would be subordinated to the old state law, even if national justice tended to prevail.

The hierarchical equality between state and indigenous forms also extends to economic, governmental and territorial matters. However, certain articles state the contrary: there are, for example, fewer powers for indigenous autonomies in relation to the departmental or central government, which maintains its unitary form; there is also the issue of representative democracy overlapping with the communitarian version, as well as the education system remaining centralized, while the market economy and industrial development enjoy more guarantees than the *ayllu* economy.

Another silence would be expressed via the concept of communitarian democracy, which was only mentioned briefly in the Constitution but had in its foundations the potential to question the modern system of individual representation. Bolivia adopted the democratic, participatory and communitarian form for its government (Article 11) (Republic of Bolivia, 2009: 15), as well as the right to exercise its political, legal and economic systems according to its world view (Article 30(II)(14)) (Republic of Bolivia, 2009: 28). The questions that arose focused on the extent to which *ayllu* democracy, with its assembly, could be integrated into a capitalist democracy without conflict. If a Constitution is judged by what it establishes as a new reality, it can only be concluded that the *ayllu* remains silent. If we view the text as a mere reflection of relations that are defined through other areas, it can be seen that, while remaining silent, the community was introduced into the legality of the state, without doubt as a consequence of mobilizations and decades of indigenous insurgent politics.

Linked to the criticism of representation and indigenous forms of democracy, the idea of direct representation, a minority claim for participation that is central to the conception of plurinationality, was incorporated from the lowlands. In discussions within the Pact of Unity that took place in the National Congress, there were 36 peoples' representatives. The opposition rejected any kind of ethnic delineation or representation that had not been determined by individual vote. The peasants of the MAS, together with those from the CSUTCB, also failed to welcome this representation of minorities. For the MAS, as Evo Morales himself went on to say, it would be this party and its deputies, elected by a majority vote, who would represent the indigenous peoples.

The constitutional resolution of this matter would remain open to discussion, since two consecutive articles established contradictory parameters on the subject. In one of them (Article 146(VII)) it was established that 'the peasant originary indigenous special circumscriptions shall be governed by the principle of density of population in each department' (Republic of Bolivia, 2009: 80), while another (Article 147(III)) states that 'the law shall define the peasant originary indigenous special circumscriptions, in which the population density and geographical continuity shall not be considered as conditional criteria' (Republic of Bolivia, 2009: 80).

The very concept of plurinationality would be the channel through which the silence of the community was expressed. One version was interpreted as a map of 36 nations, even though the Constitution officially recognized 36 indigenous languages without referring to the same number of territories. The first criticisms came from conservative sectors who suspected that the proliferation of previously unrecognized indigenous peoples constituted a means for obtaining land and other special rights. There was talk of ethnocratic government. Yet there was also criticism from those who took an unsympathetic view of the stabilizing of a dynamic process of inter-ethnic connections that did not conform to a rigid map of state nationalities. The establishment of nations, which was not asserted in the text but was assumed as a possibility, would bring rigidity to a dynamic articulation of the differences in essentialized forms that would soon become problematic for what they left out and for the impossibility of including differences in cases where they failed to adapt to these fragments of state identity.

Despite the absence of any definition, the danger and threat registered by critics, together with the force of the term 'plurinationality' as a flag that opened up the pathways and hopes of the community understood as autonomous territory, conferred a value on the term exceeding that which was explicitly set out in the text. Moreover, it was manifest when reading between the lines and exploring the extra-textual possibilities. It was a constituent silence. As such, it contained a flaw in its evasive character, in its elusiveness which came without express guarantees within the Constitution. Nevertheless, it also contained an advantage: the ontological singularity it could express was invisible in the eyes of conventional law and was therefore a gateway to its constitutionalization and public existence. The latter enabled it to survive any negotiations that placed it at a disadvantage. Both its strength and weakness lay within its silent invisibility.

9.3 The Modern Critique of an Open and Plural Constitution

In surreptitious or diffuse forms, the proposed Constitution adopted by the MAS sought to advance through what were sensitive issues for liberalism and the republic. With what can be understood as 'legal insinuations', the state appeared to seek its own decolonization from within. It was in this way that the republican form, defended by liberals in their objections to the 'indigenous peasants', was questioned through different ways of understanding property (collective territoriality and the recognition of ancestry), the representative form of government (the inclusion of direct representation of the peoples in parliament), the judicial system of substantive law (including peasant-indigenous jurisdiction) and the division of powers (including social control). Without being explicitly defined, evocations of community, indigenous values and plurinationality could or could not be adapted to the existing institutions.

In face of a proposal that only advanced at the negotiating table because of its diffuse, omnipresent and elusive form, it was possible to perceive a modern and dichotomized state form that resisted the new reforms: a conservative resistance that ran contrary to pluralism and the coexistence of non-assimilated elements.

The heterogeneous and mixed nature of the plurinational project was criticized by Juan Carlos Urenda, who utilized the image of the 'Catóblepa state'[5] to define plurinational constitutionalism as the 'contradiction', 'disorder', 'incoherence', 'violence' and 'illegality' of a 'communitaristic state' (Urenda, 2009). Jorge Lazarte, a political scientist and member of the Constituent Assembly elected in La Paz, reaches similar conclusions, but with an emphasis on what he sees as the failure of the deliberative democratic body, from a perspective that views the process as defined by chaos and improvisation, a hindrance to rational dialogue between institutional actors. Lazarte denounces the intervention of external actors, the fact that members were poorly trained in ideological argument, and the lack of debate, as well as the 'participationism' and mandatory consensus that denied the possibility of dissent, attributed to the logic of communitarian democracy and recognized by the new Constitution (Lazarte, 2011: 335–337, 350, 381 and *passim*).

What the proponents of the concept of plurinationality, or of a broad definition of the 'Bolivian people', saw as innovation by combining components of different traditions, and which I consider to be the basis for understanding the scenario of conflict and juxtaposition of ontologies, would be precisely the point targeted by many of its critics. For them, the mixture of constitutional and political matrices and paradigms was negative and threatening, in the sense that they were grafts, creating an incoherent Constitution. From the same perspective, journalist Fernando Molina, from the capital La Paz, adopts a liberal position, considering the plurinational innovations of the text to be a 'legal fiction' given that they lack the instruments needed to implement the concept, drawing a parallel with the first liberal constitutions of the country—despite the difference in content—since at that time, what is now criticized by indigenous communities was firmly established within them (Molina, 2009: 3).

For Molina, the Constitution promulgated in 2009 leads to an extreme conception of Bolivia as a non-homogeneous and diverse society (in his own words, 'non-national and fragmentary') whose foundations had already been established by the constitutional reforms of 1995, while also regressing to the matrix of a state-controlled economy with nationalist, socialist and anti-liberal influences which, for him, constitutes the principal 'Bolivian ideology' to this day. Molina describes the sources of the new Constitution as follows:

> 70% or more of the Constitution is based on Latin republicanism (popular sovereignty, separation of powers), on English liberalisms (limitation of the State through the definition of civil and personal rights) and the French (political rights, the principle of non-discrimination). The self-determination of indigenous peoples has been taken from the acquis of the European left. Decolonization is a 'post-colonial' concept; that is to say, developed in the schools of the first world.
>
> *Molina, 2009: 41*

Molina considers the combination of different aspects (in particular Indianism and anti-liberal nationalism) to be incompatible tendencies (2009: 6) which have generated attributions that do not translate into state prerogatives, as well as totalitarian elements associated with collective and communitarian property which are seen as limitations on economic freedom and private property (Molina, 2011).

From within the political and constituent process, there was a sympathetic critique of the 'process of change' which converged with the liberal challenge to the MAS more than its protagonists would have liked. Considering the modern perspective through which part of the left positioned itself in the political process, it becomes evident that any possibility of the presence of another ontology in the political game is rendered *invisible*, just as it is for the more entrenched political opposition. The 'friendly fire' against the introduction of indigenous concepts and institutional forms did sanction the need for transformations, including the necessity of indigenous empowerment, but disparagingly rejected the few non-modern elements that were being introduced or proposed. This criticism can be summarized in the controversy surrounding the so-called 'Pachamamism' which, in a more effective way than the overall challenge, resounded in the political world as a source for creating invisibility and neutralization, both for progressive liberalism and certain elements of the left.

'Pachamamism' is a term that has circulated as a reference to folk, ritualistic and religious currents which pay homage to Pachamama, but is now used to refer to the appearance of these elements in state politics. On the initiative of the Ministry of Foreign Affairs and the presidency itself, Andean ceremonial gave way to Andean symbolism, from the president's attire to the incorporation of ancestral rituals or references. Evo Morales held the inauguration ceremony for his two presidencies in the ruins of Tiwanaku, and ritualism gradually invaded certain areas of the state, as well as speeches made by those in authority. This was the way in which the strength of Indianism, registered through the mobilizations prior to the triumph of Evo Morales, was translated in terms of the new state. It represented a triumph of communication which could have important social effects for opposing the stigmatization of the indigenous peoples in a racist society and made sense as a result of the political consensus on radical changes. Aside from these aspects, which would be addressed by the Constituent Assembly, it was simply a new version of the ceremonial and, as such, was nothing more than a limited version of the full range of indigenous diversity.

Argentine journalist and researcher Pablo Stefanoni (2010a, 2010b) was one of the protagonists of this debate who openly criticized Pachamamism through his opinion columns. Yet this position extended beyond these confines to include various locations within the political process, most notably inside the cabinet of Evo Morales, and in internal disputes involving the 'Progressive' and 'Marxist' left-wing factions and the Indianism which criticizes the idea of progress and Eurocentrism. Criticism of Pachamamism is a viewpoint that fails to recognize the intrinsic (sacred, political or cosmological) value associated with it. It is a disenchanted scepticism. Stefanoni referred to referencing Pachamama, which became common practice even at the top level of state politics, as 'an almost mystical rhetoric' or 'newspeak of fashion' linked to Indianism, which

> contributes to dissolving the profound desire for change of the Bolivians through the torn sack of a supposedly alternative philosophy to the Western one, although this one is often learned in global spaces, such as the NGO

> workshops, in the calm of Duke University or on courses supervised by Catherine Walsh at the Universidad Andina or at FLACSO in Ecuador.
>
> *2010a: s.n.*[6]

The debate which ensued after the adoption of the new Constitution can be read in two ways. The first highlights the rhetorical nature of the indigenous elements which clashed directly with a developmental emphasis that did not have the least respect for Pachamama. The indigenous ceremonial could easily be confronted with the continuation and even the acceleration of a form of development which, in terms of income, could leave the state with a significant amount of resources to invest in social policies, but which, with regard to its impact on territory and the relationship created by its modes of production and exploitation, would be no different to anything previous governments had sought to implement.

The criticism reached its peak at the People's World Conference on Climate Change held in Cochabamba, in which the government was clearly exposed to accusations of double-speak, as a defender of Mother Earth but also the instigator of environmental conflicts with the indigenous peoples. Indigenous people organized a parallel session to the event, providing greater visibility for these conflicts, including the issue surrounding the construction of a highway through TIPNIS, which invoked the greatest international repercussions. This critique was important to the extent that it drew attention to the problem that transforms indigenous voices into silences. The mere mention of Pachamama would not change the world itself. However, it could bring the possibility of another politics to the discussion table, with openings for other worlds that capitalism seemed to have colonized forever. It was this level that remained invisible for those critical of Pachamamism.

The second reading of the criticism of 'Pachamamism' is of particular interest here. It was one which aimed to contest the possibilities of building an idea of a state that embraces a different theory of development, expressing distrust of an ontology that presented itself in an unusual place. Although it did not turn its back on the possible political uses of these elements, the criticism of Pachamamism denied the conflicts of ontologies, the meeting of worlds that could never coexist harmoniously: in short, the indigenous communitarian realities with modern forms consecrated alongside capitalism. In this critical reading of the indigenous symbolism that permeated the state, there were no two worlds, only institutions, politics and people or, in other words, budgets and the management of a world whose boundaries seem to be clearly and uniformly demarcated. From the perspective of political realism, the possible emergence of any difference was reduced to folklore, as is also the case with multiculturalism. Pachamama was 'symbolism' from a world in which symbols are clearly separated from things and where alternative visions are reduced to 'cultures'.

9.4 Conclusion: An Open and Post-Colonial Constitutionalism

Contrary to the positions presented in the previous section, and in what can be seen as mechanisms for eliminating 'uncomfortable' elements associated with non-modern ontologies anomalous to the state, or the inherent irreverence of the popular when not structured and hierarchical, Bartolomé Clavero questions the colonial nature of American constitutionalism since independence and proposes thinking about a 'Rule of Laws', in the plural, via the rights of the American indigenous peoples, in what is a criticism of the 'Rule of Law', in the singular, which is defined as a European invention that does not allow for liberation from the 'colonial mortgage' (2006: 684). Farit Rojas Tudela also supports the notion of a pluralistic law that incorporates indigenous voices but conceptualizes it from another setting and prefers to use the concept of Law in the singular, on condition that it is plural and porous. In the legal pluralism he defines, legal systems 'are not conceived as separate or independent entities, and coexist in the intersection, mix and inter-relationship' (Rojas Tudela, 2012: s.n.).

Rojas Tudela defends a legal perspective that could easily engage in dialogue with some of the current discussions in anthropology, in particular those which seek to explore a level of immanence in which several ontologies become audible and, at the same time, are recognized by their ability to refer to another world, rather than just a (cultural) version of a single world that would be equal for all (Schavelzon, 2016b, 2016c). For Rojas Tudela, it is a 'constant construction of the interlegality of porous legal orders' which 'are not fully open or fully closed' (2012: s.n.). It is worth analysing whether the ontologies referring to indigenous civilizations can be translated into a legal and constitutional discussion, but that is where I believe ideas such as an open and undefined institution, with constituent silences, should be used.

Leaving behind what would be a multicultural approach—a hybrid world constituted by differences, as is the case with many indigenous socialities studied by anthropology, although there is no scope to develop parallels here—Rojas Tudela states that: 'There is no talk about many laws or many legal orders, but rather of a single and open plural law and legal order in constant construction' (2012: s.n.). He goes on to define this constitutionalism in the context of a deconstructive shift toward 'post-colonial legal pluralism' which extends beyond the liberal conception of fundamental rights with the proposal of a 'ductile Law and of laws with porous qualities' which surpasses the legal monism of hierarchical gradation and the very concept of the nation state (2012: s.n.).

With regard to the 2009 Constitution, Rojas considers that, in part, the rights, duties and guarantees retain the individual nature of the Western tradition of liberal constitutionalism, 'but at the same time present a critical deconstructive possibility in forms such as legal pluralism and the rights of nations and peasant originary indigenous peoples' (2012: s.n.). He cites Article 178 of the Constitution, which paves the way for the plurality of sources of law by establishing that 'the power to impart justice emanates from the Bolivian people' (Republic of Bolivia, 2009: 101) and gives an example of the '*numerus apertus* clause' (or open number of laws), which refers to laws 'in evolution, to come', derived from other civilizational models and present in the 2009 Constitution. In this sense, Articles 1, 9, 30, 98 and 179 of the 2009 Constitution are also cited (Rojas Tudela, 2012: s.n.).

It is easy to associate these viewpoints with the idea of ontological multiplicity, the anthropology of an ontological shift as an approach that is also oriented toward the thinking of contemporary Western society (Schavelzon 2016b), and with the analysis of Boaventura de Sousa Santos regarding the struggles of law in the context of the clash between counter-hegemonic globalization and neoliberal globalization (2003: 36). Considering the conditions of a subaltern cosmopolitan legality, Santos refers to the use of hegemonic instruments in a given political struggle for non-hegemonic purposes, a subject that closely alludes to the Bolivian case and distinguishes this from their use for hegemonic purposes. Hence, he criticizes the state monopoly on declaring the legality of what is correct (and accurate) and the illegality of what is wrong (or false), postulating that the non-hegemonic use of hegemonic legal instruments can be accompanied by broad political mobilizations that include legal and illegal actions (Santos, 2003: 37).[7]

Viciano Pastor and Martinez Dalmau (2010) refer to the new Latin American Constitutionalism as the period that encompasses several reforms, ranging from the new Colombian Constitution of 1991 to the approval of the Bolivian Constitution in 2009, with the latter, alongside that of Ecuador and Venezuela, being the most relevant cases. From their reading of these processes—in which they participated as advisors—they identify the emergence of a new paradigm with elements that reformulate the division of powers, create forms of participation and include elements for constitutional control and state regulation, as well as guarantees to implement economic and social rights.[8]

The emphasis placed on peasant-indigenous issues enable me to present a counterargument to the way in which these authors characterize recent constitutional changes:

> Faced with a weak, adapted and rhetorical Constitution typical of traditional Latin American constitutionalism—historically incapable of activating political processes of social advancement—the new constitutionalism, the fruit of the constituent assemblies committed to processes of social and political regeneration, presents a new paradigm of strong, original and binding Constitution, necessary in societies that have entrusted to constitutional change the possibility of a real revolution.
>
> *Viciano Pastor and Martínez Dalmau, 2010: 9*

Focusing specifically on the Bolivian case and its elements of innovation on a communitarian and indigenous level, I would not characterize the new constitutionalism as 'strong', preferring instead to highlight its extreme fragility, malleability and mildness. In a framework that firmly maintains the foundations of traditional law, there was only an openness to the expression of other peasant-indigenous worlds and voices for the first time, in a marginal way. Moreover, the process would prove to be a fleeting moment.

In this sense, I agree with the Boaventura de Sousa Santos' characterization (2010) in discussing a constitutionalism that would be experimental and 'post-colonial' and, in the context of an irreversible crisis of liberal democracy within the modern state, would give way to a 'demodiversity' that proposes to combine various types of democracies. Rather than strong constitutionalism, it would be a matter of leaving questions open so that solutions which were not yet present could still be found in the future. In this way, 'the people would keep the constituent power in their hands and their strength would not be absorbed by the power constituted' (Santos, 2010: 22).

Although there are clear links between the different constitutional reforms within the region, it also seems important to distinguish between the different components at variance with each other within the new constitutionalism. This is what Bartolomé Clavero succeeds in doing by defining the Constitution of Bolivia as 'the first truly emancipatory Constitution in the Americas' (Clavero, 2008: 80), which has, for the first time, made a clean break with 'constitutional colonialism' (2008: 79). At the same time, he draws a distinction within the new Latin American Constitutionalism between the Bolivarian strand and another which is plurinational.

The Venezuelan Constitution of 1999, writes Clavero, was typical of another matrix, given its lack of progress with respect to pluralistic and indigenous rights issues. It was precisely what the Bolivian and Ecuadoran processes took from 'Bolivarianism' that would lead them away from the plurinational model, for example, with the exacerbation of ('unbalanced and irresponsible') presidentialism which neutralizes and conflicts with the advancement of plurinationality. Clavero emphasizes the concept of *Buen Vivir* which is present in the constitutionalism of Bolivia and Ecuador, and which he sees as an alternative to development that has no regard for nature and opposes 'good living'. The author observes that this is not found in the Venezuelan Constitution and thus concludes that there is a contrast between the Bolivarian model and the plurinational one (Clavero, 2011: 14). According to Clavero, in the case of Bolivia, this contrast translates into an insurmountable dispute between nationalist elements and the plurinational model that has been barely devised.[9]

These elements, which I relate specifically to the idea of decolonization, have led me to an interpretation of the new Constitution that highlights its open, undefined and even contradictory aspects (Schavelzon, 2012). It is these characteristics, more than its strength and capacity to establish a new framework in the field of law, which have enabled certain indigenous silences to become public and enter the Constitution, serving as a balance throughout the ontological war. It would be a constitutionalism of sensibility and subtleties that would try to find a breathing space between the individualizing liberal republican foundations, the homogenizing nationalist statism and the political pragmatism that rendered the indigenous hopelessly lost.

Its ambiguity becomes evident when we see that, despite a political rupture between the Pact of Unity indigenous organizations (the CIDOB and CONAMAQ) and the government, both continue to resort to the approved Constitution to substantiate opposing positions. With the rupture of the Pact of Unity after 2009 and the peasant-indigenous encounter, open concepts such as plurinationality and *Buen Vivir* would be closed off by the state from the ontological multiplicity that could have expressed the discussions in the Constituent Assembly. On the part of the social organizations, the rupture with the peasant sector would also lead them to adopt a more rigid stance toward opposition and protest, meaning that the process of creating concepts to measure the limits of the state form was interrupted.

Shortly after the approval of the Constitution, which was promulgated in February 2009, two positions that had been interlinked with some tension during the Assembly and within the Pact of Unity started to divide and distance themselves through a process in which the 'peasant originary indigenous' organizations would become separate indigenous and peasant unions. Other battles would continue the war of the ontological worlds that permeated the drafting of the Constitution. The Jurisdictional Demarcation Law (which materialized the asymmetry between different systems), the new electoral laws (which determined the type of direct representation that would be implemented), the Integral Development Law (which questioned principles associated with *Buen Vivir*), among others, in addition to the centralized management which restricted community access, would keep the disputes alive, providing evidence once more of the presence of silences which, although conjured from reforms that limited the difference, reappeared as threats to those who saw the rule of law and the republic put at risk.

Opposed to attempts to make the community invisible, some constituent silences would persist in peasant and indigenous struggles. They had arisen from converging differences that had gained strength by combining the search for autonomy with the struggles associated with the October Agenda and calls for a social state. The construction of the plurinational was thus aimed at introducing counter-state impulses through the will to create a state for all. The nation and the plurination worked together for a time, until they confronted each other, supporting the idea that a present and active state led to the neutralizing and silencing of voices from below, of mobilization and of alternative ancestral logics or those emerging from active collectives.

Whether more distant or closer to the state, these silences would remain as an expression of other possible worlds that had briefly interacted with a state legality that seemed receptive. Political institutions and a disenchanted common sense that rejected the indigenous people, or reduced them to 'minorities', 'culture', 'rhetoric' and 'chaos', would encounter the emergence of non-modern ontologies presenting the new voices of a cosmopolitics which resisted being transformed into a state voice, while intervening in an ontological juxtaposition that could generate new ways of living and decolonization.

Notes

1 For those interested in the dynamics of the constituent process, I refer to my doctoral thesis, which presents an ethnography of the Constituent Assembly (Schavelzon, 2012), as well as a comparative study focusing on the concept of *Buen Vivir* ('good living') and plurinationality in Bolivia and Ecuador (Schavelzon, 2015).

2 The TIPNIS (Isiboro Secure National Park and Indigenous Territory) conflict refers to a dispute between the government and the grassroots peasant and indigenous organizations that had formed the Pact of Unity in one of the greatest conflicts the government of Evo Morales had to face during his second term. The conflict had its origins in a road project that would cross the indigenous territory and National Park and connect the Chapare with the capital of El Beni. In addition to the environmental damage caused by the road, the project was seen as a means for the coca-grower settlers to expand into the aforementioned park (Schavelzon 2015).

3 The circumstances in which a new Census, in 2012, resulted in a reduction to 45% of the population self-defined as indigenous are analysed in Schavelzon (2014). As the process advanced, generic indigeneity would not only generate the capacity to constitute a considerable political force but would also oppose the processes of ontological constitution emanating from the minority, assimilating the sense of being 'indigenous' in tune with the state discourse and the discourse of the old mixed-race identity, and thus becoming totally discredited.

4 After modification by the Congress, Article 3 states that: 'The Bolivian nation consists of all Bolivians (*bolivianas y bolivianos*), the native indigenous nations and peoples, and the inter-cultural and Afro-Bolivian communities that, together, constitute the Bolivian people' (Republic of Bolivia, 2009: 11). For a study of the different versions of the article and the discussions that followed the changes, see Schavelzon (2012, Chapter 1).

5 Catóblepa (from the Greek καταβλέπω: 'looking down'). The word represents a mythological animal from Ethiopia; a quadruped similar to an antelope with a head so large and heavy that it can only look down. It was first described by Pliny the Elder. Source: Wikipedia www.wikiwand.com/pt/Catóblepa.

6 Concerning the debate, see Schavelzon (2012: Chapter 6) and different contributions by Pablo Stefanoni, Arturo Escobar and Hugo Blanco, available in 'Debate Ordenado sobre el Pachamamismo' published by David Roca Basadre at *Scribd* http://es.scribd.com/doc/33675955/Debate-Ordenado-Sobre-El-Pachamamismo.

7 Several works by Boaventura de Sousa Santos give an account of the complexity related to the problem of using hegemonic forms for emancipation. In his reflection, he considers that it is necessary to use the tools for struggle that are available, and transformative constitutionalism appears, in this context, as a considered instance, 'perhaps the most decisive', of the counter-hegemonic use of hegemonic instruments (Santos, 2010: 80). In a much earlier work, however, the question of the use of hegemonic instruments for counter-hegemonic purposes is presented as 'very conditional', involving the need to 'identify the conditions in which the hegemonic instruments can be placed at the service of a progressive and emancipatory politics' (Santos, 1997: 12). The difference between being 'very conditional' and the new constitutions as 'the most decisive instance' has to do with the emergence of the indigenous and the opening up of plurinational constitutional processes in the region. Yet it also conveys the tensions that exist between the protagonists of these processes in new and unknown ways when searching for changes and decolonization.

8 In other works, Martínez Dalmau develops the Bolivian case, emphasizing elements such as participation, state intervention in the economy, the social profile and integration in Latin America (cf. Martínez Dalmau, 2008). The indigenous communitarian and plurinational elements are mentioned but occupy a secondary place in the characterization of the new constitutionalism.

9 Regarding the case of the Bolivian Constitution, Clavero sees that 'there is a strong impulse for political nationalism against institutionalized plurinationism, which promotes an indistinct citizenship in the face of constitutional articulation'. He asks: 'Is it possible to conclude that Bolivarian constitutionalism, if "constitutional" is the appropriate term, is not even a companion of plurinational constitutionalism, but rather an agent that attacks and belittles it? In political practice, the question is open; in constitutional thinking, aggression and disregard are indubitable'. He concludes that 'the total potential of plurinationality as a constitutional paradigm has not been developed. However, the model is sufficiently delineated' (2011: 15).

References

Clavero, Bartolomé (2006), 'Estado de Direito, direitos coletivos e presença indígena na América', *in* Pietro Costa and Danilo Zolo (eds.), *O Estado de Direito. História, teoria e crítica*. São Paulo: Martins Fontes, 649–685.

Clavero, Bartolomé (2008), *Geografía Jurídica de América Latina. Pueblos Indígenas entre Constituciones Mestizas*. Mexico: Siglo XXI.

Clavero, Bartolomé (2011), 'Estado Plurinational o Bolivariano: Nuevo o Viejo Paradigma Constitucional Americano' (Borador), *Clavero.DerechosIndígenas.org*, 2nd May. Available at https://wayback.archive-it.org/org-354/20111031021543/http://clavero.derechosindigenas.org/wp-content/uploads/2011/05/Estado-Plurinacional.pdf.

Garcés, F. (2010), *El Pacto de Unidad y el proceso de construcción de una propuesta de Constitución Política del Estado. Sistematización de la experiencia*. La Paz: Pacto de Unidad/NINA/CEFREC/Caritas/CEJIS/CENDA/Agua Sustentable. Available at www.museo.umss.edu.bo/wp-content/uploads/2015/08/Garces-F-2010-El-pacto-de-unidad-y-el-proceso-de-construccion-de-una-constitucion.pdf.

Lazarte, Jorge (2008), 'Etnocracia y democracia'. *La Razón*, 3rd December D. La Paz.

Lazarte, Jorge (2011), 'La Asamblea Constituyente de Bolivia. El Pacto era necesario, ¿Por qué no fue posible?' *in* Moira Zuazo Oblitas and Cecilia Quiroga San Martín (Coords.), *Lo que unos no quieren recordar es lo que otros no pueden olvidar.Asamblea Constituyente, decolonización e interculuralidad*. La Paz: FES-ILDIS, 319–431. Available at https://library.fes.de/pdf-files/bueros/bolivien/08870.pdf

Los Tiempos (2008), 'La Esencia del proyecto del MAS', 31st October. Available at http://eju.tv/2008/10/la-esencia-del-proyecto-del-mas

Martínez Dalmau, Rubén (2008), *El Proceso Constituyente Boliviano (2006–2008). En el marco del Nuevo Constitucionalismo Latinoamericano*. La Paz: Oxfam Great Britain.

Mesa Gisbert, Carlos D. (2012), 'Tres grandes aplazos', *Pagina Siete*, 26th May. Available at https://carlosdmesa.com/2012/05/28/tres-grandes-aplazos

Molina, Fernando (2009), *La Ideología de la Constitución*. La Paz: CIPE, Fundación Milenio.

Molina, Fernando (2011), 'El puré ideológico del Gobierno', *Pagina Siete*, 7th August. Available at http://eju.tv/2011/08/el-pur-ideolgico-del-gobierno.

República de Bolivia (2009), *Constitución Política del Estado*. Available at www.procuraduria.gob.bo/images/docs/marcolegal/cpe.pdf

Rojas Tudela, Farit (2012), 'Constitucionalismo Plural', Unpublished article, mimeo.

Santos, Boaventura de Sousa (1997), 'Por uma concepção multicultural dos Direitos Humanos', *Revista Crítica de Ciências Sociais*, 48, 11–32. Available at https://ces.uc.pt/rccs/index.php?id=628

Santos, Boaventura de Sousa (2003), 'Poderá o direito ser emancipatório?' *Revista Crítica de Ciências Sociais*, 65, 3–73. DOI: https://doi.org/10.4000/rccs.1180

Santos, Boaventura de Sousa (2010), *Refundación del Estado en América Latina: Perspectivas desde una epistemología del Sur*. Lima: The Internatonal Institute on Law and Society. www.boaventuradesousasantos.pt/media/Refundacion%20del%20Estado_Lima2010.pdf.

Schavelzon, Salvador (2012), *El nacimiento del Estado Plurinacional de Bolívia: Etnografía de una Asamblea Constituyente*. La Paz: PLURAL/CLACSO/IWGIA/CEJIS. Available at http://biblioteca.clacso.edu.ar/clacso/coediciones/20130214112018/ElnacimientodelEstadoPlurinacional.pdf.

Schavelzon, Salvador (2013), 'El Pacto de Unidad como Encuentro Cosmopolitico', *Revista Boliviana de Investigación*, 10, 235–261.

Schavelzon, Salvador (2014), 'Mutaciones de la identificación indígena durante el debate del censo 2012 en Bolivia: Mestizaje abandonado, indigeneidad estatal y proliferación minoritaria', *Journal of Iberian and Latin America Review*, 20 (3), 328–354. DOI: https://doi.org/10.1080/13260219.2014.995872.

Schavelzon, Salvador (2015), *Plurinacionalidad y Vivir Bien/Buen Vivir. Dos conceptos en formación leídos desde Bolivia y Ecuador post-constituyente*. Quito: Abya Yala/CLACSO. Available at www.clacso.org.ar/libreria-latinoamericana/contador/sumar_pdf.php?id_libro=1073.

Schavelzon, Salvador (2016a), 'La Justicia Comunitaria en Bolivia y la ocupación de la casa de Víctor Hugo Cárdenas', *Direito e Democracia*, 17 (1), 43–63. Available at www.periodicos.ulbra.br/index.php/direito/article/view/2811.

Schavelzon, Salvador (2016b) 'Comunidad cosmopolítica, feminismo communario y ontologías en Bolivia: Registro de algunas debates y posibilidades constituyentes', *Revista de Antropologia*, 59 (3), 115–149. DOI: https://doi.org/10.11606/2179-0892.ra.2016.124810.

Schavelzon, Salvador (2016c), 'Cosmopolítica y Yuxtaposición en la Propuesta de Estado Plurinacional de Bolivia', *Revista de Anthropología de Chile*, 33 (1), 87–101. Available at https://revistadeantropologia.uchile.cl/index.php/RCA/article/view/43391.

Stefanoni, Pablo (2010a), '¿Adónde nos lleva el pachamamismo?' *Página* 7, 27th April and 4th May. Available at www.sinpermiso.info/textos/adnde-nos-lleva-el-pachamamismo.

Stefanoni, Pablo (2010b), 'Pachamamismo ventrilocuo', *Rebelión*, 29th May. Available at www.rebelion.org/noticia.php?id=106771.

Tapia, Luis (2011), 'Sociedad abigarrada. Repensando la democracia multicultural en Bolivia '. *Revista Estudiantil Latinoamericana de Ciencias Sociales*, 1 (1). Available at http://relacso.flacso.edu.mx/node/15.

Urenda, Juan Carlos (2009), *El Estado Catoblepas. Un Estudio Didáctico sobre la Constitución. Las contradicciones destructivas del Estado Boliviano*. Santa Cruz de la Sierra: Editorial El País [Bilingual edition (Spanish-English)].

Viciano Pastor, Roberto; Martínez Dalmau, Rubén (2010), 'Los Procesos Constituyentes Latinoamericanos y el Nuevo Paradigma Constitucional', *IUS. Revista del Instituto de Ciencias Jurídicas de Puebla A.C.*, 4 (25), 7–29. Available at www.revistaius.com/index.php/ius/article/view/214.

10

PLURINATIONAL CONSTITUTIONALISM

Plurinationality from Above and Plurinationality from Below*

Raúl Llasag

10.1 Introduction

The historical path that led to the declaration of plurinational states in Ecuador and Bolivia has been a long one. The timescale indicates that this historical process did not pursue a linear trajectory, that is, it cannot simply be analyzed as a process that aimed to move from a liberal nation state to a plurinational state, or to the refoundation of the state. At least three strategies have been adopted: (1) the plurinational state, or plurinationality from above; (2) plurinationality from below, or simply plurinationality; and (3) popular resistance. They are not exclusive, but they are also not interdependent: one strategy might be favored over the others, depending on the perspective from which it is analyzed, while popular resistance seems to be the catalyst that distinguishes between plurinationality from above and plurinationality from below. However, stating that a certain strategy may be favored does not imply exclusion, as this depends on the perspective or concept from which it is analyzed. If it is analyzed from the point of view of the social sciences and constitutionalism, the strategy of plurinationality from above is clearly favored, thus focusing on an analysis of the refoundation of the state, assuming that the revolution or the objective is that of the plurinational state. If it is analyzed via other concepts through which I intend to develop my approach, such as *yachay* or *unancha*, Andean knowledge based on the principles of *tinkunakuy*,[1] *yanantin*[2] and *randi radi*[3] (Llasag, 2011), the strategy of plurinationality from below is favored, without neglecting or delegitimizing other conceptions or making them invisible. In both cases, and fundamentally from the conception I intend to focus on, popular resistance becomes a priority.

From this perspective, the first part of this chapter summarizes the imposition of modern Western colonial and capitalist constitutionalism, which favored a

DOI: 10.4324/9781003391920-14

form of organization I refer to as the modern colonial and capitalist state, while the second part provides an overview of the process of discussing the proposal for plurinationality and the plurinational state. The third part outlines the constitutional studies developed after formal approval of the plurinational and intercultural constitutions, and the fourth part aims to summarily differentiate between plurinationality from below and from above.

10.2 Exporting a Nonviable Project: State and Modern Western Constitutionalism

I have chosen not to address the historical and theoretical discussion on the state and constitutionalism,[4] but instead to focus on modern Western constitutionalism. In using the term modern Western constitutionalism, I am referring to the constitutional model that was produced and reproduced by a Eurocentric, bourgeois, capitalist, colonialist and neocolonialist Europe. This same modern Western constitutionalism continues to lay claim to its universalization, imposed on *Abya Yala*, and specifically Ecuador and Bolivia, in the nineteenth century, the contexts which I intend to focus on.

I am also interested in making an invisible discussion visible, namely that both the colonial and capitalist modern Western state and its constitutionalism were a form of social, political and economic organization conceived in a local context which, due to its capitalist and colonial condition, generated a large number of poor people and an excessive supply of products, thus creating a gap between the many poor, who have become increasingly poor, and the few rich, who have gone on to accumulate greater wealth in the world. The perverse phenomenon that produced this nonviable capitalist project forced Europe to generate a system of internal social control through law, recently termed the 'punitive power' of the state within criminal law (Zaffaroni, Alagia and Slokar, 2000) and, in sociology, the 'monopoly of violence' (Weber, 1979). It also fueled the exportation of the negative effects to its colonies, that is, both the exportation of poverty and the exportation of the modern Western constitutionalism that renders these claims viable.

10.2.1 From the Periphery to Self-Eurocentrism

According to Dussel (2007), modernity began with the European invasion of *Abya Yala* in 1492, when Europe proclaimed itself superior. Self-proclaimed superiority or self-centrism was produced because it helped to conceal its marginality in relation to other civilizations, such as Egypt and China, which remained the sources for science, technique, ideology and political organization:

> Egypt institutionalizes the first continuous nation state, which will endure through all global political history, from approximately 3000 BC to the present.
>
> *Dussel, 2007: 26*

In order to hide its marginality, Europe created the other and disqualified it, creating the myth of inferiority and rendering it invisible. This phenomenon, in turn, generated what some call coloniality (Quijano, 2008), that is, the pattern of power that operates by naturalizing territorial, racial, cultural and epistemic hierarchies, enabling the reproduction of relationships based on domination. This pattern of power not only guarantees the exploitation, through capital, of some human beings by others on a global scale but also allows for subalternization and the obliteration of the knowledge, experiences and ways of life of those who are dominated and exploited in this way (Restrepo and Rojas, 2010:15).

This is the context within which modern Western constitutionalism developed and produced the 'universalization of the nation state as the most desirable form of political community' (Chakrabarty, 1995: 384), making the implementation of this constitutionalism a central instrument for the imposition of a twofold capitalism-colonialism, knowing that the former cannot exist without the latter, either as a political or a social relationship. Under this system of coloniality, this constitutionalism was imposed on *Abya Yala* in the nineteenth century as the sole and universal form of social organization, a model we were unable to escape, since it was not possible to think without viewing the state as an institutional structure shaped by this constitutionalism.

Yet, in reality, Europe was not central, given that it was completely peripheral. 'Smith was the last major (Western) social theorist to appreciate that Europe was a Johnny-come-lately in the development of the wealth of nations: "China is a much richer country than any part of Europe", Smith remarked in 1776' (Arrighi, 2007: 34).

Like every other region, country, state and community, Europe has a particular history within the greater history of the world but, as with all regions, countries, states and communities, it is recreated through myths and claims that it represents the center of the world. Europe has lived a particular history of invasions, frustrations and deceit. This characteristic compels it to attempt to repeat and reproduce its experiences with other peoples: hence, it invades, plunders and steals what is not its own and, in the process, appropriates other knowledge that adapts to its realities. Thus, for example, according to Dussel (2007), 3,000 years before Christ was born, Egypt institutionalized the first 'nation state', which, evidently, was not bourgeois. This model was copied by Europe and readjusted to satisfy the interests of the bourgeoisie and capitalism. Philosophy and politics did not begin in Greece: in fact, Greek philosophy and politics would have been inspired by Egypt and the Phoenician port cities. In the third and second millennia BC, the entity that would become the future Greece was colonized by Semites and Egyptians. The constitutional forms of Greek cities originate from Phoenicia and Egypt, principally due to the socioeconomic structure of slavery which was present in both.

The self-proclamation of superiority and centrality undoubtedly operates through this process of concealing the history of marginality, invaded peoples and peoples who appropriate the other's knowledge. As Dussel (2007) would observe, while Montesquieu, Voltaire and others presided over the writing of universal history, Hegel (1770–1831), from the first post-industrial generation, began to theorize on Europe as the center. Hegel (2001 [1821]) states that the Mediterranean is the center of universal history. Yet, the Mediterranean is a small sea and was the center of small cultures. These historical inventions allow Hegel to retheorize world history by projecting a hegemonic Europe after the Industrial Revolution (an event that was less than 50 years old) through the origins of Greek culture and Judeo-Christianity (both phenomena unrelated to their Eastern context) to develop a world-historical explanation.

In this way, Europe's self-proclaimed status as superior and central, later known as Eurocentrism, is nothing more than a theoretical invention which has managed to mythologize and thus impose itself on the academic field and state administration, creating a subservience or inability to think beyond it, despite the fact that it serves no function and is of no interest in everyday life, since its interest lies more in theory than in day-to-day living.

10.2.2 The Modern Western Bourgeois and Industrial State: A Local Experience that Produces Inequality and Poverty

As already indicated, it is not my concern to undertake a historical analysis of the conception of the modern Western bourgeois and industrial state. My intention is to incorporate the idea that the need to found a modern Western bourgeois and industrial state was a local experience which has since become nonviable due to its fatal negative consequences, generated by the Industrial Revolution.

It must be borne in mind that, before the Industrial Revolution, Europe lived under feudalism, an experience that not all peoples endured. The assumption was that overcoming feudalism would, paradoxically, require the emerging bourgeoisie to empower a feudal lord to rule over others in order to unite the political and military powers and thus organize a much larger market than the small medieval fiefdom. In other words, a territory with borders protected by a state army was deemed necessary.

In terms of theory, the Frenchman Jean Bodin (1530–1596) wrote *The Six Books on the Republic* (Bodin, 1997 [1576]) in order to legitimize the monarchical order required by the emerging mercantile bourgeoisie. Shortly after, in England, under a very weak monarchy, Thomas Hobbes (1588–1679) published *De Cive* (*On the Citizen*) (Hobbes, 2000 [1642]), his first political work. Hobbes' (1984 [1651]) starting point is the state of nature as a post-feudal chaos which, in the eyes of the great conservative, demands an absolute monarchy to represent civil order, a Leviathan, based on a contract whereby citizens or subjects renounce the right to exercise force and cease to use their power to prevent the exercise of sovereign power. This is precisely the content of the contract, which states that only the sovereign, the king, is allowed to exercise his freedom, as a political power, which consequently is exercised despotically. Thus, the monarchy exercises all powers, including legislative, judicial and executive power, in an indivisible manner. Ultimately, the goal is to strengthen a monarchical power that gives rise to the constitution of a state, with a larger territory to satisfy the trade requirements of the emerging bourgeoisie and the need to protect the institution of property.

As Dussel (2007) points out, John Locke (1632–1704) would have the extraordinary virtue of justifying the development of the new English state born out of the first bourgeois revolution, in proposing a pact to create the consensus that constitutes a political community based on the individual. The political community, in turn, organizes a system of *potestas*[5] through a new pact, whose ultimate reference is the parliament as a democratic regime, thus situating the absolute monarchy of the Hobbesian type in the pure state of nature. Locke was already clearly aware of the separation of legislative and executive powers under the primacy of the former, where a position of radical secularization is revealed.

However, Locke (1991 [1680]) was a cynical rhetorician: on the one hand, he asserts that all human beings are equal by nature and hold all goods in common; on the other hand, he goes on to reverse this position and prove exactly the opposite, namely that even within the state of nature there are unavoidable inequalities and private property. A similar undermining can be seen in his assertion that all human beings are, by nature, equal but that this is only valid for those who participate in the *Commonwealth* (community), since validity is reserved exclusively for adult men who are virtuous owners, thus excluding women, African slaves, American and Asian Indians, English wage earners and so on. The conclusion he draws, even for England, is that those who do not own property or who sell their work for a living wage must be excluded.

Locke (1991 [1680]) is a philosopher of Western liberalism, which now finds itself in crisis. In a rhetorical, immoral and contradictory way, this author was able to convincingly express what no one had dared to state publicly. He justified, in philosophical terms, English colonial expansion and legitimated the slave trade, usurpation and the notion that 'every man has a property in his own person [...] The labour of his body, and the work of his hands, we may say, are properly his' (2007 [1680]: 56), taking this as the basis for justifying slavery, the selling of the labor force in exchange for a wage and the idea that the wage is a phase belonging to the state of nature. For Locke (2007 [1680]), money, large properties and subsequently wages and even a political regime similar to the monarchy existed in the state of nature but, as yet, no institution that served as a judge between the monarch and the people or safeguarded private property.

For this reason, Locke (2007 [1680]) stated that it was necessary to instigate a transition to a civil state which would guarantee, through political institutions, that a certain state of affairs would prevail at the natural economic level that he calls a state of nature, which is not the state of war as cited by Hobbes (1984 [1651]). This is because Locke (2007 [1680]) was no longer facing post-feudal chaos but what he terms a glorious revolution, which proposed the state of war as a third post-civil state through which the emerging empire expands outwardly.

In order to make the defense of bourgeois private property possible, it was necessary to establish a law, a recognized and impartial judge and sufficient power to support and sustain penalties for those who act against private property, that is, those who do not own property, the wage earners and the poor, thus ensuring that the entire political-institutional structure is organized to defend a minority against the empirical majority comprising the non-owners:

> Here is the formalist 'political fallacy' of Locke (and of later liberalism): he makes 'all' the bourgeois owners pass for 'all' the 'subjects' or inhabitants, who are forced to obey the pact in which they have not participated.
>
> *Dussel, 2007: 280*

According to Dussel, the Industrial Revolution would produce an acceleration on a technical-instrumental level with major consequences. In Britain, and more slowly in France and throughout Europe, there was a civilizational take-off point which, by the end of the eighteenth century, would surpass the Yangtze valley in China and Hindustan for the first time. The Enlightenment would produce a political philosophy that would only achieve its definitive, deeply distorted, Eurocentric and universalizing splendor with Hegel.[6]

Unlike Hobbes (1984 [1651]) and Locke (2007 [1680]), Hegel (2001 [1821]) recognized that civil society is not the equal of political society. It is a less developed phase of the state or the period in which the concept of state is developed, and its members are included on a purely external basis by compulsion through policing, since there is not enough common interest to unite the antagonistic classes. In other words, civil society is a less developed phase of the state in which its members are principally motivated to participate by the protection of property, or private goods. This prevents full subjective, ethical and intersubjective adherence through mutual recognition of dignity and love for people and the homeland on the part of all its members. As an external state:

> The universal, which is contained in the particularity of the civic community, is realized and preserved by the external system of police supervision, whose purpose is simply to protect and secure the multitude of private ends and interests subsisting within it.
>
> *Hegel, 2001[1821]: 191*

For Hegel, civil society or the state in a less developed phase encounters a fatal contradiction, since the Industrial Revolution produces an inevitable and insurmountable inconsistency: on the one hand, there is the accumulation of wealth; on the other hand, 'there occur repartition and limitation of the work of the individual labourer' (2001 [1821]: 188).

In other words, industrial capitalism produces rich people who decrease in number as they become increasingly rich while, at the same time, producing poverty and an increasing number of poor people. As Santos (1995) would say, on the one hand, the liberal European capitalism of the nineteenth century triggered the concentration of wealth and concomitant social exclusion and, on the other hand, made the state the guarantor of the market:

> As it took possession of its inheritance, however, the state minimized its ethical claims and political promises so as to make them fit the regulatory needs of liberal capitalism. The sovereignty of the people became the sovereignty of the nation state in an interstate system; the general will became the rule of the majority (found among the government elites) and the *raison d'état*; law was uncoupled from ethical principles and became a docile instrument of institutional building and market regulation; the good order became order *tout court.*
>
> *Santos, 1995: 72*

This is one way in which the proposal of modern constitutionalism is revealed to be a nonviable project. As Santos (1995) states, in referring to the tension between regulation and emancipation, which he identifies as pillars of the modern project (not analyzed here since, as the author himself recognizes, this tension was absent from the colonial space, where other forms of domination prevailed, as well as other forms of resistance):[7]

> Hobbes, Locke and Rousseau, each in his own way, illustrate how the all-encompassing symmetries of their projects – state of nature/civil society; sovereign/citizens; natural law/civil law; freedom/equality; natural law/civil law; consent/coercion – are bound to collapse when translated into real life.
>
> *Santos, 1995: 69*

In overcoming civil society, Hegel presents the state law, the police and colonialism as a universal proposal and supreme form of social organization. Thus, as Dussel pointed out, 'It is not easy to find in Modernity a philosopher who has expressed in such a finished way the *dominating totality of the modern state* as Hegel' (2007: 381).

10.2.3 Peripheral Europe Exporting Its State and Bourgeois Constitutionalism to Conceal the Nonviability of the Capitalist Project

For Hegel, 'The state is the realized ethical idea or ethical spirit' (2001 [1821]: 194). In other words, it is the materialized idea, the materialized totality or materialized God, hence, for the author, freedom and the realization of individuality can only be achieved through the state. The state therefore becomes a form of universal social organization. It is within the modern Western state that the private interest pertaining to civil society preserves itself: this is how the state is substantiated and divinized.

However, the modern Western state had to overcome one of the inevitable contradictions produced by the Industrial Revolution, namely the huge gap between rich and poor. In order to address this, Hegel would construct an entire theory of the state, with internal controls, but also external dominance.

The theory of internal control is based on the creation of the rule of law, whose idea is expressed in 'the constitution or internal state organization or polity' (Hegel, 2001 [1821]: 198). This right is positive and 'only that right is binding which has become law' (2001 [1821]: 172), although 'the actual law may be different from what is in itself right' (*idem*). Hence, in positive right:

> that which is lawfully established is the source of the knowledge of what is right, or, more accurately, is the final resort in litigation. Positive jurisprudence is to that extent an historical science based on authority.
>
> *Hegel, 2001 [1821]: 172*

The law becomes relevant with regard to the internal control of the state, since the obligation in relation to the law includes the notion that: 'Since the binding force of law rests upon the right of self-consciousness, the laws ought to be universally made known' (Hegel, 2001 [1821]: 174).

Thus, their prescriptions should be simple and universal. Having presented itself as law, right 'stands in independent opposition to the particular will and opinion of right, and has to vindicate itself as a universal' (Hegel, 2001 [1821]: 178). A public power, called a judge or a magistrate, is necessary, since 'by the administration of justice, compensation is rendered for injury done to property or person' (2001[1821]: 183) and, as the ultimate reason for validating punishment, the police force is legitimated.[8]

Education, and more specifically the domestication of education, would play a key role in ensuring that the Hegelian rule of law and the police were able to guarantee internal control of the state.

However, as internal control is not enough to overcome the contradiction produced by industrial capitalism, namely the extreme poverty of the vast majority of the population, this cannot be solved by taxing the rich since:

> If upon the more wealthy classes the burden were directly laid of maintaining the poor at the level of their ordinary way of life, or if in public institutions, such as rich hospitals, foundations, or cloisters, the poor could receive direct support, they would be assured of subsistence without requiring to do any work. This would be contrary both to the principle of the civic community and to the feeling its members have of independence and honour.

> Again, if subsistence were provided not directly but through work, or opportunity to work, the quantity of produce would be increased, and the consumers, becoming themselves producers, would be proportionately too few. Whether in the case of over-production, then, or in the case of direct help, the evil sought to be removed would remain, and, indeed, would by either method be enhanced.
>
> *Hegel, 2001 [1821]: 189*

If the contradiction generated by the industrial capitalist system has solution at the internal levels, Hegel has no alternative but to resolve it by exporting poverty and overproduction outside the state, since this external dominance is necessary.

> By means of its own dialectic the civic community is driven beyond its own limits as a definite and self-complete society. It must find consumers and the necessary means of life amongst other peoples, who either lack the means, of which it has a superfluity, or have less developed industries.
>
> As the firm-set earth, or the soil, is the basis of family life, so the basis of industry is the sea, the natural element which stimulates intercourse with foreign lands.
>
> *Hegel, 2001 [1821]: 189–190*

It is therefore essential to export the poverty and overproduction generated by capitalism:

> [C]olonization [...] for a part of its population provides on a new soil a return to the family principle, and also procures for itself at the same time a new incentive.
>
> *Hegel, 2001 [1821]: 190*

Consequently, as with Locke, for Hegel the contradiction of industrial capitalism is overcome by the conquest and colonization of the periphery. It is this process alone that allows bourgeois civil society to move toward the organic and universal state:

> Further, Hegel considers the opportunity of founding the liberal state in the colonies, which shall become independent of the metropolis. This 'exportation' of population from the liberal state to the emancipated colonies is like a condition for the possibility of the constitution of the absolute state, the modern European state, having overcome the contradictions of the external state of bourgeois liberal society.
>
> *Dussel, 2009: 386*

The liberal capitalist, industrial and extractive state is not viable unless it exports poverty and overproduction to the colonies, as Europe did. In order to generate this process, it was also necessary to export the state and modern Western liberal constitutionalism to the colonies, that is to say, it became necessary to export a nonviable project to make the nonviable viable.

For this reason, the independence of the Latin American colonies would be defended by Europe itself, since they were more useful when independent under the model of state and constitutionalism which ensured the import of industrialized products and, in turn, guaranteed market freedom, private property and, above all, the law authorizing entry of the poor generated by industrial capitalism in Europe. Thus, for example, the Commission of Argentina of 1853 welcomed this objective of Europe in its preamble: 'Ensuring the benefits of freedom ... for all the inhabitants of the world who want to live on Argentine soil' (quoted by Dussel, 2007: 388).

Clearly, for *Abya Yala*, the end result would be the importing of an impoverished European surplus population. The absolute Hegelian state would then assume dominance within and outside. Hegel thought that a postcolonial era had been set in motion, 'in which, through national emancipation, the colonies would come to be neocolonial states more profitable for Europe than the ancient colonies' (Dussel, 2009: 388). The Constitution of Great Colombia of 1821 stated:

> Art. 183. All foreigners from any nation will be admitted to Colombia: their people and property will enjoy the same security as other citizens.
>
> *Borja, 1979, Tome IV: 97*

Thus, it is understood what Dussel means when he states:

> The metropolitan European modern capitalist states, having overcome their internal contradictions (relatively and by having exported them to the colonies), will be occupied with the new peripheral 'liberal' states in order to 'be the missionaries of *civilization* throughout the world'. It would be a disinterested, sublime, spiritual end.
>
> *Dussel, 2009: 390*

Something that had failed to work in Europe could not work in *Abya Yala*, far less when the intention was to convert us into the saviors of nonviable European industrial capitalism. As such, the 'independences' of the *Abya Yala* countries were a fallacy. A neocolonial liberal state was implemented, governed by a small oligarchic elite, with a colonized mindset aspiring to the colonial and the alien, and devalued itself, assuming as absolute truths the paradigms of the liberal bourgeois capitalist state and constitutionalism that exercised a double legitimation. On the one hand, it assumed as an absolute and universal truth that the state was an irreversible political structure, the optimal form of all possible organizations, and for this reason it has since been difficult to think of alternatives without a state or a modern Western constitution; on the other hand, a form of vertical organization was legitimized, marginalizing the majority of the population because they were women, minors, indigenous, Afro-Ecuadorians, Montubios and possessed neither goods nor capital.

10.3 The Discussion on the Proposal for Plurinationality and the Plurinational State

The proposal for plurinationality begins by questioning the colonial and capitalist system, and its consequences at all levels. This takes us back to before the Inca conquest, as the conquest of the peoples who populated what are nowadays the territories known as Ecuador and Bolivia implied, on the one hand, the transformation of solidarity institutions such as *minka*,[9] *anyi*[10] and *yana*[11] into production institutions and, on the other hand, the weakening of the *jatun ayllukuna*, now known as communities (since the Incas were aware of the strength of the *jatun ayllukuna*). Thus, in a way, the Inca conquest implied the imposition of a form of social organization now known as the Inca State or *Tawantinsuyu* (which was clearly neither a bourgeois nor modern Western state), and the onset of the deterioration of *yachay* or *unancha*, that is, knowledge based on the principles of interrelationality, relationality or holistic knowledge, complementary duality, correlation and reciprocity.[12]

With the Spanish invasion, given that the invaders were unable to understand the importance of the social originary organizational form of the *jatun ayllukuna*, it was deterritorialized and assigned to the *encomiendas*, converting the institutions of *jatun ayllukuna* into institutions of slavery and death. The *mita*, for example, which means 'work shift', became enslaved compulsory work resulting in deaths in the mines, thus introducing a racist colonial system. On the other hand, *unancha* or *yachay* was simply made invisible and delegitimized through accusations of idolatry, witchcraft or backwardness, thus creating what Reinaga termed in 1970 'the wall of silence' (2013: 45) and Santos (2010a) would later define as the 'abyssal line'.

When Ecuador and Bolivia became politically independent of the metropolis, this did not mean the end of the colony, of discrimination, of invisibility or subordination (Llasag, 2008: 315 ss.), since most of the *Abya Yala* countries gained independence in the nineteenth century due, on the one hand, to the Spanish crisis whereby the Creole oligarchy, who had been marginalized within the administration of the colonial state, succeeded in replacing the Spaniards, and, on the other hand, the fact that industrial capitalist Europe needed independent states to which it could export poverty and overproduction. For this reason, the move toward independence was even financed by England, where the first external debt of the new states originated. In short, the new states were born with external and neocolonial debts.

I will not explore these issues in detail as they require a broader discussion, instead confining myself to summarizing the proposal for plurinationality and the plurinational state through the indigenous movements of the last decades of the previous century, particularly from the 1970s onwards.

10.3.1 The Indigenous Movement Questioning Colonialism, Capitalism and Political Independence

The colonial and neocolonial processes of exclusion, marginalization, extermination and invisibility have not been peaceful, as there have always been forms of opposition and resistance.[13] At the beginning of the twentieth century, there was a resurgence of the indigenous movements of *Abya Yala*, this time united. This resurgence took place in different contexts, both local[14] and regional as well as international. In the regional context, I will highlight only a few of the more important examples: the long process of indigenous and peasant revolutionary activity in Mexico, beginning in 1910, whose principal demand was the recovery of lands that had been snatched by landlords; the triumph of the Cuban revolution in 1959; the Alliance for Progress program imposed by the United States in 1961, aimed at controlling indigenous movements and fighting the specter of socialism and communism; and dictatorships imposed in most Latin American countries via the North American empire, as well as policies to control and exterminate indigenous and social movements. In the international field, there was the triumph of the Russian revolution in 1917, the First and Second World Wars in which power and world control were disputed, and the creation of international institutions such as the International Monetary Fund and the World Bank, among others, to guarantee the validity of the capitalist system. All of these events were a reflection of the global crisis in the capitalist and neocolonial system sustained by the organization of the vertical state and, consequently, of constitutionalism, in addition to the socialist system that followed.

10.3.1.1 Indigenous Movements Making the Nonviability of Modern Western Constitutionalism Visible

The indigenous movements in *Abya Yala* and, in particular, Ecuador and Bolivia were the first to make visible the real problems facing not only the indigenous peoples but all those included in the so-called 'independent states' in *Abya Yala*, territory, validated by the neocolonial constitutionalism that legitimized the previous exclusionary, assimilationist, patriarchal, capitalist and monocultural colonial system. Briefly, these indigenous movements question:

a. The state as a form of uninational and monocultural organization, which intends, on the one hand, to homogenize the diversities of territories and peoples or nations into one single nation and culture, rendering them invisible within the state and, on the other hand, to create external borders to marginalize those beyond them. As stated by Ampam Karakras, in reality 'there is a diversity of cultures, so for us, the central idea is that diversity at different levels and forms – lifestyles and forms of production, etc. – constitutes a richness and must be recognized and respected' (conversation with Ampam Karakras in 2013);[15]

b. The colonial or neocolonialist state, which excludes and marginalizes not only the members of indigenous collectives known as 'Indians', but also other sections of society, such as Afro-descendants, Montubios, women, children and adolescents.[16] As Alfredo Viteri stated, 'the constitution of CONAIE allowed the peoples and nationalities of Ecuador to question the political structures of the colonial state [...] claiming the right to self-determination, to territorial law' (conversation with Alfredo Viteri in 2013);[17]
c. The predatory capitalist system, which considers nature an object for exploitation. In essence, they question the extractive system, since it has endangered not only the environment but also human life on planet Earth.[18] Tomás Huanacu[19] states that the main difficulty in achieving *Suma Qamaña*, or good living, is capitalism (conversation with Tomás Huanacu in 2014);
d. The state as an essentially vertical structure, which has resulted in racist societies and patriarchal families;[20]
e. The reproduction of the neocolonial, capitalist and vertical international system that renders designated 'third world' countries and indigenous or originary peoples invisible;[21]
f. The education system that teaches uncritical submission which fails to enhance human capacities and reproduces the colonial, capitalist, verticalist and universalist system;[22]
g. The system of knowledge production based on universalist scientific theory alien to our realities, which renders the richness of other knowledges invisible and is based on the colonial appropriation of collective knowledges.

Consequently, indigenous movements are criticizing the modern Western constitutionalism which continues to be imposed on the peoples of *Abya Yala*, even though its nonviability has been demonstrated. They also criticize imported political theory which fails to correspond to the political reality of our countries since, in the case of Ecuador and Bolivia, it has not been possible to implement the great liberal idea of the nation state. While the constitutions, and therefore constitutional law, have referred to monocultural states, in practice these states have always been heterogeneous and even multicultural: in reality, there were and still are indigenous collectives that the monocultural state apparatus has never reached. These collectives have their own[23] systems of living, which have survived the colonial and republican process of invisibility.[24]

10.3.1.2 Indigenous Movements Generating New Proposals and a Process for Discussing Plurinationality and the Plurinational State

The main demand of Ecuador's indigenous movement in the 1970s and 1980s was territorial self-determination, or the internal autonomy of communities. The political project, although oral, focused on strengthening communitarian governments and subsequently the reconstruction of peoples and nationalities, with a view to establishing self-government to counter the institutionality of the state.

In the Ecuadorian Amazon, and in particular among the Shuar nationality, the different designations that had been assigned to them from the outside, including labels such as tribes, ethnic groups and *Jíbaros*, were openly questioned. Hence, they strategically adopted the designation 'Shuar Nation', a term used by anthropologists due to the total absence of the state in those communities, since the Shuar had functioned as a historical collective entity without and outside the state. However, it should be noted that, despite referring to a society outside the state, it was called a nation, which is related to the element of the state.

The initial proposals for the territorial self-determination of communities and the reconstruction of peoples and nations were very much questioned by those who accepted the institutionality of the state, claiming that it was a proposal that would fragment the state. Yet, the questioning also came from those who were seen as possible allies of the indigenous movement, namely members of the left-wing parties, who have in turn been accused of being influenced by the CIA to obstruct the revolution.

It was under these circumstances that a Russian anthropologist named Yuri Zubritski arrived in Bolivia and Ecuador in the 1970s. In 1972, he came in contact with the Otovaleño Institute of Anthropology. He published his work in 1979 under the title *Los Incas-Qechuas.* Within this process, there was an exchange of views with several leaders concerning ethnographic research work carried out in Ecuador, Colombia and Peru, as well as theoretical, anthropological and political discussions on nationalities in the then Soviet Union.

As a result of these meetings, and given that the word 'nation' not only generated resistance but was also related to the element of the state, a consensus was reached on the use of the term 'indigenous nationalities'. Since there are several indigenous nationalities, people began to talk about plurinationality as a form of self-government or a counter-power to the state, built from the communities as grassroots organizations.

Meanwhile, in Spain there had been a debate on the regions and nationalities that make up Spain, resulting in recognition for the right to autonomy within the Constitution of 1978.

These theoretical discussions in the former Soviet Union and Spain, especially the approval of the 1978 Constitution, provided a good opportunity for Ecuador's indigenous movement to propose the refoundation of the plurinational state as a strategy. On the one hand, appropriating a proposal from a recognized reference to socialism at the time – namely, the Soviet Union – meant there was no pretext for the left-wing parties to accuse them of complicity with the CIA; on the other hand, in engaging with the proposal on Spanish autonomies, given that Spain was a reference point for Ecuador's ruling oligarchy, it was believed that it would be possible to soften the latter's complete opposition to the approaches emerging from the indigenous movements.

In line with the logic of intellectuals such as Alfredo Viteri from the Organization of Indigenous Peoples of Pastaza, who proposed the plurinational state, it was thought that the strategy for achieving the self-determination of communities, peoples and nationalities lay in the struggle for recognition of this right and that the way forward was to propose a plurinational state and Constituent Assembly, so that the constitution would explicitly recognize this right. Once this had been achieved, plurinationality could be built from below, centered on this right.

The problem was that, based on the proposal of the plurinational state and, fundamentally, due to the decision to engage in political-electoral participation via the political arm known as *Pachakutik* – created in 1995 – what I call plurinationality from above, that is, assuming the power of state institutionality and constructing the plurinational state, held sway. Obviously, this process has resulted in the marginalization of the counter-power and consequently the abandonment of strengthening community autonomies and the reconstruction of peoples and nationalities as bases for counter-power, the aforementioned plurinationality from below.

In Bolivia, however, there was no such strategic appropriation and self-identification of nationalities. As Fausto Reinaga states:

> There is no such thing. The Indian is one nation. The Indian is the animated land; it is the land vitalized; life land. The Indian is the embodiment of the rocks of the Andes. His blood flows from the most distant and hidden depths of time. The Indian is the body and soul, the heart and spirit, the elemental plasma and the fiery spark of the life of the Andean being; therefore, it is in the Indian that the quintessence of nationalism shines; the Indian is the only nationalist; outside the Indian there are but aberrations and caricatures of spurious and putrid 'nationalisms' ...
>
> The experience of four centuries has shown that the Indian is a single Nation; he is not an 'ETHNIC MINORITY'; he's just the opposite ...
>
> The famous 'indigenous nationalities' are Stalinist molds, imported from the USSR for the use and trade of unscrupulous 'communists' who abuse the good faith of the bread-hungry people and their ideals.
>
> *Reinaga, 2013: 117–118*

It is through Bolivia that the reconstruction of *coyasuyo* and the taking of power as advocated by Reinaga are proposed:

> The Indian of Bolivia cannot let the deadly crisis suffered by the West pass by. He has to take advantage of it. But not to save the enemy. He has to take advantage of this crisis to break free ... Free the Indian, form their party (GDP) and lead them to power. The power to address the issue of this Republic which, in the hands of the Creole oppressor – with each passing day – merges into the abyss.
>
> *Reinaga, 2013: 71*

In the absence of self-identification on the part of the nationalities, there was no argument for plurinationality, so the plurinational state was not initially proposed. According to Tomás Huanacu:

> Here we were not dealing with a concept of plurinationality, but really experiencing plurinationality ... But we were not tackling the concept, it was from the year 2000 onwards that we began to enhance the theme of plurinationality, based on what had been done in Ecuador, the plurinational state. The Constituent Assembly was vaguely approaching. We wanted a Constituent Assembly because indigenous peoples must be part of the state structure. Yes, but with even greater strength after the experiments in Ecuador.
>
> *Conversation with Tomás Huanacu in 2014*

This information from Huanacu is corroborated by Humberto Cholango:

> This approach to the plurinational state was carried out by the Ecuadorian indigenous movement through CONAIE. [...] This thesis quickly extended to other countries with a large indigenous presence, such as Mexico, Guatemala, Peru and, in particular, Bolivia.
>
> *Cholango, 2012: 9*

This does not mean that there has been no discussion of the plurinational state in recent years. This discussion simply had taken place from the year 2000 onward, leaving the reconstitution of *coyasuyo* through the *ayllus*[25] on hold.

10.3.2 Constituent Processes Advocating Plurinational States

By the 1980s and early 1990s, the indigenous movements had consolidated and become a very important political and social force, leading to the start of the transformation of nation states into multicultural and pluriethnic states, paving the way, according to Raquel Yrigoyen (2006), for multicultural and pluricultural constitutionalism. The former, in the author's words, began with the approval of the Constitution of Canada in 1982, continued with the Guatemalan Constitution of 1985 and the Nicaraguan Constitution of 1987, and ended with the 1988 Venezuelan Constitution. However, the latter had begun in 1989 with the adoption of the International Labour Organization Convention No. 169 on indigenous and tribal peoples in independent countries. This model expanded throughout Central and South America: to Colombia in 1991, Mexico and Paraguay in 1992, Peru in 1993, Bolivia and Argentina in 1994, Ecuador in 1996 and 1998, Venezuela in 1999 and, according to the author, extended through to 2005. However, the adoption of multiculturalism and the rights of indigenous collectives in the 1990s took place in parallel with other constitutional reforms aimed at facilitating the implementation of neoliberal policies within the scope of globalization. In other words, pluricultural and multiethnic constitutionalisms were converted into enabling instruments for neoliberalism, which obviously blocked any genuine realization of the rights that had been attained.

Although multiculturalism and multiethnicity became instruments of the neoliberal system, the indigenous movements of Ecuador[26] and Bolivia[27] did not give up on the strategy of proposing the plurinational state. Consequently, in different national contexts, Ecuador and Bolivia convened constituent assemblies that ended up declaring the plurinationality of the states in 2008 and 2009, respectively. In terms of the different contexts, I would refer, in the case of Ecuador, to the fact that the leadership of the indigenous movement had practically disconnected itself from the grassroots and lost its legitimacy, leaving the political movement *Alianza País* to take advantage of the situation by appropriating the discourses of the indigenous movements. As a result, there was no decisive role for the indigenous movement within the Constituent Assembly of 2007–2008. In Bolivia, indigenous-originary and peasant organizations had succeeded in forming the Pact of Unity, through the National Council of *Ayllus* and *Markas* of Qullasuyo (CONMAQ), the Confederation of Indigenous Peoples of Bolivia, the Trade Union Confederation of Peasant Workers of Bolivia and the 'Bartolina Sisa' National Confederation of Peasant Women of Bolivia. As such, there was a greater level of indigenous participation in the Constituent Assembly, but other problems regarding the discussion and approval of constitutional texts had to be faced.[28]

10.4 Constitutional Studies Undertaken Following the Approval of Plurinational and Intercultural Constitutions

After the implementation of the plurinational and intercultural constitutions of Bolivia and Ecuador, several studies were developed from different perspectives and trends. I identify six trends: the first is an analytical-normative theoretical trend, the second a cultural-pluralist study, the third a trend involving new constitutionalism, the fourth a sociological-analytical trend, the fifth a self-defined horizontalist and decolonialist trend and the sixth presents plurinationality or autonomy as a right and a challenge.

1. The analytical-normative trend can be divided into several groups:
   a. Those who undertake normative-historical, critical and comparative studies covering the ancient, modern, liberal, social, neoliberal constitutionalism through to the new constitutional trends in Latin America, especially in Ecuador and Bolivia, and conclude that the normative framework alone does not allow for changes which can only occur as a result of concrete struggles for political, economic and cultural democratization, which may take place at national or international level but do not tell us how to act through these concrete struggles (Pisarello, 2012). Gargarella (2011) adopts this same historical-critical path but includes a critique of the performance of progressive or left-wing politicians and theorists starting out from the contradiction between democracy and presidentialism, as well as the lack of proposals for change in the organic part of the Constitution. The vice-presidency of the Plurinational State of Bolivia (2012) followed a similar path in the *Historical Constitutional Encyclopedia* (in five volumes), but with a greater emphasis on Bolivia's final constituent process. On the other hand, Uprimny (2011) attempts to identify similarities and differences in the various constitutional processes in Latin America, classifying those in Ecuador and Bolivia as new and transformative, but with many theoretical and political challenges;
   b. Alternatively, others undertake a normative-historical analysis from the point of view of the neoconstitutional current of thought (Ávila, 2011; Grijalva, 2012);
   c. There is also a fractional normative perspective which highlights plurinationality and interculturality as part of the Constitution and, as such, is an analysis with eminently cultural connotations, without taking into account that it is an integral theoretical current (Grijalva, 2012; Ávila, 2011);
   d. Those who have opted for deconstructive-normative analysis, focusing on the actual text of the Constitution and reading it as an internal and external intercontextual text calling for open interpretation (Rodríguez & Rojas, 2011); and
   e. Trends favoring a political-normative analysis of the Constitution that essentially study the contradictions of plurinational constitutionalism and conclude that it is a virtually unattainable project (Cordero, 2012).

2. The cultural-pluralist trends can be divided into two major groups:
   a. Those based on analysis and studies of cultural diversity and its historical marginalization, both in the colony and the republic. As such, this

perspective is a recognition of diversity within the state but, since the coexistence of diversities is a complex process, proposes intercultural dialogue (Albó and Barrios, 2006; Walsh, 2009); and,

b. Those that start out by focusing on legal pluralism, which results in analyses and constitutional studies based on the recognition of indigenous justice (Yrigoyen, 1999, 2011).

3. The third trend, that of new constitutionalism, can also be divided into two groups:

   a. Those whose starting point is the perspective of the theory of modern Western constitutionalism, as advocated by Roberto Viciano Pastor and Rubén Martinez Dalmau, among others. These authors analyze European constitutional models, emphasizing that for some decades, given the weakening of a strong concept of constitution, neoconstitutionalism has insisted on differentiating between the formal and the material concepts of the constitutional state. From the early 1990s onward, guaranteeist theories were adopted by the new Latin American constitutionalism.
   b. Those that analyze the new constitutionalism through the struggles of indigenous movements. This trend argues that the struggles of indigenous movements have succeeded in bringing the constitutions of Ecuador and Bolivia into force.

4. From the sociological-analytical point of view, there are at least two main perspectives:

   a. The first, which takes the creative tensions of the revolution as its starting point, considers the plurinational state as a revolution but contains a mixture of justification for academic and state action that often conflicts with social and indigenous movements (García, s.d.);
   b. The second perspective consists of a sociological analysis from postcolonial and post-capitalist perspectives, which begins by stating that the global North finds it difficult to imagine alternatives to modern problems that societies in both the global North and the global South currently have to face, since their knowledge stems from the abyssal line that has produced the invisibility of other knowledges and experiences. Thus, it argues that a gap exists between theory and practice. These hegemonic theories have failed to realize that alternatives have been developed in the non-imperial global South, as is the case with plurinational constitutionalism. To overcome this blind spot, a new epistemology of the South is proposed that intends to develop with and through the historically marginalized and excluded knowledges, while still engaging in dialogue with other knowledges. The central premise of the epistemology of the South is the ecology of knowledges and intercultural translation. From this perspective,

plurinational constitutionalism is a transformative proposal distinct from liberal constitutionalism (Santos, 2006, 2007, 2010b).

5. The horizontalist and decolonialist trend:

   The horizontalist and decolonialist trend (Medici, 2012) is based on converting Kelsen's Pyramid into a horizontal model and the Western modern state into a decolonial state. It intends to make constitutionalism horizontal, whereby the Constitution would have supremacy since it represents the core of meaning, coordinating a plurality of culturally rooted legal knowledge and practices. The idea of substantial validity for traditional constitutionalism is preserved but constitutional meanings require a pluritopic hermeneutic for application in concrete situations.

6. Plurinationality or autonomy as a right and a challenge:

   Clavero (2016) argues that the states of Bolivia and Ecuador were born multicultural, a reality constitutionally ignored through the advancement of colonialism. Hence the nature of plurinationality is related to the decolonizing axis as a path for deconstructing the republican, colonial and liberal states. For this reason, it is argued that plurinationality involves the recognition of indigenous peoples as subjects with rights, including the right to autonomy, and that the challenge is to make these rights effective. This requires assigning constitutionally functional powers to those rights.

10.5 Plurinationality from Above and Plurinationality from Below

As previously mentioned, the plurinational state has been presented as a strategy for avoiding the opposition which made the initial proposals impossible. For this reason, it is important to differentiate between the plurinational state, or plurinationality from above, which was favored by the majority of the leaders of the indigenous movement and the theories of plurinational constitutionalism that have emerged in the meantime, and plurinationality from below, which was rendered invisible.

10.5.1 Plurinationality from Above Remains a Eurocentric Proposal and Should Be Considered Transitional

When referring to plurinationality from above, or the plurinational state, I am considering content that is given to the state via the structure of the institutionality of the modern Western state, incorporating only the 'pluri', the ecologies or the diversities, or, at best, autonomies and rights operationalized via the institutionality of the state. Consequently, the plurinational state remains a Eurocentric proposal to which the 'pluri' has been added. From the perspective of the modern Western state, this is undoubtedly an advance, just as the social state of law or the socialist state was in their times.

As the plurinational state is still a Eurocentric proposal, it is important to salvage its status as a transitory entity. The plurinational state is not the point of arrival or the end point to which the transition should lead, but the transition itself which takes us to the initial proposal, namely building a new form of social organization by strengthening the foundations of the community and expanding them beyond the indigenous.

However, the plurinational state as a transition also generates risks since, in engaging with the individualistic and vertical logic of the institutionality of the modern Western state, it is possible to become absorbed by this system and enter into disputes involving individual and vertical power that allows for survival within this model. Alternatively, from that point on, it might be possible to stop the institutionality of the state from obstructing the exercising of community autonomies and thus drive the community beyond the indigenous. However, in order to achieve this, there must be clarity on the way forward, constancy and organizational unity or strength capable of helping to prevent the institutionality of the state from becoming an obstacle to the implementation of plurinationality from below. In the latter case, popular resistance plays a key role.

The transitory quality of a hegemonic tool such as the institutionality of the state does not mean that seizing power is excluded, far less that the institutionality of the state is neglected, but simply that not all efforts are concentrated on taking power from the institutionality of the state, since the plurinational state is not the end in itself: it is a tool that has to be monitored and, at some point, confronted. Since the plurinational state is a moment of transition, this means that the initial proposal, namely plurinationality from below, becomes a priority.

10.5.2 Plurinationality from Below

Plurinationality from below means not focusing on seizing power from the institutionality of the state, but on exercising autonomy within the daily lives of the grassroots communities, extending these bases to spaces beyond the indigenous in order to facilitate the simplifying of life and regain political, economic and even knowledge autonomy. At this point, the *yachay* or *unancha* that allows for *sumak kawsay* and good living plays an important, although not exclusive, role. I would distinguish here between the *sumak kawsay* governed by the principles of *tinkunakuy*, *yanantin* and *randi radi*, which subsists in indigenous communities, the good living as an alternative to development and capitalism which is generated beyond the Andean indigenous community and is not necessarily governed by all the principles of *sumak kawsay*, and the good living in broader spaces such as the state, which must be filled with content through agreements between the *sumak kawsay* differences and the diversity of good living.

There is talk of simplifying life because the consumerist system both incapacitates us and generates a need: the more incapacitated we are, the more dependent on consumption we become. Thus, the simplification of life is nothing more than recovering the capacity for interrelationality. Only *achik runakuna*, beings interrelated with their three bodies and with everything that exists in the world, can cease to be consumers and generate natural production, and only *achik runakuna* can strengthen interrelated families and communities through *sumak kawsay*. However, plurinationality from below also implies strengthening Afro-Ecuadorian and Montubia communities, as well as replicating the voluntary and autonomous form of the community beyond the indigenous so that alternatives to development and consumption of good living systems can be generated. In this way, the simplification of life does not, and cannot, emerge through spaces such as the state or vertical and international institutions. On the contrary, these, constitute obstacles, as with the capitalist system which generates individualism, consumerism and discrimination. For this reason, it is also important to forge links between communities and create a counter-power to the state.

Since the state and the regional and international institutions are an obstacle, plurinationality from below begins in the spaces of human beings who must recover consciousness of *achik runa*, the family space formed by *achik runakuna*, and the community space in the interrelationality of the *achik runakuna*. It is in these spaces that economic liberation, liberation from scientificism, religious and scientific dogma and political liberation begin. Liberation from scientificism does not mean rejecting scientific knowledge, but regarding it as one more local knowledge of the world, such as *yachay* or *unancha*. Political liberation not only implies strengthening internal autonomy and orientation, but also the inter-communal interrelationality of the indigenous beyond the Andean indigenous. Plurinationality from below requires time and constancy, since it is developed over several generations.

Plurinationality from below produces other forms of relationship between the community and the institutionality of the state, with the latter increasingly losing power, as in the cases of the Toglla community and the Sarayaku people. Each time the indigenous communities strengthen the *sumak kawsay* and each time the community replicates beyond the Andean indigenous through alternatives to development and consumer systems for good living, multinational companies lose power. I am not sure what will happen to the state. It could reverse and become a form of horizontal organization that cannot be called a state as such, or it could assume the functions of coordination, while guaranteeing the fulfillment of the rights for everyone.

10.6 Conclusion

I may be accused of essentialism, yet essentialism is neither my intention nor my style. I seek to give visibility to hidden discussions and place them in the debate. However, I also intend to promote the production of theories from excluded contexts which, despite being excluded, have an alternative potential for alternatives. From here on, the academic and political challenges that lie ahead are decisive, and the sole intention of this chapter is to provoke and awaken these challenges.

Notes

* Translation by Neil Walker.
This chapter is a synthesis of the results of my doctoral thesis presented at the Faculty of Economics/Center for Social Studies at the University of Coimbra, which was partially funded by the ALICE Project at the Center for Social Studies, University of Coimbra.

1 *Tinkunakuy* means mutual coexistence through *Achik Runakuna* in interrelationships (not reduced solely to human beings, but extending to everything that exists). *Tinkuy* has also been translated as 'encounter'. Hence, *Tinkunakuy* has been badly translated to mean 'interculturality'. However, the meaning I wish to convey is that of 'interrelationality'.
2 *Yanantin* is the equivalent of complementary duality.
3 *Randi* is the equivalent of reciprocity.
4 See Pisarello (2012) and Santos (2007).
5 *Potestas* will henceforth be understood as the institutional power exercised by appointment, a power that is by nature delegated, in contrast to *potentia*, which is the power of the community and is called sovereignty in theoretical texts.
6 See Dussel (2007: 323).
7 See Santos (2009).
8 See Hegel (2001 [1821]: 184).
9 *Minka*, which we now know as a *minga*, is collective work, usually carried out with a view to maintaining community infrastructures.
10 *Ayni* is solidarity work involving families, neighbors and friends in specific activities that do not require much time, such as seeding, harvesting and building a house.
11 *Yana* is community work like the *Ayni*, which, with the arrival of the Incas, was transformed into forms of service to the Incas.
12 See Llasag (2011: 79–82).
13 See Albornoz (1971), Bonilla (1977), Segundo (2003) and Poma de Ayala (1980).
14 In case of the Bolivia, see Chuquimia (2012: 151–200) and, in the case of Ecuador, see Llasag (2012: 82–156).
15 Ampam Karakras, of Shuar nationality, was very close to the organizational processes involving the Shuar Federation, CONAIE and other organizations from the 1970s to the present day.
16 See Llasag (2014: 302).
17 Alfredo Viteri is an indigenous Quechuan leader and intellectual from Sarayaku who has been very close to the organizational processes since the 1970s.
18 See Llasag (2014: 302).
19 Thomas Huanacu, an Aymaran leader from Bolivia, an originary authority of Ayllu Parcomanka-Copacabana-Oruro.
20 See Llasag (2014: 303).
21 See Llasag (2014: 303).
22 See Llasag (2014: 302–303).
23 The use of the word 'own' does not necessarily refer to ancestors, since in the process of interaction between cultures there is a dynamic of creation, recreation and even adoption of other practices that the collective considers positive.
24 See Llasag (2014: 303).

25 Family clans. *(T. N.)*
26 See Llasag (2012).
27 See Santos (2010b).
28 See Llasag (2012, 2014), Santos (2010b).

References

Albó, Xavier; Barrios, Franz (2006), *Por una Bolivia Plurinacional e Intercultural con Autonomías.* La Paz: UNDP.

Albornoz, Oswaldo (1971), *Las Luchas Indígenas en el Ecuador.* Guayaquil: Claridad Editorial.

Arrighi, Giovanni (2007), *Adam Smith en Pekín. Origen y Fundamentos del Siglo XXI.* Madrid: Ediciones Akal.

Ávila, Ramiro (2011), *El Neoconstitucionalismo Transformador. El Estado y el Derecho en la Constitución de 2008.* Quito: Abya Yala.

Bodin, Jean, (1997), *Los Seis Libros de la República.* Madrid: Tecnos [orig. 1576].

Bonilla, Heraclio (1977), 'Estructura Colonial y Rebeliones Andinas', *Apuntes, Revista de Ciencias Sociales,* 7: 91–99. DOI: https:/doi.org/10.21678/apuntes.7.555.

Borja, Ramiro (1979), *Derecho Constitucional Ecuatoriano,* Tome IV. Quito: Instituto Geográfico Militar.

Chakrabarty, Dipesh (1995), 'Postcoloniality and the Artifice of History', *in* Bill Ascroft, Gareth Griffith and Helen Tiffin (eds.), *The Post-colonial Studies Reader.* London: Routledge, 383–390.

Cholango, Humberto (2012), *Movimiento Indígena del Ecuador su Participación en la Asamblea Constituyente de Montecristi, y la Lucha por el Estado Plurinacional.* Thesis prior to obtaining the third level degree, Universidad Politécnica Salesiana del Ecuador.

Chuquimia, René (2012), 'Historia, Colonia y Derecho de los Pueblos Indígenas', *in* Boaventura de Sousa Santos and José Exeni (eds.), *Justicia Indígena, Plurinacionalidad e Interculturalidad en Bolivia.* La Paz: Abya Yala and Fundación Rosa Luxemburg, 151–200. www.rosalux.org.ec/producto/justicia-indigena-plurinacionalidad-e-interculturalidad-en-bolivia.

Clavero, Bartolomé (2016), *Constitucionalismo Latinoamericano: Estados Criollos entre Pueblos Indígenas y Derechos Humanos.* Santiago de Chile: Olejnik.

Cordero, Sofía (2012), 'Estados Plurinacionales en Bolivia y Ecuador, Nuevas Ciudadanías, ¿Más Democracia?', *Revista Nueva Sociedad,* 240 (julio – agosto), pp. 134–148. https://nuso.org/revista/240/democracias-en-ebullicion.

Dussel, Enrique (2007), *Política de la Liberación, Historia Mundial y Crítica,* Tome 1. Madrid: Trotta Editorial.

Dussel, Enrique (2009), *Política de la Liberación,* Tome 2. Madrid: Trotta Editorial.

García, Álvaro (s.d.), *Las Tensiones Creativas de la Revolución: La Quinta Fase del Proceso de Cambio.* La Paz: Vice-presidency of the Plurinational State. www.vicepresidencia.gob.bo/IMG/pdf/tensiones_revolucion.pdf.

Gargarella, Roberto (2011), 'Pensando sobre la Reforma Constitucional en América Latina', in César Rodríguez Gravito (coord.), *El Derecho en América Latina, un Mapa para el Pensamiento Jurídico del Siglo XXI.* Buenos Aires: Siglo XXI, 87–108.

Grijalva, Agustín (2012), *Constitucionalismo en Ecuador.* Quito: Constitutional Court of Ecuador. http://bivicce.corteconstitucional.gob.ec/bases/biblo/texto/Constitucionalismo/Constitucionalismo_en_Ecuador.pdf.

Guamán Poma de Ayala, Felipe (1980), *Nueva Crónica y Buen Gobierno.* Mexico: Siglo XXI Editores.

Hegel, Georg W.F. (2001), *Philosophy of Right*. Kitchener: Batoche Books [orig.1821].
Hobbes, Thomas (1984), *Leviatán*. Madrid: Sarpe [orig.1651].
Hobbes, Thomas (2000), *De Cive: Elementos Filosóficos sobre el Ciudadano*. Madrid: Alianza [orig.1642].
Llasag, Raúl (2008), 'Plurinacionalidad: una Propuesta Constitucional Emancipadora', *in* Ramiro Ávila (ed.), *Neoconstitucionalismo y Sociedad*. Quito: Ministry of Justice and Human Rights of Ecuador, 311–355.
Llasag, Raúl (2011), 'Derechos de la Naturaleza: Una Mirada desde la Filosofía Indígena y la Constitución', *in* Carlos Gallegos and Pérez, Camilo (eds.), *Los Derechos de la Naturaleza y la Naturaleza de sus Derechos*. Quito: Ministry of Justice, Human Rights and Worship, 75–92.
Llasag, Raúl (2012), 'Movimiento Indígena del Ecuador a partir del Siglo XX: Visibilizando el Resurgir, sus Avances y Retrocesos', *in* Boaventura de Sousa Santos and Agustín Grijalva (eds.), *Justicia Indígena, Plurinacionalidad e Interculturalidad en el Ecuador*. Quito: Abya Yala and Fundación Rosa Luxemburg, 83–156. www.rosalux.org.ec/producto/justicia-indigena-plurinacionalidad-e-interculturalidad-en-ecuador.
Llasag, Raúl (2014), 'Constitucionalismo Plurinacional e Intercultural de Transição: Equador e Bolívia', *Meritum*, 9(1): 265–294. www.fumec.br/revistas/meritum/article/view/2497/1487.
Locke, John (2007), *Segundo Tratado do Governo*. Lisbon: Calouste Gulbenkian Foundation [orig. 1680]. https://gulbenkian.pt/publication/segundo-tratado-do-governo.
Medici, Alejandro (2012), *La Constitución Horizontal, Teoría Constitucional y Giro Decolonial*. San Luis de Potosí, Mexico: Centro de Estudios Jurídicos y Sociales Mispat.
Pisarello, Gerardo (2012), *Un Largo Termidor, Historia y Crítica del Constitucionalismo Antidemocrático*. Quito: Constitutional Court of Ecuador.
Quijano, Hannibal (2008), 'Coloniality of Power, Eurocentrism, and Social Classification', *in* Mabel Moraña, Enrique Dussel, Carlos A. Jáuregui (eds.), *Coloniality at Large: Latin America and the Postcolonial Debate*. London: Duke University Press.
Reinaga, Faust (2013), *La Revolución India*. La Paz: WA-GUI.
Restrepo, Eduardo; Rojas, Axel (2010), *Inflexión Decolonial: Fuentes, Conceptos y Cuestionamientos*. Popayán, Colombia: University of Cauca.
Rodríguez, Eduardo; Rojas, Farit (2011), *Lectura(s) Plural (es) de la Constitución: Ductilidad, Porosidad, Despliegue y Deconstrucción. Un Acercamiento desde los Estudios Constitucionales*. La Paz: Bolivarian Catholic University 'San Pablo', Faculty of Law and Political Sciences, Center for Constitutional and Political Studies.
Santos, Boaventura de Sousa (1995), *Toward a New Common Sense: Law, Science and Politics in the Paradigmatic Transition*. New York: Routledge.
Santos, Boaventura de Sousa (2006), *Conocer desde el Sur. Para una Cultura Política Emancipatoria*. Lima: Editorial Universidad Bolivariana.
Santos, Boaventura de Sousa (2007), *La Reinvención del Estado y el Estado Plurinacional*. Santa Cruz de la Sierra, Bolivia: CENDA, CEJIS and CEDIB.
Santos, Boaventura de Sousa (2009), *Una Epistemología del Sur*. Buenos Aires: CLACSO.
Santos, Boaventura de Sousa (2010a), *Para Descolonizar Occidente, más allá del Pensamiento Abismal*. Buenos Aires: CLACSO.
Santos, Boaventura de Sousa (2010b), *Refundación del Estado en América Latina, Perspectivas desde una Epistemología del Sur*. Quito: Abya Yala.
Second, Moreno Yánez (2003), *Alzamientos Indígenas en la Audiencia de Quito, 1534–1803*. Quito: Campaña Nacional Eugenio Espejo por el Libro y la Lectura.

Uprimny, Rodrigo (2011), 'Transformaciones Constitucionales Recientes en América Latina: Tendencias y Desafíos', *in* César Rodríguez Gravito (coord.), El *Derecho en América Latina, un Mapa para el Pensamiento Jurídico del Siglo XXI.* Buenos Aires: Siglo XXI Editores, 109–137.

Vice-presidency of the Plurinational State of Bolivia (2012), *Enciclopedia Histórica Constitucional,* Tome 5. La Paz: Vice-presidency of the Plurinational State of Bolivia.

Walsh, Catherine (2009), *Interculturalidad, Estado, Sociedad: Luchas (de) Coloniales de Nuestra Época*. Quito: Abya Yala.

Weber Max, (1979), *El Político y el Científico.* Madrid: Alianza Editorial.

Yrigoyen, Raquel (1999), *Pautas de Coordinación entre el Derecho Indígena y el Derecho Estatal.* Guatemala: Fundación Myrna Mack.

Yrigoyen, Raquel (2006), 'Hitos del Reconocimiento del Pluralismo Jurídico y el Derecho Indígena en las Políticas Indigenistas y el Constitucionalismo Andino', *in* Mikel Berraondo (coord.), *Pueblos Indígenas y Derechos Humanos.* Bilbao: Universidad de Deusto, 337–567.

Yrigoyen, Raquel (2011), 'El horizonte del constitucionalismo pluralista: del multiculturalismo a la descolonización', *in* César Rodríguez Garavito (coord.), *El Derecho en América Latina, un Mapa para el Pensamiento Jurídico del Siglo XXI.* Buenos Aires: Siglo XXI Editores, 139–159.

Zaffaroni, Raúl; Alagia, Alejandro; Slokar, Alejandro (2000), *Derecho Penal. Parte General.* Buenos Aires: Ediar.

11

TRANSFORMATIONAL CONSTITUTIONALISM, INTERCULTURALITY AND THE REFORM OF THE STATE

Looking through the Eyes of the Originary Peoples

Nina Pacari

This chapter provides a critical reading of constitutional advances in Ecuador from the perspective of indigenous peoples. It is a testimonial and a critical reflection constructed from the author's experience as a jurist, an activist working for the recognition of indigenous peoples, and a member of the National Constituent Assembly, the National Assembly of Ecuador and the Constitutional Court. It draws attention to the continuity of power structures based on Western hegemony imposed on the originary peoples and seeks to show the epistemic complexity underlying indigenous claims.

11.1 Introduction

I do not intend to describe the historical background of the institutional process that led to the characterization of Ecuador as a plurinational and intercultural state and to an emerging constitutionalism. Nor is it my intention to lament the uphill struggles which the originary peoples have experienced. On this occasion, the aim is to reflect on some 'doctrinal' themes from the perspective of indigenous peoples, a reflection that is essential given the nature of a *magna carta* that could lead to transformational constitutionalism and the possibility of constructing a truly plurinational and intercultural state.

Much has been said about the European invasion and subsequent colonization, and the imposition of a vertical structure and institutionality, as well as an economic system that produces social disparities. Due to the hegemony of the Eurocentric vision, the resistance of the originary peoples was, and continues to be, regarded as 'struggles' for specific demands, for rights inherent to their specific situation or protests relating to claims associated with issues such as access to education or overcoming the state of poverty in which they find themselves.

DOI: 10.4324/9781003391920-15

Analysis of the various texts referring to the 'indigenous revolts' of the colonial or republican era reveals that they are considered to be specific and isolated episodes. In recent times, very few sociologists and experts in the social sciences have made any kind of effort to understand that the 'indigenous protests' have to do with the management of power and the structuring of a state capable of overcoming the supremacy of the Western concept, as well as inequalities.

A more in-depth reading of the most diverse expressions of resistance undertaken by indigenous peoples and nationalities (uprisings, revolts, mobilizations, marches, etc.) shows the presence of a 'continuous vision' in reviving a sense of horizontal power, the concept of the state (as plurinational) and the praxis of the community economy (*sumak kawsay*) as interrelated elements that have been disturbed.

Depending on the historical context, during the period from the 1960s to the 1990s, while organizational reconstruction was taking place due to the plight of peoples and nationalities, the idea of a state that could respond to the new historical dimensions, acknowledge the presence and contributions of the various originary nations and work to eliminate economic and material inequalities was being refined. A hermeneutic task was required to strengthen the principles, structure and life system transmitted from generation to generation, dating back to our ancestors.

As the disparities deepened and the Western-framed state structure strengthened to the detriment of the pre-colonial states, the indigenous movement had to develop new strategies, including epistemic ones, in order to focus on institutional restructuring in terms of policies and rights, including self-determination.

This was the context in which the framework of the plurinational state came to public attention, against the backdrop of an unprecedented national indigenous uprising which took place in June 1990 and was organic in its projection.

Since then, the need to restructure the state has become apparent, and the indigenous movement has therefore presented a number of demands, including the formation of a National Constituent Assembly and legal-constitutional reforms, drafting proposals for new normative frameworks and promoting territorial and identity reconstitution. In the face of a new juridical-constitutional and socio-political context, the task that remains pending is that of applying the constitutional advances, which requires an epistemic approach, at the very least in order to understand the social fabric and the concepts embedded in proposals from the originary peoples of Latin America, in particular those of Ecuador. Moreover, taking this epistemic variable into account must be considered an essential component in promoting South-South dialogue.

11.2 The Nature of the State

In university classrooms, students learn that a state must possess certain elements, including a defined territory, population, laws, governing bodies, internal sovereignty, which consists of the power to apply its laws within the territory without the need for intervention by other states, and external sovereignty, which allows it to call on its inhabitants to defend the territory from external attack.

They also have the opportunity to study theories presented by intellectuals such as Max Weber, who asserts that: 'The state has the monopoly of a legitimate use of physical force within a given territory', that is, the state is an organization supported by its *monopoly of legitimate violence*, since it is composed of powerful bodies such as the armed forces, the police and the courts that are responsible for, among other matters, guaranteeing the functions and obligations of the government, defense, security and justice.

It is also necessary to understand other philosophical currents that are opposed to the existence of the state in its manifest form. Anarchism, for example, advocates the complete removal of states and their replacement with free entities and organizations based on participation. Marxism, on the other hand, considers that the state is a resource controlled by a ruling class that uses it to exercise dominion and, consequently, proposes its replacement by a proletarian state as part of the transition to socialism and communism.

These conceptual frameworks are important but do not address the concept that has been constructed by the originary peoples in this respect. Through an eagerness to make the indigenous proposal for a plurinational state viable, and thus affirm identity as that of 'nations or nationalities', it has become common practice to confer equal status, in principle, on elements such as territory, population, laws, governing bodies, language, history and culture in order to argue that when dealing with nationalities by combining these elements or requirements, the nature of the state should effectively reflect this condition. However, the concept of 'own', in one way or another, has still been ignored.

When, via a reflexive exercise, attempts are made to find terms or concepts within the world of the originary nations equivalent to those that have emerged from the Western formation, it may be concluded that they do not exist. In the 1980s, they used to ask us: how do you say 'state', 'nation' or 'nationality' in Quechuan? In recent times, in the context of the constitutional recognition of *sumak kawsay*, a female Bolivian anthropologist declared that during her entire career working with peasants and Indians, she had never heard of *sumak kawsay*, thus reasoning that it must be a political fantasy of the indigenous elites. The fact that the anthropologist's 'ear' offers her no proof of this, or that we have not provided an answer in the form of a literal translation into an epistemic construction that derives from the West, does not mean that there are no theories or production of knowledge in the world of the indigenous peoples on matters such as those related to the state, nations or power.

In the Quechuan language, the term *Ayllu* cannot be reduced to only one concept. Yet, in this case, for the purposes of domination, it has often been reduced to a literal translation equivalent to the *family*, understood as the bloodline or, at best, the *extended family*. Concomitant with this conceptual reduction, other substitute terms such as *ayllu-llacta*, referring to a commune or community, were applied. In exploring these two issues of reduction and substitution further, it has been imperative to adopt two measures: the first is related to restoring the conceptual meaning of *ayllu* and the other to incorporating the term 'commune' or 'community' as part of the 'own culture', so that the word, although from another language and culture, is regarded as our own by attributing a concept of 'own' that has been developed by the peoples.

Thus, analyzing the term *ayllu* in greater depth, it can be found to refer not only to ties of consanguinity but also to a population established in a territory, which has authorities, has developed a system for producing authorities, practices norms, uses and customs of its own and has a language, a history and procedures for administrating justice, as well as an institutionality that reflects its world view: ultimately, it is about historical territorial entities or units, which is nothing more than *being an ayllu or belonging to an ayllu*, as, for example, in the phrase *the Ayllu of Quéchua* or the '*Kichwacunapak Jatun Ayllu Tantanakui*' – the Confederation of Peoples of Kichwa Nationality.

In the 1990s, at one of the continent-wide conferences of the indigenous movement, one of the leaders of the Quechuan nation of Bolivia spoke to me, asking, rightly so in my opinion: 'Why do we continue to identify ourselves as provincial organizations based on the political-administrative division imposed on us instead of restoring our self-identification as *ayllu*?' In fact, one of the consequences of the constitutional reform that took place through the Constituent Assembly of 1998 which, in Article 84, recognized the right of native indigenous peoples to self-define as *indigenous nationalities of ancestral roots* was territorial and identity reconstitution. The intensive work undertaken by the Confederación Kichwa-Ecuarunari resulted in the Quechuan peoples reinforcing their identity in each of the provinces of the inter-Andean region. Some 24 years later, it can now be noted that the sense of belonging and the *Kichwa Ayllu* identity have gained strength and vitality, evident in the following cases, to name but a few: Karanki, Natabuela, Otavalo, Kayambi, Renildo-Kara, Panzaleo, Chibuleo, Salasaca, Waranka, Puruhá, Kanari, Sarakuro and Palta. Such examples have, in large measure, succeeded in overcoming the ideological oppression and the derision to which we have been subjected through a wide range of derogatory epithets.

However, due to the appropriation of the term 'commune' or 'community' in the understanding of the *Ayllu-llacta* or *Ayllu-marca* (territory, population and core institutionality of the *ayllu*), it was specified that, with regard to establishing authority, these are to be known as *communitarian governments of horizontal practice* (*ayllu apuk* or *ayllu pushak*). Thus, the subject that integrates the community is not limited to an individual but is a 'collective being', giving rise to a collective subject of rights. In this sense, Article 10 of the current Constitution states that: 'Persons, *communities, peoples, nationalities and collectives* are bearers of rights and shall enjoy the rights guaranteed to them in the Constitution and in international instruments' (Ecuador, 2008:27, italics added).

In the Constituent Assembly of 2008 the process of consolidating the *Jatun Ayllukuna* – indigenous nations or nationalities –was the key to insisting not only on recognition of indigenous nationalities but also the impact of this for the nature of the state itself, with all the repercussions that this implies, whether in terms of the structure of the state, the division of powers, the formulation of public policies, the economic model or the construction of new forms of relationship between the state-government and indigenous nationalities.

Thus, a plurinational state is one that shares and promotes the self-determination of the peoples, nations or nationalities that coexist in a territory. A state is plurinational not simply because it incorporates indigenous peoples into the institutional sphere of the state, but because it has a political content that respects the originary peoples and is put into practice by the state, that is, by the government in office and through institutions in general. A plurinational state must effectively recognize and foster a new structural arrangement so that indigenous territorial autonomies can come to terms with their respective duties and responsibilities within the political-administrative division that prevails today, so that the political autonomy derived from indigenous institutions that have been created within the state[1] (as well as those that may subsequently be created) can be administered by the originary peoples according to their uses, customs, norms and procedures, and thus strengthen democracy.

In this context, the decision that the current government of the citizen revolution has adopted with regard to intercultural bilingual education is contrary to the Constitution and to the very nature of the state. A brief reflection on this matter is outlined below.

Since the colonial era, access to education for the indigenous peoples has been marked by the imposition of new cultural and epistemic codes that have fostered alienation and an emptying of the teaching process. The political project from which the states were born was based on the ideal of homogeneity in the form of a *single nation*, taking for granted the disappearance of the peoples as a consequence of their 'domination'. Yet, the historical continuity of the native peoples has been present throughout the most varied forms of resistance. Since the mid-1980s, when there was a return to democracy, resistance took the form of a proposal for an education that liberates, is capable of rescuing the originary languages and their grammars, thus strengthening the philosophy of the peoples and addressing their reality, their needs and their life project, and is based on exercising the cultural diversity that should be recognized, adopted and respected by the state. Achieving political autonomy in education through the creation of the National Directorate of Intercultural Bilingual Teaching (between 1986 and 1987) represented a great victory, since the indigenous peoples were responsible for the management of bilingual cultural education and its implementation. A national director, together with the provincial directors, was to be appointed by the peoples themselves in accordance with their uses and customs, and any decision adopted by the indigenous nationalities would be ratified by the appropriate ministry.

Despite negligence on the part of every government without exception, evident in cuts to funds in their budgets, it was possible to revive all the languages of the indigenous nationalities and their respective grammars. Moreover, the drafting of curricula suitable for teaching in pluricultural or plurinational societies has been recognized internationally, to the extent that government authorities from several countries have taken this educational model as a reference point, with a view to incorporating it into their educational policies for originary peoples.

As a way of guaranteeing this political autonomy in intercultural bilingual education, the indigenous movement not only supported the corresponding legal framework, but also the respective constitutional reforms, as defined in Article 84(11) of the 1998 Constitution, concerning the right to the existence of an intercultural education system (Ecuador, 1998), and in Article 69, which states that 'the state will guarantee the intercultural bilingual education system' (Ecuador, 1998).

Despite this normative advance, which is enshrined in the 1998 Constitution, governments have endeavored to postpone it. The indigenous movement therefore supports the strengthening of intercultural bilingual education as stipulated in the current Constitution, which establishes, in Article 57(14), that the plurinational state guarantees the right to

> develop, strengthen and improve the intercultural bilingual education system, on the basis of criteria of quality, from its incentivization in childhood to the higher levels of education, in accordance with cultural diversity, for the care and preservation of identities in keeping with its teaching and learning methodologies. A dignified teaching career will be guaranteed. The administration of this system shall be collective and participatory, with temporal and spatial rotation, based on community monitoring and accountability.
>
> *Ecuador, 2008:46*

Similarly, Article 347(9) states that it is the obligation of the state to

> guarantee the intercultural bilingual education system, in which the principal language for educating shall be the language of the respective nation and Spanish as the language for intercultural relations, under the guidance of the State's public policies and with full respect for the rights of communities, peoples and nationalities.
>
> *Ecuador, 2008:161*

Clearly contradicting these constitutional provisions, after the plurinational state had been declared by Decree-Law 1585 of February 18, 2009, the government of Rafael Correa suppressed the political autonomy that the National Directorate of Intercultural Bilingual Education was entitled to and excluded the indigenous nationalities from its management under the pretext of having supposedly ascertained (from the hegemonic viewpoint of the other) the shortcomings of bilingual teaching.

According to Decree 1585,[2] the Minister of Education is responsible for defining the policy for bilingual education, appointing the undersecretary for Intercultural Dialogue, the National Director of the DINEIB and its provincial directors, defining who may be admitted to the Consultative Council on Bilingual Education and determining the competence of each of these entities.

This exclusion of indigenous peoples and nationalities from developing education in their own languages and in accordance with their world views is a setback to the exercise of collective rights: Decree 1585 not only violates collective rights but is openly unconstitutional and reflects a return to the path of coloniality. In order to defend their rights, the indigenous movement, through the Confederation of Indigenous Nationalities, filed a petition on March 8, 2009, to the Constitutional Court on the unconstitutionality of the decree in question, but there had been no ruling on its part, as had been supposed. It was later replaced by Decree 196, which contains the same shortcomings as Decree 1585. What is the outcome of this for the petition on unconstitutionality presented by indigenous peoples? The Constitutional Court has publicly justified itself by noting that it is not within its competence to decide on a decree which is not in force because it has been replaced. This is the kind of game to which we are subjected in the age of the new constitutional framework.

11.3 Fundamental Principles in the Structural Redefinition of State Powers

With regard to the fundamental principle of 'unity in diversity', it has been stated that horizontal or communitarian democracy is not based on representation or on the secret, universal or direct vote which simply delegates decision-making to others through elections. Instead, it is based on decision-making *by consensus* rooted in the direct intervention of the *Ayllu-llacta*, *Ayllu marca* or, in other words, the communitarian collective. Through this process of constructing a plurinational state, a proposal was put forward to reform the state's first power, the national parliament. In order to pave the way for its integration (from 1994 to 1995), it was proposed to create an indigenous national jurisdiction, together with indigenous provincial jurisdictions, in which the nationalities would participate, when appropriate, choosing members according to their customs, rules and procedures. In this way, a plurinational parliament would not be restricted to including indigenous peoples from indigenous nationalities: the rules and concepts relating to democracy and the electoral procedures of indigenous nationalities would constitute the substantive basis for the institutional restructuring of a state that implements the principle of cultural diversity. However, none of these proposals were accepted during the period of constitutional reform in the 1990s or in the 1998 and 2008 Constitutions.

With reference to another state power, namely the judiciary, the question of recognizing legal pluralism has been raised. Both the 1998 Constitution and the Constitution currently in force have recognized the competences of the indigenous peoples' authorities in resolving conflicts according to their own uses, customs, norms and procedures (Article 171) (Ecuador, 2008:98). The judicial system encompasses not only the ordinary justice system but also the specific indigenous regime which the originary peoples also use in matters of justice, albeit in a different way. Essentially, whereas in ordinary justice the ruling is delivered by a judge or judges (depending on the circumstances), in *Quechuan justice* the decision is community-based: it is shared between the authorities and participants convened by the assembly to resolve the conflict; deliberations are undertaken within the assembly; a committee or committees of 'inquiry' are set up by the assembly; and 'confrontation' (*chimbapura* – face-to-face) takes place within work of the assembly, as part of the procedure itself. At the end of the process, the decision or judgment is adopted by the assembly, that is, by the authorities and members of the communitarian assembly. It might therefore be considered that the decision is not taken by the authorities, but this is not the case. Article 171 of the present Constitution recognizes the uniqueness of the originary peoples and, by virtue of this recognition, their authorities are vested with the power to administer justice according to their uses and customs (Ecuador, 2008:98). The Constitution does not determine that the decision is made only by the indigenous authorities but refers to the uses, customs, norms and procedures practiced by the peoples. Consequently, the way in which the rupture of harmony (*llaki* – conflict) is resolved depends on the practices and concepts developed by the peoples, including not only customs but also norms and procedures. Having been adopted collectively, it may be considered that no one can be held responsible in matters of constitutional control. However, that is not the case either: this is not an instance of *Fuenteovejuna*.[3] It is precisely this communitarian entity that participates in the assembly and whose authorities are those vested with legal, judicial and extrajudicial representation.

As can be seen, the administration of indigenous justice (as with Quechua) is different from that of ordinary justice, yet this may also be the case if the indigenous procedure is being applied to the administration of ordinary justice. As clearly understood in the ordinary justice system, the principle corresponding to the law which is relevant to the case in question must be applied: for this reason, the way in which indigenous justice and ordinary justice are administered is different or even opposite but also complementary, insofar as their coexistence facilitates access to justice in plurinational societies. Strictly speaking, what becomes evident through this constitutional recognition is the interaction involving the principle of 'complementary differences' or 'complementary opposites' (an epistemic construction developed by the originary peoples) within a plurinational state.

By applying the same principle of complimentary differences or opposites at the level of state organization, it can be said that the powers that constitute it, although different in terms of their composition or attributions, must effectively respond to the nature of their societies, which are the basis on which state and government institutionality is established: consequently, co-responsibility is a manifestation of complementarity. Nevertheless, in this section I do not intend to dwell on analyzing the application of the principle of *complimentary differences* to the materiality of balance and control between the powers of the state which, according to Western conceptions, constitutes the fundamental basis for living in a democracy.

11.4 The Constitutional Court and the Paradoxes of Its Composition

Although the state was not recognized as plurinational in 1994, after the indigenous revolt against the Agrarian Development Act approved by parliament, the Confederation of Indigenous Nationalities of Ecuador (CONAIE) proposed a reform of Article 144 of the Constitution, demanding that the Constitutional Court should accept a member elected by indigenous nationalities.

Although this was a constitutional provision that would open up a slim possibility for indigenous peoples to count on having one member in the Constitutional Court on the basis of a list shared with the trade unions, it is ironic that their application has failed to materialize precisely because trade unionism also sought to have its own representation.

The fact that the application has failed does not mean that the norm should disappear. On the contrary, what is required is that the norm should be effective. We should therefore ask where the inefficacy of this norm specifically resides, a question which begs contextual analysis.

At the time (early 1990), politicians and many academics agreed that indigenous peoples' organizations constituted 'guilds' or 'corporate entities', that is, they were composed of indigenous citizens who were affiliated, had organized themselves and even had legal personality (since they were legally constituted). The indigenous peoples, for their part, emphasized their historical continuity as peoples or nations, together with the fact that their identity was neither union nor guild-based, and neither proletarian nor corporate or associative. This 'conceptual' disagreement showed that there was an epistemic and cognitive conflict.

One of the social rights that Western culture has developed is that of freedom of association, taking as its specific starting point the subject recognized by law, that is, the person, the individual. This is why a number of people can spontaneously and freely organize on the basis of a common objective, such as a sports club, a trade union, a company or a committee for improvements and, when registering at the relevant ministry, obtain their own legal personality.

This concept of the social right to freedom of association is also applied to the originary peoples. It is worth noting, for example, that in 1944 when the first indigenous organization was recognized, despite being termed the Ecuadorean

Federation of Indians, two central questions were raised: the first, despite invoking the term 'Indian', highlights the individual subject (the summation of indigenous people); the second relates to 'classist' content. In other words, the imposition of normative content became clear through a specific epistemic concept attributed to peoples with different epistemic codes.

This is not a reflection aimed at determining whether this view is better or worse: the issue here is that the cognitive construction of the organizational form developed by indigenous peoples is based mainly on identity, territory and historical continuity, that is, on their continued status as Quechuan, Shwar, Siona, Secoya, Aymara, Maia, Aztec and so on, with languages, uses, customs, norms, established authority and other forms of institutionality that differ from Western forms. According to this conception, on the one hand, being Quechuan or Shwar is not based on an individual desire to belong to a certain indigenous nationality, but rather on the continuity of societal constructions established prior to the invasions and colonization, nor does it comprise the sum of individual and spontaneous wills that seek a common good. As a consequence of being excluded historical entities, what is required is the recognition and exercise of their rights in the context of a plurinational state whose institutional construction should be defined and implemented with the full participation of these peoples.

This concept was not understood by the political elite between 1994 and 1998, and thus they failed to consider the direct or differentiated participation of the indigenous peoples in the appointment of members of the Constitutional Court, other than to assume that this was a corporate entity of workers or, at best, a set of 'recruited' trade unions which, in defense of their legitimate right, had also not given up their 'quota'.

Thus, at the time of its application, the reformed constitutional norm revealed its lack of effectiveness in failing to respond to the reality of a society and a plurinational history.

11.5 The Constitutional Court and Institutional Independence Tied to the Origins of the Nomination of Its Members

In addition to establishing the plurinational and intercultural character of Ecuador, Article 1 of the current Constitution also defines it as 'a constitutional state of rights and justice' (Ecuador, 2008:23).

In the academic debate, there are two pivotal standpoints on the constitutional nature of *rights*. On the one hand, there are those who argue that the term 'rights' refers to recognition of the differentiated (individual and collective) rights that attend to the needs of the indigenous nationalities, Afro-descendants or mixed race (Ecuador, 2008:27). On the other hand, there are those who affirm that this is a specific recognition of legal pluralism, since it refers to the different legal systems that indigenous peoples have preserved. In addition to the arguments presented by each side, there is a consensus on the fact that Ecuador has had the opportunity to generate profound changes, including those affecting its legal culture and institutional independence.

It is evident that Ecuador has traditionally been characterized by its legalistic culture, giving precedence to the application of secondary legislation to the detriment of constitutional provisions. This culture of legality has superimposed itself on the primacy of the Constitution. There have always been obstacles to the exercise of collective rights, since the time when the 'civilian' view of law, for example, prevailed over the appropriate constitutional interpretation that should be applied to resolve conflicts or demands. In the heat of the *March for Life* in 1992, led by the Confederation of Indigenous Nationalities of the Ecuadorian Amazon (CONFENIAE) – a member of the Confederation of Indigenous Nationalities of Ecuador (CONAIE) – the confederations proposed the 'legalization of their territories'. The Amazonian nationalities are not only found on the mountain slopes of the Oriente region and the central parts of the Amazon basin but have also historically occupied the border territories between Ecuador and Peru, since they are peoples whose history predates the demarcation of borders between states. However, in applying the National Security Law, several territorial areas failed to be 'legalized', that is, 'attributed' to the originary peoples, even though they were ancestral possessions.

It may be thought that this issue, which predates the constitutional reforms of 1998 and 2008, would have subsequently been resolved but this is not the case. The problem does not lie in temporality, but in the traditional inherited doctrine, which has a strong Franco-European component that supports the notion that the law is the legal basis of social regulation *par excellence*; a doctrine that is further manipulated when the intention is to introduce or disrupt its adoption in societies with different epistemic concepts.

In the administration of ordinary justice, for example, legality still carries more weight than constitutional justice. Landmark cases include La Cocha 2, which ruled against the indigenous authorities of Saraguro on the grounds that they were exercising judicial powers through a constitutional mandate when administering justice, and that of Azuay, in which the judges and the criminal court did not uphold the petition for competence lodged by the indigenous authority of the community and sentenced a member of the community to several years in prison.

Further examples that are not limited to the sphere of the indigenous peoples could also be cited, but my reflections have a common thread, namely to highlight the political-institutional action of the state and the hegemonic view that is imposed on the originary peoples.

Regardless of this, a shift in legal culture from the supremacy of legality to that of the Constitution, which guarantees collective and human rights (not the least since the Constitution is directly applicable), while possibly resulting in a gradual modification of the culture of legality, would not mean that access to justice is automatically improved or respect for the exercise of rights is guaranteed.

Without dwelling on a case-by-case analysis of La Cocha 2 and other proceedings, it is worth setting out some additional reflections.

According to Article 429 of the present Constitution, 'the Constitutional Court is the supreme body for controlling, constitutionally interpreting and administering justice in this matter' (Ecuador, 2008:192).

While it is true that submission to constitutional limits or human rights constitutes a relatively recent innovation, some of the most serious conflicts affecting the Constitutional Court in terms of its relationship with the state powers have to do with its competences as a constitutional control body when these powers exceed their limits in exercising their constitutional competences, deviate from the procedure set out in the supreme norm or result in abuses of power. In a democratic system, the division of powers, the system of checks and balances and institutional independence not only constitute a procedural guarantee but also the continuity of a constitutional state that respects rights.

The Constitutional Court is not subject to the jurisdiction of other organs. On the contrary, it is endowed with functional autonomy and comprehensive authority, enabling it to exercise its judicial function with full independence in constitutional matters (Articles 436 to 440) (Ecuador, 2008:194–196). However, it is also true that during the transitional period, a lack of independence could be observed in several of the rulings handed down by the majority of its members. It is enough to review and analyze most of the speeches of its members regarding the process of reforming the Constitution proposed by the executive in 2011, the judgment concerning the petition on the unconstitutionality of the Mining Law or the dictates of repeated ordinances relating to states of emergency associated with petroleum or security issues emanating from the Legislative Assembly after the events of '30 S',[4] which contradict the provisions outlined in Article 166 of the Constitution, among others (Ecuador, 2008).

Added to this is the fact that the controversy over independence has also been questioned due to the composition of the current Constitutional Court.

According to the provisions in Article 434 of the Constitution, nominations for members of the Constitutional Court are drawn up by the legislative, executive and transparency and social monitoring authorities (Ecuador, 2008:193).

The concentration of power in the hands of the President of the Republic is common knowledge. This is not due exclusively to the hyper-presidentialist system contemplated in the current Constitution. It is also true that the parliamentary majority resides in the party in office, but this does not mean that 'the first power of the state' is subordinate to the executive power, thus leaving the field open to hyper-presidentialism and undermining democracy, since the required checks and balances disappear, and subordination manifests itself openly.

In these circumstances, the lists presented by the legislative and transparency and social monitoring authorities are answerable to the hegemony of the executive power. Consequently, due to the origins of the nominations put forward, it may be said that the Constitutional Court will remain subordinate to the executive power, except in decisions that demonstrate the opposite.

11.6 Raising Interculturality

Several concepts of culture have been developed in Western thinking, in some cases related to art, education, intellectuality and folklore, as well as the sciences of anthropology, sociology and philosophy, among others.

According to the thinking of originary peoples such as the Quechua, for whom the *Kawsay* represents life, in exercising the principle of relationality (taking a holistic view), the culture of the peoples does not conform to some specific or isolated dimension, but instead refers to the ways of living, producing knowledge, creating authority and spirituality of each *Ayllu marca*, *Ayllu-llacta* or *Jatun Ayllu* – the peoples and nationalities. Hence, in the organizational process of the indigenous movement of Ecuador, the *Equador Runakunapak Riccharimuy* (ECUARUNARI), founded in 1972 and currently known as the Confederation of Peoples of Kichwa Nationality, has fought its struggle under the slogan: '*Allpamanta, Kawsaymanta, Kishpirinkakaman*' ('Land, Culture and Freedom').

The question does not revolve around the fact that both Western and indigenous perspectives refer to similar elements, namely that all the peoples of the world develop their culture, which is expressed in forms of social organization, art, economics, history, language, literature and so on, whether from an atomistic or holistic outlook. The issue here is that the 'Western notion of *culture*' is based on the hegemony of the individual subject who can constitute an organized collective, contrary to the indigenous nations, who take the collective subject as their starting point, necessarily linked to historical continuity and territory, as previously mentioned. Moreover, what characterizes this Western notion of culture is its hegemonic role in relation to other cultures. As such, in the face of exclusion and oppression stemming from the new socioeconomic and political fabric imposed since the colonial period, the *originary cultures – indigenous nations or nationalities* – question the uninational or monocultural state, as well as the system of inequalities.

This is how the proposal to restructure the state and make it plurinational emerged from the indigenous movement, reflecting the debates that took place within the organizations during the 1980s and 1990s.

On the national and international stage, there is also a debate on multiculturalism, in which the 'American or European multicultural interpretations, despite the social heterogeneity highlighted, do not affect or challenge the foundations of the organization of power (the state)' (ECUARUNARI, 2012:132), while the notion constructed by the originary peoples is endowed with a political and ideological principle that manifests itself in its demands and is opposed to the colonial and exclusionary state: this is where the epistemic value formulated by the originary peoples resides.

In other words, what is at stake is the fact that while the indigenous peoples, in questioning the political-social model and the asymmetric relations between the state and originary nations, conceive of culture as a political-ideological struggle against the hegemonic model, Western culture conceives of pluri- and interculturality as a form of harmonious relations between different cultures, but from the same dominant hegemonic perspective. The case of intercultural bilingual education reflects this conception.

Currently, the state is defined as plurinational and *intercultural*, and this definition emanates from the principle of *interculturality*, which is not limited to the relationship based on equality between the different cultures that coexist in a country or the mutual respect that should prevail among them but is subordinated to the dominant Western thinking.

Inasmuch as every culture, people or nationality is a producer of knowledges, interculturality refers to a dialogue of knowledge, an epistemic dialogue that must prevail in plurinational societies. Consequently, applying interculturality in relation to power or democracy obliges the state to apply procedures or rights such as consultation or 'ruling through obeyance' (*mandar obedeciendo*).

At this point, it is worth questioning whether, and how, the principle of *ruling through obeyance* would apply in countries such as ours, where the exercise of power is vertical.

The construction of these appropriate forms or mechanisms as the product of intercultural interpretation is what would enable a transformational constitutionalism to materialize, capable of promoting a true plurinational state sustained by an economic model free of inequalities.

In short, the current Constitution establishes paradigms such as *sumak kawsay*, together with plurinationality or interculturality, which, had they been duly implemented, would have paved the way for a profound transformation of the traditional state. As certain experts in the field have pointed out, the fact that an 'advanced' Constitution exists but fails to recognize collective rights such as those of the originary peoples, among others, suggests that the only option left is to develop interculturality.

In this situation, a South-South dialogue would have to overcome the hegemonic barrier of the epistemic variable, since in this South-South context, especially in Latin America, originary civilizations exist which, by virtue of their struggles, have managed to influence a constitutionalism and a state that can effectively become transformative when generating ruptures in all types of hegemonies, including the epistemic.

Notes

1 The National Directorate of Intercultural Bilingual Education (DINEIB), National Directorate of Indigenous Health, Council for the Development of Nationalities and Peoples of Ecuador (CODENPE) and Fund for the Development of Indigenous Peoples (FODEPI).

2 Ordinance 1585, February 18, 2009.
3 This is a reference to a play by Lope de Vega, in which the community assumes collective responsibility for a crime, thereby refusing to recognize the perpetrators individually. *(N. T.)*
4 A reference to September 30, 2010, the beginning of a political crisis in which there was never a consensus as to whether a *coup d'état* had been attempted or not. *(N. T.)*

References

Ecuador (1998), 'Constitución Política de la República del Ecuador', *The Official Register* 1, of 11th August. Available at www.cancilleria.gob.ec/wp-content/uploads/2013/06/constitucion_1998.pdf.

Ecuador (2008), 'Constitución de la República de Ecuador', *The Official Register* No. 449, of 20th October. Available at www.asambleanacional.gob.ec/sites/default/files/documents/old/constitucion_de_bolsillo.pdf.

ECUARUNARI (2012), *Una Mirada a Nuestra Historia. Movimiento Nacional Ecuador Runakunapk Rikcharimuy*. Quito: Confederación de Pueblos de la Nacionalidad Kichwa – ECUARUNARI.

12

PARTICIPATION AND PRESIDENTIALISM IN THE ECUADORIAN CONSTITUTION OF 2008*

Agustín Grijalva

12.1 New Constitutionalism[1]

Neoconstitutionalism,[2] a term which is European in origin, refers to constitutions that feature extensive rights and safeguards (Ahumada, 2009). This is the fundamental trait which this constitutional trend shares with the new Latin American constitutionalism, or transformative constitutionalism, and which aims to bring about necessary institutional consequences, such as the strengthening of the role of judges, in particular, constitutional court judges.

However, there are other aspects that constitute specific and important characteristics of the new Latin American constitutionalism, such as the strengthening of political participation, the concern for equality and diversity, social and collective rights, the constitutional regulation of the economy, openness to international human rights law and secularism (Uprimny, 2011). As is the case with both Ecuador and Bolivia, these differences in characteristics are accentuated by the inclusion of principles such as the plurinational state, communitarian democracy, the rights of nature and 'good living' (*buen vivir*) in the constitutional texts. These concerns, specific to the new Latin American constitutionalism, can be summed up in a broad and radical conception of democracy which, in terms of its political, cultural and economic dimensions, is understood as amounting to more than elections.[3] The differences between European neoconstitutionalism and this new Latin American constitutionalism are not incidental. In fact, they have emerged, both directly and indirectly, as a response to the historical conditions that preceded the respective constituent processes. Nothing new comes from nowhere, and this new constitutionalism cannot escape the constitutional tradition of the region.

DOI: 10.4324/9781003391920-16

With regard to the mediated conditions, the new Latin American constitutionalism has its own specific roots in the constitutional currents of radical democracy that developed on the continent (Gargarella, 2014) in other historical periods. Interest in democratic issues has been a constant in Latin American societies, which are deeply marked by exclusion and inequality. A concern for social and economic rights, for example, is highlighted in several Latin American constitutions that appeared in the first decades of the twentieth century, among which the Mexican Constitution stands out. The need to take onboard new models of economic constitution is directly related to the history of the role of the state in Latin America regarding the economy, and the declaration of a plurinational state expresses our historical colonial experience and the corresponding struggle of the indigenous peoples.

It should be remembered that these constitutions have been seeking to increase the political participation of citizens and their organizations since the 1990s, as a response to disillusionment with representative democracy and, specifically, the political parties and legislature in many countries in the region. On the other hand, the importance of strengthening the state's role in relation to the economy was clearly a response to the privatization and deregulation processes of the preceding neoliberal period. Thus, as Boaventura de Sousa Santos has stated, the strengthening of rights, in particular social, economic and cultural rights, has brought about a new commitment from the left in the face of the crisis in socialist countries (Santos, 2010). It is within this context of the protection and promotion of rights that the importance of these constitutional charters can be understood from a formal point of view, in terms of guarantees and justices.

However, there is one variable that demonstrates the strong continuity between the neoliberal constitutional model and that of twenty-first-century socialism. It is a continuity that, in turn, has distant antecedents in Latin American history. In this respect, it has led to the inveterate strengthening of the executive and, specifically, the position of the President of the Republic. This continuity is expressed in the form of greater powers for the president, the weakening of the legislative and judicial fields and, in the case of the new constitutionalism, the possibility of indefinite re-election. How can this paradox be explained?

In fact, both neoliberal and twenty-first-century socialist governments have elected presidents who have achieved high levels of popularity, legislative majorities and significant influence over constitutional court judges. Under these conditions, presidents have promoted their re-election as a means of carrying out their programs. In the case of neoliberalism, macroeconomic stabilization and structural adjustment programs have been developed, while so-called socialist governments have chosen to boost the modernization of infrastructures and pursue policies of economic redistribution by increasing state revenues through exports of oil, minerals or other primary goods. In each case, whether deregulating or regulating, privatizing or nationalizing, strong executives were required, with the capacity to impose themselves on the social resistance that generates these processes. This logic has led to hyperpresidentialism.

The problem with hyperpresidentialism is that it constitutes a dimension or structural component which clearly contradicts the other postulates of new constitutionalism. The concentration of power inherent in hyperpresidentialism is contrary to deepening democracy through participation. It is also contrary to respecting rights which, in the light of their prerequisites, always limit and guide power.[4] In particular, this centralization of power is contrary to the plurinational state, founded on the decentralization of power and recognition of the diversity of indigenous peoples. Likewise, it is contrary to the independence of both the judicial system and the constitutional jurisdiction, as well as the autonomy of the supervisory bodies. There is also a clear antipathy between hyperpresidentialism and any territorial decentralization scheme.

Moreover, as explained by research in Ecuador and Bolivia (Santos and Grijalva, 2012) led by Boaventura de Sousa Santos, the state's extractive economic policy requires preventing or, at least, limiting participatory processes (such as indigenous autonomy, including justice itself). In fact, this participation can be directly or indirectly expressed as mechanisms of resistance to the extractive activities carried out by the state and multinationals. In one sense, the present study extends the hypothesis developed in the aforementioned research to other forms of participation.

12.2 Direct Democracy and Political Participation

It is clear that democracy as defined in several of the most recent Latin American constitutions extends beyond the representative form of democracy, while still incorporating it. Moreover, since the constitutional reforms of the 1990s, representative democracy itself has been redefined in the region to encompass forms of direct and semi-direct democracy, together with other mechanisms for participation including referendums, the repeal of mandates and legislative initiatives.

Even if these mechanisms can potentially enrich representative democracy, they should not be adopted without proper investigation. Nuria Cunill (1997)[5] summarized and analyzed several cases in Latin America and other parts of the world in which the supposed majority or participatory expressions of democracy did not serve to transform power relations and redistribute resources in a more egalitarian way, but rather to legitimize the *status quo* and even facilitate conservative reforms. In fact, the constitutional reforms in Latin America in the 1990s, which introduced direct participation mechanisms such as the popular legislative initiative, the referendum, the plebiscite and various participatory democracy mechanisms, coincided with processes designed to reduce the state and transfer resources and powers to the private sector. It so happens that, as previously noted, participation has often been reduced to a purely functional mechanism to meet the information and management requisites of bureaucracy or the needs of corporate control under populist and authoritarian governments, including dictatorships.[6]

It is particularly important to specify the conditions under which participation is truly democratic and conducive to the realization of human rights, especially in Latin America. Several of the governments in the region that presented themselves as progressive during the first decade of this century organized various kinds of citizen councils. It is necessary to study these experiences critically in order to determine how they either transformed or reproduced power relations and how they have redistributed resources. One key condition that should be taken into account is the assessment of how these forms of popular organization have related to the state and, specifically, to the government in office. Without autonomy and enabling rights, participatory experiences degenerate into political control mechanisms with exclusionary and authoritarian effects, that is to say, effects contrary to those which strengthen democracy.

Following the establishment of Latin American governments recognized as progressive and by enacting new constitutions and reviewing the existing ones, the state has continued to grow. Has this growth meant greater or less citizen political participation? How has this participation influenced the effectiveness of rights and the redistribution of power and economic resources?

12.3 Participation in the Ecuadorian Constitution of 2008

Unlike the constitution drafted in 1998, which established the classic division between the legislative, executive and judicial powers, the 2008 Constitution establishes five functions, adding two more, namely the electoral function, and transparency and social control, to the three classic functions. The latter aims to promote participation, rights, control of public services and the fight against corruption.[7]

The 2008 Constitution has nominally strengthened citizen participation in public management, oversight and the fight against corruption. The previous Ecuadorian Constitution, enacted in 1998, had already set up a Civic Corruption Control Commission which received complaints of alleged crimes that could be referred to the judicial authorities for trial and sentencing (Article 220). The 2008 Constitution has transferred these powers to this new state function, which operates at the same hierarchical level as the executive, legislative, judicial and electoral functions and is called the Transparency and Social Control Function (Article 204).

The main body within this new state function is the National Council for Citizen Participation and Social Control (Article 207). The members of this council are appointed via a contest, held after the candidate selection process has taken place, overseen by citizens. The Council's functions include the fight against corruption, the promotion of citizen participation and the appointment of the Ombudsman, the Public Defender's office, the Financial Inspectorate, the Attorney General and members of the National Electoral Council and the Electoral Litigation Tribunal (Article 208). After a decade under this Constitution, it can be concluded that, despite being conceived of as a new state function and despite the innovation that the creation of the Citizen Participation Council represented, neither citizen participation nor control of corruption has improved. On the contrary, this new function has contributed to weakening supervision by citizens and control bodies. At the same time, it has led to a shift in legislative power, both in terms of its supervisory tasks and the appointment of members of public control and human rights bodies.[8]

In fact, the Council suffers from serious problems of representation and even political legitimacy. While the notion of participation concerns the direct, unmediated intervention of citizens in matters of public interest, the composition of this Council has been based on contests, that is, confusing assumptions and evaluations as a means for selecting officials who have no social or political representation since they have not been elected by anyone. Thus, instead of complementarity, it has resulted in a confusion between participatory democracy, representative democracy and meritocracy.

Article 100 of the Ecuadorian Constitution also establishes the possibility of organizing various other mechanisms for citizen participation,[9] such as public hearings, popular committees, assemblies, advisory councils, observatories and inspections to approve development plans in various territorial and institutional bodies within the Ecuadorian state. This is how the National Councils for Equality are created, composed of representatives from the executive and civil society, whose function is to combat discrimination, marginalization and exclusion. Along the same lines, what is referred to in the Constitution as direct democracy is strengthened by expanding the repeal of the mandate for all public authorities (Article 105), as well as the ratification and greater constitutional regulation of the citizen initiative through the presentation of draft legislation (Article 103). Innovative institutions such as the 'empty chair' (the possibility of having a citizen representative in public sessions of decentralized autonomous governments) (Article 101) are also outlined.

There are still few empirical studies on the implementation of these multiple constitutional mechanisms for participation. Nevertheless, the hypothesis of largely uneven development and an insufficient or negative balance sheet regarding implementation can be formulated. For example, due to delays in setting up, during the formative years several of the new councils operated on the basis of a majority of government delegates and were chaired by them (Ospina, 2013) or showed little development (Cordoba, 2013) and a low level of involvement in processes such as planning (Orrantia, 2015). The expansion and regulation of the repeal of the mandate resulted in a certain manipulation and abuse of this institution (Malacatus, 2016). Innovative institutions such as the 'empty chair' are still scarcely used and, when applied, have been confusing or even distorted (Castro, 2014). One example, highlighting a particularly troubling result of this strategy, can be found in the citizen inspection set up to review public contracts in favor of a brother of President Correa. In this case, criminal proceedings were initiated against two of the four inspectors after it was concluded that the president was aware of the contracts. The inspectors were sentenced to one year in prison.

Furthermore, Article 95 of the Constitution defines participation as a right that is exercised through the mechanisms of representative, direct and communitarian democracy. Article 96 even recognizes all forms of societal organization as an 'expression of popular sovereignty', as a means of ensuring involvement in all decisions and public policies. Nevertheless, what has emerged in practice is the criminalization of human rights defenders and a systematic attack on the right to social protest[10] and association, through legal statutes established in the new Integral Criminal Code dictated by the regime (sabotage, terrorism, rebellion, etc.) This Code has been applied to numerous protests,[11] together with Decree 16, enacted in June 2013, which has allowed the executive to dissolve organizations deemed contrary to its policies.[12] This is a deeply paradoxical situation in a country whose Constitution enshrines the right to resist actions or omissions by public authorities that constitute a violation of rights (Article 98).

The constitutional formulation of participation in the Ecuadorian Constitution of 2008 is thus contradictory in itself and, furthermore, compromised by government policies that constitute additional violations of the right to participate. On the one hand, this formulation includes a proliferation of participation mechanisms while, on the other hand, it 'statizes' participation, reducing it to a differentiated 'state function' when, in fact, it ought to be a transversal mechanism applicable to all public institutions and all state functions in their relationships with society, establishing itself as the main axis for the latter. Yet, appointees to the participatory function are selected through a contest that has, in practice, facilitated their co-option by the executive,[13] which has, in turn, enabled interference in appointments to the supervisory bodies.[14] In this way, an institutionality that should promote social participation has actually served to deprive parliament of its political supervision and control functions, by controlling or reducing citizen participation and, in its place, ensuring the onset of hyperpresidentialism.

In point of fact, and from a conceptual perspective, two forms of participation can be distinguished here: *participation as legitimation* and *participation as democratization*. The former is vertically induced within society and its organizations through the power of the state. The latter seeks to legitimize what has already been decided or will be decided later at the level of the political elites and public administration, displaying a preference for the number of workshops, meetings, assemblies and so on, rather than their quality. Since this form of participation fails to democratize decisions, it also fails to distribute political power or, necessarily, economic power. Non-binding consultation is one very clear example of this.

In contrast, *participation as democratization* is born from the organizations and social movements that are seeking to effectively democratize decisions, which is why it truly guides the state bureaucracy, avoiding the need to sacrifice quality for quantity through the number of meetings or participatory mechanisms and thereby safeguarding genuine conditions for collecting information, building equality and monitoring. By its very nature, this type of participation tends to provide a genuine redistribution of public power and economic and cultural assets. The best practices of participatory budgets are clear examples of this (Fung and Wright, 2003).

By analyzing the case of popular consultation authorized in Ecuador by President Rafael Correa in 2011, I seek to illustrate this difference between the two types of participation. As will be seen, this is an obvious example of legitimizing participation which, in restricting judicial independence, has concentrated power rather than redistribute it. Two further exercises in popular consultation, which were frustrated or blocked by the Correa government and serve to corroborate the above thesis of instrumentalizing participation, will also be analyzed.

In Ecuador, particularly since the return of democracy in 1978, numerous referendums and popular consultations have been held on a wide range of issues. The nation shares with Uruguay the distinction of being one of the countries in the region with the highest number of referendums and plebiscites. Nevertheless, there are important differences since, in Uruguay, with the return of democracy from 1989 onward, many plebiscites and referendums have been organized by the citizens themselves and their organizations, whereas in Ecuador, since 2008 it has been the presidents who have used this mechanism to consolidate or legitimize their power.

12.4 The Popular Consultation of 2011

In Ecuador, the popular consultation of May 7, 2011, showed precisely how participation in a plebiscite can be used to legitimize greater concentration of power rather than its democratization. This consultation enabled President Correa to significantly increase the interference of the executive and other public bodies under his influence in the designation of members of the Judiciary Council, thereby eroding the formulation that the Constitution had provided as a way of preserving judicial independence.

In February 2011, Correa simultaneously called a referendum and a popular consultation. In Ecuador, the former is aimed at revising the Constitution while the latter focuses on issues that the president considers to be of great public importance.[15] A total of ten questions on a wide range of topics were included in the referendum and consultation. However, it was fundamentally a constitutional review regarding the composition of the Judiciary Council. Questions 4 and 5 of the referendum convened by President Correa implied a revision of the Constitution, as well as several articles in the Organic Code of the Judicial Function. The main change involved the dissolution of the Judiciary Council and the appointment, for an 18-month period, of a Transitional Judiciary Council composed of three members, one appointed by the Executive, another by the Legislature and a third by the Transparency and Social Control.[16] After this period, a definitive Judiciary Council would be appointed, with a different composition based on the new rules governing the Constitution. The new Judiciary Council was now composed of five delegates and their deputies, elected by the Council for Citizen Participation and Social Control from groups of three people proposed by the President of the National Court of Justice, the Attorney General, Legal Protection and the National Assembly. This review also included several changes to the functional structure and tasks of the internal bodies of the Judiciary Council.

The reform fundamentally changed the institutional formulation for the composition of the Judiciary Council originally conceived in the 2008 Constitution. In this Constitution, the Judiciary Council was a body whose composition and functioning were autonomous in relation to other state functions, given that delegates were not appointed by any of those functions. The Constitution provided for the appointment of the nine members of the Judiciary Council by means of a public contest in which legal and public administration professionals participated. This contest was to be organized by the Council for Citizen Participation and Social Control (Constitution of the Republic of Ecuador, 2008).[17] The referendum proposed by the president changed this model completely.

The amendment proposed by President Correa entailed a constitutional revision of an organic order subject to constitutional scrutiny. For this reason, the Constitutional Court examined the questions to determine whether the procedure adopted was appropriate. According to Article 441 of the Ecuadorian Constitution, the president may only submit referendum revisions to the Constitution that do not alter the fundamental structure or the character and constituent elements of the state. Consequently, there was a debate between those who opposed the consultation, arguing that the revision of the composition of the Judiciary Council altered the structure of the state and the executive, who stated that the reform remained within the legal parameters.[18] This division of criteria also occurred within the Constitutional Court, where the majority of magistrates stated, in line with the executive, that the way in which the members of the Judiciary Council were appointed was a separate matter, unrelated to their independence.

In short, the majority in the Court put forward two central arguments: (1) the way in which members of the Judiciary Council are elected does not affect the independence or structure of the state; (2) in any event, the democratic decision of the majority of citizens, who can and shall express their opinion in the referendum, will prevail. In light of these arguments, the minority in the Court presented an opposite view, stating that the way in which members of the Judiciary Council are appointed has direct relevance for judicial independence. The reason put forward, as previously stated, is that in Ecuadorian constitutional history, both the executive and legislative functions had sought to control judges for party-political reasons by means of their dismissal and appointment. It is precisely for this reason that the Ecuadorian Constitution eliminated the involvement of these functions in the election of the members of the Council.

In the end, the results of the referendum favored the government in all questions, although with respect to the questions on the Judiciary Council the president won by a narrow margin (53.8%). Hence, the case of Ecuador highlights how plebiscitary democracy can erode judicial independence. Several questions and concerns have been raised regarding the independence of judges and the institutional conditions of the justice system. In fact, international inspections and reports which addressed the appointment of new judges and the Ecuadorian judicial system in general[19] have made observations confirming the existence of these problems.

Clearly, the limits on executive power have been affected by the results of the referendum in at least two ways. Firstly, the executive in Ecuador has again directly interfered in the appointment and removal of judges and, thus, in their decisions.[20] Secondly, the weakening of judicial independence implies less control over the executive, thereby eroding the rule of law and favoring corruption.

12.5 Blocking New Consultations

The need for a national consultation was discussed on three more occasions within the framework of the 2008 Constitution. The first was regarding the Yasuní ITT Project, initiated in 2007, while the second concerned a set of constitutional reforms promoted by Correa at the end of 2015, including indefinite re-election. The third occasion saw Rafael Correa call a popular consultation for February 19, 2017, relating to a ban on investments in tax havens by civil servants.

The Yasuní ITT Project basically consisted of not exploiting 856 million barrels of oil existing underground in a protected area of the Ecuadorian Amazon, an area with extensive biodiversity in which uncontacted indigenous peoples live. By keeping the oil underground, Ecuador would reduce environmental contamination and, in the process, lessen the ecological and cultural damage, preventing the emission of 407 million metric tons of carbon dioxide in exchange for international compensation worth US$350 million per year for lost revenues.

This initiative to keep oil under the ground corresponded to what had been established in Article 407 of the Ecuadorian Constitution, which clearly and expressly prohibits any extractive activity in protected areas, unless a declaration of national interest is requested by the president. This exception did not apply in the case of Yasuní, since the final part of Article 57 of the Constitution categorically prohibits such exploitation in areas inhabited by uncontacted indigenous peoples.[21] Nevertheless, on August 15, 2013, after raising insufficient international funds, Correa's government took the decision to end the ITT initiative for the non-exploitation of Yasuní. In view of this, several popular organizations and the

Yasunidos collective started a national petition campaign to convene a popular consultation on whether or not to support the non-exploitation of Yasuní.[22] After several months and difficulties related to the procedure, they were able to collect 673,862 signatures that were submitted to the National Electoral Council on April 12, 2014. Nevertheless, after several actions aimed at violating the proceedings, together with repression and media aggression, thousands of these signatures were unlawfully annulled, thus preventing the consultation.

The frustrated consultation on Yasuní clearly illustrates the gap between, on the one hand, the constitutional provisions for participation, the rights of nature and indigenous peoples in a state that proclaims itself plurinational and intercultural and, on the other hand, the concrete actions of the Correa government. Despite broad public support for opposing the exploitation of Yasuní, which sought to express itself through consultation, President Correa ended the ITT initiative by means of a decree and declared the exploitation of Yasuní a matter of national interest, subsequently ratified by a pro-government majority in the National Assembly. At the same time, the Constitutional Court and the National Electoral Council, also aligned with the government's position, acted to block popular consultation.

In short, the full array of state institutionality acted in a systematic and coordinated way to violate the rights of participation, environmental rights and indigenous peoples' rights, in pursuing the extractive policy of the regime. Paradoxically, as in other Latin American countries, the government used the need to obtain economic resources to satisfy the social rights of the poorest as its main argument for this exploitation.

A second discussion on the relevance of a popular consultation took place in 2015, following the 16 constitutional amendments presented by the government party, Alianza País, to the National Assembly. Among these amendments were restrictions on popular consultation, on rights concerning the association and strike action and on communication, as well as a reduction in the powers of the Finance Inspectorate in tandem with an expansion of the powers of the Armed Forces in order to maintain internal order. In addition, the amendments would allow for the indefinite re-election of the President of the Republic and other openly elected authorities. Opposition to Correa's government insisted that this constitutional revision should be carried out through a popular consultation or referendum, given its political importance and, more precisely, its effects on rights and democracy. Nevertheless, the Correa government refused to carry out the reform through a referendum and, taking advantage of its legislative majority and interference in the Constitutional Court, submitted and approved the revision through a National Assembly amendment in December 2015. However, following a transitory provision, the revision introducing indefinite re-election was not applied immediately, thus excluding the possibility of Correa's re-election for now.

It is evident that the amendments proposed by the pro-government legislative bloc all pointed in the direction of restricting various rights of participation. The constitutional revision limited the very establishment of popular consultation by requiring it to refer to matters within the legal competences of municipalities and other autonomous regional governments. As subsequently analyzed, the review also restricted the rights of unionization, collective bargaining and strike action by public administration workers. Moreover, it strengthened the capacity for control and internal repression by extending these functions to the armed forces. Unfortunately, this has not been an isolated phenomenon. As in other Latin American countries that have progressive constitutions, during the post-constituent phase in Ecuador, legislation, jurisprudence, public policies and even constitutional revisions have openly restricted or violated rights, instead of developing them. The establishment of indefinite re-election in Ecuador has also occurred in Venezuela, Nicaragua and Bolivia, for example, revealing a serious deterioration in representative democracy in these countries. Instead of complementing and enriching representative democracy by exercising the multiple mechanisms of direct democracy and participation envisaged in the constitutions of these countries, in practice what is evident is a serious distortion of the electoral processes.[23] Both parliament and the constitutional judges, together with the government, have participated in this distortion.

In fact, indefinite presidential re-election highlights the personalist support for the leader on the part of the movements and organizations that back the government in office. Thus, instead of strengthening the participation of popular organizations as a means of continuing projects for change, a general deinstitutionalization of political parties and movements has been created around a political culture increasingly focused on the 'warlord' that, consequently, excludes more extensive and improved participation.

Subsequently, President Correa convened a popular consultation on banning elected authorities and civil servants from holding assets or capital of any kind in tax havens. This consultation was held on February 19, 2017, the same date as the presidential and legislative elections. Once again, it was an initiative taken by presidential decree and endorsed by the Constitutional Court within a context of strong polarization and electoral rivalry in a country which, since the *Panama Papers*, has faced major scandals related to funds directed to tax havens.

The 2011 popular consultation, which included the Correa government's refusal to allow democratic participation in the Yasuní ITT initiative, the 2015 constitutional amendments establishing indefinite re-election and the latest popular consultation on tax havens highlight the selective and biased use of the referendum and popular consultation. These mechanisms have not been used to effectively extend popular participation in state decision-making throughout society. On the contrary, participation has become a selective political resource used to promote and impose on society, vertically via the state, the reforms and initiatives that the government wants to carry out and legitimize, a process which even violates the Constitution itself.

12.6 Participation and Extractivism

As a rule, extractivism is identified exclusively as an economic policy model but, as has been suggested throughout this chapter, its influence can be felt beyond economic processes in areas as diverse as participation, education, work and the justice system. In order to exploit natural resources, extractive policies require strong social control by the state, which converts participation into a source of legitimacy rather than a mechanism for expanding democracy. This social control requires a centralization of power which, by its nature, is contrary to, or at least restricts, democratic participation, plurinational autonomy and often the exercise of other rights, such as association, expression and opinion. In short, extractivism, as an economic model, requires certain political conditions. On the other hand, although the constitution expressly gives priority to cooperative forms of economic organization in which workers participate more in decision-making processes, economic policy has strengthened the state sector of the economy without producing any structural change in the cooperative sector.

In the case of Ecuador, while recognizing a significant modernization of infrastructures and economic redistribution, it is undeniable that the same productive matrix remained after the 2008 Constitution. The dynamics of Ecuador's economy are still tied to oil exports, and government expectations are now focused on mining. Among other variables, it is the political needs of the extractive model that have driven the centralization of power within a hyperpresidential regime in Ecuador. One clear example of this is the government's blocking of a popular consultation on the Mining Law and the exploitation of the Yasuní, as well as cuts aimed at reducing the autonomy and participation of indigenous peoples in areas such as intercultural education and community justice, peoples who could have generated direct and indirect forms of resistance to these policies, as they had done before.[24]

The resources obtained through extractivism – oil revenues in the case of Ecuador – have, in turn, financed the activities of a large bureaucracy and public companies in strategic sectors of the economy, such as energy, telecommunications and non-renewable natural resources. The aim is to finance services, especially those that are public, which contribute to some economic redistribution. Nevertheless, once again, this process is produced through centralization and the vertical exercise of power which – by restricting constitutional rights with respect to unionization, strike action and collective bargaining – implies less worker participation.

Conversely, in Ecuador, cooperatives, communities and other forms of social- and solidarity-based economy have not developed to the extent that the constitution provides for, as the authorities recognize. Since these forms of productive organization combine capital and labor, thus extending the participation of the workers themselves, this lack of development also implies little growth in participation in productive processes.

12.7 What We Have Learned

Truly democratic participation must be induced autonomously from below, through society, and the state must respond to this requirement. State-induced vertical participation is, as a rule, more a form of legitimation and concentration of power than redistribution of power.

Hyperpresidentialism not only leads to the concentration of power in the executive or the president at the level of state institutionality: this centralization of power also has consequences that extend into civil society through the instrumentalization, reduction, regulation and even criminalization of the participation of social organizations and individuals.

Hyperpresidentialism is a functional political form linked to extractivism, which requires the authoritarian imposition of the extraction of natural resources. In the process, rights are manipulated as rhetoric in order to justify this exercise of power, while failing to constitute effective guidelines or to place limits on it.

Simply lapsing into 'being disappointed by the state' is neither strategic nor does it has political effects. These years of experience of the progressive cycle must lead to serious reflection on the relationships between society and the state, between social movements and institutions, and between social struggle and the Constitution.

The independence of ordinary, constitutional and electoral judges and courts is indispensable if democracy is to exist and deepen. These judges protect rights that are essential to democracy, such as freedom of association, freedom of opinion, freedom of information and electoral rights. Conversely, the judges' political dependence on the executive can be used to criminalize social protest and to limit or violate other inherent rights attributed to a deeper form of democracy.

The Constitution is not the end, but the beginning of a process for social change. It should be seen as a political program that must be defended through each law, each regulation and each public policy and through the composition and performance of each public institution. Otherwise, constitutional principles can be profoundly distorted and weakened during the post-constituent phase, giving rise to a process of deconstitutionalization.

Social change cannot be induced by the state which, rather than a means to an end, becomes an end in itself. The vertical and authoritarian voluntarism of the state, expressed through the expansion of bureaucracy, regulations, control and even resources, can be highly inefficient in terms of structural transformation. It is the society which, through active and autonomous participation, must permeate the state in order to release and monitor structural processes for social and economic change.

Notes

* Translation by Neil Walker.

1 I have already highlighted some of these ideas, in particular concerning new constitutionalism, in a previous essay (Grijalva, 2015).

2 In fact, it is a rather misleading term since the theory sometimes refers to very disparate and even contradictory subjects and approaches. It can be better understood as a set of criticisms and debates that emerged within the theory of law as a response to classical legal positivism and constitutionalism.

3 For this analysis of Bolivia and Ecuador, see Santos (2010).

4 In fact, this tension between strong government, participation and rights has been a constant in Latin American constitutional history, previously expressing itself in the conflict between conservative, republican and liberal constitutionalisms. See Gargarella (2014). For a perspective on this tension in the Ecuadorian Constitution of 2008, see Pablo Andrade (2012).

5 Regarding constitutional reforms in Latin America during the 1990s, Cunill points out that

> the recurrent reforms are aimed at introducing forms of popular initiative in the formation of laws and referendums at national level, conceived of as political rights for citizen participation. The Argentinian Constitution, revised in August 1994, includes both forms as rights, as do the new constitutions of Peru (September 1993) and Colombia (October 1991). Previously, they had been incorporated into the Constitution of Brazil, enacted in October 1988.
>
> *Cunill, 1997: 83*

6 A very clear example of the former is the case of the Fujimori government in Peru, while the latter situation is well exemplified by the Pinochet government in Chile. Both, to a lesser extent, called for the participation of society as a means to justify privatization and dismantling the state. Some so-called progressive governments, such as that of Ecuador, seem to have called for participation not simply to 'recover' the state but to juxtapose it with society.

7 Article 204 of the Ecuadorian Constitution.

8 The widespread corruption in the country is public knowledge. For example, in Ecuador, only the Odebrecht company paid fines for fraudulent public contracts, totaling $33.5 million according to the U.S. Department of Justice, while the names of the civil servants involved are still not known.

9 For a comprehensive institutional and legal overview of these institutions, see Albert Noguera and Marco Navas (2016).

10 See the report: *Criminalización de la Protesta Social Frente a Proyectos Extractivos en Ecuador* (FIDH, 2015).

11 There were several examples of urban protests, marches and indigenous protests, including that of Saraguro, in the south of the country, where several demonstrators were put on trial, as well as conflicts in the Amazon related to the advance of mining projects backed by the government which were rejected by these indigenous organizations, with social leaders subsequently facing arrest and criminal proceedings. There have also been abuses involving declarations of a state of emergency during some of these protests.

12 This was the case with environmental organizations, even extending to broad-based organizations such as Pacha Mama and Acción Ecológica, along with professional organizations, such as the National Union of Educators (UNE). The decree established a system of re-registration and delivery of information from all NGOs in the country, as well as broad criteria for the creation and dissolution of these organizations, which has given rise to a high level of discretion on the part of the state.

13 Many advisors were previously linked to the government as senior officials or advisors to ministers.
14 Even the incumbents reapplied for subsequent contests, as was the case with the Attorney General, the Inspector of Finance and the Ombudsman.
15 Article 147(14) and Article 441(1) (Constitución de la Republic del Ecuador, 2008).
16 As indicated, this function was created by the Constitution of 2008 and is composed of the Ombudsman, the Inspector of Finance and a council focused on citizen participation, among others. Its main competences are related to accountability, controlling corruption and encouraging participation.
17 *Official Registry* No. 449, October 20, 2008, Articles 179 and 180 (prior to revision).
18 It should also be noted that Questions 1 and 2 of the consultation proposed by the President referred, in turn, to restrictions on the power of judges regarding the declaration of precautionary measures, that is, urgent judicial measures for the protection of rights. In the case of such reforms, the Constitution, in Article 442, also limits the President's initiative, as it states that he will not be able to propose constitutional revisions restricting constitutional rights or guarantees.
19 See, for example, the report by Judge Baltazar Garzón and other international inspectors on justice in Ecuador, available at www.pensamientopenal.com.ar/system/files/2014/12/doctrina35446.pdf. See also the collective work: *Insufficient Judicial Independence, Distorted Preventive Prison*, Washington, Due Process of Law Foundation, 2013. For case studies, see Luis Pásara (2014).
20 In fact, the constitutional revision had a purely organic character, but clearly illustrates how the organization of power directly affects rights and principles such as those of fair trial, judicial independence and, thus, all judicial rights.
21 This constitutional proscription has been analyzed in Grijalva (2010).
22 As part of its response, the government also mobilized dependent organizations and 33 Amazonian mayors to collect signatures supporting oil exploration in Yasuní Park.
23 See Richard Ortiz (2017).
24 In the Saraguro case, for example, an indigenous court tried the indigenous people involved in protests against mining projects in their region. Ordinary justice did not recognize the competence of indigenous judges. It is also clear that the education provided by indigenous community schools is closely linked to valuing the land and nature as a source of life, rather than just as resources for economic exploitation.

References

Ahumada, María de los Ángeles (2009), 'Neoconstitucionalismo y Constitucionalismo' *in* Paolo Comanducci, Maria de los Angeles Ahumada and Daniel González (eds.), *Positivismo Jurídico y Neoconstitucionalismo*. Madrid: Fundación Coloquio Legal Europeo.

Andrade, Pablo (2012), 'El Reino (de lo) Imaginario: Los Intelectuales Políticos Ecuatorianos en la Construcción de la Constitución de 2008', *Ecuador Debate*, 85: 35–47. Available at http://hdl.handle.net/10469/3993.

Castro, José Luis (2014), *La Silla Vacía como Mecanismo de Participación Ciudadana*. Thesis for obtaining the title of lawyer, Pontificia Universidad Católica del Ecuador, Quito.

Constitución de la República del Ecuador (2008), Official *Registry* No. 449, 20th October. Available at www.registroficial.gob.ec/index.php/registro-oficial-web/publicaciones/registro-oficial/item/4864-registro-oficial-no-449.html.

Cordoba, Holguer (2013), *Derechos sin Poder Popular*. Quito: Centro Andino de Estudios Estratégicos.

Cunill Grau, Nuria (1997), *Repensando lo Público a Través de la Sociedad*. Caracas: Editorial Nueva Sociedad.

FIDH—Federación Internacional de Derechos Humanos (2015), *Criminalización de la Protesta Social Frente a Proyectos Extractivos en Ecuador.* Available at www.fidh.org/IMG/pdf/equateur666espagn2015hd_1_.pdf.

Fung, Archon; Wright, Eric Olin (2003), *Democracia en Profundidad: Nuevas Formas Institucionales de Gobierno Participativo con Poder de Decisión.* Bogotá: Universidad Nacional de Colombia.

Gargarella, Roberto (2014), *La Sala de Máquinas de la Constitución.* Buenos Aires, Katz Editors. DOI: https://doi.org/10.2307/j.ctvm7bcjw.

Grijalva, Agustín (2010), 'Régimen Constitucional de Biodiversidad, Patrimonio Natural, Ecosistemas Frágiles, y Recursos Naturales Renovables', *in* Agustín Grijalva, Efraín Pérez and Rafael Oyarte (eds.), *Desafíos del Derecho Ambiental Ecuatoriano Frente a la Constitución Vigente.* Quito: Centro Ecuatoriano de Derecho Ambiental (CEDA).

Grijalva, Agustín (2015), 'Nuevo Constitucionalismo, Democracia e Independencia Judicial', *Cálamo – Revista de Estudios Jurídicos,* 3: 27–38. Available at www.calamo.ec/number/3.

Malacatus, Edwin (2016), *La Revocatoria del Mandato, como Derecho Establecido en la Actual Constitución y Legislación del Ecuador, Respecto a sus Alcances, Requisitos y Limitaciones.* Master's thesis in Law, Area of Constitutional Law, Universidad Andina Simón Bolívar, Quito.

Noguera, Albert; Navas, Marco (2016), *Los Nuevos Derechos de Participación Derechos Constituyentes o Constitucionales?* Valencia: Tirant lo Blanch.

Orrantia Parra, Daniela (2015), *Análisis Crítico de la Planificación Participativa en la Elaboración del Plan Nacional del Buen Vivir 2013-2017.* Master's thesis in Latin American Studies, Politics and Culture, Area of Social and Global Studies, Universidad Andina Simón Bolívar, Quito.

Ortíz, Richard (ed.) (2017), *Reforma Electoral en Ecuador.* Quito: Udla.

Ospina, Pablo (2013), 'La Participación Ciudadana en Ecuador (2009–2012)', *in* Gina Benavides and María Gardenia Chávez (eds.), *Horizonte de los Derechos Humanos – Ecuador 2012.* Quito: Universidad Andina Simón Bolívar, 147–161. Available at http://hdl.handle.net/10644/4105.

Pásara, Luis (2014), *Independencia Judicial en la Reforma de la Justicia Ecuatoriana.* Washington: DPLF.

Santos, Boaventura de Sousa (2010), *Refundación del Estado en América Latina.* Quito: Ediciones Abya Yala.

Santos, Boaventura de Sousa; Grijalva, Agustín (eds.) (2012), *Justicia Indígena, Plurinacionalidad e Interculturalidad en Ecuador.* Quito: Fundación Rosa Luxemburg.

Uprimny, Rodrigo (2011), 'Las Transformaciones Constitucionales Recientes en América Latina: Tendencias y Desafíos', *in* César Rodríguez Garavito (ed.), *El Derecho en América Latina: Un Mapa para el Pensamiento Jurídico del Siglo XXI.* Buenos Aires: Siglo Veintiuno Editores, 109–137.

Jurisprudence

Corte Constitucional del Ecuador, Sentencia Nro. 113-14-SEP-CC Case Nro. 0731-10-EP.

13

TRANSFORMING TRANSFORMATIVE CONSTITUTIONALISM

Lessons from the Political-Legal Experience of Cherán, Mexico*[1]

Orlando Aragón Andrade

13.1 Introduction

The aim of this chapter is to contribute to enriching the discussion on the transformation of constitutionalism, focusing on one of the most enlightening experiences of political-legal struggle recently encountered in Mexico. Drawing on the movement of the Purépecha community of San Francisco Cherán[2] and, in particular, my work as a community lawyer accompanying this struggle,[3] I propose the existence of a different type of transformative constitutionalism to the one founded on the South American (especially Bolivian and Ecuadoran) experiences: a type of constitutionalism that has its foundations in lay knowledge and, being derived from an indigenous community, has been able to transform the very basis of the Mexican state, opening up new pathways to indigenous autonomy in Mexico.

It should be noted that the analysis presented in this work is the result of my dual role as a militant academic and as a lawyer in the legal and political processes explored here. For this reason, the following threads are based on the tensions that stem from the study, participation, application, observation and reformulation of the theoretical-political proposal of *subaltern cosmopolitan legality* (Santos and Rodríguez-Garavito, 2007) within the political-legal struggle of Cherán.

It is therefore necessary to outline the path followed for the development of my arguments. Regarding legal pluralism and the epistemologies of the South, I begin by analyzing the elements which characterize a constitution. I also examine some of the main points that provide transformative constitutionalism with emancipatory characteristics and, based on the experience of Cherán, raise the possibility of the existence of another form of transformative constitutionalism. I then set out the necessary conditions required for transformative constitutionalism on a local

DOI: 10.4324/9781003391920-17

level, or from below, to become transformational on a national scale. Finally, I conclude by reflecting on the limitations and potentialities of transformative constitutionalism from below.

13.2 The Constitution of Peoples without a Constitution: A Look at Constitutionalism from the Perspective of the Epistemologies of the South

On April 15, 2011, the recent history of the Purépecha community of San Francisco Cherán, in the municipality of Cherán, Mexico, changed radically. On that day, the Cheránense confronted illegal loggers and members of organized crime syndicates who, for several years, had been destroying their forests while subjecting them to an existence dominated by violence and fear. On the same day the movement for 'security, peace, justice and the reconstitution of the territory' began, driven by the need to protest that 'enough is enough' to the political parties which divided them and had allied themselves with organized crime and to reject the *modus operandi* and security institutions of the Mexican state due to their ineptitude and collusion with organized crime. Faced with this twofold assault on their community, in the midst of popular insurrection, the Cheránense reached a decision within their assemblies: a resounding 'no' to political parties and state police, while embracing a municipal government system based on their 'uses and customs' and a community militia founded by the Cheránense themselves.

From this new political consensus, one of Mexico's most outstanding examples of the process of indigenous struggle has been developing for more than five years, accompanied by a series of judicial victories in the most important courts in Mexico,[4] resulting in reforms to constitutional texts and secondary laws. The impact of this political movement within the legal domain was so significant that it led to the recognition in law of the first indigenous municipality of Mexico, with the authority to elect its own municipal authorities and define its formation through a system based on 'uses and customs'.

So, what is the relationship between this new political pact of Cherán and our understanding of a constitution? At first glance, the answer is nothing. In general terms, a constitution is conceived of as a body of fundamental legal norms that structure and shape what is, quintessentially, the political organization of modernity: the nation state. In this sense, constitutions may have different characteristics (for instance, their content may be written or oral, defense mechanisms may vary, etc.), but all of them are limited to a definition of the nation state and are based on scholarly knowledge, as is the case with state law. For this reason, it is easy to understand that, even in many areas of legal studies, only the nation state as unit is considered capable of producing a constitution via a political pact formalized through a set of legal norms. However, this idea has been losing ground for some years now due to the emergence of new global political entities. The establishment of a constitution for the European Union may well be the most eloquent example, illustrating that this set of fundamental legal norms is capable of changing to adapt to the global scales of postmodern capitalism.

Another fundamental element of the modern understanding of a constitution that has changed dramatically in recent years is that of popular sovereignty. In fact, this idea, anchored in a constitution and particularly in constituent power, has been called into question by the hegemony of various expressions of global legality and the increasing pressure that international financial bodies exert over national states (Santos, 2012; Negri, 2015). Consequently, it can clearly be seen that, in practice, sovereignty is no longer held by the popular will of the citizens of a given nation state but principally by the hegemonic hubs of capitalist financial power.

The prevailing idea that the constitution fails to correspond completely to the political dimensions of modernity can not only be perceived through analysis of the current situation. A brief review of the history of the West confirms the fact that, over the centuries, important changes have been made to the way in which constitutions are conceived (Fioravanti, 2001). If we add a post-colonial critique—elaborated through the *sociology of absences*[5]—to these considerations, the way in which constitutions are rendered invisible can be observed on different scales, at different times and through different cultures. Although they articulate their own laws and result from political pacts, from the perspective of legal *abyssal thinking*[6] these constitutions emerge as if devoid of these characteristics because they are not presented in accordance with the formalities of the hegemonic Western tradition.

Consequently, the notion of a constitution or constitutions developed through the epistemologies of the South would have to take into account the limitations associated with the formulations of hegemonic legal thinking. Progress has been made in this respect via the idea of transformative constitutionalism, centered largely on the new constitutions of Bolivia and Ecuador. The two *magna cartas* brought into play a series of substantive innovations, to the extent of signaling a difference in the Eurocentric tradition of constitutionalism. These innovations include their plurinational nature, the creation of new subjects of law—such as nature—popular representation within the constituent process and the replacement of neoliberal multiculturalism with an intercultural commitment (Clavero, 2008; Gargarella, 2011; Santos, 2012).

Despite these undeniable gains achieved through the notion of transformative constitutionalism, I consider it necessary to question whether such achievements are sufficient for an understanding of constitutions from the perspective of the epistemologies of the South. After all, transformative constitutionalism, as it stands, retains several exclusionary elements characteristic of Western modernity: for example, it is centered on the state, is built around professional legal knowledge that excludes most citizens from becoming involved in its construction and application and preserves the formal characteristics of the Western tradition of a constitution. Any formulation of a constitution viewed through the epistemologies of the South should, I believe, go further. As with other fields of knowledge, it should undertake a more radical rethinking of the law and the constitution.

The approaches to law embedded in theories of legal pluralism provide a good basis for initiating this task. It is widely acknowledged that in the 1980s the prevailing legal anthropology began to challenge the naturalized idea that the law is an exclusive attribute of the state and, in particular, the nation state. Based on this critique of 'legal centralism' (Griffiths, 1986), a series of empirically based studies were developed with a greater emphasis on other laws practiced by different human collectives that do not correspond to state law which, from the standpoint of hegemonic common sense, regulates the entire social life of a nation state.

In the case of Latin America, and more specifically in Mexico, interest has focused on the forms of justice practiced in indigenous communities in terms of the history of the region and the country. Despite the important contributions to academic and political fields provided by this research on indigenous peoples and communities, they have prospered with a fundamental problem in their midst which, in my view, can be overcome by applying the epistemologies of the South.

In fact, although studies in the field of legal anthropology in Mexico have highlighted the diversity of existing laws within the Mexican state, as well as their complex and sometimes paradoxical interactions with state law, they have reproduced the same epistemological fragility that accompanies most of the research on legal pluralism in the world, in trying to clearly delineate the aim of the study. Thus, from a pluralistic framework, it has not been possible to define law as no longer the exclusive domain of the state and to recognize its far wider and diverse scope (Tamanaha, 1993).

In an attempt to overcome this obstacle, important debates have opened up, the most celebrated in the field of legal anthropology being that of normativism versus processualism (Sierra and Chenaut, 2002). Several strategies have also been proposed in response to this challenge which have facilitated the analysis of these and other legal constructions, but have also made their limitations clear.

In the case of Mexican legal anthropology, the emphasis has been placed on conflict as the unit of analysis. This perspective, combined with processualism, focuses on how actors mobilize law in specific situations and at different levels of justice. The limitation of this perspective has already been pointed out, namely the fact that it is excessively instrumentalist and, by extension, emerges as disconnected from references and principles that condition and limit these decisions and practices (Martínez, 2007).

Thus, although many of these studies have made important contributions to the knowledge of Mexico's indigenous justices, they have also left important questions unanswered. More precisely, in terms of their approach to the notion of law, they have limited indigenous justices to strategic practices which they mobilize at their convenience. While confirming the existence of 'other laws', this approach fails to articulate them in terms of certain basic principles that endow them with coherence.

Other authors have emphasized that indigenous justices possess general philosophical and ethical principles that are articulated from a normative standpoint, thus lending them coherence (López, 2014). Unlike other perspectives on indigenous justice, these approaches tend to vindicate principles that often seem timeless and essential, yet can also be challenged by the daily practices of the actors present in the communities.[7]

Beyond these two approaches, is it possible to consider that indigenous justices are not just about strategic practices which actors use at their convenience or are governed by timeless and essential normative principles? Is it possible, therefore, to consider that indigenous justice can be articulated through more contingent and political principles? Is it possible to affirm, as Boaventura de Sousa Santos (2015) has already suggested, that indigenous justices have their own constitutions? Leaving aside the relevance that indigenous struggles in Mexico may have, as their consensuses and political pacts can be labeled as constitutions, it seems clear that the legal analysis proposed via the epistemologies of the South endows these issues with unquestionable relevance. Before getting to the heart of the matter, it is worth clarifying that I do not intend to deny the two dimensions already problematized in the literature on indigenous justices, nor reject the need to work through these two levels to understand indigenous justices, but rather to point out that, just as these can be expressed through strategic practices or general normative principles, there is an intermediate level that rearticulates and hierarchizes the general normative principles at certain historical junctures on the basis of political pacts and consensuses adopted within the communities. These political pacts clearly depend on the challenges they face and consequently lead to the ordering and ranking of legal practices.[8]

For this reason, with regard to the question of whether indigenous justices can be considered constitutions, I advocate an affirmative response, if three elements of constitutions that are present in almost all the stages of their history are taken into account, namely: (1) They constitute the most important political pact of a collectivity, (2) they construct institutions which are compatible with this political pact, and (3) they contain the legal and political mechanisms required to defend this pact.

I have already presented the fundamental elements of the political pact established by the community of San Francisco Cherán in 2011, observing that it was structured around two pillars: a municipal government premised on 'uses and customs' and a security system based on its communitarian militia. The questions which determine how successful the outcome might be are the following: Have institutions been built that develop and strengthen this pact? Is the structure provided with mechanisms to protect this pact? From my experience of working with this community, I can once again answer in the affirmative.

During the months of insurrection in the city, which started in 2011, up to the inauguration of a new municipal government established in accordance with 'uses and customs' on February 5, 2012, the Purépechas of Cherán operated within the four neighborhoods that make up their community, using a new political model based on their old organizational forms. A series of committees were formed, entrusted with dealing with the needs of the community in the absence of the municipal government which had, to all intents and purposes, been dissolved a few days after the movement began. Sixteen committees were created: a general committee and others dedicated to specific areas such as honor and justice, education, the forest, press and propaganda, and food. The principles for forming the committees ensured that their composition depended on the assemblies of each of the four neighborhoods of Cherán. For this reason, all the committees were composed of members from each of the districts. In addition, the work of the members was undertaken *pro bono* as a service to the community.

On February 5, 2012, a similar logic was applied and, while still functioning under a judicially recognized government, representation for the municipality was entrusted to a series of councils led by the *Concejo Mayor de Gobierno Comunal* (CMGC), all appointed on an equal footing through the *fogatas* (large campfire meetings which represented the organizational cells of this structure) from each of the four neighborhoods of Cherán. The CMGC, which replaced the figure of the municipal president, is composed of twelve people: each ward elects three representatives to hold office for three years, without mediation from any political party or recourse to voter registration, using a system of public voting with no campaigning.

During the 2011 insurrection, the community reinstated the former representative body of the communitarian militia and invented a new body for justice unprecedented in any other Purépecha community, which became known as the Commission for Honor and Justice. By coordinating these two institutions, the community was able to build a communitarian security system in which the militia is responsible for order and security, while the Commission for Honor and Justice controls the functioning of judicial proceedings within the municipality. Both institutions, like all the councils in the new municipal structure of Cherán, are subordinate to the neighborhood assemblies and the General Assembly which, from 2011 to the present day, constitute the highest authority within the municipality.

It is the neighborhood assemblies that carry out the main function of defending or altering the political pact established in Cherán in 2011. In 2014, for example, various members of political parties attempted to promote a consultation process aimed at reinstating the system of electing political parties and the municipal council. This proposal was submitted for consideration by the neighborhood assemblies and was rejected, thus ratifying the agreement to be governed by 'uses and customs' established in 2011. However, only a few months later, the neighborhood assemblies determined that the original composition of the councils which are part of the Cherán municipal government should be altered to promote two of the sectors that had played a decisive role during the 2011 uprising. As a result, the Council of Women and the Youth Council have been added to the existing councils since 2015.

In 2016, the government of the province of Michoacán, to which Cherán belongs, launched a campaign aimed at restoring police control in all municipalities. This led to the provincial government lobbying in the face of resistance from municipalities and a number of communities which had been attempting to devise alternative security schemes for several years. When the provincial government tried to do the same with the municipality of Cherán, the assemblies of the four neighborhoods deliberated and then ratified the communitarian security model initiated in 2011. Consequently, the municipality of Cherán distanced itself from the scheme referred to as 'single-command policing' leaving the provincial government with no choice but to accept the decision of the assemblies.

Following the case of Cherán, it should be noted that not only is it necessary to consider the various scales (local, national and global) in order to understand law, but the analysis of constitutions per se also requires this multi-scalar approach.

13.3 What Makes Transformative Constitutionalism Transformational? Plurinationality, Self-determination and Decolonization

Even assuming that the struggle in Cherán has succeeded in giving substance to a constitution on the basis of which its legal practices and political institutions are formulated, this does not necessarily mean that it is transformational in nature. For this reason, it is worth recalling the meaning of 'transformative' in the type of constitutionalism under analysis.

As has been argued, the principal force for transformative constitutionalism, emanating from the Bolivian and Ecuadorean experiences, stems from the nature of the demands of indigenous struggles which, due to their historical precedence and cultural autonomy, are capable of questioning the modern colonial state dominant in Latin America on the basis of this history (Santos, 2012). Consequently, it is the recognition of indigenous justice that gives meaning to this type of constitutionalism:

> It is not about the recognition of the cultural diversity of the country or of a process that allows local and remote communities to resolve small conflicts from within, thus guaranteeing the social peace that the State could never guarantee for lack of material and human resources. It is, rather, the conception of indigenous justice as an important part of a political project of decolonizing and anti-capitalist vocation, a second independence that finally breaks the Eurocentric ties that have conditioned the processes of development over the past 200 years.
>
> *Santos, 2012:15*

So, does the constitution of Cherán contain this power of transformative constitutionalism? My response is affirmative, at least in one important sense. In claiming the right to self-determination specifically based on an identity and a sustained autonomy that predates the Mexican state, Cherán has managed to create a rift at the base of the state, in the municipality, which clearly surpasses the mandate of neoliberal multiculturalism.

As with the Bolivian and Ecuadorean forms of transformative constitutionalism, Cherán's experience constitutes a robust recognition of, and approach to, legal and political pluralism. This is not the Oaxaca model of 'uses and customs' which, at best, is procedural in the manner in which municipal authorities are elected:[9] the experience of Cherán represents a transformation to the structure, rationale and relationships of the municipal government through different rules, mechanisms, practices and logics based on their 'uses and customs'. This same difference has been ascertained in relation to other levels of government within the Mexican state.

It can be argued, however, that the constitution of Cherán is not endowed with the plurinational dimension of transformative constitutionalism evident in the Bolivian and Ecuadorean versions and that, as such, it lacks the potential this element confers. Nevertheless, I consider that the broader claim for the right to self-determination of indigenous peoples and communities expressed through the political-juridical struggle of Cherán has functioned in a manner equivalent to the requirement for plurinationality, to the extent that indigenous peoples and communities from other regions of Mexico have followed in their footsteps, including the two inter-ethnic municipalities of San Luis Acatlán and Ayutla de los Libres in the province of Guerrero and the four new indigenous municipalities of Xoxocotla, Hueyapan, Coatetelco and Tetelcingo in the province of Morelos.

In addition to these shared elements, it is important to note that the political-juridical struggle of Cherán corresponds to the precept outlined by Boaventura de Sousa Santos for the emancipatory character of state law. As Santos states, the law (and perhaps the same can be said for a constitution) is not in itself emancipatory or otherwise; instead, it is the social group or movement that propels, promotes and defends it (Santos, 2003).

On this point, the legal mobilization that has taken place in defense of Cherán's political pact and, by extension, its constitution is another element which seems to me to endow it with an emancipatory character. Cherán's struggle in the judicial and political field aimed to safeguard the political-social pact achieved via the emergence of the 2011 movement, but this has been generated within a broader context. The Cherán movement did not come about simply as a result of local factors, nor did it have an effect only on one or more indigenous communities: instead it occurred in the context of widespread problems for the indigenous peoples in other regions of Mexico and the mixed-race population in general. The plunder of natural resources, the violence, the states of exception, the ruling class's collusion with organized crime and the crisis of the electoral institutions were part of the national context in which the struggle in Cherán emerged (Aragón, 2016), and largely explain the sympathy and solidarity expressed by broad sectors of Mexican society in relation to this movement.

Given this context, the legal and political battles waged by Cherán since 2011 are framed by a series of attempts by different groups and social sectors to bring about changes to the injustice and oppression that Mexican society in general is currently facing. In fact, within these struggles, the Cheránense have been liaising with indigenous organizations, artistic collectives, media, unions and committed academics, among many others (Aragón, 2013, 2015). For this reason, a reading of Cherán's struggles and contributions in terms of a counter-hegemonic mobilization of the law goes beyond the ethnic equation and includes elements of more widespread efforts calling for a fairer society.

One last point I wish to address in this section focuses on two strengths that feature in the Cherán constitution and which contrast directly with the South American experiences. I am referring, on the one hand, to its dynamic character that serves to maintain constituent power and, on the other hand, to the space it creates, enabling it to produce different political and legal practices and principles to those of state law.

As is readily acknowledged, the Bolivian and Ecuadorean constitutions of the first decade of the twenty-first century were the product of important social mobilizations that succeeded in conquering power in the two states after several years of struggle. The most relevant consequence of these triumphs of the progressive forces consisted precisely in formulating new constitutions that condensed their aspirations and demands into new political pacts formalized through constitutions.

This succession of events brought a new relevance and a unique innovative quality to the two new constitutions. However, the first results of this new process were not as favorable as expected. In both Bolivia and Ecuador, a deepening rupture developed between governments and the various social movements that had brought them to power. This led to a situation in which the old inertia re-established itself and new processes that initially seemed to have opened up via the new constitutions became blocked. In the final analysis, it must be remembered that the constitutions of Bolivia and Ecuador did not presume an outcome that would be achieved simply by promulgating the constitutions and waving a magic wand to change social realities: they were to be a starting point, opening up new possibilities for transformation (Santos, 2012).

In both countries, unexpected developments in relations between the governments and several of the social movements that had brought them to power and somehow succeeded in inscribing their aspirations in the constitution can be interpreted in theoretical terms on the basis of the ever-complex relationship between (transformative and even revolutionary) constituent power and (generally conservative) instituted power. In the case of the South American experiences, the constituent power that brought about this renewing and transforming energy seems to have frozen in the face of an instituted power which, for various reasons, has suppressed the achievements enshrined in the constitutional text.

In contrast, I have provided some examples of how the constitution of Cherán presents a very different dynamic through which the constituent power, permanently assigned to the assemblies, has sufficient strength to modify the political project or rein in its representatives if they consider that they are deviating in their function or performance.

Moreover, the South American experiences of transformative constitutionalism created a space (the Constituent Assembly) framed by a logic and subordinated to the principles of state law, not those of the communities. This situation has resulted in the establishment of a *contact zone* favoring a Eurocentric and colonial equilibrium.

For its part, the Cherán constitution maintains its own space—while remaining aware of state legality—which, in accordance with its own logic, facilitates the reproduction and reinvention of political and juridical practices and principles that are then mobilized in contexts of struggle to hybridize with state and international law in other judicial, legislative and political spaces.

This logic of articulation seems to build more advantageous *contact zones* for the Cherán constitution, in which its destabilizing potential is not confined or crystallized but is able to create fractures and contradictions in the legal framework and hegemonic constitutionalism of Mexico.

13.4 Can a Local-scale Constitution Challenge the Hegemonic Model of the Nation State in Mexico? The Ecology of Knowledges as a Trans-scale Instrument

Even if we accept that Cherán instituted a constitution via the 2011 movement and that its content is analogous to that of transformative constitutionalism, it can still be argued, as is often the case with *lazy reason* (Santos, 2002), that, due to its local character, it is simply irrelevant in the face of Mexico's hegemonic constitutional and political order.

I would like to begin my argument by stating that, in my experience, one precondition that would ensure that a constitution like Cherán's may eventually transcend a local context is the existence of a state of pressing need which cannot be resolved by legality and hegemonic politics. This condition applies to the legal-political struggle of Cherán, but also to the multiple communities, collectives, organizations and social movements of Mexico in general and the world at large that have come to learn from the Cherán experience.

It was precisely the confrontation with institutionalized corruption and insecurity that led the Cheránense to seek new forms, instruments and allies to restore a legitimate government and address the lack of security. Cherán walked tall, first by resorting to its past and adapting it to the needs of the present through a political and legal pact, but also by recourse to the counter-hegemonic use of state law via an alliance with the mixed-race lawyers of the *Colectivo Emancipaciones*, thus broadening the movement and later strengthening the new political consensus established in 2011 in legal terms.

Hence, in September 2011, during the period of insurrection, Cherán went to the *Tribunal Electoral del Poder Judicial de la Federación* (TEPJF), the highest judicial body of the Mexican state in matters concerning political rights, to request recognition of its right to elect municipal authorities in accordance with a procedure based on 'uses and customs' rather than political parties. In addition, the Cheránense requested that they be allowed to overhaul the structure of the municipal authority beyond the tradition of municipal government inherited from colonial times and applied throughout Mexico, in order to adapt it to their organizational logic and collective authorities briefly described in the first section of this chapter (Aragón, 2013).

After winning this dispute, Cherán again needed to appeal to the courts following the reform of Article 3 of the Constitution by the province of Michoacán. Although it improved legal recognition of the indigenous peoples and communities of Michoacán, this amendment omitted the right to grant municipal governments the status of 'uses and customs' which Cherán had won a few weeks earlier through the TEPJF. The political logic of this constitutional reform was precisely to contain—through seemingly favorable legal recognition, but clearly framed within the contours of neoliberal multiculturalism—the transformative potential that Cherán had obtained by means of the TEPJF decision, in relation to the entire structure of the Mexican state.

Consequently, in 2014, it was necessary to initiate a second legal dispute, which was resolved on this occasion by the highest constitutional court in the Mexican state, the *Suprema Corte de Justicia de la Nación* (SCJN). The objectives of this new legal dispute were multiple. To begin with, it sought a strong political charter that would enable it to maintain a less disadvantaged and more visible relationship with a new provincial government openly hostile to the Cherán process. Secondly, in tandem with political advantage, it sought legal certainty for the political pact initiated in 2011 and to increase the recognition obtained through the TEPJF ruling and, by extension, its transformative potential. This second dispute was settled in favor of the municipality of Purépecha de Cherán and succeeded in setting a precedent in Mexico, and perhaps in Latin America, in annulling a constitutional reform for violating the right to prior, free and informed consultation of an indigenous community.

In addition to the proceedings in the highest judicial bodies of the Mexican state and the legal precedents that have proved fundamental for other indigenous peoples and communities, it is important to register here that all this was possible due to an *ecology of legal knowledges*[10] in which the constitution of Cherán and its indigenous legal practices played a central role. Today, Cherán is recognized as the first indigenous municipal government in the history of the Mexican state, and many other municipalities and indigenous communities are following its path toward self-determination.[11]

Elsewhere, I have explained in detail the legal strategy used in these two lawsuits that are considered paradigmatic in the legal history of Mexico, while also emphasizing that the formulation of both cases was carried out through a progressive hybridization of the practices of indigenous justice and the professional or technical legal knowledge of state law and the laws on international human rights and indigenous peoples (Aragón, 2013, 2015).

In the first of the processes, highlighting the example of the *ecology of legal knowledges*, it was necessary to explain to the TEPJF the existence of a municipality regulated in practice by its 'uses and customs'. At the same time, according to the rights enshrined in the political constitution of Mexico and, significantly, in international treaties, it had the right—together with the state allowing it to elect its authorities along different lines from the principles of political representation based on political parties—to be legally recognized as a government structure, also in accordance with its 'uses and customs'.

In the case presented to the SCJN, it was necessary to apply this progressive combination of scales of legality in order to argue that the Congress of the State of Michoacán had not followed the consultation process for the contested constitutional reform, in line with the 'uses and customs' of Cherán (which had been recently formalized and institutionalized) and that it had therefore violated their human rights, as guaranteed in the Mexican Constitution and in international treaties.

In addition to these two general approaches, it is relevant here to draw attention to the fact that these two lawsuits have created different *contact zones* associated with their development, which have facilitated different checks and balances in the *ecology of legal knowledges*. While in both cases the time spent formulating the legal arguments and the resolution of the dispute was dominated by a technical knowledge of state law, in the final judgment (and very clearly in the ruling of 2011), knowledge of indigenous justice was decisive throughout the entire judicial struggle in ensuring an outcome as favorable as possible with regard to the provisions laid out in the Cherán constitution of 2011.

In terms of technical knowledge, the first situation does not require further explanation, since recourse to a state court implies accepting and assuming in advance the formal logic by which it is governed and, consequently, its rules. On the other hand, with regard to the final judgment, particularly that of 2011, a relatively long phase was initiated in which a consultation process with the people of Cherán was ordered to ascertain whether, in fact, the majority of the population agreed with the change of political regime. The interpretation given by the community during the final judgment—presented before other state authorities that were obliged to participate in this process, in the absence of any regulation relating to this right at federal and provincial level—was based on the criteria established by the Inter-American Court of Human Rights (Saramaka *vs.* Suriname) in which it was anticipated that the consultation should be carried out according to the 'uses and customs' of the community. With this point defined for the authorities involved in making a judgment, the knowledge of the Cheránense regarding their indigenous justice was of paramount importance to the strategic choice of practices that would ensure a swift and safe outcome for the political struggle that had been undertaken, and which ultimately sought to protect the political pact established months before.

Thus, instead of conducting a consultation process similar to those used in the electoral system based on political parties, with polls, a secret ballot, voter registration and so on, indigenous justice practices and means of political organization were chosen in accordance with the political agreement of 2011, that is, a consultation process held at the meetings of each of the four districts, with a public vote carried out by a show of hands, using traditional identification mechanisms such as an attendance list and recognition by neighbors, a tabled debate for assemblies and so on.[12]

One final example I wish to present to illustrate how the constitution of Cherán has been able to challenge the dominant legal and political order of the colonial state in Mexico is the initiative to reform Article 115 of the Constitution of Mexico, presented by the CMGC in April 2016 to the Senate of the Republic.

This task consisted of a legislative initiative developed in various assemblies by the Cheránense, their authorities and their lawyers. The proposal was in response to the inactivity of the legislators in the province of Michoacán and the Mexican state itself with regard to harmonizing the constitution with the provisions issued by the two highest constitutional courts concerning the judicial victories of Cherán. The initiative was built up from the political pact assumed by the community in 2011, applying a technical knowledge of the state laws and the human rights of indigenous peoples with the aim of including the indigenous municipalities, as well as their powers and obligations, in the Constitution of the Mexican state.

On the day of the presentation, five of the six senators from Michoacán, representatives from all the political parties, took the initiative upon themselves, having been joined by six other senators from Oaxaca, Guerrero and Chiapas. It would be remiss of me not to draw attention to the fact that Cherán was the first community to present a constitutional reform initiative to the Senate and, in just one day—the final day of the legislative work—succeeded in gaining the support of 10% of the Senate from across the three major political parties in Mexico.

13.5 The Limitations and Potential of Transformative Constitutionalism from Below

In comparison to the transformative constitutionalism based on South American experiences, the version emanating from Cherán's political-juridical struggle which I have set out to substantiate here—described as originating 'from below'—has clear limitations. The most obvious is that, while the former experiences became the general reference for the interpretation of the law of the states of Ecuador and Bolivia, with all the ensuing depletion and deconstitutionalization, the general context in which the latter has proceeded is much more colonial and capitalist. This means that the struggle based on transformative constitutionalism from below is entirely subversive, that is, a struggle intended to increase the number of loopholes and contradictions present in the constitution of the Mexican state and hegemonic law, so that indigenous peoples and communities can employ them in their struggles for autonomy.

Another evident limitation is the absence, in the Cherán experience, of a robust approach to development, as has been the case with transformative constitutionalism in Ecuador and Bolivia. Although there are communitarian management initiatives for development in Cherán, it has not yet been possible to consolidate a sufficiently robust proposal that could override the neoliberal development model.

Yet, although this transformative constitutionalism from below has its limitations, it also possesses potentialities. The first emerges as the reversal of a limitation, since this type of transformative constitutionalism from below demonstrates that it is not necessary to have an ideal constitutional context in place on a national scale. Indigenous peoples can exercise their right to self-determination and, at the same time, transform the old structures of colonial nation states.

Secondly, unlike the South American approach, this transformative constitutionalism is stimulated from below by a vibrant social movement which, in times of struggle, builds an anti-colonial and transformative political undertaking through the constituent power permanently lodged in its assemblies that challenge Mexico's hegemonic constitutional and political system.

Thirdly, the thinking regarding the Cherán experience of transformative constitutionalism operates in *contact zones* where the balance between a knowledge of state and international law presents fewer disadvantages for the pursuit of indigenous justice. As outlined earlier, the different phases in the processes of political-legal struggle have allowed for different checks and balances in which, in many cases, the main role given to the *ecology of legal knowledges* was precisely that of indigenous justices.

Finally, this transformative constitutionalism from below constitutes a true laboratory for utopias in the field of law. On the basis of this real, day-to-day, concrete and practical work that has been developed for more than five years among the Cheránense, the mixed-race lawyers, the committed academics, the human rights organizations and all the indigenous or non-indigenous actors who have contributed (to a greater or lesser extent) to this process, as well as to the construction of this hybrid law, I attest to the possibility of building a much-needed new Mexico, founded on interculturality and solidarity between different struggles and in support of a more progressive knowledge.

Notes

* Translation by Neil Walker.

1 This work was carried out with the support of the PAPIIT AI303516 project at the National Autonomous University of Mexico.

2 The community of San Francisco Cherán is located in the heart of the Michoacán state region in an area known as the Purépecha Plateau. It is one of the largest of these indigenous people's communities in terms of territorial extension (20,826 hectares), a feature that allows it to be both a community and the seat of the municipality known only by the name of Cherán. The municipality of Cherán was created in 1861. At present, its population has risen, according to the 2010 Census, to 18,141 inhabitants divided mainly between the two communities that comprise the municipality: San Francisco Cherán, with 14,245 inhabitants, and Santa Cruz Tanaco, with 2,947.

3 The analysis of the lawsuits referred to in this chapter was carried out in collaboration with other lawyers from the *Colectivo Emancipaciones*, to which I belong.

4 In particular, in the case of protecting the political-electoral rights of the citizen, which was settled by the upper chamber of the *Tribunal Electoral del Poder Judicial de la Federación* (TEPJF) in 2011, reference SUP-JDC 9167/2011, and the constitutional dispute trial 32/2012, resolved in 2014 by the plenary of the *Suprema Corte de Justicia de la Nación* (SCJN). Both judicial precedents are considered of the highest order in terms of relevance in defending the human rights of indigenous peoples in Mexico.

5 Boaventura de Sousa Santos defined the sociology of absences as

> research aimed at showing that what does not exist is, in fact, actively produced as non-existent, that is, as a non-credible alternative to what exists. Its empirical object is impossible from the point of view of the conventional social sciences. It is about transforming impossible objects into possible objects, objects that are missing into objects that are present.
>
> *Santos, 2010:37*

6 This notion is understood through the proposal of the epistemologies of South as

> a system of visible and invisible distinctions, the invisible constitute the foundation of the visible. Invisible distinctions are established through radical lines that divide social reality into two universes, the universe 'this side of the line' and the universe of 'another side of the line'. The division is such that 'the other side of the line' disappears as a reality, becomes non-existent and is, in fact, produced as non-existent. Non-existent means not to exist in any relevant or understandable way of being.
>
> *Santos, 2009:160*

7 María Teresa Sierra (2011) understood this dilemma of legal anthropology several years ago and, taking up Benda-Beckman's theoretical proposal, highlighted the need to combine the analysis of legal practices with the study of the ideologies of legal orders to account more fully for the inter-legality present in the indigenous regions.

8 In the case of Cherán, for example, the literature on the history of the community in the twentieth century shows a very different political pact from that of 2011. In earlier academic work, anthropologists and historians had conceived of Cherán as a community where the strength of chiefs, political parties, disputes between factions and worship of the figure of Lázaro Cárdenas del Río were the prevailing reality (Castile, 1974; Beals, 1992; Calderón, 2004). Despite this, it cannot be said that the general normative principles of the indigenous justices in Cherán were necessarily different from those in force today, but that, with the movement of 2011, these principles were recalibrated and adapted to a new political pact.

9 The two most important texts on elections according to 'uses and customs' in the municipalities of Oaxaca (Anaya, 2006; Recondo, 2007) note that, in general terms,

this recognition of indigenous communities and peoples results in the continuation of the old authoritarian regime of the PRI in that province.

10 For Boaventura de Sousa Santos,

> The ecology of knowledge is based on the pragmatic idea that it is necessary to re-evaluate concrete interventions in society and in nature that different knowledges can offer. It focuses on the relationship between knowledge and hierarchies that are produced between them from the point of view that concrete practices would not be possible without these hierarchies. However, rather than subscribing to a unique, universal and abstract knowledge hierarchy, the ecology of knowledges favors hierarchies that depend on the context, in light of the concrete results intended or achieved by different practices of knowledge.
>
> *Santos, 2009:189*

11 In section two of this chapter, I mentioned the case of two municipalities in Guerrero and four in Morelos which tried to follow the footsteps of Cherán. However, it would be a mistake to think that they are the only ones: in fact, Cherán's case represented a separation of the waters in the TEPJF, which since then has been producing a rich vein of jurisprudence on the self-determination of indigenous peoples and communities. The cases that have generated this new jurisprudence span almost the entire territory of the Mexican state, ranging from recognition of the traditional authorities of indigenous communities not provided for in the laws of the state through to recognition of the exercising of communitarian autonomy in disposing of the resources that correspond to the public budget.

12 It is clear that many of these forms are not indigenous in the sense of being essential but have been adapted and modified by indigenous communities through different experiences and historical processes to make them compatible with their forms of organization.

References

Anaya Muñoz, Alejandro (2006), *Autonomía Indigena, Gobernabilidad y Legitimidad en México. La Legalización de Usos y Custumbres Eelectorales en Oaxaca*. Mexico DF: Ibero-American University/Plaza y Valdes.

Aragón Andrade, Orlando (2013), 'El Derecho en Insurrección. El Uso Hegemónico del Derecho en el Movimiento Purépecha de Cherán', *Journal of Studies & Research on the Americas*, 7 (2), 37–69. Available at http://periodicos.unb.br/index.php/repam/article/view/20220.

Aragón Andrade, Orlando (2015), 'El Derecho Después de la Insurrección. Cherán y el Uso Hegemónico del Derecho en la Suprema Corte of Justicia de México', *Sortuz: Oñati Journal of Emergent Socio-Legal Studies*, 7 (2), 71–87. Available at http://opo.iisj.net/index.php/sortuz/article/view/702.

Aragón Andrade, Orlando (2016), 'Otra Democracia es Posible. Aprendizajes para una Democracia Radical en México desde la Experiencia Política de Cherán'. Conference presented at the University of California, Berkeley, on November 4, 2015, in the '*Mexico at the Crossroads*' cycle.

Beals, Ralph Larson (1992), *Cherán: Un Pueblo de la Sierra*. Zamora: The College of Michoacán.

Calderón Mólgora, Marco Antonio (2004), *Historia, Procesos Políticos y Cardenismos*. Zamora: The College of Michoacán.

Castile, George Pierre (1974), *Cherán: La Adaptación de una Comunidad Tradicional*. Mexico DF: The National Indigenist Institute.

Clavero, Bartolomé (2008), *Geografía Jurídica de América Latina. Pueblos Indígenas entre Constituciones Mestizas*. Mexico DF: Siglo XXI.
Fioravanti, Maurizio (2001), *Constitución. De la Antigüedad a nuestros Días*. Madrid: Trotta.
Gargarella, Roberto (2011), 'Pensando sobre la Reforma Constitucional en América Latina', *in* César Rodríguez Garavito (ed.), *El Derecho en América Latina. Un Mapa para el Pensamiento Jurídico del Siglo XXI*. Buenos Aires: Siglo XXI, 87–108.
Griffiths, John (1986), 'What Is Legal Pluralism?', *The Journal of Legal Pluralism*, 18 (24), 1–55.DOI: https://doi.org/10.1080/07329113.1986.10756387.
López Bárcenas, Francisco (2014), 'Normas y Principios Jurídicos entre los Ñuú Savi', *Diarios de Campo*, 4–5, 42–47. Available at www.revistas.inah.gob.mx/index.php/diariodecampo/article/view/5722.
Martínez, Juan Carlos (2007), 'La Crisis Interna de Santiago Amoltepec. Reflexiones sobre las Relaciones de Poder y la Formalidad en el Campo Jurídico en una Localidad Oaxaqueña', *in* Jorge Hernández-Díaz (ed.), *Ciudadanías Diferenciadas en un Estado Multicultural: Los Usos y Costumbres en Oaxaca*. Mexico: Siglo XXI/The Benito Juárez Autonomous University of Oaxaca, 229–249.
Negri, Antonio (2015), *El Poder Constituyente*. Madrid: Traficantes de Sueños.
Recondo, David (2007), *La Política del Gatopardo. Multiculturalismo y Democracia en Oaxaca*. México DF: Center for Research and Advanced Studies in Social Anthropology.
Santos, Boaventura de Sousa (2002), *A Crítica da Razão Indolente. Contra o Desperdício da Experiência*. Porto: Afrontamento.
Santos, Boaventura de Sousa (2003), 'Poderá o Direito ser Emancipatório?' *Revista Crítica de Ciências Socias*, 65, 3–76. DOI: https://doi.org/10.4000/rccs.1180.
Santos, Boaventura de Sousa (2009), *Una Epistemología del Sur. La Reinvention del Conocimiento y la Emancipación Social*. Mexico: Siglo XXI.
Santos, Boaventura de Sousa (2010), *Refundación del Estado en América Latina. Perspectivas desde una Epistemología del Sur*. Lima: International Institute of Law and Society.
Santos, Boaventura de Sousa (2012), 'Cuando los Excluidos Tienen Derecho: Justicia Indígena, Plurinacionalidad e Interculturalidad', *in* Boaventura de Sousa Santos and Agustín Grijalva Jiménez (eds.), *Justicia Indígena, Plurinacionalidad e Interculuralidad en Ecuador*. Quito: Abya Yala, 13–50.
Santos, Boaventura de Sousa (2015), 'Para que Servem as Constituições?' Master Class at the Faculty of Economics of the University of Coimbra, April 10.
Santos, Boaventura de Sousa; Rodríguez-Garavito, César (2007), 'El Derecho, la Política y lo Subalterno en la Globalización Contrahegemónica', *in* Boaventura de Sousa Santos y César Rodríguez-Garavito (coords.), *El Derecho y la Globalización desde Abajo. Hacia una Legalidad Cosmopolita*. Barcelona: Anthropos, 7–28.
Sierra, María Teresa (2011), 'Pluralismo Jurídico y Interlegalidad. Debates Antropológicos en Torno al Derecho indígena y las Políticas de Reconocimiento', *in* Victoria Chenaut, Magdalena Gómez, Héctor Ortiz y María Teresa Sierra (coords.), *Justicia y Diversidad en América Latina. Pueblos Indígenas ante la Constitución*. Quito: FLACSO/CIESAS, 385–406. Available at https://biblio.flacsoandes.edu.ec/shared/biblio_view.php?bibid=126754&tab=opac
Sierra, Maria Teresa; Chenaut, Victoria (2002), 'Debates Recientes y Actuales en la Antropología Jurídica: Las Corrientes Anglosajonas', *in* Esteban krotz (ed.), *Antropología Jurídica: Perspectivas Socioculturais en el Estudio del Derecho*. Barcelona: Anthropos/The Metropolitan Autonomous University—Iztapalapa, 113–170.
Tamanaha, Brian (1993), 'The Folly of the "Social Scientific" Concept of Legal Pluralism', *Journal of Law and Society*, 20 (2), 192–217. DOI: https://doi.org/10.2307/1410167

14

THE LAW OF THE EXCLUDED

Indigenous Justice, Plurinationality and Interculturality in Bolivia and Ecuador

Boaventura de Sousa Santos

14.1 Transformative Constitutionalism: A Challenge to Abyssal Legal Thinking

This chapter reflects on the political processes and constitutional transformations that dominated the social, political and cultural life of Ecuador and Bolivia during the period 2000–2015. The decision to choose indigenous or originary justice as a subject of analysis stems from two reasons that have been very much present in my work.[1] The first reason is that law and justice are the privileged windows through which to analyze the contradictions, ambivalences, rhythms, advances and setbacks in processes of social transformation, especially those which claim to be bearers of new political projects or decisive moments in political transition.[2] Both the modern state and the legal system it upholds have a key contradictory characteristic: in order to effectively consolidate unequal power relations in society, they must deny the existence of this inequality in a credible way. The ideal is that the oppressed themselves believe that there is no inequality because the state is legitimate and sovereign and because the law is autonomous and universal. When this belief is widespread, it can be said that the judicial-political (dis)order is hegemonic. However, during processes of profound transformation, this judicial-political construction, seemingly unassailable in normal times, is the first to collapse. Hence the interest in analyzing the contrast between the surface structure of this construction and its deep structure.

The second reason is that what truly distinguishes indigenous struggles from other social struggles on the American continent, namely the claim of historical precedence and cultural autonomy, challenges the entire legal and political edifice of the modern postcolonial state. Indigenous struggles therefore have a specific potential to radicalize (in the sense of going back to their roots) processes of social

DOI: 10.4324/9781003391920-18

transformation, especially when they assume a constituent dimension. When the state and the law are under discussion in a constituent process, the leading political forces seek to maintain control of the discussion and impose limits, so that key issues which can challenge the political system are never discussed. Hence the state and the Eurocentric law at the core of the modern nation state, even when undermined, maintain an abyssal line which separates what is subject to dispute and open to criticism (the legitimate questions) from what is not (the illegitimate or unthinkable questions).[3] This abyssal line has particularly affected social groups who demand that the illegitimate or unthinkable questions should be discussed. In other words, the abyssal line conditioning the constitutional process is the constitutional version of a thoroughgoing abyssal line that shapes modern epistemological and political thought as a whole, including Eurocentric critical thought.

I have been arguing that the three main modes of modern domination are capitalism, colonialism and patriarchy. They are certainly not the only ones; in several contexts or periods, religion or the caste system have also been crucial modes of domination. Nevertheless, these three modes seem to be present everywhere. Contrary to what has been assumed by conventional theory, including Eurocentric Marxist theory, colonialism did not end with the independence processes; it only changed its operational code. Independence brought an end to a specific form of colonialism, namely the historical colonialism based on territorial occupation by a foreign country. Yet colonialism continued under different guises, all involving the ontological inferiority of the group subjected to colonial domination. Racism, internal colonialism, neocolonialism, imperialism, white supremacism, anti-migration and anti-refugee policies and xenophobia (and most recently, Islamophobia) are some of the forms by which colonialism is perpetuated as a mode of domination (Santos, 2014a, 2018). The coexistence of capitalism, colonialism and patriarchy, as well as the profound interconnections between them, is the material basis for the abyssal thinking that both creates the radical separation between metropolitan sociability and colonial sociability and makes it invisible. Metropolitan sociability is the realm of free and equal humans, as formulated by the French Revolution. This realm is socially and politically constituted by the tension between social regulation and social emancipation. Colonial sociability is the realm of the masses of people who are considered ontologically inferior, mainly for reasons of race or gender. Since they cannot be treated as free and equal, their realm is socially and politically constituted by the tension between appropriation and violence. In terms of social exclusion, there is a radical difference between the two forms of sociability. Whenever social exclusion occurs in metropolitan sociability, because they are free and equal, the victims are protected by general and universal laws and are therefore entitled to legal redress. In other words, exclusions occurring within metropolitan sociability are not abyssal. In colonial sociability, on the other hand, the exclusions are abyssal because the victims, in the course of being victimized, are not considered fully human and hence do not deserve the protection afforded by laws that only apply to free and equal human beings. Thus, any norms that are valid or ethical on the metropolitan side of the line do not apply to the colonial side of the line. However, this does not compromise their universality because colonial sociability lacks the human element that would require or justify the application of such norms. The abyssal line dividing the two forms of sociability is so radical that it remains invisible. The negation and invisibility of this separation is the modern way of guaranteeing its reproduction. This is as valid today as it was in the period of historical colonialism. We still live in societies that are capitalist, colonialist and patriarchal. Being on the other side of the abyssal line—the colonial side—means being prevented by the dominant Eurocentric knowledge from representing the world in one's own terms. Herein lies the crucial role of Northern epistemologies in the reproduction of colonial-capitalist and patriarchal relationships in modern societies. In producing, while concealing, the abyssal line, Northern epistemologies are unable to recognize the distinction between abyssal exclusions (those occurring on the colonial side of sociability) and non-abyssal exclusions (those occurring on the metropolitan side of sociability). Moreover, Northern epistemologies conceive of the epistemological North as the only valid source of knowledge, no matter where, geographically speaking, knowledge is produced. By the same token, the South, that is to say, everything that is on the "other" side of the line, is the realm of ignorance. Thus, the North remains the solution whereas the South is represented as the problem. Under these conditions, the only valid understanding of the world is the Eurocentric, socio-juridical construction of the world. The struggles of the indigenous peoples in Bolivia and Ecuador and the social and political visibility they conquered as active participants in the constitutional processes in the first decade of the millennium were attempts to denounce the abyssal line and eventually overcome it. At the end of the first decade of the millennium, Bolivia and Ecuador were the two Latin American countries that had undergone the deepest constitutional transformations during the course of the political mobilizations carried out by indigenous movements.[4] It is therefore hardly surprising that the constitutions of these two countries contain the embryos of a paradigmatic transformation of modern law and the state, whose main characteristic would be to put an end to the centuries-old abyssal line haunting their social, cultural and political life. In light of this, we can legitimately speak of a process of political, social, economic and cultural refoundation (Gargarella and Courtis, 2009; Rodríguez Garavito, 2011; Grijalva, 2012; Llasag Fernandéz, 2014). Recognition of the existence and legitimacy of indigenous justice therefore acquires a new political significance. It is not just recognition of the country's cultural diversity or an expedient to enable local and remote communities to resolve minor conflicts within their own sphere, thus guaranteeing the social peace which the state could not safeguard under any circumstances due to a lack of material and human resources. It is rather about conceiving of indigenous justice as an important part of a political project with a decolonizing and anti-capitalist mission, a second independence that finally breaks with the Eurocentric abyssal line that has conditioned the processes of development over the past two hundred years. This chapter addresses the reforms carried out during the first years of the twenty-first century, which sought to transform the nature of the state in Ecuador and Bolivia through a process of transformative constitutionalism. However, although these reforms have produced significant advances for the indigenous and Afro-descendant populations, an in-depth analysis of the ways in which they have been experienced and resisted illustrates the limits of the transformative projects of the nation state, and consequently, the resilience of the abyssal line.[5]

14.2 The Indigenous Nationalist Revolutions in Ecuador and Bolivia

In Latin America, regional and national indigenous organizations grew in number and strength during the 1980s and 1990s. Indigenous political movements and political parties emerged in several countries, such as Mexico, Venezuela, Colombia, Bolivia, Ecuador and Guatemala.[6] The tidal wave of indigenous movements entering the major political institutions brought several key legal debates to the fore, including the land claims of Europeans (and their descendants) and acts of violence and conquest involving indigenous and colonizing forces (Keal, 2003: 84–87). Modern property laws emerged, together with colonial modes of appropriation; they became a source of legitimization, then globalization, of the Eurocentric mode of legality (Santos, 2009a, 2009b). These laws, a reminder that colonialism did not end with the independence of the former colonies, operate as a set of techniques and mechanisms encapsulated in legislation, legal judgments and many everyday practices of ownership structuring the contemporary colonial-capitalist modes of accumulation (Chakrabarty, 2000). Clearly, property laws[7] are a central feature of the modern abyssal line underlying the philosophical and political projects associated with the imposition of a teleological vision of the modern paradigm that has set the standard for what can or cannot be considered civilized. This explains why, throughout Latin America, indigenous peoples worked for the Portuguese and Spanish elites in colonial times and then for the elites of the newly independent countries in haciendas and plantations since the early nineteenth century. Other forms of forced labor in place in the colonial and postcolonial contexts of the Americas included elaborate systems of debt peonage, taxation, work passbooks and required labor quotas (Maybury-Lewis, 2002: 347). Property laws are a key feature of capitalism/colonialism. As Peter Fitzpatrick has argued, "law becomes generally and integrally associated with the mythic settling of the world—its adequate occupation and its bestowal on the rightful holders, the Occidental 'possessors and builders of the Earth'" (1992: 83). Colonial polities were sustained by a racial regime of ownership that has survived to the present day, creating a conceptual apparatus in which justifications for private property remain bound to a concept of being human that is racial from the outset and also reproduces the abyssal line as racial (Bhandar, 2018: 4).

Racial segregation did not mean that indigenous peoples did not resist or gave up their legal structures and norms. From the onset of the violent colonial occupation, indigenous communities contested the dominant colonial ideology and the institutionalized exploitation and oppression it legitimized (Warren and Jackson, 2002: 13). However, the relationship between the state, the formal judicial system and the legal practices of indigenous groups has a long and varied record. As Anna Barrera emphasizes (2011: 6), the modes of accommodation ranged from tolerance to criminalization of local normative orders.

These features are present in both Bolivia and Ecuador, countries with a significant indigenous population and therefore good examples of multiethnic, multicultural and multilingual nations.[8] Since the 1990s, the indigenous organizations in these countries have gained national and international prominence through the struggles they have mounted.[9] The political outcome of the indigenous resistance was the emergence of strong ethno-political forces that sought to challenge the dominant political structure by participating at every electoral level (Albó, 2002; Van Cott, 2005), including in the design of the current constitutions (Becker, 2011; Grijalva, 2012; Exeni Rodríguez, 2017; Llasag Fernandéz, 2018).

14.3 The Process of Transition and Indigenous Justice

Eurocentric concepts conditioned the independence of the Latin American colonies in the nineteenth century, comprising the monolithic and monocultural state and law, dependent capitalism, internal colonialism, racism, authoritarianism and bureaucratic centralism: in a word, the entire Eurocentric cultural canon (Benton, 2005; Clavero, 2016; Premo, 2017). Thus, economic, educational, cultural, linguistic, health, security, welfare and territorial policies were drawn up which relied on excluding, repressing or rendering invisible ways of living, thinking, acting and feeling that clashed with liberal nationalist principles.[10]

Severing the ties with Eurocentrism is a historical process, rather than a political process subject to the electoral cycle of liberal democracy. Transformative constitutional projects are only starting points for epochal changes, opening up new benchmarks and new grammars for political struggle (Bonilla Maldonado, 2013). In short, these processes are the beginning of an extensive process of long-term historical transition (Gargarella, 2013).

However, this type of paradigmatic, transitional process is subject to many distortions, boycotts and deviations; its worst opponents are not always those who claim this role. What invariably happens is that those who begin by leading the transition are rarely the ones who continue to do so. The constituent momentum of the early days always runs the risk of surrendering to the inertia of the constituted power. Thus, more likely than not, transformative constitutional projects will eventually be subjected to processes of deconstitutionalization.

These vicissitudes are particularly visible and severe in the case of indigenous justice, which is why it is one of the themes that best reveals the contradictions of the political transition in Bolivia and Ecuador. On the one hand, unlike plurinationality, indigenous justice is not a project in the sense that it is something new to be constructed. Instead, it is a reality which, whether recognized by the state or not, has been part of the life of the communities. Once integrated into a project to construct plurinationality, indigenous justice becomes the vanguard of such a project, since it is already a living and realistic demonstration of the possibilities created by plurinationality. On the other hand, it quickly becomes the easiest target for conservative policies with ambitions to reduce constitutional transformation to what can be controlled by the abyssal thinking of the elites (Santos, 2010, 2018; Llasag Fernandéz, 2018). Politically accepted at first by the modernist Eurocentric constitutional canon as harmless or nothing more than a minor eccentricity and perhaps even useful for colonialist and capitalist domination, once it became part of the plurinational project, indigenous justice became the most visible and therefore the most threatening face of this project (Nolte and Schilling-Vacaflor, 2012). It also became the project's most vulnerable face, since its grassroots practices left it at the mercy of hostile and prejudiced interpretations by the opponents of plurinationality. The demonization of indigenous justice thus became one of the main strategies in the politics of deconstitutionalization. The media and political treatment of certain real or fictitious cases of indigenous justice in the period immediately after the promulgation of the new constitutions is an eloquent expression of this process.[11]

14.4 Tensions in a Complex Transitional Process with an Uncertain Outcome

The recognition of indigenous justice as an integral part of a project for plurinationality changes its political significance completely. It is a firm recognition based on a conception of legal pluralism in the strongest terms. The dimensions of this change involve many other areas of tension and dispute. Although related, these different areas have some autonomy, which helps to identify asymmetries in the development of each one. The impact they have on each other illustrates the enormous complexity of the transition process as a whole, whose main facets are analyzed below.

14.4.1 From Judicial Monolithism to Judicial Pluralism

The first area of tension and dispute occurs between the broad recognition of indigenous justice and the Eurocentric legal tradition shaped by the architecture of ordinary or state justice, steeped in legal theory, educational curricula and the professional training of lawyers in law schools, and the dominant legal culture. Moreover, this legal culture is not only dominant but also hegemonic, which means that the indigenous peoples themselves do not always recognize the methods for resolving disputes and organizing social life within their own communities to be those of "true" justice.

Plurinational recognition of indigenous justice is challenged for allegedly jeopardizing three fundamental principles of modern Eurocentric law: the principle of sovereignty, the principle of unity and the principle of autonomy.

The principle of sovereignty is nowadays called into question by numerous factors, among which indigenous justice is certainly not the most contentious. This principle establishes that the state holds a monopoly over the production and application of the law. The regional integration processes and sharing of sovereignty which this often implies, as well as the conditionalities imposed by multilateral agencies (the World Bank, International Monetary Fund and World Trade Organization) alongside international economic agreements involving multinational companies operating in a given country and the general clauses attached to them—known as the new *lex mercatoria*—comprise some of the legal constraints and limitations which restrict the state's monopoly over the legal system.

In historical terms, indigenous justice is older than any of these and was recognized without major upsets during the colonial period. Even when it was not officially recognized, indigenous justice remained in force in the countries emerging out of colonialism because the state was unable to maintain an effective presence throughout the country. The official recognition was, in general, the combined result of the demands of indigenous struggles and the political acknowledgment that recognition could prove useful as a means of managing minor social conflicts and thereby maintaining social peace. It was only with the legal positivism of the nineteenth century and the way in which it conceived of the state's consolidation of modern law—the state requires one nation, one culture, a single educational system, a single army and one system of law in order to consolidate itself—that indigenous justice came to be seen as a violation of the state's monopoly (Benton, 2005; Postero, 2017).

Indigenous justice is also called into question because it threatens the principle of the unity of law. This principle establishes that, since a law has only a single source which is internally homogenous, the law is a well-defined totality that can be understood in all its dimensions at any given moment due to the methods that modern legal science has developed and placed at the service of the law and legal experts. This principle is being undermined today by a plurality of factors. For decades we have witnessed the enacting of endless new laws which often contradict each other, not to speak of norms that cease to be used without formal revocation. Moreover, peripheral countries have been subjected to successive international political and legal impositions that often contradict domestic law, including constitutional law. For all these reasons, it is now virtually impossible to accurately and exhaustively determine all the laws effectively in force in a given country at any given moment. On the other hand, throughout the twentieth century the state itself assumed so many new functions that its institutional architecture was profoundly modified. Since these modifications were not always implemented with full respect for the coherence of state action, the unity of the law was further undermined. In addition, asymmetric pressures, both internal and external, on the activities of the state led to the internal heterogeneity of state regulation, giving rise to what I call internal legal pluralism, the political form of which is the heterogeneous state (Santos, 2002: 95). For example, legal norms promulgated to protect the environment often contradict legal norms enacted to promote the mining and energy industry, with the result that instead of resolving this contradiction, governments use it to keep competing social demands under control. For all these reasons, the unity of the law, understood as the homogeneity of law, does not make much sense today. It should be noted that internal heterogeneity, which seems to be a serious problem for ordinary law, does not constitute a problem for indigenous justice, since the latter has never claimed to be a unitary system. Indigenous justice is internally very diverse. There are enormous variations in the type of authorities administering justice, the manner in which they apply it, the normative guidelines governing its application, the types of disputes in which they consider themselves competent, the penalties that are applied most often, the relationship between orality and writing, the relative normative and institutional distance in relation to ordinary justice and the forms of connections and cooperation that are maintained throughout this process. There are communities in which indigenous authorities resolve all the relevant cases within the community and others which engage and coordinate with state justice to solve problems they consider are not within their jurisdiction or would generate difficulties, and preferably call for recourse to ordinary or state justice in order to safeguard the cohesion of the community. This diversity makes it more appropriate to speak of indigenous justice in the plural, that is, indigenous justices. Indigenous justices have in common the fact that they are exercised within the communities by their own recognized authorities.

Legal pluralism consists of recognizing the existence of more than one legal system in the same geopolitical space (the state). Indigenous justice constitutes one of the most widely studied cases of legal pluralism; as previously stated, its existence is officially recognized in several countries on different continents. Legal pluralism does not call into question the unity of law as long as coordinating mechanisms between indigenous and ordinary justice are established. This matter will be discussed below.

Finally, indigenous justice is regarded as undermining the autonomy of law. The autonomy of modern law is one of the most problematic principles. In its own terms, the legal system is a specific field of social regulation endowed with its own logic, which is not only different but also autonomous in relation to other fields of social regulation, whether they concern the political or the economic system. Niklas Luhmann's theory of systems led to the extreme theorization of the autonomy of law (1995). The professionalization of training and judicial functions is regarded as an expression of the autonomy of law that simultaneously guarantees its preservation.

However, the truth is that the autonomy of law emerges in modern liberal judicial thinking at the precise moment when the state establishes a monopoly over the production of law and the administration of justice, that is, at the moment when the law becomes more vulnerable to the interference of (political, economic, social and cultural) factors and forces that influence the actions of the state. It is therefore not surprising that critical legal theory and the sociology of law have challenged the principle of autonomy and focused on the analysis of the political, economic and cultural factors that condition the production and application of modern law.

The problem of the autonomy of law does not arise in the context of indigenous justice, because the latter is not thought of as a separate dimension within the social regulation of communities. The authorities who administer justice often have other functions which, from the perspective of modern social regulation, can be regarded as political or economic. Moreover, these functions often have a spiritual dimension that scarcely conforms to the institutional or cultural imagination of ordinary law.

14.4.2 From Liberal Multiculturalism to Interculturality

Liberal multiculturalism recognizes the presence of non-Eurocentric cultures in society provided they are only present in the communities that adopt them and do not interfere with the dominant culture in the rest of society. For liberal legal multiculturalism, the same also applies to law. However, this is not the multiculturalism enshrined in the constitutions of Bolivia and Ecuador. The new emerging plurinational state and its intercultural component not only require recognition of diversity but also the celebration of cultural diversity and reciprocal enrichment among the various existing cultures.

The difficulty in recognizing and valuing intercultural diversity is due to the persistence of colonialism in contemporary societies. Colonialism is any system of domination based on the ontological inferiority of the individuals and groups subjected to it, whether on the basis of ethnic or racial criteria. The modern state is monocultural and, in this sense, colonial, since its institutions assume the naturalized superiority of Eurocentric norms. At best, diversity has to be accommodated, but under no circumstances celebrated. When the United Nations was created in 1948, the Latin American countries, with few exceptions, declared that they had no ethnic minorities, despite the fact that some of them even had ethnic majorities. This shows the invisibility of the other, of the inferior, of what does not exist. I call such invisibility the "sociology of absences" (Santos, 2014a, 2018).

In the two countries under analysis, the existence of colonialism has officially been acknowledged. In Ecuador, services were set up for the "decolonization of the state", while in Bolivia a Vice-Ministry of Decolonization was created. The decolonization of institutions, practices and mentalities is, however, a process that will last a long time because colonialism is much more pervasive than can be imagined. It manifests itself in multiple ways, racism being simply the best-known.

Studies carried out in Ecuador and Bolivia (Santos and Exeni Rodríguez, 2012; Santos and Grijalva, 2012) included in-depth analyses of two cases of racism which have had an impact on indigenous justice. Based on a case study in Riobamba (Ecuador), Karla Encalada shows the structural racism of judicial officials, which is clearly expressed in the way they treat indigenous people, how they look at them, laugh at the way they dress and speak and how they go about producing their absence or invisibility, for example, by making an indigenous person wait twice as long as another citizen for the same procedure (Encalada, 2012, 2016). It is a diffuse racism that is as present in the everyday life of the institutions today as it was in colonial times. The other case of racism highlighted in the studies is the way in which indigenous justice is demonized, especially in the media, and characterized as "savage" or "barbaric justice" (Llasag Fernandéz, 2012).

Obviously, indigenous justice, with its enormous diversity, is not free from excesses, in the same way that state justice is not. In the case of indigenous justice, colonial prejudice manages to transform exceptional cases into the rule, and what is seen as excessive is represented as the "normal" way of deciding things. It is a means of showing indigenous justice for what it is not, when for centuries it has displayed all its richness and effectiveness, resolving conflicts in places where the state had no presence. The persistence of colonialism explains why governments and the media, usually at odds over most current issues, agree on the idea that indigenous justice is savage and barbaric.

14.4.3 From Nation to Plurination

In the political contexts analyzed here, indigenous justice should not be conceived of as an alternative method of dispute resolution like any other, such as arbitration, conciliation, justices of the peace or communitarian justice. It is rather the ancestral justice of the originary peoples, anchored in a system of self-governing territories, who have their own world views. It has a particularly long history and an equally long memory, composed of much suffering but also a great deal of resistance, which persists to the present day.[12]

As part of a constitutional project for plurinationality, indigenous justice directly questions the concept of a nation presiding over the modern liberal nation state. According to this concept, the nation is the set of individuals, the citizens, that belong to the same geopolitical space. The concept of the civic nation, although seemingly completely inclusive, hides many exclusions. On the one hand, it disregards the fact that societies are not only made up of individuals but also social groups that have different ways of belonging to the territory covered by the state. On the other hand, it reserves the right to exclude entire social groups that are sometimes the majority in terms of population size from the most comprehensive form of belonging, namely citizenship. Historically, workers, women, slaves, children and indigenous peoples have been excluded from the civic nation. It was only through social struggles and at great human cost that these groups succeed in gaining citizenship.

In fighting for citizenship, indigenous peoples do not necessarily call into question the legitimacy of the civic nation. They simply refuse to accept that this is the only concept of nation recognized by the state (Gargarella and Courtis, 2009; Ávila Santamaría, 2012; Santos and Exeni Rodríguez, 2012). They demand that, alongside the civic nation, the ethno-cultural nation be recognized, a nation based on a collective way of belonging through sharing the same cultural and symbolic universe, the same ancestry and the same relationship with land and territory (Yrigoyen Fajardo, 2010; Gotkowitz, 2012; Porto-Gonçalves and Betancour, 2013). This recognition of the existence of various concepts of nationhood and their coexistence within the same state lies at the heart of the plurinational state project: Bolivian or Ecuadorean nationality coexisting with the Quechuan, Aymara or Guarani nationalities (González *et al.*, 2003; Llasag Fernandéz, 2014; Postero, 2017).

Although several states now consider themselves plurinational—from Canada to Belgium, from Switzerland to New Zealand and from Ethiopia to Nigeria—the plurinational project remains controversial and has many opponents. The liberal ideology of the modern state as a unitary and monolithic entity, both on a cultural and an institutional level, still firmly prevails. In Latin America, the most common argument against the plurinational project is that plurinationality endangers the already fragile social unity and cohesion in countries that have emerged from colonial domination. The imaginary or real threats of secession (highlighted by the case of the Media Luna in Bolivia) have served to confirm this danger (Assies, 2006; Centellas, 2016).

It is a serious argument, whose genuine grounds for concern should be taken into account when constructing plurinationality, but it is not an argument that prevents this from happening (González *et al.*, 2003; Bautista, 2010). The threats to social unity and cohesion have never come from indigenous peoples. On the contrary, they have been violently excluded from any project for national unity and cohesion. It is only through considerable struggle and immense suffering that they have achieved some inclusion which, incidentally, has always been precarious, even today when plurinational constitutions are in force. It was the abyssal exclusion of indigenous peoples (even in countries in which they were demographically the majority, as is the case in Bolivia) that largely discredited the idea of the civic nation and paved the way for the emergence of the ethno-cultural nation (Yashar, 2005; Van Cott, 2005).

In my opinion, colonialism is present in the plurinationality debate for yet another reason rarely addressed in the public sphere. The colonialism-authoritarianism-capitalism complex operates in the debate on plurinationality through a twofold division whose fundamental objective is to isolate indigenous peoples and neutralize their most advanced causes (Santos and Grijalva, 2012; Santos and Exeni Rodríguez, 2012). The first division consists of separating indigenous peoples from the rest of society, so that the plurinationality project is no longer presented as an inclusive project and a solution for society as a whole. Instead, it becomes an indigenous problem whose indigenous solution can only cause problems for society as a whole. The second division seeks to divide indigenous peoples themselves, fueling divisions between organizations and, above all, separating the indigenous peoples from the leaders of their organizations. This division operates by demonizing indigenous leaders and criminalizing the protests they organize.

The plurinational project is a long-term, perhaps irreversible, project but is certainly far less linear than constitutionalists and social scientists imagined at the end of the previous decade (Albó and Barrios, 2006; Grijalva, 2012). The social and political isolation of indigenous peoples may be one of the perverse effects of constitutional changes, resulting in indigenous leaders themselves thinking that the plurinationality project is only an indigenous issue, not an issue for the country as a whole.

Since it is now linked to the plurinational project, indigenous justice cannot fail to reflect the vicissitudes surrounding the question of plurinationality. Together with the autonomies envisaged in the constitutions, indigenous justice is perhaps the most visible and therefore the most vulnerable face of the plurinational project (Barrera, 2011; Thomas, 2017). It is also important to bear in mind that the categories of formal official law and indigenous customary laws are far less rigidly defined in daily life than they are in theoretical terms. In the case of Ecuador, although indigenous legal systems are given separate semi-autonomous status in national law, the reality on the ground is that members of indigenous communities do not always choose indigenous over formal official law. Moreover, they do not necessarily perceive state and indigenous legal systems as being completely separate at all (Thomas, 2017; Cevallos Vivar, 2019).

The challenge of legal pluralism is how to craft coordinating rules, procedural mechanisms and institutional designs without eliminating the legal pluralism that is intrinsic to daily life. However, various examples of contested legal pluralism[13] suggest that if this project fails, indigenous justice will continue on its path, but gradually lose its identity and become trivialized. It will be reduced to an alternative mechanism for resolving minor disputes that the state has an interest in recognizing or tolerating (Santos, 2006; Twining, 2012: 123).

14.4.4 From Eurocentric Political Pluralism to Intercultural Political Pluralism

Eurocentric political pluralism has liberal roots that manifest themselves in numerous forms, including the following.[14]

- *Individualism*: The unity of the political system rests in individuals and the dual political obligation that binds them. This duality consists of the horizontal political obligation, which binds citizens to each other through the idea that all are equal before the law, and the vertical political obligation, which binds citizens to the state (Bazurco Osorio and Exeni Rodríguez, 2012; Llasag Fernandéz, 2018). The dual political obligation gives rise to the distinction between private and public law.
- *The precedence given to representative democracy* over other possible forms of democracy. In representative democracy, citizens do not make political decisions; instead, they elect political decision-makers by means of individual votes. The exercise of democracy takes place in the public sphere and is reserved for citizens. Democracy is not envisaged as belonging to private or community spaces or as being exercised by non-citizens.
- *The state's role as a representative of the general interest.* As theorized by Hegel, the state opposes the fragmentation of interests in civil society.
- *The aggregation of sectoral interests through the political party*, which assumes sole responsibility for the political representation of interests. Other forms of aggregating interests, such as trade unions and social movements, which are recognized but political representation are generally reserved for parties.
- *Nationalism.* This is regarded as the highest expression of the unity of the civic nation, as previously mentioned. Nonetheless, the presence of ethno-political parties suggests the presence of other forms of national belonging both in Ecuador and in Bolivia, built from common ancestral references (Albó, 2002; Van Cott, 2005; Assies, 2006; Exeni Rodríguez, 2017).
- *Secularism*: The separation between church and state is the structural foundation of political society (the set of interactions between the state and civil society). Religious freedom is possible because the public space is free of religion.
- *Capitalism as a natural means for achieving the liberal project in the socio-economic sphere.*

In the light of these characteristics, it is easy to conclude that indigenous peoples, like Afro-descendants, have long been excluded from this kind of pluralism. It was a pluralism that was inherently hostile to them, not only because for a long time it did not recognize them as citizens, but also because it was based on philosophical and cultural assumptions that contradict their collective practices, ways of life and social organization. Marxism itself has retained the exclusion and even the social and political invisibility of indigenous peoples, one notable exception being José

Mariátegui.[15] Undoubtedly, Marxism introduced the factor of social class into its political model, removed the aura of defender of the general interest from the state, addressed the contradiction between the question of class and the national question and defended socialism as a way of overcoming capitalism. Yet, despite all this, the Latin American left, both Marxist and non-Marxist, has, in general, maintained a racist and colonialist attitude toward the indigenous peoples which at times has resulted in exclusion and persecution and at other times translated into paternalistic guardianship and clientelistic co-optation.[16] In Latin America, the struggles of indigenous peoples after their countries achieved independence in the nineteenth century were a clear sign that they had never accepted this model of political pluralism uncritically. Instead, they have oscillated between rejecting it completely and accepting it as a point of entry to a level of political inclusion that would allow them to advance to transforming the political model. The constitutions of Ecuador (2008) and Bolivia (2009) represent the culmination of the second strategy. Promulgated by left-wing governments following important social struggles spearheaded by indigenous peoples, these constitutions envisage important transformations in the political system, many of which are responses to the claims of indigenous movements (Exeni Rodríguez, 2017). It is particularly significant that Article 11 of the Bolivian Constitution establishes three forms of democracy, namely representative democracy, participatory democracy and communitarian democracy, the latter being the form of democracy that corresponds to the practices of political organization within the indigenous communities. The difficulties, obstacles, barriers and decharacterization to which this process of political transformation has been subjected in recent years show that Eurocentric political pluralism remains dominant and that the governing left-wing parties still have not freed themselves from the racism and colonialism that have always characterized them.

14.4.5 From Dependent Capitalist Development to the Sumak Kawsay *or* Suma Qamaña[17]

The most substantive difference between interculturality within the nation state and plurinational interculturality is that the latter encompasses the cultural as well as the political, territorial, and economic dimensions of diversity. In other words, plurinational diversity implies the constitutional recognition that there are a number of ways, all equally legitimate, of organizing political action, conceiving of ownership, managing territory and organizing economic life. Although registered in different ways and with distinct emphases, recognition of this diversity is established in the constitutions of the two countries analyzed (Santos, 2010; Grijalva, 2012; Llasag Fernandéz, 2014).

Indigenous justice has always been a part of the constellations of social and economic relations that are alien to the possessive individualism of liberalism, the primacy of individual property over all other forms of ownership and the logic of infinite accumulation and commodification of life that underlies capitalism. Although indirectly subordinated to capitalism through the market and wage labor outside the community, indigenous communities have maintained, over time, internal logics of production and social reproduction of societies and peasant economies founded on different indigenous world views. This has never been a matter of rigid time-boundedness or pure logics. On the contrary, they have sought to evolve through an understanding of how to adapt their time logic in conjunction with other economic logics, in particular the capitalist logic (Ramirez Gallegos, 2014). Nevertheless, they have always known how to maintain a relative autonomy. This is how they have survived throughout the long period of colonial and capitalist domination. The Ecuadorian and Bolivian constitutions emphatically recognize the diversity of economic logics prevailing in society. Moreover, they seem to give precedence to the indigenous logics as organizing principles for society as a whole. It is not a question of returning to imagined pre-capitalist pasts or leaping forward to socialist futures. Instead, it points to a post-capitalist horizon which is not defined as socialist (Gudynas, 2011; Escobar, 2016). The difficulty in naming these constitutional goals in colonial languages has resulted in the constitutions making use of originary languages to express the concepts, for the first time in the history of modern Latin American constitutionalism. Examples include the *sumak kawsay* and the *suma qamaña*, among other related concepts (Acosta and Martinez, 2009; Ávila Santamaría, 2011: 121–130).

The most prudent approaches to such concepts incorporate the idea that the plural organization of the economy and property must be administered globally through the principles of reciprocity, complementarity, the primacy of collective well-being and by respecting the rights of the natural world, *Madre Tierra* ("Mother Earth"), the originator and guarantor of human and non-human life. These principles are much closer to the social and economic realities regulated by indigenous justice than the realities regulated by ordinary justice. This would imply that indigenous justice should be valued precisely because its operational logics are particularly suited to constitutional purposes. Management of the land, resources and territory within the indigenous communities has, in general, fallen within the remit of indigenous justice (Ramírez-Cendrero *et al.*, 2017).

However, the truth is that none of this is being put into practice; on the contrary, indigenous justice has been challenged, among other reasons, because it is seen as an obstacle to development, preventing indigenous peoples from fully participating in the new cycle of development initiated by the new constitutional governments. The practice points to a broad continuity with the dependent capitalist development that characterized the periods prior to the constitutional processes. The social mobilizations and constitutional processes which followed coincided with the intensification of neoliberal global capitalist development and financial speculation in commodities and natural resources. For these reasons, the historically unequal international trade which harmed those who exported natural resources rather than manufactured goods was reversed. Suddenly, natural resources were valued on the international markets and became a desirable source of funding for state policies, in particular the social policies inscribed in the constitutional texts. The surpluses were used to develop infrastructures, which were lacking in both countries, and for social redistribution through programs aimed at strengthening public policies (health and education) and financing the family budgets of those deemed most vulnerable by means of compensatory bonuses. The new redistributive policies helped to convince large sections of the population that such an opportunity could not, and should not, be wasted. One of the main consequences of this economic option was the political isolation of indigenous peoples and their organizations (Llasag Fernandéz, 2018; Cevallos Vivar, 2019). Neo-extractivism, as the new (old) development strategy came to be called, was consolidated through a new nationalist justification, in a more comprehensive manner than the oligarchies had previously deployed. Social support for neo-extractivism came, as might be expected, from the sectors that had traditionally gained from it and were now seeing their profits grow without having to bear the political burden of social contestation which this entailed. Support also came from the urban middle classes and rural or suburban communities where the indigenous identity was not as strong as the identity of the peasant, miner, worker, small or middle-scale entrepreneur or *Cocalera* (Restrepo Botero and Peña Galeano, 2017).[18]

The social costs included occupation of indigenous lands without prior consultation, contamination of their waters, environmental destruction, hideous violations of the rights of *Madre Tierra* as a result of open-cast mining, the reinforced presence of conservative churches (taking advantage of the disorientation and despair of the populations) and the assassination of leaders, as well as the mass displacement of populations and their resettlement with no respect for their grievances, their sacred territories or their ancestors (Urioste, 2015). As the social costs of neo-extractivism hit the indigenous communities, resistance was organized and the state response was, in general, repressive (Cevallos Vivar, 2019).[19]

When communities resist in order to maintain control over their territories, they resort to their authorities and indigenous justice which, in many cases, is the means by which issues concerning access to land have always been managed. This resistance has quite often been portrayed as the enemy of development and is stigmatized in public opinion. Such stigmatization has been manipulated in order to divide the indigenous movement and its organizations, a strategy that has strengthened the position of the political opponents of the new Constitutions (Belinda Fontana, 2014: 301; Almaraz, 2015: 52–53).

As indigenous justice starts to be seen as an obstacle to development; it becomes necessary to neutralize it in order to persuade the indigenous communities of the benefits of progress (obviously defined in Eurocentric terms). To this end, in addition to criminalizing social protest, the state makes use of several other measures: defining indigenous territory as surface territory, thereby excluding the subsoil; reducing the territorial or material jurisdiction of indigenous justice to make it harmless; assigning control over access to land to other state-controlled institutions; and so on (Llasag Fernandéz, 2018; Eichler, 2019).[20]

This policy is nuanced in many other ways. One of them involves accusing indigenous communities of being in the service of American imperialism and American environmental NGOs. This accusation is convincing since it contains a grain of truth. In fact, the USA has changed its strategies for continental domination in recent times and now seems to prefer financing promising indigenous leaders, their organizations, their foundations and their local development projects. In the course of this "development aid", they seek to mold the leaders and members of the organizations in order to turn them away from their national political leaders, who are seen as enemies of the USA, anti-imperialist communists or atheists (the accusation may vary according to the particular population being indoctrinated). This indoctrination makes the political struggle more complex for all participants. However, the anti-imperialism of the progressive leaders of the two countries (Evo Morales, President of Bolivia until his forced resignation in November 2019, and Rafael Correa, who was President of Ecuador between 2007 and 2017) has been atypical. In apparent contradiction to their discursive stance, both countries have adopted neo-extractivism as an integral part of the neoliberal development model. There is a consensus within the social and political camp supporting the constitutional project that the economic fabric and the financial basis of state action cannot be changed from one day to the next. It would be necessary to define a politics of transition that would provide progressively more convincing signals that society is changing in the terms proposed in the Constitution, albeit far more slowly than previously expected. In this process of transition, one of the most conclusive signs would be a refusal to permit the anarchic disorganization of the communities.

14.5 Coordination between Indigenous and Ordinary Justice: From the Duality of Justices to the Ecology of Judicial Knowledges and Practices

The constitutions of the two countries stipulate that indigenous and ordinary justice have the same constitutional dignity. In view of this, forms of coordination and cooperation must be defined, in order to avoid any overlapping or contradictions between them. In general, as these two justices have coexisted for a long time, numerous forms of relationships between the two justices have been developed over time. Comparative historical experience points to four ideal-types of relationship: *denial*, *coexistence at a distance*, *reconciliation* and *conviviality*. *Denial* is the ground-zero of the relationship. It consists in refusing to acknowledge the existence of the other justice. This refusal has taken different forms according to whether the source of refusal originates in the state or the indigenous communities themselves. When the initiative comes from the state, the indigenous authorities have often met with violent repression or an arrogant overriding of their decisions, as if they were invalid. When denial has been initiated by the indigenous authorities, it has taken the form of clandestine self-determination and escaping to territories beyond the reach of ordinary justice.

Coexistence at a distance consists of reciprocal recognition, yet prohibited contact. The most complete expression of this form of relationship could be found in the apartheid system in South Africa, where African communitarian justice, for example, was applied solely in the townships and Bantustans, the areas reserved for the black population.

Reconciliation consists of a type of relationship in which the politically dominant justice system (official law) recognizes the existence of subaltern justice and provides it with some degree of dignity, as reparation for the way in which it was ignored or suppressed in the past. Reconciliation is past-oriented. It seeks to heal the past, but in a way that does not interfere with the present or the future.

Finally, conviviality is only an ideal, the aspiration that ordinary and indigenous justice might recognize and enrich each other in the process of developing this relationship, naturally respecting each other's autonomy and the respective areas of reserved jurisdiction. It is a very complex form of relationship, especially because it cannot be realized by decree. It presupposes a convivial judicial culture, which is shared by those involved in the two justices. If we consider the history of relations between indigenous and ordinary justice in Ecuador and Bolivia, it can be said that denial, coexistence and reconciliation (the latter in the most recent period) have all applied in different times and places. Conviviality is the form of relationship prescribed by the respective plurinational constitutions. However, as previously observed, prescription proves to be of little value if it is not sustained by a judicial culture that sees conviviality as a more realistic and effective new way of envisaging and applying the law. From what has been stated above, it is evident that such a judicial culture does not exist among those involved in ordinary justice. On the contrary, a positivist judicial culture dominates. Its replacement by another anti-positivist and intercultural judicial culture is a process that will last for decades. It is therefore to be expected that the relationship between ordinary and indigenous justice will be haphazard during the initial post-constitutional period and will fall far short of what has been established in the respective constitutions in terms of their norms and spirit. Moreover, in the light of the analysis proposed in this text, certain forces in society and the state will act to ensure that the new judicial culture never emerges. Given these conditions, it is important to begin by emphasizing that, over time, very rich and diverse forms of coordination between the two justices have been created in the margins of the legislation. This is known as coordination from below, through the concrete practices of the operators or authorities in the two justice systems as part of their daily work of resolving disputes. It is an empirical, interstitial, routine coordination that does not attract media attention. There are many illustrations of this empirical coordination in studies carried out in Bolivia and Ecuador (Santos and Exeni Rodríguez, 2012; Santos and Grijalva, 2012). In fact, the construction of the new relationship between ordinary and indigenous justice should begin with a detailed analysis of grassroots coordination practices. It should also be borne in mind that coordination between the two justice systems does not have to be achieved through legislative means, but may be left to a judicial body such as the Constitutional Court, as is the case in Colombia and South Africa.[21] In the case of judicial coordination, the mission and the philosophy which create and appoint the court are decisive. This solution has several arguments in its favor. Principally, as a constitutional mandate and a new matter for all concerned, the subject of coordination requires a period of learning and experimentation. It is a period of searching for paths, which are not always complementary, seeking out solutions and progressing by trial and error. In such circumstances, a jurisdictional solution is always better than a legislative one. The legislative solution is rigid and, as it corresponds to a given political and ideological conjuncture, will not adapt easily to any new conditions that may arise.

This observation is particularly relevant in the light of the experience in Bolivia, when a law on coordination between ordinary and indigenous justice, the *Ley de Deslinde Jurisdiccional* (Jurisdictional Demarcation Law), was enacted in 2010.[22] Our analysis (Santos and Exeni Rodríguez, 2012) shows that the normative definitions of coordination and demarcation constitute an attack on the plurinational state, since this law is not a true law of coordination, but rather a law of subordination. While equal status for ordinary and indigenous justice is recognized in its first section, indigenous justice is demoted in terms of the scope of its validity. It identifies communal indigenous justice as "alternative modes of conflict resolution" (Orias, 2015: 17). It is therefore a law of denial in terms of the legal pluralism established in the Constitution. More recently, the Plurinational Constitutional Court of Bolivia interpreted the principle of inter-legality in Resolution SCP 00874/2014, granting jurisdiction over a mine to an indigenous community. According to the decision, inter-legality is defined as "the participation of indigenous peoples [...] whose presence is fundamental to the reframing and reinterpretation of the law—of access to justice" (*apud* Kennemore *et al.*, 2017: 415). Hence the relevance of the presence of their representatives—representative of indigenous origin—in the Plurinational Constitutional Court.[23] According to this resolution, "indigenous and ordinary juridical systems are related through their differences, 'generating institutions, spaces and processes of interaction and interpenetration', which will allow the construction of a plural legal system" (*apud* Kennemore *et al.*, 2017: 415). By proclaiming the significance of inter-legality in Bolivia, this Resolution of the Court emphasizes the importance of indigenous justice in improving access to justice, as well as in expressing the diverse legal practices in the country. In Ecuador, there is no law on coordination between jurisdictions. The Constitutional Court issued mandatory judgments to limit the exercise of indigenous jurisdiction, based not only on the Constitution and complementary legislation but also on expert sociological and anthropological studies, many of which lie within the scope of hegemonic human rights (Llasag Fernandéz, 2018).

The legislative solution does not dispense with the existence of a jurisdictional body. For this reason, I would again stress the importance of the mission, philosophy and composition of the Constitutional Court. In order to respect the constitutional project, the mission of this court should be directed toward gradually promoting what I call the ecology of judicial knowledges, the mode of judicial thought that corresponds to the form of inter-judicial relationship that I have termed conviviality. For now, coexistence, a duality of judicial knowledges, dominates. If it remains, this duality will eventually impoverish both indigenous and ordinary justice.

The ecology of judicial knowledges, as expressed in Resolution SCP 00874/2014, is based on the reciprocal learning of the two systems and the enrichment that can result from both. Drawing on contemporary debates on the administration of justice in increasingly complex societies and taking Ecuador as a reference, Ramiro Ávila (2012) identified various areas in which ordinary justice can learn from indigenous justice. It is not difficult to imagine other areas in which indigenous justice can, in turn, learn from ordinary justice. In fact, at the level of grassroots coordination, our study (Santos and Grijalva, 2012) reveals that indigenous justice has been enriched through guidance from ordinary justice. These exchanges of legal solutions lead to what I have termed inter-legality and judicial hybrids. This inter-legality results from the greater knowledge citizens have of the two justices, which allows them to choose, in certain circumstances, between one or the other. It also allows for situations in which certain social relationships are simultaneously regulated by more than one judicial system, namely situations in which it is possible to distinguish between different dimensions of relationships—for example, within family relationships, marriage, inheritance, relationships with children, divorce and domestic violence. In certain circumstances, citizens may opt for either judicial system to regulate specific dimensions.

Judicial hybrids are concepts or procedures in which it is possible to identify the presence of various judicial cultures. The concept of the rights of nature, for example, is a judicial hybrid. The concept of right comes from Eurocentric culture and modern law, but its application to nature, conceived as *Madre Tierra* or *Pachamama*, is a contribution from the originary Andean culture. The use of forms and minutes in the administration of indigenous justice can be considered another judicial hybrid. Through the use of the written word, indigenous justice aims to improve memory, register recidivism and avoid double judgments.

14.6 Building Respect for the Constitution and International Human Rights Law

Within the architecture of the modern state, infra-constitutional law cannot violate the constitution due to the primacy assigned to it as a fundamental law.

When judicial pluralism is officially acknowledged, all recognized systems of justice must likewise comply with the Constitution. Thus, the compliance that binds indigenous justice to the Constitution is the same as that which binds ordinary justice. Additionally, given the primacy of international human rights law (IHRL), both indigenous and ordinary justice are duty-bound to comply with it. Yet, whenever this theme is approached with respect to indigenous justice, it acquires its own dramatic force. The reasons for this are not always good and have to be distinguished from their more positive counterparts. Commencing with the negative reasons, the following can be noted.

The dominant legal and political culture, which I sought to define above in general terms, tends to consider indigenous justice from the perspective of a hermeneutic of suspicion. As this culture is Eurocentric and monocultural, it views indigenous justice with mistrust, as something strange, since it has difficulty in understanding the premises on which it is established. The colonial past of the modern state on the continent reinforces this attitude: the justice of an inferior people cannot fail to be inferior, hence the repeated references to the excesses or shortcomings of indigenous justice. In addition, the significance attributed to each of these bears no comparison to the significance attributed to the excesses and shortcomings of ordinary justice, despite the latter being widely acknowledged and frequent. This attitude of suspicion in relation to indigenous justice ends up serving the interests of those who want to demonize it in order to politically isolate indigenous peoples and liquidate the constitutional project. The positive reasons for the complexity of the subordination of indigenous justice to the Constitution and IHRL lie in the fact that indigenous justice is founded on a culture of its own, in a symbolic universe that is very different from those presiding over the Constitution and IHRL. Therefore, it is highly likely that conflicts will arise, together with complex problems of interpretation. The experience of Colombia's constitutional jurisprudence is a good example of this (Rodríguez Garavito, 2011).

In order to resolve these problems with the full attention they deserve and in compliance with the constitutional mandate, three principal conditions are necessary. The first relates to the composition of the constitutional courts, the second concerns the interpretation of the Constitution itself and the third refers to preventing difficult issues and problems from being avoided through silence and omission.

Regarding *the composition of the constitutional courts*, ideally they should reflect the actual judicial pluralism that is recognized as existing at the infra-constitutional level. In other words, it is important that they are made up of experts from both justices. In the case of indigenous justice, the best experts will, in principle, be indigenous authorities with experience in the administration of justice. This was the solution adopted for the first version of the Bolivian Constitution, although it did not prevail. Should this not prove possible for political or other reasons, it is essential that the members of the Constitutional Court comply with the constitutional objective of constructing intercultural justice over time, based on the ecology of judicial knowledges. In the case of Bolivia, it is essential that the authorities in the Plurinational Constitutional Court, elected through an unprecedented and complex process of popular voting, assume plurinationality in justice and commit themselves to actively implementing the constitutional mandate. In the case of Ecuador, the Council for Citizen Participation and Social Control (CPCCS) elected the new Constitutional Court on February 5, 2019, after a documented contest. The CPCCS is the fifth power of the state, in charge of appointing various state authorities. The new Constitutional Court was chosen in accordance with the principles of equality and participation by peoples and nationalities and raised many expectations among the public regarding the quality and independence of their future judgments.

The second condition concerns *intercultural translation*. This condition is related to the previous one and establishes that it is necessary to develop mechanisms for intercultural translation that facilitate the interpretation of the Constitution and IHRL in intercultural terms. In other words, fundamental rights themselves must be subjected to intercultural interpretation. The values embodied in these rights must be respected, but since the concrete actions that violate or respect them are not ethically neutral, they may be subject to opposing interpretations depending on the cultural norms on which they are based. This may be the case with, for example, flogging with nettles or being subjected to baths of ice-cold water, which are considered to be corporal punishment. In what context and under what conditions might these be construed as torture? Are there other sanctions that ordinary justice applies which are considered even more violent from the point of view of indigenous justice, such as imprisonment for many years?

One highly controversial issue concerns equality between men and women, which is defended in the Constitution and in IHRL. Do indigenous conceptions of complementarity between men and women, namely *chacha-warmi*, contradict the principle of equality or, conversely, do they implement it in a different but equally valid way? In this area, two issues should be identified. The first is the problem of equivalence between two principles that originate from different cultures. Are they incommensurable, or is it possible to engage in intercultural translation and accept that, in principle, they point to two equally valid paths to ensure parity between men and women in all areas of public and private life?

The other issue relates to the discrepancy between what the principles proclaim in abstract and the concrete practices that take place in their name. This issue is not unique to indigenous cultures and communities: on the contrary, it is a universal problem. Currently, in Europe, the continent of alleged gender equality, sociological studies show that women still receive on average between 75% and 80% of the wages men are paid for the same work; in other words, equality in theory, inequality in practice. Our studies (Santos and Exeni Rodríguez, 2012; Santos and Grijalva, 2012) also reveal that the indigenous concept of complementarity, *chacha-warmi*, often conceals the subordination of women (Burman, 2011; Choque

Aldana *et al.*, 2013). This is particularly true in three aspects: political participation, family violence and access to land.

The issue which this raises suggests that the most correct approach is to promote intercultural translation between the concepts of gender equality typical of Eurocentric feminism and the forms of complementarity inherent to the indigenous world view, in order to determine which practices promote them and which violate them. This is even suggested by many of those involved in the indigenous women's struggles. If, on the one hand, they remain at a distance from Eurocentric feminism (for instance, in their reluctance to argue that their struggle is against men), on the other hand, they fight for women's rights and gender equality within their communities without abandoning their own culture or world views (Espinosa Miñoso *et al.*, 2014).

Thus, cultures must be seen as dynamic, creating conflicts that serve to transform them: this is the richness of all indigenous and non-indigenous cultures. It is why, in this case, there are particularly interesting forms of cultural hybrids containing elements of a Eurocentric feminism which are then treated in a very different way within the indigenous world view. It is for this reason that women are often seen as agents of inter-legality in these countries.

Another possible example of intercultural translation is the concept of a "fair trial". From an intercultural perspective, it is imperative to admit that each system of justice has different ways—its own ways—of ensuring the constitutional value of the fair trial. To give one example among many, the Colombian Constitutional Court ruled that the concept of a "fair trial" should be understood interculturally.[24] The absence of lawyers representing the respective parties, for instance, may not be a violation of the fair trial process if the parties are accompanied by close friends or family, that is, by people who, acting as lawyers, support, help and speak on their behalf. As such, forms of intercultural translation are needed to define what torture is, what gender equality is and what the concept of a fair trial is. Clearly, there are excesses that are commonly acknowledged. However, the point is that both ordinary or state justice and indigenous justice have their own means of preventing such excesses. The originary authorities themselves are aware that excesses discredit justice and weaken communities and their authorities. The third condition is *preventing omission and silence from becoming an insidious way of resolving constitutional conflicts.* This condition was jeopardized by the Constitutional Court of Ecuador in the 2010 La Cocha 2 case, when the alleged murderers of the young Marcus Olivo were sanctioned by both indigenous and ordinary justice. After four years, the Constitutional Court settled the case.[25] The resolution sets an important precedent for cases concerning indigenous justice (Guamán Anilema, 2015). The judges stated that there was no double judgment in this case. The murderers of Marco Olivo were sanctioned by their indigenous community to flogging and cold-water baths, but the public prosecution and judges also sanctioned them in accordance with ordinary law. Secondly, the court ruled that, from that moment on, crimes against life would only be judged by ordinary and not indigenous justice, regardless of whether or not the incident occurred in an indigenous community or the victim/perpetrator was indigenous. A third point that raised concerns the regulation of the media when dealing with incidents and events associated with indigenous justice. According to Patricio Pazmiño, former president of the Constitutional Court,

> It is the obligation of all public, private or community media to disclose cases of indigenous justice, obtain prior authorization from the indigenous authorities involved and communicate the facts ensuring their truthfulness and contextualization, reporting fully on the processes for the resolution of internal conflicts and not only the acts of sanction.

The Constitutional Court ordered the Ministry of Justice and the Council of the Judiciary to ensure the widespread dissemination of this resolution. It is particularly relevant that the conflict underlying this case is not very different from other cases in the past, including La Cocha 1 in 2002, although the previous cases had been resolved without major problems, thus strengthening the communities and respect for rights in the communities.

The difference in the La Cocha 2 case is that it was presented as a pretext for an intense political confrontation between the government and the indigenous communities and served to deepen the division within the indigenous communities. The delay in the decision of the Constitutional Court created a strange and extremely disturbing situation. In the end, it was not the indigenous community or justice that were discredited, but ordinary justice and the Constitutional Court itself that fell into disrepute. It is necessary to coordinate a win-win situation between ordinary and indigenous justice. The case of La Cocha 2 shows that judicial decisions should be appropriate and conducted over a reasonable period of time but, more specifically, that they should also be decisions that respect and strengthen both indigenous and state justice. This "*empate catastrófico*" (catastrophic draw) for justice—a term used by the Bolivian vice-president, Álvaro García Linera (2008), with reference to the broad political context—could lead to a deterioration in the coordination mechanisms already used between justices, such as those in the communities of La Cocha where, until now, there has been a very rich dialogue and widespread coordination between indigenous and ordinary justice at grassroots level, involving the police authorities and ordinary justice officials.

14.7 The Defense of Indigenous Justice through International Law

It is true that, within the constitutional framework analyzed here, indigenous justice must recognize the primacy of IHRL, which must be defended insomuch as this normative area is interpreted in intercultural terms rather than solely in terms of the liberal philosophy from which it originates. IHRL itself contains standards that protect indigenous justice, such as Convention 169 of the International Labor Organization (ILO, 1989) and the UN Declaration on the Rights of Indigenous Peoples (UN, 2007). This international law has, for better or worse, been shaping the activities of the institutions of different regional human rights systems. This is the case with the inter-American human rights system and its two main institutions, the Inter-American Commission on Human Rights and the Inter-American Court of Human Rights. Particularly in the past decade, the Commission and the Court have taken important decisions in favor of recognizing indigenous positions on the principle of self-determination that have a direct impact on indigenous justice as an essential component of indigenous peoples' internal autonomy and control over their territories. On June 27, 2012, the court issued a ruling on a dispute that had been going on for a decade and a half between the Kichwa Sarayaku people and the Ecuadorian government (*Pueblo Indígena Kichwa de Sarayaku versus Ecuador*).[26] This ruling is significant for its detailed analysis of the facts and careful legal treatment of the regulatory framework that was able to serve as a basis for resolving the dispute. It condemned the Ecuadorian state for not safeguarding the rights of the Sarayaku people, namely their right to consultation.

The ruling was celebrated as a victory by the Sarayaku people. In the socio-political context from which it emerged, it is a truly significant decision. However, the court's ruling falls short of fully recognizing the indigenous right to self-determination. The limitations are embedded in many other controversial areas of international jurisdiction over indigenous peoples: recognition of the principle of the internal autonomy of indigenous peoples as the principle from which all others emanate; the impact of plurinationality on understanding and extending the principle of autonomy; the timing, nature, process and objectives of consultation (consultation or acquiescence?); the subsoil (namely, the natural resources) as an intrinsic part of the territories; the possible contradiction between the relationality that presides over indigenous world views and the exploitation of resources for commercial purposes; the identification of transgressors (restricted to the state or including multinational companies?); the criteria for an equitable sharing of benefits; and so on.

14.8 Conclusion

Research on indigenous justice in Bolivia and Ecuador (Santos and Exeni Rodríguez, 2012; Santos and Grijalva, 2012) shows that studying relations between indigenous justice and ordinary or state justice does not mean studying the traditional and the modern: it is a study of two rival modernities, one Indigenocentric and the other Eurocentric. Both are dynamic and each has its own rules for adapting to the new and responding to threats; in short, for reinventing itself.

It also shows that colonialism and patriarchy exist side by side with capitalism and feed on each other. As a consequence, not all people are free and equal, even in abstract terms. Those subjected to colonial or patriarchal domination are considered ontologically inferior for reasons of race or gender and therefore are not fully human. Hence, an abyssal line separates those that are considered free and equal from those that are considered inferior for ontological reasons. This is as true today as it was during the long period of historical colonialism.

Despite the intense constitutional project that shaped the socio-judicial landscape of Ecuador and Bolivia in the early twenty-first century, the new constitutions did not radically subvert the dominant political and juridical project. Clearly, these new constitutions made a major effort to incorporate previously ignored demands and integrate social groups that had been neglected for centuries. However, although these constitutional projects continued to assert their democratic and inclusive nature in the sections dedicated to rights, many of the demands of the indigenous movements concerning an effective refoundation of the state, in order to accommodate the various socio-legal fields, were not applied. In fact, the state structure retained the hierarchical, top-down features of the organization of power (Gargarella, 2013: 200). The abyssal line may have been dislocated as a consequence of the most recent political period—expanding the zone of metropolitan sociability and shrinking the zone of colonial sociability—but it has not been superseded.

The path toward democratizing democracy (Santos and Mendes, 2017) is based on the idea that social justice cannot be achieved without cognitive justice. As I have stated elsewhere, we have the right to be equal when difference demeans us, and we have the right to be different when equality decharacterizes us. Hence there is a need for an equality that recognizes differences and a difference that does not produce, reproduce or feed on inequalities (Santos, 2008: 316). An intercultural egalitarian constitutionalism must therefore challenge the cognitive, economic, social and political injustices at the core of the modern nation state and its landmark, the Constitution. This is a key aspect in promoting a different institutional model, aimed at recognizing distinct justice systems and semi-autonomous systems, a plural juridical system integrating different institutions and normative projects in a more fluid and interconnected way.

If the constitutional mandate for the coordination of justices in a plurinational state is to be fulfilled, it must tread slowly along a path that leads away from the dualities of judicial knowledges and toward the ecologies of judicial knowledges. In political terms, it will be a very difficult path, involving a great deal of human suffering, political struggle, misunderstanding and polarization. It may well be a utopia, but it is a realistic utopia. The constitutional project will advance insofar as the current conflicting dualities—dual knowledges, temporalities, recognized identities, scales and productivities—are converted into ecologies, systems based on the coexistence of different conceptions of culture, justice, power and economics.

In a nutshell, the ecologies of legal knowledges and inter-legality emerging from the recent political and legal experiences in Bolivia and Ecuador would suggest the following signposts should guide the journey:

1. The specificity of indigenous justice is that indigenous peoples are not only individuals who have rights enshrined in ordinary law: they are communities that have their own law.
2. Taking indigenous justice seriously also involves taking the project for the pluralistic decolonizing and democratizing transformation of society and the state seriously.
3. Dealing with indigenous justice is not a matter of legal expertise, even though it has a strong technical dimension. It is above all a political issue.
4. In the two countries studied, the future of ordinary justice is inextricably linked to the future of indigenous justice and vice versa.
5. A healthy equality between the two justices implies, at least temporarily, positive discrimination in favor of indigenous justice.
6. The plurijudicial and plurinational unity of the state is guaranteed by the subordination of both justices, rather than indigenous justice alone, to the Constitution and IHRL.
7. The two justice systems must be coordinated according to the logic of the ecology of judicial knowledges, not the logic of the duality of judicial knowledges.

Notes

1 See Santos (1995, 2002, 2007, 2009a, 2014a, 2014b, 2015, 2018). In this chapter, the term "indigenous peoples" is used interchangeably with "indigenous communities", as there is no consensus on the definition of the term "indigenous peoples". The Declaration on the Rights of Indigenous Peoples (UN, 2007) leaves the decision on the identification criteria for "indigenous peoples" to the respective groups themselves (see Article 33).

2 See Santos and Gomes (1998), Santos and Villegas (2001), Santos and Trindade (2003), Santos (2010), Santos and Exeni Rodríguez (2012), Santos and Grijalva (2012), Santos and Van Dúnen (2012) and Santos and Mendes (2017).

3 On my theoretical approach to modern abyssal thinking, see Santos (2009b, 2014a, 2018).

4 Constitution of the Republic of Ecuador, October 20, 2008, Official Registration no. 449; and Constitution of the Plurinational State of Bolivia, February 7, 2009.

5 These topics are at the core of two projects I carried out in Ecuador and Bolivia, whose results are published in Santos and Exeni Rodríguez (2012) and Santos and Grijalva (2012).

6 On this topic see Rivera Cusicanqui (1987), Hernández Castillo (2002), Van Cott (2003), Jackson and Warren (2005), Dávalos (2005), Bengoa (2007), Dangl (2010), Yrigoyen Fajardo (2010), Aragón Andrade (2016) and Tzul Tzul (2018).

7 Colonial-capitalist property laws are rather different from relationships based on communal property/ownership, especially those regarding land, a reality present

in many contexts in the global South—see, for example, Waldron (2004) and Wily (2018). This difference is fundamental to understanding *sumak kawsay* or *suma qamaña*, which will be analyzed below.

8 See https://minorityrights.org/country/bolivia and https://minorityrights.org/country/ecuador, both accessed in June 2019.

9 Many publications discuss this topic. See, among others, CONAIE (1989), Ayala Mora *et al.* (1992), Ticona (2000), Selverston-Scher (2001), Pallares (2002), Van Cott (2005), Albó and Barrios (2006), Walsh (2009), Reinaga (2013), Postero (2017) and Dangl (2019).

10 In many colonial situations, genocide went hand in hand with episodes of linguicide and epistemicide, as I have analyzed elsewhere (Santos, 1995, 2018).

11 One eloquent illustration of this is the media-political treatment of the *La Cocha 2* case in Ecuador (Guamán Anilema, 2015), as well as the automatic, derogatory association made in Bolivia concerning cases of lynching as a supposed expression of "communitarian justice" (Yates, 2017).

12 On this topic, see, among others, Rivera Cusicanqui (1987), Chuquimia Escobar (2012), Godoy (2012), Premo (2017) and Dangl (2019).

13 See Santos (2014b, 2015), Santos and Villegas (2001), Santos and Trindade (2003) and Santos and Van Dúnen (2012).

14 This topic is developed in Santos (1995, 2002, 2006, 2009a).

15

> If the original sin of Peru was to be born against the Indians, the socialist project could not ignore the reality of an agrarian country where the Indian was the traditional farmer and represented three quarters of the population; the Indian is the bedrock of our nationality in formation. [...] Without the Indian, there is no possible Peruvianness.
>
> *Mariátegui, 2008 [1928]: 87*

16 For an overview of Marxist thought in Latin America, see Liss (1984) and Aricó (2017).

17 The 2008 Ecuadorian Constitution defines the concept of *Buen Vivir* or *Sumak Kawsay* as a central principle of the state. The 2009 Bolivian Constitution enshrines a similar idea of *Vivir Bien* or *Suma Qamaña*. This notion of Good Life (also translated as Living Well), presented as a way of life inspired by ancestral, indigenous (Kichwa and Aymara) experiences, seeks to establish an alternative to growth, development and capitalism (Acosta and Martinez, 2009).

18 *Cocalera*: related to the cultivation or use of coca as a source of income.

19 For example, in Ecuador in 2017 figures indicate that around 200 leaders were indicted on allegations of terrorism or sabotage for fighting for their territories and defending them (Koenig, 2017; Human Rights Watch, 2018).

20 The new developmentalist state (as the actions of the state have come to be called) and neo-extractivism flatly contradict the realization of the rights of nature in Ecuador (Article 71 of the Constitution) and the application of the *Ley de los Derechos de la Madre Tierra* adopted in Bolivia in 2010.

21 See, for South Africa, www.gov.za/about-government/judicial-system and, for Colombia, http://hrlibrary.umn.edu/iachr/indig-col-ch11.html.

22 Jurisdictional Demarcation Law No. 73, of December 29, 2010.

23 Currently the Plurinational Constitutional Court has no indigenous Justice.

24 See, for example, Resolution C-054-13, accessed May 2019, at www.corteconstitucional.gov.co/RELATORIA/2013/C-054-13.htm.

25 The judgment was issued on July 30, 2014 (The Constitutional Court of Ecuador, Judgment No. 113-14-SEP-CC, Case No. 0731-10-EP).

26 The text of the Resolution is available at http://corteidh.or.cr/docs/casos/articulos/seriec_245_esp.pdf.

References

Acosta, Alberto; Martinez, Esperanza (eds.) (2009), *El buen vivir. Una vía para el desarrollo*. Quito: Ediciones Abya Yala.

Albó, Xavier (2002), "Bolivia: from Indian and Campesino Leaders to Councillors and Parliamentary Deputies", in Rachel Sieder (ed.), *Multiculturalism in Latin America: Indigenous Rights, Diversity and Democracy*. New York: Palgrave Macmillan, 74–102.

Albó, Xavier; Barrios, Franz (2006), *Por una Bolivia plurinacional e intercultural con autonomías*. La Paz: PNUD.

Almaraz, Alejandro (2015), "Luchas Políticas y Legales por la Tierra en Bolivia: Las Luchas Indígenas y Campesinas en los Dos Ciclos de la Reforma Agraria", in Fundación Tierra (ed.), *Recientes Transformaciones Agrarias en Bolivia*. La Paz: Fundación Tierra, 49–54. Available at www.ftierra.org/index.php?option=com_mtree&task=att_download&link_id=141&cf_id=77.

Aragón Andrade, Orlando (2016). *De la "vieja" a la "nueva" justicia indígena. Transformaciones y continuidades en las justicias indígenas de Michoacán*. Michoacán: Ediciones del Lirio.

Aricó, José (2017), *Dilemas del Marxismo en América Latina*. Buenos Aires: CLACSO.

Assies, Willem (2006), "La 'Media Luna' sobre Bolivia: Nación, Región, Etnia y Clase Social", *América Latina Hoy*, 43, 87–105. Available at https://dialnet.unirioja.es/ejemplar/147862.

Ávila Santamaría, Ramiro (2011), *El Neoconstitucionalismo Transformador. El Estado y el Derecho en la Constitución de 2008*. Quito: Universidad Andina Simón Bolívar/Abya-Yala.

Ávila Santamaría, Ramiro (2012), "¿Debe Aprender el Derecho Penal Estatal de la Justicia Indígena?", in Boaventura de Sousa Santos and Agustín Grijalva (eds.), *Justicia Indígena, Plurinacionalidad e Interculturalidad en Ecuador*. Quito: Fundación Rosa Luxemburg/Abya Yala, 279–304. Accessed in May 2018, at www.rosalux.org.ec/producto/justicia-indigena-plurinacionalidad-e-interculturalidad-en-ecuador.

Ayala Mora, Enrique *et al.* (eds.) (1992), *Pueblos Indios, Estado y Derecho*. Quito: Corporación Editora Nacional.

Barrera, Anna (2011), "Turning Legal Pluralism into State-Sanctioned Law: Assessing the Implications of the New Constitutions and Laws in Bolivia and Ecuador", *GIGA Working Papers No. 176*. DOI: https://doi.org/10.2139/ssrn.1920297.

Bautista, Rafael (2010), "¿Qué Significa el Estado Plurinacional?", in Gonzálo Gosálvez and Jorge Dulon (eds.), *Descolonización en Bolivia: Cuatro Ejes para Comprender el Cambio*. La Paz: Vicepresidencia del Estado/Fundación Boliviana para la Democracia Multipartidaria, 169–206.

Bazurco Osorio, Martín; Exeni Rodríguez, José Luis (2012), "Bolivia: Justicia Indígena en Tiempos de Plurinacionalidade", in Boaventura de Sousa Santos and José Luis Exeni Rodríguez (eds.), *Justicia Indígena, Plurinacionalidad e Interculturalidad en Bolivia*. Quito: Fundación Rosa Luxemburg/Abya Yala, 49–144. Accessed in May 2018, at www.rosalux.org.ec/producto/justicia-indigena-plurinacionalidad-e-interculturalidad-en-ecuador.

Becker, Marc (2011), "Correa, Indigenous Movements, and the Writing of a New Constitution in Ecuador", *Latin American Perspectives*, 38(1), 47–62. DOI: 10.2307/29779306.

Belinda Fontana, Lorenza (2014), "Indigenous Peoples vs Peasant Unions: Land Conflicts and Rural Movements in Plurinacional Bolivia", *Journal of Peasant Studies*, 41(3), 297–319. DOI: https://doi.org/10.1080/03066150.2014.906404.

Bengoa, José (2007), *La Emergencia Indígena en América Latina*. Santiago de Chile: Fondo de Cultura Económica.
Benton, Laura (2005), *Law and Colonial Cultures*. Cambridge: Cambridge University Press.
Bhandar, Brenna (2018), *Colonial Lives of Property. Law, Land, and Racial Regimes of Ownership*. Durham, NC: Duke University Press.
Bonilla Maldonado, Daniel (ed.) (2013), *Constitutionalism of the Global South: The Activist Tribunals of India, South Africa, and Colombia*. Cambridge: Cambridge University Press. DOI:10.1017/CBO9781139567114.
Burman, Anders (2011), "*Chachawarmi*: Silence and Rival Voices on Decolonisation and Gender Politics in Andean Bolivia", *Journal of Latin American Studies*, 43(1), 65–91. DOI: https://doi.org/10.1017/S0022216X10001793.
Centellas, Miguel (2016), "The Santa Cruz *Autonomía* Movement in Bolivia: A Case of Non-indigenous Ethnic Popular Mobilization?", *Ethnopolitics*, 15(2), 245–264. DOI: https://doi.org/10.1080/17449057.2015.1018710.
Cevallos Vivar, Fabián A. (2019), *Travesías dentro y fuera del Estado. Contribuciones de las Waorani del Yasuní frente al desarrollismo neo-extractivo en Ecuador*. PhD thesis submitted to Coimbra University, Doctoral program in Postcolonialisms and Global Citizenship.
Chakrabarty, Dipesh (2000), *Provincializing Europe: Postcolonial Thought and Historical Difference*. Princeton, NJ: Princeton University Press.
Choque Aldana, Marlene; Torres García, Isabel; Goyes Quelal, Solanda (2013), *La Apuesta por la Paridad: Democratizando el sistema político en América Latina. Los casos de Ecuador, Bolivia y Costa Rica*. Stockholm: International IDEA.
Chuquimia Escobar, René Guery (2012), "Historia, Colonia y Derecho de los Pueblos Indígenas", in Boaventura de Sousa Santos and José Luis Exeni Rodríguez (eds.), *Justicia Indígena, Plurinacionalidad e Interculturalidad en Bolivia*. Quito: Fundación Rosa Luxemburg/Abya Yala, 151–200. Accessed in May 2018, at www.rosalux.org.ec/producto/justicia-indigena-plurinacionalidad-e-interculturalidad-en-ecuador.
Clavero, Bartolomé (2016), *Constitucionalismo Colonial. Economía de Europa, Constitución de Cádiz y más acá*. Madrid: UAM Ediciones. DOI: https://doi.org/10.15366/const.colonial2016
CONAIE—Confederación de Nacionalidades Indígenas del Ecuador (1989), *Las Nacionalidades Indígenas del Ecuador. Nuestro proceso organizativo*. Quito: Ediciones Tincui/Abya Yala.
Dangl, Benjamin (2010), *Dancing with Dynamite: States and Social Movements in Latin America*. Edinburgh: AK Press.
Dangl, Benjamin (2019), *The Five Hundred Year Rebellion: Indigenous Movements and the Decolonization of History in Bolivia*. Edinburgh: AK Press.
Dávalos, Pablo (2005) (ed.), *Pueblos indígenas, Estado y democracia*. Buenos Aires: Clacso Libros.
Eichler, Jessika (2019), "Neo-extractivist Controversies in Bolivia: Indigenous perspectives on global norms", *International Journal of Law in Context*, 15(1), 88–102. DOI: https://doi.org/10.1017/S1744552318000150.
Encalada, Karla (2012), "Racismo en la Justicia Ordinaria", in Boaventura de Sousa Santos and Agustín Grijalva (eds.), *Justicia Indígena, Plurinacionalidad e Interculturalidad en Ecuador*. Quito: Fundación Rosa Luxemburg/Abya Yala, 185–205. Accessed in May 2018, at www.rosalux.org.ec/producto/justicia-indigena-plurinacionalidad-e-interculturalidad-en-ecuador.

Encalada, Karla (2016), *Rusticidad, Indígenas en la Cárcel y Racismo Legal: Una Etnografía del Sistema de Justicia Estatal y las Élites en Riobamba, Ecuador.* Buenos Aires: Antropofagia.

Escobar, Arturo (2016), "Sentipensar con la Tierra: Las Luchas Territoriales y la Dimensión Ontológica de las Epistemologías del Sur", *AIBR—Revista de Antropología Iberoamericana*, 11(1), 11–32. DOI: https://doi.org/10.11156/aibr.110102.

Espinosa Miñoso, Yuderkys; Gómez Correal, Diana; Ochoa Muñoz, Karina (eds.) (2014), *Tejiendo de Otro Modo: Feminismo, epistemología y apuestas descoloniales en Abya Yala.* Popayán, Colombia: Editorial Universidad del Cauca. Available at www2.congreso.gob.pe/sicr/cendocbib/con4_uibd.nsf/498EDAE05058753605258004007698 5F/$FILE/Tejiendo.pdf.

Exeni Rodríguez, José Luis (2017), "A Longa Caminhada das Autonomias Indígenas na Bolívia: Demodiversidade plurinacional em exercício", in Boaventura de Sousa Santos and José Manuel Mendes (eds.), *Demodiversidade: Imaginar Novas Possibilidades Democráticas.* Lisboa: Edições 70, 545–570.

Fitzpatrick, Peter (1992), *The Mythology of Modern Law.* London: Routledge.

García Linera, Álvaro (2008), "Empate Catastrófico y Punto de Bifurcación", *Crítica y Emancipación: Revista Latinoamericana de Ciencias Sociales*, 1(1), 23–33. Available at http://bibliotecavirtual.clacso.org.ar/ar/libros/secret/CyE.

Gargarella, Roberto (2013), *Constitutionalism, 1810–2010. The Engine Room of the Constitution.* Oxford: Oxford University Press.

Gargarella, Roberto; Courtis, Christian (2009), *El Nuevo Constitucionalismo Latinoamericano: promesas e interrogantes.* Santiago de Chile: CEPAL.

Godoy, Scarlett O'Phelan (2012), *Un Siglo de Rebeliones Anticoloniales: Perú y Bolivia, 1700–1783.* Lima: Institut français d'études andines/Instituto de Estudios Peruanos.

González, Miguel; Burguete Cal y Mayor, Araceli; Ortiz-T., Pablo (eds.) (2003), *La Autonomía a Debate. Autogobierno indígena y Estado plurinacional en América Latina.* Quito: FLACSO/GTZ/IWGIA/CIESAS/UNICH. Available at https://biblio.flacsoandes.edu.ec/shared/biblio_view.php?bibid=122516&tab=opac.

Gotkowitz, Laura (2012), *La Revolución antes de la Revolución. Luchas indígenas por tierra y justicia en Bolivia, 1880–1952.* La Paz: Plural.

Grijalva, Agustín (2012), *Constitucionalismo en Ecuador.* Quito: Corte Constitucional del Ecuador.

Guamán Anilema, María Nelly (2015), *Caso La Cocha II análisis de la problemática de la justicia indígena y justicia ordinaria en el contexto ecuatoriano, a partir de la sentencia de La Corte Constitucional en la que establece límites a la justicia ancestral.* Thesis submitted to the Universidad San Francisco de Quito, Colegio de Jurisprudencia.

Gudynas, Eduardo (2011), "Buen Vivir: Today's tomorrow", *Development*, 54(4), 441–447. DOI: https://doi.org/10.1057/dev.2011.86.

Hernández Castillo, R. Aída (2002), "Indigenous Law and Identity Politics in Mexico: Indigenous Men's and Women's Struggles for a Multicultural Nation", *Political and Legal Anthropology Review*, 25(1), 90–109. DOI: https://doi.org/10.1525/pol.2002.25.1.90.

Human Rights Watch (2018), *Amazonians on Trial. Judicial Harassment of Indigenous Leaders and Environmentalists in Ecuador.* Accessed in May 2019, at www.hrw.org/sites/default/files/report_pdf/ecuador0318_web.pdf.

ILO—International Labour Organisation (1989), *Convention Concerning Indigenous and Tribal Peoples in Independent Countries.* Geneva: ILO. Accessed in May 2018, at www.ilo.org/dyn/normlex/en/f?p=NORMLEXPUB:12100:0::NO::P12100_ILO_CODE:C169.

Jackson, Jean E.; Warren, Kay B. (2005), "Indigenous Movements in Latin America, 1992–2004: Controversies, Ironies, New Directions", *Annual Review of Anthropology*, 34, 549–573. DOI: https://doi.org/10.1146/annurev.anthro.34.081804.120529.

Keal, Paul (2003), *European Conquest and the Rights of Indigenous Peoples: The Moral Backwardness of International Society*. Cambridge: Cambridge University Press.

Kennemore, Amy; Pachaguaya Yurja, Pedro Celestino; Salazar Nieves, Cynthia Berenice; Almeida, Marina Correa; Marcani Yapura, Juan Carlos; Telésforo, João (2017), "El Derecho de Acceso a la Justiça a partir de la Constitución Política del Estado Plurinacional de Bolivia de 2009: El pluralismo jurídico como nuevo escenario", in Juan José Martínez Layuno (ed.), *Derecho de Acceso a la justicia: Aportes para la construcción de un acervo latinoamericano*. Santiago de Chile: CEJA—Centro de Estudios de Justicia de las Américas, 403–448. Accessed in June 2019, at http://biblioteca.cejamericas.org/handle/2015/5551.

Koenig, Kevin (2017), "Indigenous Mobilization Results in Steps to End Criminalization in Ecuador", *Amazonwatch*, May 31, 2017. Accessed in May 2019, at https://amazonwatch.org/news/2017/0531-indigenous-mobilization-results-in-steps-to-end-criminalization-in-ecuador.

Liss, Sheldon B. (1984), *Marxist Thought in Latin America*. Berkeley, CA: University of California Press.

Llasag Fernández, Raúl (2012), "Justicia Indígena ¿Delito o Construcción de la Plurinacionalidad? La Cocha", in Boaventura de Sousa Santos and Agustín Grijalva (eds.), *Justicia Indígena, Plurinacionalidad e Interculturalidad en Ecuador*. Quito: Fundación Rosa Luxemburg/Abya Yala, 321–372. Accessed in May 2018, at www.rosalux.org.ec/producto/justicia-indigena-plurinacionalidad-e-interculturalidad-en-ecuador.

Llasag Fernández, Raúl (2014), "Constitucionalismo Plurinacional e Intercultural de Transición: Ecuador y Bolivia", *Revista Meritum de Direito da Universidade FUMEC*, 9(1), 295–319. Available at www.fumec.br/revistas/meritum/article/view/2498.

Llasag Fernández, Raúl (2018), *Constitucionalismo Plurinacional desde los Sumak Kawsay y sus Saberes. Plurinacionalidad desde abajo y plurinacionalidad desde arriba*. Quito: Huaponi Ediciones/INIGED.

Luhmann, Niklas (1995), *Social Systems*. Stanford, CA: Stanford University Press.

Mariatégui, José (2008), *Sete Ensaios de Interpretação da Realidade Peruana*. São Paulo: Expressão Popular and CLACSO [orig. 1928]. Available in Spanish at https://es.wikisource.org/wiki/7_ensayos_de_interpretación_de_la_realidad_peruana.

Maybury-Lewis, David (2002), "Conclusion", in David Maybury-Lewis (ed.), *The Politics of Ethnicity: Indigenous Peoples in Latin American States*. Cambridge, MA: Harvard University Press, 347–361.

Nolte, Detlef; Schilling-Vacaflor, Almut (eds.) (2012), *New Constitutionalism in Latin America: Promises and Practices*. Burlington, VT: Ashgate.

Orias Arredondo, Ramiro (2015), *Reforma Judicial en Bolivia. Elementos para el diagnóstico y desafíos*. La Paz: Friedrich Ebert Stiftung-Bolivia. Available at https://library.fes.de/pdf-files/bueros/bolivien/11647.pdf.

Pallares, Amalia (2002), *From Peasant Struggles to Indian Resistance: The Ecuadorian Andes in the Late Twentieth Century*. Norman, OK: University of Oklahoma Press.

Porto-Gonçalves, Carlos Walter; Betancour, Milson (2013), *Encrucijada Latinoamericana en Bolivia: el conflicto del TIPNIS y sus implicaciones civilizatorias*. La Paz: Autodeterminación.

Postero, Nancy (2017), *The Indigenous State: Race, Politics, and Performance in Plurinational Bolivia*. Oakland, CA: California University Press.

Premo, Bianca (2017), *The Enlightenment on Trial. Ordinary Litigants and Colonialism in the Spanish Empire*. New York: Oxford University Press.

Ramírez-Cendrero, Juan M.; García, Santiago; Santillán, Alejandro (2017), "*Sumak kawsay* in Ecuador: The Role of Communitarian Economy and the Experience of the Rural Communities in Sarayaku (Ecuadorian Amazonia)", *Journal of Rural Studies*, 53, 111–121. DOI: https://doi.org/10.1016/j.jrurstud.2017.05.018.

Ramírez Gallegos, René (2014), *La Vida (Buena) Como Riqueza de los Pueblos: Hacia una Sociecoología Política del Tiempo*. Madrid: Viejo Topo.

Reinaga, Fausto (2013), *La Revolución India*. La Paz: WA-GUI.

Restrepo Botero, Darío I.; Peña Galeano, Camilo Andrés (2017), "Territories in Dispute: Tensions between 'Extractivism', Ethnic Rights, Local Governments and the Environment in Bolivia, Colombia, Ecuador and Peru", in Gilles Carbonnier, Humberto Campodónico and Sergio Tezanos Vázquez (eds.), *Alternative Pathways to Sustainable Development: Lessons from Latin America*. Leiden: Brill Nijhoff, 269–290. DOI: https://doi.org/10.1163/9789004351677_013.

Rivera Cusicanqui, Silvia (1987), *Oppressed but not Defeated: Peasant Struggles among the Aymara and Qhechwa in Bolivia, 1900–1980*. Geneva: United Nations Research Institute for Social Development.

Rodríguez Garavito, César (ed.) (2011), *El Derecho en América Latina, un Mapa para el Pensamiento Jurídico del siglo XXI*. Buenos Aires: Siglo XXI.

Santos, Boaventura de Sousa (1995), *Toward a New Common Sense: Law, Science and Politics in the Paradigmatic Transition*. New York: Routledge.

Santos, Boaventura de Sousa (2002), *Toward a New Legal Common Sense. Law, Globalization, and Emancipation*. London: Butterworths.

Santos, Boaventura de Sousa (2006), "The Heterogeneous State and Legal Pluralism in Mozambique", *Law & Society Review*, 40(1), 39–76. DOI: https://doi.org/10.1111/j.1540-5893.2006.00258.x.

Santos, Boaventura de Sousa (2007), *Para uma Revolução Democrática da Justiça*. São Paulo: Editora Cortez.

Santos, Boaventura de Sousa (2008), *A Gramática do Tempo: para uma Nova Cultura Política*. São Paulo: Editora Cortez.

Santos, Boaventura de Sousa (2009a), *Sociología Jurídica Crítica. Para un Nuevo Sentido Común en el Derecho*. Madrid: Editorial Trotta.

Santos, Boaventura de Sousa (2009b), *Una Epistemología del Sur*. México DF: Siglo XXI Editores.

Santos, Boaventura de Sousa (2010), *Refundación del Estado en América Latina. Perspectivas desde una Epistemología del Sur*. La Paz: Plural Editores.

Santos, Boaventura de Sousa (2014a), *Epistemologies of the South. Justice against Epistemicide*. Boulder, CO: Paradigm.

Santos, Boaventura de Sousa (2014b), *A Justiça Popular em Cabo Verde*. Coimbra: Almedina.

Santos, Boaventura de Sousa (2015), *O Direito dos Oprimidos*. Coimbra: Almedina.

Santos, Boaventura de Sousa (2018), *The End of the Cognitive Empire: The Coming of Age of Epistemologies of the South*. Durham, NC: Duke University Press.

Santos, Boaventura de Sousa; Exeni Rodríguez, José Luis (eds.) (2012), *Justicia Indígena, Plurinacionalidad e Interculturalidad en Bolivia*. Quito: Fundación Rosa Luxemburg/

Abya-Yala. Available at www.rosalux.org.ec/producto/justicia-indigena-plurinacionalidad-e-interculturalidad-en-bolivia.

Santos, Boaventura de Sousa; Gomes, Conceição (1998), *Macau: O Pequeníssimo Dragão*. Porto: Afrontamento.

Santos, Boaventura de Sousa; Grijalva, Agustín (eds.) (2012), *Justicia indígena, Plurinacionalidad e Interculturalidad en Ecuador*. Quito: Fundación Rosa Luxemburg/Abya Yala. Available at www.rosalux.org.ec/producto/justicia-indigena-plurinacionalidad-e-interculturalidad-en-ecuador.

Santos, Boaventura de Sousa; Mendes, José Manuel (eds.) (2017), *Demodiversidade: Imaginar Novas Possibilidades Democráticas*. Lisboa: Edições 70.

Santos, Boaventura de Sousa; Trindade, João Carlos (eds.) (2003), *Conflito e Transformação Social: Uma Paisagem das Justiças em Moçambique*. Porto: Afrontamento.

Santos, Boaventura de Sousa; Van Dúnen, José Octávio Serra (eds.) (2012), *Sociedade e Estado em Construção: Desafios do Direito e da Democracia em Angola*. Coimbra: Almedina.

Santos, Boaventura de Sousa; Villegas, Mauricio García (2001), *El Caleidoscopio de las Justicias en Colombia*. Bogotá: Ediciones Uniandes-Siglo del Hombre.

Selverston-Scher, Melina (2001), *Ethnopolitics in Ecuador: Indigenous Rights and the Strengthening of Democracy*. Coral Gables, FL: North-South Center Press.

Thomas, Marc Simon (2017), *The Challenge of Legal Pluralism: Local Dispute Settlement and the Indian-State Relationship in Ecuador*. Abingdon, Oxon: Routledge.

Ticona, Esteban (2000), *Organización y Liderazgo Aymara. La experiencia indígena en la política boliviana, 1979–1996*. La Paz: Universidad de la Cordillera/AGRUCO.

Twining, William (2012), "Legal Pluralism 101", in Brian Z. Tamanaha, Carol Sage and Michael Woolcock (eds.), *Legal Pluralism and Development: Scholars and Practitioners in Dialogue*. Cambridge: Cambridge University Press, 112–128.

Tzul Tzul, Gladys (2018), *Gobierno Comunal Indígena y Estado Guatemalteco: algunas claves críticas para comprender su tensa relación*. Ciudad de Guatemala: Instituto Amaq'/Ediciones Bizarras.

UN—United Nations Organization (2007), *Declaration on the Rights of Indigenous Peoples*. Resolution adopted by the General Assembly on September 13, 2007. New York: UN. Accessed in April 2018, at www.un.org/development/desa/indigenouspeoples.

Urioste, Miguel (2015), "La Contrarreforma Agraria en Bolivia", *Página* 7, July 31, 2015. Accessed in May 2019, at www.paginasiete.bo/ideas/2015/8/2/contrarreforma-agraria-bolivia-65019.html.

Van Cott, Donna Lee (2003), "Andean Indigenous Movements and Constitutional Transformation: Venezuela in Comparative Perspective", *Latin American Perspectives*, 30(1), 49–69. DOI: https://doi.org/10.1177/0094582X02239144.

Van Cott, Donna Lee (2005), *From Movements to Parties in Latin America: The Evolution of Ethnic Politics*. Cambridge: Cambridge University Press.

Waldron, Jeremy (2004), "Property and Ownership", in *The Stanford Encyclopedia of Philosophy*. Accessed on June 2019, available at https://plato.stanford.edu/archives/win2016/entries/property.

Walsh, Catherine (2009), *Interculturalidad, Estado, Sociedad: luchas (de)coloniales de nuestra época*. Quito: Abya Yala.

Warren Kay B.; Jackson, Jean E. (2002), "Introduction", in Kay B. Warren, Jean E. Jackson (eds.), *Indigenous Movements, Self-Representation and the State in Latin America*. Austin: University of Texas Press, 1–46.

Wily, Liz Alden (2018), "Collective Land Ownership in the 21st century: Overview of Global Trends", *Land*, 7(2), 68. DOI: https://doi.org/10.3390/land7020068.

Yashar, Deborah (2005), *Contesting Citizenship in Latin America: The Rise of Indigenous Movements and the Postliberal Challenge*. New York: Cambridge University Press.

Yates, Donna (2017), "'Community Justice', Ancestral Rights, and Lynching in Rural Bolivia", *Race and Justice*, 10(1), 3–19. DOI: https://doi.org/10.1177/2153368717713824.

Yrigoyen Fajardo, Raquel Z. (ed.) (2010). *Pueblos Indígenas, Constituciones y Reformas Políticas en América Latina*. Lima: IIDS.

CONCLUSION

The Epistemologies of the South is a cosmopolitan epistemological and pedagogical project that challenges the social sciences and legal thinking to identify, denounce and strive to overcome the abyssal exclusions characteristic of Eurocentric modernity arising from its modes of domination, namely a fluctuating combination of capitalism, colonialism and patriarchy. This was the challenge that has guided this book on law, state and constitutionalism. Law represents one of the most complete manifestations of abyssal thinking, making everything that is not recognized by official state or international law illegal, invisible and illegitimate. The supposed universality of law conceals the abyssal line separating human beings who are fully recognized as such from human beings who are systematically treated as subhuman and therefore cannot count on the protection of the law. The epistemologies of the South thus formulate the question: Can law be post-abyssal?

This question extends beyond the limits of conventional legal debate, including critical debate. The reflections do not focus on the number or percentage of those who fit into the social contract, since it is not enough to expand the metropolitan area by extending access to rights. It is necessary to recognize the subjects, social struggles, knowledges and legal experiences that do not identify with, or cannot be translated into, the language and premises of the social contract, thus introducing questions, conditions and proposals that unsettle Eurocentric legal theory and its limits. In other words, it is not enough to grant rights to the 'other'. What is required is the dismantling of the hierarchies that have produced otherness and crystallized diversity into categories of opposition that have rendered the possibilities for legal and political imagination invisible. This process does not involve romanticizing knowledges on the other side of the line or showing contempt for modern institutions. The objective is to promote debates based on

DOI: 10.4324/9781003391920-19

the logic of radical co-presence, that is, dialogue in which the contemporary/primitive dichotomy is replaced by transversal recognition of the incompleteness of knowledges and the provincialization of modern understanding and law.

Reflection and debate are extremely complex and involve both a legal sociology of absences which reveals the design of modern abyssal lines, pointing to what has been left out, and a legal sociology of emergences, which operates in the realm of utopias, reflecting on the future through experiences and knowledges that have been ignored. This broad epistemological, theoretical and political landscape serves as a backdrop to the concrete theme that is addressed in detail in this book, namely the possibility of decolonizing contemporary constitutionalism. Why are constitutions important? Who are they important to? Can they be important to the 'wretched of the earth' or the abyssally excluded? Can Europe learn from the constitutionalisms of the South? Under what conditions would it be possible to transform legal pluralism into a founding principle of the constitution? To what extent have theories and empirical studies on legal pluralism, as well as the different recognition policies, contributed to broadening or strengthening the Eurocentric legal canon? What possibilities emerge from combining social struggles, namely the struggles for decolonization and depatriarchalization? Which elements of apartheid remain as continuities in the post-apartheid constitution and what transformative possibilities does it contain? Is it possible for a constitution to undertake a decolonizing project, replacing the monoculture of constitutional law with intercultural dialogue? What can we learn from the constitutional struggles of Latin America? What are the constituent silences and how do they reveal themselves? How do we ensure that achievements avoid suffering due to processes of unconstitutional erosion? What is the difference between plurinationality from above and plurinationality from below? What is the relationship between law and extractivism? What makes constitutionalism transformative? Is it possible to say that indigenous justices possess their own constitutions? Can a local-scale constitution challenge the hegemonic nation-state model? What have we learned from the transformative constitutional experiences that have occurred in recent decades?

As stated in the preface, we did not intend to offer a universal answer here, nor did we intend to exhaust all the answers. We wanted to take on board the discomfort that post-abyssal questions provoke and learn from the discussions they promote. In refuting the idea of a general theory, it is not up to us to translate what the authors have argued through their formulated positions into a conclusion. We issue a challenge to readers to produce their own reflections and continue the exercise of formulating questions, anticipating the identification of abyssal lines, challenging them and broadening the horizon for constructing decolonized, depatriarchalized and decommodified legal thinking.

INDEX

Note: Endnotes are indicated by the page number followed by 'n' and the endnote number e.g., 20n1 refers to endnote 1 on page 20.

For Product Safety Concerns and Information please contact our EU
representative GPSR@taylorandfrancis.com
Taylor & Francis Verlag GmbH, Kaufingerstraße 24, 80331 München, Germany

www.ingramcontent.com/pod-product-compliance
Ingram Content Group UK Ltd.
Pitfield, Milton Keynes, MK11 3LW, UK
UKHW020154200926
475702UK00016B/2707

* 9 7 8 1 0 3 2 4 9 0 2 7 4 *